JAPANESE
AT A GLANCE
PHRASE BOOK AND DICTIONARY FOR TRAVELERS

BY NOBUO AKIYAMA, M.A.
Instructor in Japanese
School of Advanced International Studies
The Johns Hopkins University
Washington, DC

CAROL AKIYAMA, M.A.
Language Training Consultant
Washington, DC

D0311385

BARRON'S EDUCATIONAL SERIES, INC.
New York ■ London ■ Toronto ■ Sydney

Cover and Book Design   Milton Glaser, Inc.
Illustrations   Juan Suarez

©Copyright 1985 by Barron's Educational Series, Inc.

All inquiries should be addressed to:
Barron's Educational Series, Inc.
250 Wireless Boulevard
Hauppauge, New York 11788

Library of Congress. Number 84-20468

Paper Edition
International Standard Book No. 0-8120-2850-3

Library of Congress Cataloging in Publication Data

Akiyama, Nobuo.
  Japanese at a glance.

  Includes index.
  1. Japanese language—Conversation and phrase books—
English.   I. Akiyama, Carol.   II. Series.
PL539.A65 1984   495.6'83421   84-20468
ISBN 0-8120-2850-3

PRINTED IN THE UNITED STATES OF AMERICA
901   900   19 18 17 16 15 14 13 12 11

CONTENTS

PREFACE

So you're taking a trip to one of the many fascinating countries of the world. That's exciting! This new phrase book will prove an invaluable companion that will make your stay far more interesting.

This phrase book is part of a new series being launched by Barron's Educational Series, Inc. In these books we present the phrases and words that a traveler most often needs for a brief visit to a foreign country, where the customs and language are often different. Each of the phrase books highlights the terms particular to that country, in situations that the tourist is most likely to encounter. With a specially developed key to pronunciation, this book will enable you to communicate quickly and confidently in colloquial terms. It is intended not only for beginners with no knowledge of the language, but also for those who have already studied it and have some familiarity with it.

Some of the unique features and highlights of the Barron's series are:

■ Easy-to-follow *pronunciation keys* and complete phonetic transcriptions for all words and phrases in the book.

■ Compact *dictionary* of commonly used words and phrases— built right into this phrase book so there's no need to carry a separate dictionary.

■ Useful phrases for the *tourist*, grouped together by subject matter in a logical way so that the appropriate phrase is easy to locate when you need it.

■ Special phrases for the *business traveler*, including banking terms.

■ Thorough section on *food and drink*, with comprehensive food terms you will find on menus; these terms are often difficult or impossible to locate in dictionaries, but our section gives you a description of the preparation as well as a definition of what it is.

■ *Emergency phrases* and terms you hope you won't need:

medical problems, theft or loss of valuables, replacement or repair of watches, camera, and the like.

■ *Sightseeing itineraries*, shopping tips, practical travel tips to help you get off the beaten path and into the countryside, to the small towns and cities, and to the neighboring areas.

■ A *reference section* providing: important signs, conversion tables, holidays, telling time. days of week and months of year.

■ A brief *grammar section*, with the basic elements of the language quickly explained.

Enjoy your vacation and travel with confidence. You have a friend by your side.

ACKNOWLEDGMENTS

We would like to thank the following individuals and organizations for their assistance on this project: Constance O'Keefe, Japan National Tourist Organization, New York, New York; Robert Fisher, *Fisher Travel Guides,* New York; Patricia Brooks, author, *Japan, Land of Culinary Surprises;* Mitsuki Kovacs, author and culinary expert; Tomoko Tanaka Campen, Foreign Service Institute, Washington, DC; Madeline Ehrman, Foreign Service Institute, Washington, DC; Chieko Akiyama, critic and commentator, Tokyo, Japan; The Japan Society, New York, New York; Barbara Gilson, editor; Keiko Okamoto; Carol Bryan.

Also, the Japan Society, Japan Air Lines, the Japan National Tourist Organization, the Association of American Travel Writers, the *New York Times, Signature* Magazine, *Travel and Leisure* Magazine, U.S. Tour Operators, and the U.S. Travel Data Center.

INTRODUCTION TO THE
JAPANESE LANGUAGE

Speaking some Japanese will make your trip to Japan a more pleasurable experience. The Japanese people appreciate any efforts foreigners make to communicate in their language. Even a few words or phrases elicit an encouraging response.

You'll probably find Japanese unlike any language you are familiar with. It's not like English, French, Spanish, German, or any other Indo-European language. It's not like most other Asian languages either. Although it borrows some vocabulary and much of its writing system from China, spoken Japanese is completely different from Chinese.

Some linguists think Japanese may have originated in the Altaic language family of Central Asia, but its relationship to any existing language hasn't been proved.

Japanese is rich in the intricacies and sophistication of a 2000-year-old culture. You will find that in many ways it is complex and subtle, in other ways simple and direct. It reflects how the Japanese people think and reason, and their deeply held values, many quite different from western ones. As you use the phrases in this book, you may begin to perceive how the Japanese look at life, and your interactions will become easier and more natural.

QUICK PRONUNCIATION GUIDE

Japanese pronunciation is relatively simple, especially for English speakers. Although there are regional dialects, most people will understand the standard (Tokyo) dialect presented here.

The pronunciation is given for each Japanese item listed. Pronunciation entries are based on English spelling conventions, so you can read them without learning complicated rules. For each entry, the English expression is followed by the Japanese, and then the pronunciation.

Good morning.　　　　　おはようございます *oh-HAH-yoh goh-ZAH-ee-mahs*

Spelling Conventions

The capital letters in the pronunciation on the right mean a slight rise in the pitch of the voice, not stress or emphasis as in English. The line above a syllable means lengthening: hold the vowel sound twice as long as you normally would. This lengthening is very important because it often distinguishes otherwise identical words.

In places where it would be helpful, we have also included the so-called Hepburn spelling. This is the most common system of romanization of Japanese words; it's called romaji. You will see a lot of Hepburn romaji in Japan: on street signs, in railroad stations, in advertisements, and in various other places.

Vowels

Japanese vowels are more like those of Spanish than English. The following vowels are short and pure, with no glide—that is, they are not diphthongs.

Hepburn Vowel	English Spelling	Pronunciation Convention Used in This Book	
a	as in father	*ah*	*ah-KAH-ee*
e	as in men	*eh*	*eh-BEE*
i	as in see	*ee*	*EE-mee*
o	as in boat	*oh*	*oh-EE-shee*
u	as in food	*oo*	*oo-MAH*

The following vowels are like the ones above, but held longer.

Hepburn Vowel	English Spelling	Pronunciation Convention Used in This Book	
ā	as in father, but lengthened	*ah*	*BAH-tah*
ei	as in men, but lengthened	*eh*	*eh-goh*
ii	as in see, but lengthened	*ee*	*ee-stoh*
ō	as in boat, but lengthened	*oh*	*oh-sah-mah*
ū	as in food, but lengthened	*oo*	*poo-roo*

And keep in mind:

1. Take long vowels seriously; pronouncing a long vowel incorrectly can result in a different word or even an unintelligible one. For instance, **obasan** (*oh-BAH-sahn*) means aunt; **obāsan** (*oh-BAH-sahn*) means grandmother. **Ojisan** (*oh-JEE-sahn*) means uncle; **ojiisan** (*oh-JEE-sahn*) means grandfather. **Seki** (*SEH-kee*) means seat; **seiki** (*SEH-kee*) means century.

2. Sometimes the **i** and the **u** are not pronounced. This usually occurs between voiceless consonants (p, t, k, ch, f, h, s, sh), or at the end of a word following a voiceless consonant. An example you may already know is **sukiyaki** (*skee-YAH-kee*). This word for a popular Japanese dish begins not with **soo**, but with **skee**. You omit the **u** entirely. In **tabemashita** (*tah-beh-MAHSH-tah*), which means "I ate," the last **i** is omitted.

Consonants

With a few exceptions, Japanese consonants are similar to those of English. Note the differences:

f   The English **f** is pronounced by a passage of air between the lower teeth and the upper lip. The Japanese **f** is different: The air passes between the lips as if you were just beginning a whistle. The sound is made with a slight blowing of air. Example: foo-TOHN.

g   As in **go**. You may also hear it pronounced as the **ng** sound in ri**ng**, although not at the beginning of a word. Example: NAH-goh-yah.

r   This is different from the English **r**. The Japanese **r** is made by lightly touching the tip of the tongue to the bony ridge behind the upper teeth, almost in the English **d** position. It's more like the Spanish **r**, but it's not flapped or trilled. Example: koh-reh.

s   It is always hissed, as in **so**; it is never pronounced as in hi**s** or plea**s**ure. Example: sah.

Please note:

1. If you have trouble making these consonants the Japanese way, your English pronunciation will be intelligible and not considered incorrect.

2. Some Japanese consonants may be doubled. In English, this is just a feature of spelling and often doesn't affect pronunciation. In Japanese, the doubling is important and may change the meaning of a word. Here are some examples: **kite kudasai** (*kee-TEH koo-dah-SAH-ee*) means "please put it on (clothing)." **Kitte kudasai** (*KEET-teh koo-dah-SAH-ee*) means "please cut it." In a word with a doubled consonant, don't say the consonant twice—just hold the sound longer.

Pitch

In English we emphasize syllables by stress—an increase in loudness. For example, in the word "morning," the first syllable is stressed; that is, it is a little louder than the second. In Japanese, however, stress is not an important part of pronunciation. Pronounce each syllable clearly, with equal emphasis. Pitch (high tone or low tone) is a factor. A rise in pitch (not loudness) is indicated for you by capital letters in the pronunciation. Remember, it does not mean that the syllable is stressed, but that the pitch of the voice is slightly higher.

Loan Words

If you know English, you may already know more Japanese than you think. There are thousands of English loan words in everyday use in Japan. Most of these common words have been borrowed with no change in meaning. But there _is_ a change in pronunciation. This can be tricky: On the one hand you're secure with the familiar words; on the other, if you pronounce them as you're used to doing, you won't be understood and you won't understand the words when Japanese use them. For example, baseball won't work; **besuboru** (_BEH-soo-BOH-roo_) will! If you order a beer, you might not get one; say **biru** (_BEE-roo_) and you will. (Note the long vowel: **biru** with a short vowel means "building.")

Here are a few more examples of familiar words with somewhat different pronunciations in Japanese:

gasoline	**gasorin**	_gah-SOH-reen_
pocket	**poketto**	_poh-KEHT-toh_
pink	**pinku**	_PEEN-koo_
ballpoint pen	**boru pen**	_BOH-roo-pehn_
supermarket	**supa**	_SOO-pah_
yacht	**yotto**	_YOHT-toh_
handkerchief	**hankachi**	_HAHN-kah-chee_

THE BASICS FOR GETTING BY

MOST FREQUENTLY USED EXPRESSIONS

The expressions in this section are the ones you'll use again and again—the fundamental building blocks of conversation, the way to express your wants or needs, and some simple forms you can use to construct all sorts of questions. It's a good idea to practice these phrases until you know them by heart.

Greetings

Good morning.	おはようございます。	*oh-HAH-yoh goh-ZAH-ee-mahs*
Good afternoon.	こんにちは。	*KOHN-nee-chee-wah*
Good evening.	こんばんは。	*KOHN-bahn-wah*
Good night.	おやすみなさい。	*oh-YAH-soo-mee nah-sah-ee*
Pleased to meet you.	はじめて，おめにかかります。	*hah-JEE-meh-teh, oh-MEH-nee kah-kah-ree-mahs*
How do you do?	はじめまして。どうぞ，よろしく。	*hah-JEE-meh-mahsh-teh. DOH-zoh yoh-ROH-shee-koo*
How do you do? (reply)	はじめまして。こちらこそ，よろしく。	*hah-JEE-meh-mahsh-teh. koh-CHEE-rah koh-soh, yoh-ROH-shee-koo*
How are you?	お元気ですか。	*oh-GEHN-kee dehs KAH*
Fine, thank you.	はい，おかげさまで。	*HAH-ee, oh-KAH-geh-sah-mah deh*
Goodbye.	さようなら。	*sah-YOH-nah-rah*

Common Expressions

Yes.	はい。／ええ。	*HAH-ee/EH*
No.	いいえ。	*ee-EH*
Mr./Mrs./Miss/Ms.	さん	___ *sahn*
Thank you.	どうもありがとう。	*DOH-moh ah-REE-gah-toh*
You're welcome.	いいえ，どういたしまして。	*ee-EH, doh-ee-TAH-shee-mahsh-teh*
I'm sorry.	ごめんなさい。／すみません。	*goh-MEHN-nah-sah-ee/soo-MEE-mah-sehn*
Excuse me.	ごめんなさい。／失礼します。	*goh-MEHN-nah-sah-ee/shee-TSOO-reh shee-mahs*
Please.	どうぞ／お願いします。	*DOH-zoh/oh-NEH-gah-ee shee-mahs*
Hello (for telephone calls, for getting someone's attention).	もしもし。	*MOH-shee-moh-shee*
Of course.	もちろん。	*moh-CHEE-rohn*
Maybe.	多分。	*TAH-boon*
Pardon me, but____.	すみませんが。	*soo-MEE-mah-sehn gah,____.*
It's all right.	だいじょうぶです。	*dah-ee-JOH-boo dehs*
It doesn't matter.	かまいません。	*kah-MAH-ee-mah-sehn*
With pleasure.	喜んで。	*yoh-ROH-kohn-deh*
I don't mind.	いいですよ。／かまいません。	*EE-dehs-yoh/kah-MAH-ee-mah-sehn*
Oh, I see.	ああ，そう。	*ah, SOH*
Is that so?	そうですか。	*SOH dehs kah*
Really?	本当。／そうですか。	*hohn-TOH/SOH dehs KAH*
Let's go.	行きましょう。	*ee-KEE-mah-shoh*
Shall we go?	行きましょうか。	*ee-KEE-mah-shoh KAH*

Let's (go/eat/etc.)	さあ。	$\overline{SAH}$...
No thank you.	いいえ，けっこうです。	$\overline{ee}$-EH, KEHK-koh dehs
I don't want it.	いりません。／けっこうです。	ee-REE-mah-sehn / KEHK-koh dehs
I think so.	そうだと，思います。	$S\overline{OH}$ dah-toh, oh-MOH-ee-mahs
I don't think so.	そう思いません。	soh oh-MOH-ee-mah-sehn
It's interesting/fun.	おもしろいです。	oh-MOH-shee-roh-ee dehs
It's over/I'm finished.	終わりました。	oh-WAH-ree-mahsh-tah
Yes, it is.	はい，そうです。	HAH-ee, $S\overline{OH}$ dehs
No, it isn't.	いいえ，ちがいます。	$\overline{ee}$-EH, chee-GAH-ee-mahs
Just a moment, please.	ちょっと待って下さい。	CHOHT-toh MAHT-teh koo-dah-sah-ee
Not yet.	まだです。	MAH-dah dehs
Soon.	もうすぐです。	$M\overline{OH}$ soo-goo dehs
Right away (request).	すぐ。	soo-goo
Right away (response).	ただいま。	tah-DAH-ee-mah
Now.	今。	EE-mah
Later.	あとで。	AH-toh deh

Some Questions and Question Words

What's the matter?	どうか、しましたか。	*DOH-kah shee-MAHSH-tah KAH*
What's this?	これは，何ですか。	*koh-REH wah NAHN dehs KAH*
Where's the____?	____は，どこですか。	*____wah DOH-koh dehs KAH*
bathroom	お手洗／トイレ／お便所	*oh-TEH-ah-rah-ee/ TOH-ee-reh/ oh-BEHN-joh*
dining room	食堂	*shoh-KOO-doh*
entrance	入口	*ee-REE-goo-chee*
exit	出口	*DEH-goo-chee*
telephone	電話	*dehn-wah*
When?	いつ。	*EE-tsoo*
Where?	どこ。	*DOH-koh*
Why?	なぜ。／どうして。	*NAH-zeh/DOH-shteh*
Who?	だれ。／どなた。	*DAH-reh/DOH-nah-tah*
Which?	どれ。／どちら。	*DOH-reh/DOH-chee-rah*
What?	何	*NAH-nee*
How?	どうやって。	*DOH-yaht-teh*
How much?	どのくらい。	*doh-NOH-koo-rah-ee*
How much (money)?	いくら。	*EE-koo-rah*

Needs

Could you tell me where the____is?	____がどこか，教えて下さい。	*____gah DOH-koh kah, oh-SHEE-eh-teh koo-DAH-sah-ee*
Could you give me____?	____を下さい。	*____oh koo-DAH-sah-ee*
I need____.	____がいります。	*____gah ee-REE-mahs*

I want____.	____が欲しいです。	____gah hoh-SHEE dehs
I want to go to____.	____に, 行きたいです。	____nee ee-kee-TAH-ee dehs
I want to see____.	____を見たいです。	____oh mee-TAH-ee dehs
I want to buy____.	____を買いたいです。	____oh kah-ee-TAH-ee dehs
I want to eat____.	____を食べたいです。	____oh tah-beh-TAH-ee dehs
I want to drink____.	____を飲みたいです。	____oh noh-mee-TAH-ee dehs

Your Personal Condition

I'm thirsty.	のどが, かわいています。	NOH-doh gah, kah-WAH-ee-teh ee-mahs
I'm hungry.	おなかが, すいています。	oh-NAH-kah gah, soo-EE-teh ee-mahs
I'm full.	おなかが, いっぱいです。	oh-NAH-kah gah, eep-PAH-ee dehs
I'm tired.	つかれています。	tsoo-KAH-reh-teh ee-mahs
I'm sleepy.	ねむいです。	neh-MOO-ee dehs
I'm sick.	病気です。	BYOH-kee dehs
I'm fine.	元気です。	GEHN-kee dehs
I'm all right.	だいじょうぶです。	dah-ee-JOH-boo dehs

Some Adjectives

It's cold.	寒いです。	sah-MOO-ee dehs
It's hot.	暑いです。	ah-TSOO-ee dehs
It's hot and humid.	蒸し暑いです。	moo-SHEE ah-TSOO-ee dehs
pretty, beautiful/ ugly	きれい／みにくい	KEE-reh/ mee-NEE-koo-ee
delicious/awful-tasting	おいしい／まずい	oh-EE-shee/ mah-ZOO-ee

good, fine/bad	いい／悪い	$\overline{EE}$/wah-ROO-ee
fast, quick/slow	速い／おそい	hah-YAH-ee/ oh-SOH-ee
high/low	高い／低い	tah-KAH-ee/ hee-KOO-ee
expensive/cheap	高い／安い	tah-KAH-ee/ yah-SOO-ee
hot/cold	熱い／冷たい	ah-TSOO-ee/ tsoo-MEH-tah-ee
same	同じ	oh-NAH-jee
warm/cool	暖かい／涼しい	ah-TAH-tah-kah-ee/ soo-ZOO-shee
big/small	大きい／小さい	$\overline{OH}$-kee/ CHEE-sah-ee
long/short	長い／短い	nah-GAH-ee/ mee-JEE-kah-ee
strong/weak	強い／弱い	tsoo-YOH-ee/ yoh-WAH-ee
far/near	遠い／近い	$\overline{TOH}$-ee/ chee-KAH-ee
wide/narrow	広い／せまい	hee-ROH-ee/ seh-MAH-ee
heavy/light	重い／軽い	oh-MOH-ee/ kah-ROO-ee
new/old	新しい／古い	ah-TAH-rah-shee/ foo-ROO-ee
young	若い	wah-KAH-ee
dark/light	暗い／明るい	koo-RAH-ee/ ah-KAH-roo-ee
quiet/noisy	静か／やかましい	SHEE-zoo-kah/ yah-KAH-mah-shee
a lot, many/a little, few	たくさん／すこし	tahk-SAHN/ SKOH-shee
intelligent/stupid	利口／ばか	ree-$\overline{KOH}$/BAH-kah

right/wrong	正しい／悪い	*tah-DAH-shee/* *wah-ROO-ee*
easy/difficult	易しい／難しい	*yah-SAH-shee/* *moo-ZOO-kah-shee*
early/late	早い／おそい	*hah-YAH-ee/* *oh-SOH-ee*

Pronouns

I	私	*wah-TAHK-shee*
you (singular)	あなた	*ah-NAH-tah*
he/she	彼／彼女	*KAH-reh/KAH-noh-* *joh*
we	私たち	*wah-TAHK-shee-tah-chee*
you (plural)	あなたたち	*ah-NAH-tah-tah-* *chee*
they	彼ら	*KAH-reh-rah*

Note: To form the possessives, simply add the particle <u>noh</u> to the above pronouns:

| my | 私の | *wah-TAHK-shee noh* |

More Basic Words

here/there/over there	ここ／そこ／あそこ	*koh-KOH/soh-KOH/* *ah-SOH-koh*
this/that/that over there (nouns)	これ／それ／あれ	*koh-REH/soh-REH/* *ah-REH*
this/that/that over there (adjectives)	この／その／あの	*koh-NOH/soh-NOH/* *ah-NOH*
and (between nouns)	と	___*toh*___
and (between sentences)	そして	___*sohsh-TEH*___
but	けれども／でも	*KEH-reh-doh-moh/* *DEH-moh*
or	それとも／または／ あるいは	*soh-REH-toh-moh/* *mah-TAH-wah/ah-* *ROO-ee-wah*
also	も／また	*moh/mah-TAH*

before	_____の前に	_____noh MAH-eh nee
during	_____の間に	_____noh ah-EE-dah nee
after	_____のあとで	_____noh AH-toh deh
to	_____へ	_____eh
from	_____から	_____kah-rah
at	_____で	_____deh
in	_____に	_____nee
up	_____の上に	_____noh oo-EH nee
down	_____の下に	_____noh SHTAH nee
inside	_____の中に	_____noh NAH-kah nee
outside	_____の外に	_____noh SOH-toh nee
on	_____の上に	_____noh oo-EH nee
near	_____の近くに	_____noh chee-KAH-koo nee

Communicating

Do you understand?	わかりますか。	wah-KAH-ree-mahs KAH
Yes, I understand.	はい，わかります。	HAH-ee, wah-KAH-ree-mahs
No, I don't understand.	いいえ，わかりません。	ee-EH, wah-KAH-ree-mah-sehn
Do you understand English?	英語がわかりますか。	EH-goh gah, wah-KAH-ree-mahs KAH
I speak a little Japanese.	日本語が，少し話せます。	nee-HOHN-goh gah, SKOH-shee hah-NAH-seh-mahs
I know very little Japanese.	日本語は，ほんの少ししか知りません。	nee-HOHN-goh wah, hohn noh SKOH-shee shkah shee-REE-mah-sehn

I don't understand Japanese.	日本語は，わかりません。 *nee-HOHN-goh wah, wah-KAH-ree-mah-sehn*
Could you repeat it, please?	もう一度，お願いします。 $\overline{MOH}$ *ee-chee-doh, oh-NEH-gah-ee shee-mahs*
Please speak slowly.	もう少し，ゆっくり話して下さい。 *MOH SKOH-shee yook-KOO-ree hah-NAHSH-teh koo-dah-sah-ee*
Write it down on the paper, please.	紙に書いて下さい。 *kah-MEE nee, KAH-ee-teh koo-dah-sah-ee*
Is there anyone who understands English?	だれか，英語がわかる人がいますか。 *DAH-reh kah EH-goh gah wah-KAH-roo hee-toh gah ee-mahs KAH*
Do you speak English?	英語を話しますか。 $\overline{EH}$-*goh oh hah-NAH-shee-mahs KAH*
What's this called in Japanese?	これは，日本語で何といいますか。 *koh-REH wah, nee-HOHN-goh deh NAHN toh ee-mahs KAH*
What do you call this?	これは，何といいますか。 *koh-REH wah, NAHN toh ee-mahs KAH*
Excuse me, could you help me, please?	すみませんが，助けていただけませんか。 *soo-MEE-mah-sehn gah, tahs-KEH-teh ee-tah-dah-keh-mah-sehn KAH*
Please point to the phrase in this book.	この本から，適当な文を選んで，示してください。 *koh-noh HOHN kah-rah teh-kee-TOH nah boon oh eh-RAHN-deh, shee-MEH-shee-teh koo-dah-sah-ee*

POLICE

Japan is a very safe country: the crime rate is one of the lowest in the world. It's unlikely that you'll ever need to talk to the police for anything but directions. Nevertheless, here are a few "just in case" phrases.

Excuse me.	すみませんが. *soo-MEE-mah-sehn gah*
Would you call the police for me please?	警官をよんでもらえますか. *KEH-kahn oh YOHN-deh moh-rah-eh-mahs KAH*
What's the telephone number for the police?	警察の電話は，何番ですか. *KEH-sah-tsoo noh dehn-wah wah, NAHN-bahn dehs KAH*
I seem to have lost my <u>wallet</u>.	<u>さいふ</u>を，なくしてしまったみたいです. *sah-EE-foo oh, nah-KOO-shteh shee-maht-tah mee-tah-ee dehs*
passport	パスポート *pah-SOO-poh-toh*
plane tickets	飛行機の券 *hee-KOH-kee noh kehn*
What shall I do?	どうしたらいいでしょうか. *DOH shee-tah-rah ee deh-shoh KAH*
I want to report <u>a theft</u>.	<u>盗難</u>を，報告したいのですが. *toh-nahn oh, HOH-koh-koo shee-tah-ee noh dehs gah*
an accident	事故 *JEE-koh*
I think my money has been stolen.	お金を，盗まれてしまったみたいです. *oh-KAH-neh oh, noo-SOO-mah-reh-teh shee-maht-tah mee-tah-ee dehs*
Someone just grabbed my <u>camera</u>.	ほんの今，<u>カメラ</u>をひったくられてしまいました. *HOHN noh ee-mah, KAH-meh-rah oh heet-TAH-koo-rah-reh-teh shee-mah-ee-mah-shtah*
purse	ハンド・バッグ *HAHN-doh bahg-goo*
Can you help me?	ちょっと，助けてもらえませんか. *CHOHT-toh, tahs-KEH-teh moh-rah-eh-mah-sehn KAH*
My name is ____.	私の名前は，____です. *wah-TAHK-shee noh nah-mah-eh wah, ____ dehs*
I'm an <u>American</u> citizen.	<u>アメリカ人</u>です. *ah-MEH-ree-kah-jeen dehs*
a British	イギリス人 *ee-GEE-ree-soo-jeen*

I'm in Japan <u>on business</u>.	日本へは，<u>仕事</u>で来ています．	*nee-HOHN eh wah, shee-GOH-toh deh kee-teh ee-mahs*
as a tourist	観光	*KAHN-koh*
I'm staying at ____.	____に，泊まっています．	____ *nee, toh-MAHT-teh ee-mahs*
My telephone number is ____.	私の電話番号は，____番です．	*wah-TAHK-shee noh dehn-wah bahn-goh wah,* ____ *bahn dehs*
I've lost my way.	道に，迷ってしまいました．	*mee-chee nee, mah-YOHT-teh shee-mah-ee-mah-shtah*
Can you direct me to ____?	____への行き方を，教えてください．	____ *eh noh ee-KEE-kah-tah oh, oh-shee-eh-teh koo-dah-sah-ee*

NUMBERS

Cardinal Numbers

0	ゼロ／零	*ZEH-roh/reh*
1	一	*ee-CHEE*
2	二	*nee*
3	三	*sahn*
4	四	*shee/yohn*
5	五	*goh*
6	六	*roh-KOO*
7	七	*shee-CHEE/NAH-nah*
8	八	*hah-CHEE*
9	九	*kyoo/koo*
10	十	*joo*
11	十一	*joo ee-CHEE*
12	十二	*joo nee*
13	十三	*joo sahn*
14	十四	*joo shee/joo yohn*

15	十五	*joo goh*
16	十六	*joo roh-KOO*
17	十七	*joo shee-CHEE/joo NAH-nah*
18	十八	*joo hah-CHEE*
19	十九	*joo koo*
20	二十	*NEE joo*
30	三十	*SAHN joo*
40	四十	*YOHN joo*
50	五十	*goh JOO*
60	六十	*roh-KOO joo*
70	七十	*nah-NAH joo*
80	八十	*hah-CHEE joo*
90	九十	*KYOO joo*
100	百	*hyah-KOO*
200	二百	*nee HYAH-koo*
300	三百	*SAHN byah-koo*
400	四百	*YOHN hyah-koo*
500	五百	*goh HYAH-koo*
600	六百	*rohp-PYAH-koo*
700	七百	*nah-NAH hyah-koo*
800	八百	*hahp-PYAH-koo*
900	九百	*KYOO hyah-koo*
1,000	千	*SEHN*
2,000	二千	*nee SEHN*
10,000	一万	*ee-CHEE mahn*
20,000	二万	*nee MAHN*
100,000	十万	*JOO mahn*
200,000	二十万	*nee JOO mahn*
1,000,000	百万	*hyah-KOO mahn*
2,000,000	二百万	*nee HYAH-koo mahn*

3,000,000	三百万	*SAHN byah-koo mahn*
4,000,000	四百万	*YOHN hyah-koo mahn*
5,000,000	五百万	*goh HYAH-koo mahn*
6,000,000	六百万	*rohp-PYAH-koo mahn*
7,000,000	七百万	*nah-NAH hyah-koo mahn*
8,000,000	八百万	*hahp-PYAH-koo mahn*
9,000,000	九百万	*KYOO hyah-koo mahn*
10,000,000	千万	*SEHN mahn*
20,000,000	二千万	*nee SEHN mahn*
100,000,000	一億	*ee-CHEE oh-koo*

Cardinal Numbers (Another System)

1	一つ	*hee-TOH-tsoo*
2	二つ	*foo-TAH-tsoo*
3	三つ	*meet-TSOO*
4	四つ	*yoht-TSOO*
5	五つ	*ee-TSOO-tsoo*
6	六つ	*moot-TSOO*
7	七つ	*nah-NAH-tsoo*
8	八つ	*yaht-TSOO*
9	九つ	*koh-KOH-noh-tsoo*
10	十	*toh*
11	十一	*JOO ee-chee*
12	十二	*JOO nee*

Ordinal Numbers

first	一番目／第一	*ee-CHEE bahn meh/ DAH-ee ee-chee*

second	二番目／第二	*nee BAHN meh/ DAH-ee nee*
third	三番目／第三	*SAHN bahn meh/ DAH-ee sahn*
fourth	四番目／第四	*YOHN bahn meh/ DAH-ee yohn*
fifth	五番目／第五	*goh BAHN meh/ DAH-ee goh*
sixth	六番目／第六	*roh-KOO bahn meh/ DAH-ee roh-koo*
seventh	七番目／第七	*nah-NAH bahn meh/ DAH-ee nah-nah*
eighth	八番目／第八	*hah-CHEE bahn meh/DAH-ee hah-chee*
ninth	九番目／第九	*KYOO bahn meh/ DAH-ee koo*
tenth	十番目／第十	*JOO bahn meh/ DAH-ee joo*

THE LAND AND PEOPLE

GEOGRAPHY

Japan is an island nation in the North Pacific, off the eastern coast of Asia. Its four major islands are:

Honshu (main)	本州	*HOHN-shoo*
Hokkaido (north-ernmost)	北海道	*hohk-KAH-ee-doh*
Kyushu (south-ernmost)	九州	*KYOO-shoo*
Shikoku (smallest)	四国	*shee-KOH-koo*

The major cities, in order of population size, are:

Tokyo	東京	*TOH-kyoh*
Yokohama	横浜	*yoh-KOH-hah-mah*
Osaka	大阪	*OH-sah-kah*
Nagoya	名古屋	*NAH-goh-yah*
Kyoto	京都	*KYOH-toh*
Sapporo	札幌	*sahp-POH-roh*
Kobe	神戸	*KOH-beh*
Fukuoka	福岡	*foo-KOO-oh-kah*

TALKING ABOUT THE COUNTRY

Japan	日本	*nee-HOHN*
population	人口	*jeen-koh*
land area	面積	*MEHN-seh-kee*
Pacific Ocean	太平洋	*tah-EE-heh-yoh*

Sea of Japan	日本海	*nee-HOHN-kah-ee*
Pacific side	表日本	*oh-MOH-teh nee-hohn*
Sea of Japan side	裏日本	*oo-RAH nee-hohn*
volcano	火山	*KAH-zahn*
hot springs	温泉	*OHN-sehn*
earthquake	地震	*jee-SHEEN*
ocean	海	*OO-mee*
coast	海岸	*kah-EE-gahn*
bay	湾	*wahn*
island	島	*shee-MAH*
mountain range	山脈	*SAHN-myah-koo*
mountain	山	*yah-MAH*
hill	丘	*oh-KAH*
river	川	*kah-WAH*
lake	湖	*mee-ZOO-oo-mee*
waterfall	滝	*tah-KEE*
capital	首都	*SHOO-toh*
city	市	*shee*
big city	都会	*toh-KAH-ee*
countryside	地方／田舎	*chee-HŌH/ee-NAH-kah*
town	町	*mah-CHEE*
village	村	*moo-RAH*
prefecture	県	*kehn*
prefectural capital	県庁所在地	*KEHN-choh shoh-ZAH-ee-chee*
map	地図	*CHEE-zoo*
national park	国立公園	*koh-KOO-ree-tsoo KOH-ehn*

SEASONS AND WEATHER

season	季節	*KEE-seh-tsoo*
four seasons	四季	*SHEE-kee*
spring	春	*HAH-roo*
March/April/May	三月／四月／五月	*SAHN-gah-tsoo/shee-GAH-tsoo/GOH-gah-tsoo*
summer	夏	*nah-TSOO*
June/July/August	六月／七月／八月	*roh-KOO-gah-tsoo/ shee-CHEE-gah-tsoo/ hah-CHEE-gah-tsoo*
fall	秋	*AH-kee*
September/ October/ November	九月／十月／十一月	*KOO-gah-tsoo/JOO-gah-tsoo/JOO-ee-chee-gah-tsoo*
winter	冬	*foo-YOO*
December/ January/ February	十二月／一月／二月	*JOO-nee-gah-tsoo/ee-CHEE-gah-tsoo/nee-GAH-tsoo*
warm	暖かい	*ah-TAH-tah-kah-ee*
hot	暑い	*ah-TSOO-ee*
hot and humid	蒸し暑い	*moo-SHEE-ah-tsoo-ee*
cool	涼しい	*soo-ZOO-shee*
cold	寒い	*sah-MOO-ee*
dry	乾燥している	*KAHN-soh shteh ee-roo*
humid	湿っている	*shee-MEHT-teh ee-roo*
climate	気候	*kee-KOH*
weather	天気	*TEHN-kee*
clear (sky)	晴れ	*HAH-reh*

cloudy	曇り	*koo-MOH-ree*
wind	風	*kah-ZEH*
rain	雨	*AH-meh*
rainy season	梅雨	*tsoo-YOO*
snow	雪	*yoo-KEE*
typhoon	台風	*tah-EE-foo*

When does the rainy season begin?	梅雨は，いつ始まりますか．	*tsoo-YOO wah, EE-tsoo hah-jee-mah-ree-mahs KAH*
When does the rainy season end?	梅雨は，いつ終わりますか．	*tsoo-YOO wah, EE-tsoo oh-wah-ree-mahs KAH*
When do the cherry blossoms bloom?	桜は，いつ咲きますか．	*sah-KOO-rah wah, EE-tsoo sah-kee-mahs KAH*
When do the autumn leaves begin?	紅葉は，いつ頃ですか．	*KOH-yoh wah, ee-TSOO-goh-roh dehs KAH*
It's a nice day, isn't it?	いい（お）天気ですねえ．	*EE (oh)-TEHN-kee dehs NEH*
It's terrible weather, isn't it?	いやな（お）天気ですねえ．	*ee-YAH nah (oh)-TEHN-kee dehs NEH*
It's <u>hot</u> today, isn't it?	今日は，<u>暑い</u>ですねえ．	*KYOH wah <u>ah-TSOO-ee</u> dehs NEH*
cool	涼しい	*soo-ZOO-shee*
cold	寒い	*sah-MOO-ee*
warm	暖かい	*ah-TAH-tah-kah-ee*
It's <u>fine</u>.	<u>晴れ</u>です．	*<u>HAH-reh</u> dehs*
cloudy	曇り	*koo-MOH-ree*
raining	雨	*AH-meh*
snowing	雪	*yoo-KEE*
Will it stop raining/snowing soon?	もうじき，やむでしょうか．	*MOH jee-kee yah-MOO deh-shoh kah*
I hope it will clear up.	晴れる<u>と</u>いいのですが．	*hah-REH-roo toh ee noh dehs gah*

| What's tomorrow's weather forecast? | あしたの天気予報は． *ah-shtah noh TEHN-kee-yoh-hoh WAH* |
| Do you think a typhoon is coming? | 台風は，来そうですか． *tah-EE-foo wah, kee-SOH dehs KAH* |

GETTING TO KNOW THE JAPANESE

Japanese culture is not only very old, it's also remarkably intact. Perhaps geography played a role, perhaps history—Japan was virtually isolated from the rest of the world for two and a half centuries, ending in 1868. Because the Japanese people were free from outside contacts for so long, their own traditions became stronger. Even today, with the influence of the West so visible, the Japanese adhere to their unique customs and values. Some Japanese cultural requirements may differ from your own. No one expects foreign visitors to act like Japanese. But a few insights into new and different customs can help you speak Japanese more easily.

Introductions

In general, the Japanese prefer "proper" introductions. Some people will be glad to strike up a conversation with a stranger under casual circumstances. You can introduce yourself if you like. But formal introductions are preferable; they can set the tone of the ongoing relationship. Whenever possible, have a mutual friend, acquaintance, or colleague introduce you to someone he or she already knows.

Who is that?	あの方は，どなたですか． *ah-NOH-kah-tah wah, DOH-nah-tah dehs KAH*
Do you know who that is?	あの方は，どなたかごぞんじですか． *ah-NOH-kah-tah wah, DOH-nah-tah kah goh-ZOHN-jee dehs KAH*
I would like to meet him/her (literally, <u>that person</u>).	あの方に，おめにかかりたいのですが． *ah-NOH-kah-tah nee, oh-MEH nee kah-kah-ree-tah-ee noh dehs gah*
Would you introduce me to him/her (that person)?	あの方に，紹介していただけませんか． *ah-NOH-kah-tah nee, SHOH-kah-ee shee-teh ee-TAH-dah-keh-mah-sehn KAH*

Mr./Ms. A, may I introduce Mr./Ms. B?	Aさん，Bさんを御紹介します． *A-sahn, B-sahn oh goh-SHOH-kah-ee shee-mahs*
I would like you to meet Mr./Ms. C.	Cさんを，御紹介します． *C-sahn oh, goh-SHOH-kah-ee shee-mahs*
Have you met Mr./Ms. D?	Dさんを，ごぞんじですか． *D-sahn oh, goh-ZOHN-jee dehs KAH*
Mr./Ms. F, this is Mr./Ms. G.	Fさん，こちらはGさんです． *F-sahn, koh-CHEE-rah wah G-sahn dehs*
Pardon me, may I introduce myself?	突然失礼ですが，自己紹介してもよろしいですか． *toh-TSOO-zehn shee-TSOO-reh dehs gah, jee-KOH-shoh-kah-ee shee-teh-moh yoh-ROH-shee dehs KAH*
This is my <u>friend</u>.	私の友人です． *wah-TAHK-shee noh YOO-jeen dehs*
husband	主人 *SHOO-jeen*
wife	家内 *KAH-nah-ee*
son	息子 *moo-SOO-koh*
daughter	娘 *moo-SOO-meh*
father	父 *chee-CHEE*
mother	母 *HAH-hah*
How do you do?	初めまして．どうぞよろしく． *hah-JEE-meh-mahsh-teh, DOH-zoh yoh-ROH-shee-koo*
How do you do? (reply)	初めまして．こちらこそよろしく． *hah-JEE-meh-mahsh-teh, koh-CHEE-rah koh-soh yoh-ROH-shee-koo*
I'm honored to meet you.	おめにかかれて，光栄です． *oh-MEH nee kah-KAH-reh-teh, KOH-eh dehs*
I'm glad to meet you.	よろしくお願いします． *yoh-ROH-shee-koo oh-NEH-gah-ee shee-mahs*
I'm <u>Joe Smith</u>.	ジョー・スミスと申します． *joh SOO-mee-soo toh moh-shee-mahs*

My name is <u>Jean Brown</u>. 　私の名前は，ジーン・ブラウンで
す． *wah-TAHK-shee noh nah-mah-eh
wah, <u>jeen boo-RAH-oon</u> dehs*

Cards

Japanese routinely exchange business cards during introductions. Japan has been called a vertical society; people deal with each other according to their relative positions on that vertical ladder. Knowing a person's profession or business affiliation, including position within a company, is important. It helps in choosing the right level of language, the right gestures, and other, more subtle interactions. It's also convenient to have the card to refer to later. You'll be given a lot of cards in Japan, and you will find it useful to have your own to offer in exchange. Some airlines that fly to Japan help you to get cards printed with English on one side and Japanese on the other. Or you can have them made once you arrive. You might prefer just to take your own cards with you, since many Japanese can read English.

card 　名刺 *MEH-shee*

Here's my card. 　名刺をどうぞ． *MEH-shee oh DOH-zoh*

Thank you very much. 　ありがとうございます． *ah-REE-gah-toh goh-ZAH-ee-mahs*

Here's mine. 　私のもどうぞ． *wah-TAHK-shee noh-moh DOH-zoh*

May I have your card? 　名刺をちょうだいできますか． *MEH-shee oh CHOH-dah-ee deh-kee-mahs KAH*

Names

Japanese rarely use first names with people they've just met. They use the last name followed by the respectful **san** (*sahn*). Even among themselves, most friends of long standing use last names. When friends or family members do use first names, they too are followed by **san**. In the case of children, the first names are followed by **chan** (*chahn*). Because few Japanese are comfortable with the use of their own or others' first names, it's safer for foreigners to use last names plus **san** when addressing Japanese, unless specifically asked to do otherwise. Note that when referring to oneself, the **san** is dropped. Also keep in mind that Japanese use the family name first: it's Jones Mary, not Mary Jones.

What's your name?	お名前は． *oh-NAH-mah-eh WAH*
My name is (last name).	（苗字）です．／（苗字）と申します． *(last name) dehs/(last name) toh moh-shee-mahs*

Personal Information

Where are you from?	どちらから，いらっしゃいましたか． *DOH-chee-rah kah-rah ee-RAHSH-shah-ee-mah-shtah KAH*
I'm from <u>America</u>.	<u>アメリカ</u>から来ました． *ah-MEH-ree-kah kah-rah kee-MAHSH-tah*
England	イギリス *ee-GEE-ree-soo*
Canada	カナダ *KAH-nah-dah*
Australia	オーストラリア *OH-soo-toh-rah-ree-ah*
New Zealand	ニュージーランド *nyoo-jee-rahn-doh*
Which country are you from?	お国はどちらですか． *oh-KOO-nee wah DOH-chee-rah dehs KAH*
I'm from the United States.	アメリカです． *ah-MEH-ree-kah dehs*
Where were you born?	お生まれはどちらですか． *oh-OO-mah-reh wah DOH-chee-rah dehs KAH*
I was born in Rome.	ローマです． *ROH-mah dehs*
Where do you live?	お住いはどちらですか． *oh-SOO-mah-ee wah DOH-chee-rah dehs KAH*
I live in Paris.	パリです． *PAH-ree dehs*
Are you married?	結婚していらっしゃいますか． *kehk-KOHN shteh ee-rahsh-shah-ee-mahs KAH*
I'm married.	結婚しています． *kehk-KOHN shteh ee-mahs*
I'm single.	独身です． *doh-KOO-sheen dehs*

Do you have any children?	お子さんがいらっしゃいますか． *oh-KOH-sahn gah ee-rahsh-shah-ee-mahs KAH*
How old are you?	おいくつですか． *oh-EE-koo-tsoo dehs KAH*
I'm over 20.	二十才は過ぎています． *nee-JOOS-sah-ee wah, SOO-gee-teh ee-mahs*
I'm <u>20</u> years old.	<u>二十才</u>です． *nee-JOOS-sah-ee /HAH-tah-chee dehs*
25	二十五才 *NEE-joo-GOH-sah-ee*
30	三十才 *sahn-JOOS-sah-ee*
35	三十五才 *SAHN-joo-GOH-sah-ee*
40	四十才 *YOHN-joos-sah-ee*
45	四十五才 *YOHN-joo-GOH-sah-ee*
50	五十才 *goh-JOOS-sah-ee*
55	五十五才 *goh-JOO-goh-sah-ee*
60	六十才 *roh-KOO-joos-sah-ee*
65	六十五才 *roh-KOO-joo-GOH-sah-ee*
70	七十才 *nah-NAH-joos-sah-ee*
75	七十五才 *nah-NAH-joo-GOH-sah-ee*
80	八十才 *hah-CHEE-joos-sah-ee*
What do you do?	お仕事は． *oh-SHEE-goh-toh WAH*
I'm <u>a student</u>.	<u>学生</u>です． *gahk-SEH dehs*
a teacher	教師 *KYOH-shee*
a professor	教授 *KYOH-joo*
a housewife	主婦 *SHOO-foo*
an office worker	サラリーマン *sah-RAH-ree mahn*
a secretary	秘書 *HEE-shoh*
an engineer	エンジニア *EHN-jee-nee-ah*
in the military	軍人 *GOON-jeen*
a company president	会社の社長 *kah-EE-shah noh shah-CHOH*

a company executive	会社の重役 *kah-EE-shah noh JOO-yah-koo*
an industrialist	実業家 *jee-TSOO-gyoh-kah*
a doctor	医者 *ee-SHAH*
a dentist	歯医者 *HAH-ee-shah*
a nurse	看護婦 *KAHN-goh-foo*
a lawyer	弁護士 *BEHN-goh-shee*
an architect	建築家 *KEHN-chee-koo-kah*
a writer	作家 *sahk-KAH*
a politician	政治家 *SEH-jee-kah*

Daily Greetings and Leavetakings

Japanese ritual greetings and leavetakings differ somewhat from those of English. There are some phrases that you might not think of saying yourself, but that you will need for daily ritual exchanges.

There's no real equivalent for the English "Hi" or "Hello." In Japanese, the initial greeting is based on the time of day:

Good morning.	おはようございます。 *oh-HAH-yoh goh-ZAH-ee-mahs*
Good afternoon.	こんにちは。 *KOHN-nee-chee-wah*
Good evening.	こんばんは。 *KOHN-bahn-wah*

This is said by both people, and the exchange is not usually followed by anything like the English "How are you?" There is, however, a phrase that Japanese say when they meet after not having seen each other for a while (several weeks or longer):

| It's been a long time. | お久しぶりです。 *oh-HEE-sah-shee-boo-ree dehs* |

Next comes a statement of gratitude for any kindness or favor the other person may have done for the speaker during their previous meeting or since. The translation seems a bit awkward in English, but knowing what it means will help you to understand why Japanese keep saying to <u>you</u> in English, "Thank you for last time."

| Thank you for last time. | このあいだは，どうもありがとう。 *koh-NOH ah-ee-dah wah, DOH-moh ah-REE-gah-toh* |

Another greeting is the ubiquitous "welcome," spoken with a smile and a lilt. Friends will welcome you to their homes or offices that way, and shopkeepers, especially in restaurants, will sing it out to anyone entering the door.

Welcome.	いらっしゃい。	*ee-RAHSH-shah-ee*

There is an exchange that translates as the equivalent of the English "How are you?"/ "Fine thank you," but it is not used among people who see each other daily. Save this for when you haven't seen someone in a while—several weeks or more:

How are you?	お元気ですか。	*oh-GEHN-kee dehs KAH*
Fine, thanks, and you?	はい、お陰様で、(名前) さんは。	*HAH-ee. oh-KAH-geh-sah-mah-deh. (name)-sahn WAH*

Jpanese has many ways to say goodbye. Here are some. There are more choices here than for the greetings!

Good night.	おやすみなさい。	*oh-YAH-soo-mee nah-sah-ee*
Goodbye.	さようなら。	*sah-YOH-nah-rah*
Well, goodbye.	それでは、さようなら。	*soh-REH deh-wah, sah-YOH-nah-rah*
See you again.	では、また。	*DEH-wah, mah-TAH*
See you tomorrow.	またあした。	*mah-TAH ahsh-TAH*
See you soon.	では、また近いうちに。	*DEH-wah, mah-tah chee-KAH-ee oo-chee nee*
See you later.	では、のちほど。	*DEH-wah, noh-CHEE-hoh-doh*
So long.	ごきげんよう。	*goh-KEE-gehn-yoh*
Take care.	気をつけて。	*kee oh TSKEH-teh*
I must go.	おいとまします。	*oh-EE-toh-mah shee-mahs*
I'm afraid I'll have to go soon.	そろそろ、おいとまします。	*SOH-roh-soh-roh oh-EE-toh-mah shee-mahs*
Sorry for taking your time.	おじゃましました。	*oh-JAH-mah shee-mahsh-tah*

| Thank you for the delicious food. | 本当に、ごちそうになりました。 |
| | *hohn-toh nee, goh-chee-SOH nee nah-ree-mahsh-tah* |

If you're not going to see someone for a long time, there's no equivalent of "I'll miss you." It's a natural thing for English speakers to express, but Japanese feel that some things are better left unsaid!

GESTURES

The Handshake and the Bow

Japanese rarely shake hands with each other. They know that Westerners do this, so it isn't offensive to them if you extend your hand for a handshake. Some might even offer theirs first. But anything more, like a greeting hug or kiss, could be offensive unless you know the person <u>very</u> well. Open displays of affection are rare.

| bow | おじぎ *oh-JEE-gee* |
| to bow | おじぎする。 *oh-JEE-gee soo-roo* |

When meeting new people or greeting friends, Japanese bow. It's an old and important custom. They bow according to prescribed rules of etiquette and respect that become second nature. The kind and degree of the bow depends on the relationship between the two people, the relative status, age, obligation, and feeling of respect. There are even rules for who bows lower to whom. This custom is so instinctive that Japanese often bow when they're talking on the telephone! They say it helps them to convey verbally the proper nuances.

What should <u>you</u> do? To bow or not to bow, indeed, <u>how</u> to bow will be up to you. Remember, non-Japanese are not expected to bow. But people <u>will</u> bow to you, and you're free to follow suit if you feel comfortable. Just lean forward from the waist, keep your head down, and you'll do just fine.

GIFT GIVING AND RECEIVING

Japan is a country of gift giving and receiving. If you have Japanese friends or acquaintances, you'll probably receive some gifts yourself while you're in Japan. They may be token souvenirs, or much more. These phrases will help!

gift	おみやげ	oh-MEE-yah-geh
return gift	おかえし	oh-KAH-eh-shee

Although Japanese will give you gifts, they don't expect anything in return. Whether you participate in the exchange or not is up to you; either way is fine.

Giving

Here's something for you.
これを、どうぞ。 koh-REH oh DOH-zoh

It's from Virginia.
これは、バージニアからです。 koh-REH wah, BAH-jee-nee-ah kah-rah dehs

It's just a token.
これは、ほんのおしるしです。 koh-REH wah, HOHN noh oh-SHEE-roo-shee dehs

I hope you like it.
お気にめすと、いいのですが。 oh-KEE nee MEHS toh, EE noh dehs gah

This is a small present for you.
ささやかな物ですが、どうぞ。 sah-SAH-yah-kah nah moh-NOH dehs gah, DOH-zoh

It's not anything special, but...
たいした物ではありませんが。 TAH-eesh-tah moh-NOH deh-wah, ah-REE-mah-sehn gah

And Receiving

Thank you very much.
どうも、ありがとうございます。 DOH-moh, ah-REE-gah-toh goh-ZAH-ee-mahs

Thank you very much for such a wonderful gift.
大変けっこうな物を、ちょうだいして。 tah-ee-hehn KEHK-koh nah moh-NOH oh, CHOH-dah-ee-shteh

It's very kind of you.	本当に，ご親切に。 *hohn-toh nee, goh-SHEEN-seh-tsoo nee*
That's very thoughtful of you.	わざわざ，ご丁寧に。 *WAH-zah-wah-zah, goh-TEH-neh nee*
Thank you very much for your kindness.	本当に，恐縮です。 *hohn-toh nee, KYOH-shoo-koo dehs*
I'm very much obliged for your generosity.	恐れいります。 *oh-SOH-reh ee-ree-mahs*
I'm most grateful.	感激です。 *KAHN-geh-kee dehs*
How nice of you!	ご親切さまです。 *goh-SHEEN-seh-tsoo sah-mah dehs*
How generous of you!	そんなにまで，していただいて。 *SOHN-nah nee mah-deh, SHTEH ee-tah-dah-ee-teh*
I'm indebted.	どうも，もうしわけありません。 *DOH-moh, MOH-shee-wah-keh ah-ree-mah-sehn*

When you give or receive a gift, it's good manners to use both hands. Don't be surprised if, when you give a Japanese a gift, he or she doesn't open it in front of you, but waits to open it after you leave. If you want to open a gift you've received, it's quite all right. Japanese know that Westerners do this. Just say:

| May I open it? | あけても，よろしいですか。 *ah-KEH-teh-moh, yoh-ROH-shee dehs KAH* |

Now you can open your gift, and make the appropriate responses; it's hard to thank someone for a beautifully wrapped package when you don't know what's inside!

WHEN YOU ARRIVE

ENTRANCE REQUIREMENTS

Entrance formalities for foreigners arriving in Japan are handled quickly and efficiently. If you come by air, you'll probably arrive at New Tokyo International Airport at Narita, or at Osaka International Airport; if by sea, the ports of Yokohama or Kobe. In either case, you'll find English-speaking personnel and well-organized procedures to help speed you on your way to your hotel or other destination.

airport	空港	*KOO-koh*
airplane	飛行機	*hee-KOH-kee*
flight number	便名	*been-meh*
Northwest #003	ノースウェスト3便	*NOH-soo wehs-toh SAHN been*
JAL#005	日航5便	*neek-KOH goh BEEN*
passenger	乗客	*JOH-kyah-koo*

Quarantine

Unless you are arriving in Japan from an infected area, you are not required to show proof of smallpox or cholera inoculations. If you are coming from such areas, here are a few phrases. If not, you usually pass right through.

quarantine	検疫 *KEHN-eh-kee*
vaccination certificate	種痘証明書 *shoo-TOH shoh-meh-shoh*
Do you need to see my vaccination certificate?	種痘証明書は必要ですか。 *shoo-TOH shoh-meh-shoh wah, hee-TSOO-yoh dehs KAH*

Immigration

At both Immigration and Customs, there are separate, clearly marked lines for Japanese and nonresidents. At Immigration, or

Passport Control, show your passport, with proper visa (check before you leave home to see if you need one—Americans do!), and your Embarkation/ Disembarkation Card (a small form you will be given before the plane lands).

My name is ____.	私の名前は，____です。	*wah-TAHK-shee noh nah-mah-eh wah, ____ dehs*
I'm <u>American</u>.	<u>アメリカ人</u>です。	*ah-MEH-ree-kah jeen dehs*
British	イギリス人	*ee-GEE-ree-soo jeen*
Canadian	カナダ人	*kah-NAH-dah jeen*
Dutch	オランダ人	*oh-RAHN-dah jeen*
Australian	オーストラリア人	*OH-soo-toh-rah-ree-ah jeen*
I'm staying at ____.	____に，泊まります。	*____ nee toh-MAH-ree-mahs*
Here's my <u>passport</u>.	これが，私の<u>パスポート</u>です。	*koh-REH gah, wah-tahk-shee noh pah-SOO-poh-toh dehs*
documents	書類	*SHOH-roo-ee*
Embarkation/ Dis- embarkation Card	出入国記録	*shoo-TSOO-nyoo-goh-koo KEE-roh-koo*
I'm on <u>vacation</u>.	<u>バケーション</u>です。	*bah-KEH-shohn dehs*
a sightseing tour	観光旅行	*KAHN-koh ryoh-koh*
a busineess trip	仕事の旅行	*shee-GOH-toh noh ryoh-koh*
I'll be staying here <u>a few days</u>.	数日滞在の予定です。	*soo-jee-tsoo tah-EE-zah-ee noh yoh-TEH dehs*
a week	一週間	*ees-SHOO-kahn*
two weeks	二週間	*nee-SHOO-kahn*
a month	一か月	*eek-KAH-geh-tsoo*
two months	二か月	*nee-KAH-geh-tsoo*
I'm traveling <u>alone</u>.	一人で，旅行しています。	*hee-TOH-ree deh, ryoh-koh shteh ee-mahs*

with my husband	主人と *SHOO-jeen toh*
with my wife	家内と *KAH-nah-ee toh*
with my family	家族で *KAH-zoh-koo deh*

BAGGAGE CLAIM

Where is the baggage claim?	荷物の受取所は，どこですか。 *NEE-moh-tsoo noh oo-KEH-toh-ree-joh wah, DOH-koh dehs KAH*
baggage/ luggage	荷物 *NEE-moh-tsoo*
Get that black suitcase for me please.	その黒いスーツケースを取ってください。 *soh-noh koo-ROH-ee SOO-tsoo-keh-soo oh TOHT-teh koo-dah-sah-ee*
white	白い *shee-ROH-ee*
red	赤い *ah-KAH-ee*
blue	青い *ah-OH-ee*
brown	茶色い *chah-EE-roh-ee*
big	大きい *OH-kee*
small	小さい *CHEE-sah-ee*

That's mine.	それは，私のです。	*soh-reh wah, wah-TAHK-shee noh dehs*
I can't find my luggage.	荷物が，みつかりません。	*NEE-moh-tsoo gah, mee-TSOO-kah-ree-mah-sehn*
Where's my luggage?	私の荷物は，どこですか。	*wah-TAHK-shee noh NEE-moh-tsoo wah, DOH-koh dehs KAH*
My luggage is lost.	荷物を，なくしました。	*NEE-moh-tsoo oh, nah-KOO shee-mahsh-tah*

CUSTOMS

You must present your bags for customs inspection, and they may be opened. An oral declaration of your personal effects will be sufficient except for the following circumstances, in which case, you'll have to fill out a written declaration: arrival by ship, unaccompanied baggage, or articles in excess of the duty free allowance.

Duty free allowances (for nonresidents of Japan):

tobacco	500 grams, <u>or</u> 400 cigarettes <u>or</u> 100 cigars
liquor	3 bottles
perfume	2 ounces
other items	total value 100,000 yen or less

customs	税関	*ZEH-kahn*
customs inspection	税関検査	*ZEH-kahn KEHN-sah*
Where's customs?	税関は，どこですか。	*ZEH-kahn wah DOH-koh dehs KAH*
Here's my passport.	これが，私のパスポートです。	*koh-reh gah, wah-TAHK-shee noh pah-SOO-poh-toh dehs*
Here's my customs declaration form.	これが，私の関税の書類です。	*koh-reh gah, wah-TAHK-shee noh KAHN-zeh noh shoh-roo-ee dehs*

This is my luggage.	これが，私の荷物です。 *koh-reh gah, wah-TAHK-shee noh NEE-moh-tsoo dehs*
This is all I have.	これで，全部です。 *koh-reh deh, ZEHN-boo dehs*
I have nothing to declare.	申告するものは，何もありません。 *SHEEN-koh-koo soo-roo moh-noh wah, nah-NEE moh ah-ree-mah-sehn*
I have two cartons of cigarettes.	タバコのカートンを二箱持っています。 *tah-BAH-koh noh KAH-tohn oh foo-TAH-hah-koh MOHT-teh ee-mahs*
three bottles of whiskey	ウイスキーを三本 *oo-EE-skee oh SAHN-bohn*
three bottles of wine	ワインを三本 *WAH-een oh SAHN-bohn*
These are my personal effects.	これは，私のてまわり品です。 *koh-reh wah, wah-TAHK-shee noh teh-MAH-wah-ree-heen dehs*
It's not new.	新品では，ありません。 *SHEEN-peen deh-wah, ah-REE-mah-sehn*
These are gifts.	これは，おみやげです。 *koh-reh wah, oh-MEE-yah-geh dehs*
May I close the bag now?	しめてもいいですか。 *SHEE-meh-teh-moh ee dehs KAH*
Do I have to pay duty?	税金を，払わなければなりませんか。 *zeh-keen oh hah-RAH-wah-nah-keh-reh-bah nah-ree-mah-sehn KAH*
How much do I pay?	いくらですか。 *EE-koo-rah dehs KAH*
Where do I pay?	どこで払いますか。 *DOH-koh deh, hah-rah-ee-mahs KAH*
Can I pay with dollars?	ドルで払えますか。 *DOH-roo deh hah-rah-eh-mahs KAH*

PORTERS

There's a fixed price (300 yen) for each bag. This is a fee, not a

tip, and you don't need to give the porter anything more.
Convenient, free luggage carts are available.

Could you get me a porter?	ポーターをよんでもらえますか。 *POH-tah oh yohn-deh moh-rah-eh-mahs KAH*
Could you help me?	ちょっと，お願いします。 *CHOHT-toh, oh-NEH-gah-ee shee-mahs*
My luggage is <u>here</u>.	荷物は<u>ここ</u>です。 *NEE-moh-tsoo wah <u>koh-KOH</u> dehs*
there	そこ *soh-KOH*
over there	あそこ *ah-SOH-koh*
I have <u>two pieces</u> of luggage altogether.	全部で<u>二つ</u>あります。 *ZEHN-boo deh, <u>foo-TAH-tsoo</u> ah-ree-mahs*
three pieces	三つ *meet-TSOO*
four pieces	四つ *yoht-TSOO*
five pieces	五つ *ee-TSOO-tsoo*
This one is fragile.	われやすい物が，入っています。 *wah-REH-yah-soo-ee moh-NOH gah, HAH-eet-teh ee-mahs*
Please be careful.	気をつけてください。 *kee OH tskeh-teh koo-dah-sah-ee*
I'll carry this one my-self.	これは，自分で運びます。 *koh-reh wah, jee-BOON deh hah-KOH-bee-mahs*
To the <u>taxi stand</u>, please.	<u>タクシー乗り場</u>まで行ってください。 *<u>tahk-SHEE noh-ree-bah</u> mah-deh eet-teh koo-dah-sah-ee*
bus stop	バスの乗り場 *BAH-soo noh noh-REE-bah*
hotel bus	ホテルのバスの乗り場 *HOH-teh-roo noh BAH-soo noh noh-REE-bah*
limousine bus (TCAT–Hakozaki)	箱崎へのリムジン・バスの乗り場 *hah-KOH-zah-kee eh noh ree-MOO-jeen bah-soo no noh-REE-bah*
Keisei shuttle bus	京成のシャトル・バス *KEH-seh noh shah-TOH-roo bah-soo*

JNR shuttle bus	国鉄のシャトル・バス *kohk-TEH-tsoo noh shah-TOH-roo bah-soo*
I want the limousine bus to <u>Haneda Airport</u>.	羽田空港へのリムジン・バスに乗りたいのですが。 *hah-NEH-dah koo-koh eh noh, ree-MOO-jeen bah-soo nee noh-REE-tah-ee noh dehs gah*
Yokohama City Air Terminal	横浜シティーターミナル *yoh-KOH-hah-mah shee-tee TAH-mee-nah-roo*
Here is fine.	ここで，けっこうです。 *koh-koh deh, KEHK-koh dehs*
Put them down here please.	ここに置いてください。 *koh-koh nee oh-EE-teh koo-dah-sah-ee*
How much do I owe you?	いくらですか。 *EE-koo-rah dehs KAH*

HOTEL RESERVATIONS AND OTHER QUESTIONS

You've probably made your hotel reservations before arriving in Japan. If not, or if you have questions about transportation to town, or anything else, the following phrases will be helpful. You'll find someone who speaks English at each counter.

Where's the information counter?	案内所は，どこですか。 *AHN-nah-ee-joh wah, DOH-koh dehs KAH*
Where's the hotel reservation counter?	ホテルの予約カウンターは，どこですか。 *HOH-teh-roo noh yoh-YAH-koo kah-OON-tah wah,DOH-koh dehs KAH*
Where's the Japan Travel Bureau counter?	交通公社は，どこですか。 *KOH-tsoo KOH-shah wah, DOH-koh dehs KAH*
Where's the Japan National Tourist Organization (JNTO) Tourist Information Center?	国際観光振興会の観光案内所は，どこですか。 *kohk-SAH-ee kahn-koh SHEEN-koh kah-ee noh ahn-nah-ee-joh wah, DOH-koh dehs KAH*

Note: For information on changing money at the airport, see pp. 45–50 in Banking and Money Matters.

NARITA-TOKYO TRANSPORTATION

New Tokyo International Airport at Narita is a modern facility; it's also farther from downtown Tokyo than you might expect—about 40 miles, or 65 kilometers. There are convenient ways to get from the airport to your destination, but the trip will take some time and could involve a transfer. The length of the ride varies according to the means of transportation, the time, and traffic conditions. So—once you've landed at Narita, you still have a trip ahead of you!

How can you get to town? There are several possibilities. Check at the appropriate counter in the terminal for information on schedules and tickets.

Bus to Your Hotel

Check to see if there is one.

Limousine Bus to Tokyo City Air Terminal (TCAT)

TCAT (often called "tee-cat") is located at Hakozaki in downtown Tokyo. The limousine bus takes from 70 to 90 minutes, depending on traffic. Once you arrive at TCAT, ask about direct bus service to your hotel, or take a taxi.

Trains to Tokyo

Inquire at the Keisei Line ticket counter and the Japanese National Railways ticket counter for schedule and ticket information.

FROM NARITA AIRPORT TO TOKYO

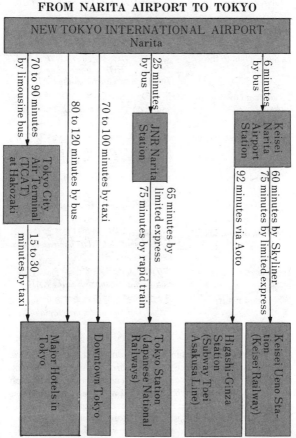

I want to go to the limousine bus counter.	リムジン・バスのカウンターに，行きたいのですが。 *ree-MOO-jeen bah-soo noh kah-OON-tah nee ee-kee-TAH-ee noh dehs gah*
JNR counter	国鉄のカウンター *kohk-TEH-tsoo noh kah-OON-tah*
Keisei counter	京成電鉄のカウンター *KEH-seh DEHN-teh-tsoo noh kah-OON-tah*
Is there a bus to the ___ hotel?	＿＿ホテルへ行く，バスがありますか。 *___ HOH-teh-roo eh ee-koo, BAH-soo gah ah-ree-mahs KAH*
I want to go to ___ in Tokyo.	東京の＿＿へ行きたいのですが。 *toh-kyoh noh ___ eh ee-KEE-tah-ee noh dehs gah*
What's the best way to go?	どの行き方が，一番いいですか。 *DOH-noh ee-kee-kah-tah gah, ee-CHEE-ban EE dehs KAH*
the fastest	一番速い *ee-CHEE-bahn hah-YAH-ee*
the cheapest	一番安い *ee-CHEE-bahn yah-SOO-ee*
How long does it take?	時間は，どの位かかりますか。 *jee-KAHN wah, doh-NOH koo-rah-ee kah-kah-ree-mahs KAH*
When does the next one leave?	次のは，いつ出ますか。 *tsoo-GEE-noh wah, EE-tsoo deh-mahs KAH*
Where do I get it?	それは，どこで乗れますか。 *soh-reh wah, DOH-koh deh noh-reh mahs KAH*

Taxis

This takes 70 to 100 minutes, depending on traffic. Taxis have meters, so it's an expensive ride. Keep in mind that you should not try to open or close the door yourself. The driver operates the left rear door automatically from his seat. It will swing open when you get in and close behind you after you leave. Because some hotels have different names in English and Japanese, you might want to have someone write your destination for you in Japanese before you leave the terminal, to show to the taxi driver.

Where can I get a taxi?	どこで，タクシーに乗れますか。 *DOH-koh deh, TAHK-shee nee noh-REH-mahs KAH*
How long does it take to Tokyo?	東京まで，どの位時間がかかります か。 *toh-kyoh mah-deh, doh-NOH koo-rah-ee jee-KAHN gah kah-kah-ree-mahs KAH*
How much will it cost?	いくら，かかりますか。 *EE-koo-rah, kah-kah-ree mahs KAH*
Take me to the ____ Hotel, please.	____ホテルまで，行ってください。 *____ HOH-teh-roo mah-deh, eet-TEH-koo-dah-sah-ee*
Take me to this address please.	この住所まで，行ってください。 *koh-NOH JOO-shoh mah-deh, eet-TEH koo-dah-sah-ee*

Car with Driver

This is the Japanese equivalent of limousine service, but don't expect a limousine! What you <u>can</u> expect is a standard size, immaculate car, with a polite, efficient driver. The Japanese call this "Hire." Be sure to pronounce it in the Japanese way, HAH-ee-yah. It takes about the same time as a taxi and costs about twice as much. It's customary to tip the driver about 7 or 8 percent at the end.

Where can I get a car with driver?	ハイヤーは，どこでやとえますか。 *HAH-ee-yah wah, DOH-koh deh yah-toh-eh-mahs KAH*
How much will it cost to ___ in Tokyo?	東京の___まで，いくらかかりますか。 *toh-kyoh noh ___ mah-deh, EE-koo-rah kah-kah-ree-mahs KAH*
Is the rate <u>by the hour</u>?	料金は，時間制ですか。 *R<u>YOH</u>-keen wah, <u>jee-KAHN</u> seh dehs KAH*
by the half-day	半日 *HAHN nee-chee*
by the day	一日 *ee-CHEE nee-chee*
I'd like to get one.	一台お願いします。 *ee-CHEE dah-ee oh-NEH-gah-ee shee-mahs*

Rental Cars

You can arrange for a car in the airport terminal. You'll need an International Driving Permit (you can get it through the American Automobile Association or similar organizations in other countries). You'll also need a good knowledge of Japanese road signs and some kanji, or Japanese writing. See page 313 for more information on renting a car.

BANKING AND MONEY MATTERS

Japanese banks are open weekdays from 9 A.M. to 3 P.M. and Saturdays from 9 A.M. to noon, except for the second Saturday of each month, when all financial institutions are closed. You can change money at authorized currency exchanges only. These are well-marked, and located at such places as banks, major Western-style hotels, leading shops that foreigners frequent, and international airports. You <u>must</u> have your passport with you for all money-exchanging transactions, and you should keep your receipt. The yen is the basic unit of Japanese currency. The symbol for yen is ¥.

yen   円 *ehn*

Yen Denominations
COINS

1	yen	aluminum
5	yen	copper color
10	yen	bronze color
50	yen	silver color
100	yen	silver color
500	yen	silver color

BILLS 500 yen, 1,000 yen, 5,000 yen, 10,000 yen

For the yen value of your own currency, check the daily exchange rate at your hotel front desk, credit card office, bank, or other authorized currency exchange. Some currencies cannot be exchanged for yen and should be converted to a negotiable currency before the bearer arrives in Japan. It's best to check before you leave home.

Since exchange rates fluctuate, the following table may be helpful in converting yen into your own currency for easy comparison of prices and values.

Yen	Your Own Currency	Yen	Your Own Currency
50		1,000	
100		5,000	
500		10,000	

EXCHANGING MONEY

Where can I change money?	お金は，どこでかえられますか。 *oh-KAH-neh wah, DOH-koh deh kah-eh-rah-reh-mahs KAH*
dollars	ドル *DOH-roo*
pounds	ポンド *POHN-doh*
travelers checks	トラベラー・チェック *toh-RAH-beh-rah chehk-koo*
a personal check	個人用小切手 *koh-JEEN yoh koh-GEET-teh*
Is there a hotel nearby where I can change my travelers checks to yen?	近くに，トラベラー・チェックを円にかえられるホテルがありますか。 *chee-KAH-koo nee, toh-RAH-beh-rah chehk-koo oh EHN nee kah-eh-rah-reh-roo hoh-teh-roo gah ah-ree-mahs KAH*
Can I change foreign currency into yen at the front desk?	フロントで，外貨を円にかえられますか。 *foo-ROHN-toh deh, GAH-ee-kah oh EHN nee kah-eh-rah-reh-mahs KAH*
Where is a bank?	銀行は，どこにありますか。 *geen-koh wah, DOH-koh nee ah-ree-mahs KAH*
the American Express Office	アメリカン・エクスプレスのオフィス *ah-MEH-ree-kahn eh-KOOS-poo-reh-soo noh oh-fee-soo*
the Carte Blanche office	カルテ・ブランチのオフィス *kah-ROO-teh boo-RAHN-chee noh oh-fee-soo*

the Diners Club office	ダイナーズ・クラブのオフィス *dah-EE-nah-soo KOO-rah-boo noh oh-fee-soo*
the MasterCard office	マスターカードのオフィス *mah-SOO-tah kah-doh noh oh-fee-soo*
the Visa office	ビザのオフィス *BEE-zah noh oh-fee-soo*
I'd like to change <u>dollars</u> into yen.	ドルを円にかえたいのですが。 *DOH-roo oh EHN nee kah-EH-tah-ee noh dehs gah*
pounds	ポンド *POHN-doh*
What's today's <u>dollar</u>—yen exchange rate?	今日のドルと円の交換率は，どの位ですか。 *kyoh noh DOH-roo toh EHN noh koh-kahn ree-tsoo wah, doh-NOH koo-rah-ee dehs KAH*
pound	ポンド *POHN-doh*
I'd like to change <u>100</u> dollars to yen.	100ドルを，円にかえたいのですが。 *hyah-KOO doh-roo oh, EHN nee kah-EH-tah-ee noh dehs gah*
200	*nee-HYAH-koo*
300	*SAHN-byah-koo*
400	*YOHN-hyah-koo*
500	*goh-HYAH-koo*
600	*rohp-PYAH-koo*
700	*nah-NAH-hyah-koo*
800	*hahp-PYAH-koo*
900	*KYOO-hyah-koo*
1,000	*SEHN*
Do I need to fill out a form?	書式に記入の必要がありますか。 *shoh-SHEE-kee nee, kee-NYOO noh hee-tsoo-yoh gah ah-ree-mahs KAH*
Here's my passport.	これが，私のパスポート／旅券です。 *koh-REH gah, wah-tahk-shee noh pah-SOO-poh-toh／ryoh-KEHN dehs*

I'd like the money in <u>large</u> bills.	大きい（お）札でください。 *OH-kee (oh) sah-tsoo deh koo-dah-sah-ee*
small	小さい *CHEE-sah-ee*
I want some change, too.	硬貨も，すこしください。 *KOH-kah moh, SKOH-shee koo-dah-sah-ee*
Give me one 10,000 yen, two 5,000 yen, and three 1,000 yen bills, please.	一万円札を一枚と，五千円札を二枚と，千円札を三枚ください。 *ee-CHEE-mahn-EHN-sahts oh ee-CHEE-mah-ee toh, goh-SEHN-EHN-sahts oh NEE-mah-ee toh SEHN-EHN-sahts oh SAHN-mah-ee koo-dah-sah-ee*

Airport Money Exchange

If you need to change currency at the airport, these phrases can help. There are different lines for currency and for travelers checks.

Where's the money exchange?	両替所は，どこですか， *RYOH-gah-eh-joh wah, DOH-koh dehs KAH*
Is the money exchange open?	両替所は，あいていますか。 *RYOH-gah-eh-joh wah, ah-EE-teh ee-mahs KAH*
May I cash travelers checks?	トラベラー・チェックを，現金化できますか。 *toh-RAH-beh-rah chehk-koo oh, GEHN-keen-kah deh-kee-mahs KAH*
Which window do l use to change <u>foreign money</u> to yen?	外貨を円にかえるのは，どの窓口ですか。 *GAH-ee-kah oh EHN nee kah-eh-roo noh wah, DOH-noh mah-doh-goo-chee dehs KAH*
travelers checks	トラベラー・チェック *toh-RAH-beh-rah chehk-koo*

Personal Checks

Personal checks, especially those on foreign banks, are
not going to be of much use to you in Japan. Cash,
travelers checks, and major credit cards are all fine.
The major credit card companies have offices in large
Japanese cities, and they provide the usual services;
you can count on them to cash personal checks in an
emergency (if you're a cardholder).

Banking Terms

amount	金額	*KEEN-gah-koo*
banker	銀行家	*geen-koh-kah*
bill	紙幣	*SHEE-heh*
to borrow	借りる	*kah-REE-roo*
capital	資本	*shee-hohn*
cashier	支配人	*shee-HAH-ee-neen*
cashier's office	支配人のオフィス	*shee-HAH-ee-neen noh OH-fee-soo*
check	小切手	*koh-GEET-teh*
to endorse	裏書する	*oo-RAH-gah-kee-soo-roo*
income	収入	*shoo-nyoo*
interest rate	利率	*ree-REE-tsoo*
investment	投資	*toh-shee*
to lend	貸す	*kah-soo*
loss	損失	*SOHN-shee-tsoo*
to make change	こまかくする	*koh-MAH-kah-koo soo-roo*
mortgage	住宅ローン	*JOO-tah-koo rohn*
to open an account	口座を開く	*KOH-zah oh hee-RAH-koo*
premium	プレミアム	*poo-REH-mee-ah-moo*
profit	利益	*REE-eh-kee*

secretary	秘書	*HEE-shoh*
safe	金庫	*KEEN-koh*
signature	署名／サイン	*shoh-MEH/ SAH-een*
window	窓口	*mah-DOH-goo-chee*

TIPPING: SOME GENERAL GUIDELINES

You're about to deal with a variety of people who provide the kinds of services for which you'd normally expect to tip. Resist the impulse. Hotels and restaurants add a 10 to 15 percent service charge to your bill or check, so individual employees do not usually expect tips. People in service positions take pride in what they do; they consider their wages or salaries sufficient, and they don't look to the customer for something extra. The few exceptions are pointed out for you under appropriate headings in this book.

In some large Western-style hotels, porters, bellhops, and room service staff have been given tips by Westerners so often that they may expect them; and you'll see signs in a few hairdressing salons saying that the operators should be tipped. The amounts are up to you. It's also customary to tip the room maid in Japanese-style inns.

The general "no tipping" rule does <u>not</u> extend to small gifts (monetary or otherwise) for extra or special service. The Japanese are a gift-giving people, and a token gift is always appreciated, but not expected. In most cases, a smile and a "thank you" will do quite well.

AT THE HOTEL

ACCOMMODATIONS

When you stay in Japan, you have a choice between Western-style and Japanese-style accommodations. The terms "Western-style" and "Japanese-style" categorize both the facilities and the service that each type of lodging offers. In each of the two broad categories, you'll find a wide range of possibilities, from costly and luxurious to inexpensive and simple. You might stay at a Western-style hotel when you first arrive, and then a Japanese-style inn, or **ryokan** (*ryoh-KAHN*) for a few nights as you travel around. You might even enjoy staying at a family guest house, or **minshuku** (*MEEN-shoo-koo*). Sometimes it's possible to have a bit of both worlds: Some Western-style hotels have a few Japanese-style rooms or suites, and some Japanese-style hotels may have a few guest rooms with beds.

The differences between the two styles of accommodations often require different kinds of language. You say certain things at Japanese inns that you would not have to say at Western-style hotels, and you need a slightly more formal or polite level of Japanese as well. Because of these special language needs, you'll find a section for each category here.

WESTERN-STYLE LODGING

Hotels and Business Hotels

First-class hotels in Japan equal fine hotels anywhere for facilities and quality of service. They may equal them in costs as well. There are options, however. Japan has a great many Western-style hotels of various types and standards. A relatively new kind of hotel, and an exceedingly popular one, is the business hotel. Some say the name comes from the fact that this category of hotel is popular with Japanese businessmen. Others maintain it comes from the businesslike competence with which they are run.

Whatever the origin of the name, these hotels are convenient, efficient, and usually quite reasonable. They offer clean, comfortable rooms and "no frills" service. They're often located near the center of town, within easy walking distance of train and subway stations. They're not fancy: The lobbies are plain, the rooms are *very* small, and few have room service. But they're well-run, and for many travelers, the price is right.

hotel	ホテル HOH-teh-roo
business hotel	ビジネス・ホテル bee-JEE-nehs HOH-teh-roo

GETTING TO YOUR HOTEL

I'd like to go to the ____ Hotel.	____ホテルへ行きたいのですが。 ____HOH-teh-roo eh ee-KEE-tah-ee noh dehs gah
Where can I get a taxi?	タクシーは，どこでひろえますか。 TAHK-shee wah, DOH-koh deh hee-roh-ee-mahs KAH
What buses go into town?	どのバスに乗れば，市内へ行けますか。 DOH-noh bah-soo nee noh-REH-bah, SHEE-nah-ee eh ee-KEH-mahs KAH
Where is the bus stop?	バス停は，どこですか。 bah-SOO-teh wah, DOH-koh dehs KAH
How much is the fare?	料金は，いくらですか。 RYOH-keen wah, EE-koo-rah dehs KAH

CHECKING IN

The registration form that you are asked to fill out in Western-style hotels has an English translation. Hotels add a 10 percent tax and the 10 to 15 percent service charge to the bill.

My name is ____.	私の名前は，____です。 wah-TAHK-shee noh nah-mah-eh wah, ____ dehs

I have a reservation.	予約が，してあります。 *yoh-YAH-koo gah, shteh ah-ree-mahs*
I don't have a reservation, but can I get a room?	予約がないのですが，泊まれますか。 *yoh-YAH-koo gah NAH-ee noh dehs gah, toh-MAH-reh-mahs KAH*
I'd like <u>a single room</u>.	<u>シングルの部屋が欲しい</u>のですが。 *<u>SHEEN-goo-roo noh heh-yah gah</u> hoh-SHEE noh dehs gah*
two single rooms	シングルが二部屋 *SHEEN-goo-roo gah foo-TAH-heh-yah*
a double room	ダブルの部屋が *DAH-boo-roo noh heh-yah gah*
a single room and a double room	シングルを一部屋とダブルを一部屋 *SHEEN-goo-roo oh hee-TOH heh-yah toh, DAH-boo-roo oh hee-TOH heh-yah*
a suite	スイートが *soo-EE-toh gah*
I'd like a room <u>with twin beds</u>.	<u>ツイン・ベッド</u>の部屋が欲しいのですが。 *<u>tsoo-EEN BEHD-doh</u> noh heh-yah gah, hoh-SHEE noh dehs gah*
with bath	浴室付きの *yoh-KOOSHTS tskee noh*
with a shower	シャワー付きの *shah-WAH tskee noh*
with a good view	ながめのいい *nah-GAH mch noh EE*
facing the mountain	山に面した *yah-MAH nee MEHN-shtah*
facing the ocean	海に面した *OO-mee nee MEHN-shtah*
facing the street	通りに面した *TOH-ree nee MEHN-shtah*
facing the courtyard	中庭に面した *nah-KAH-nee-wah nee MEHN-shtah*
I need a baby crib in the room, please.	ベビー・ベッドが欲しいのですが。 *beh-BEE BEHD-doh gah, hoh-SHEE noh dehs gah*

What's the rate?	一泊，いかほどですか。 *eep-pah-koo, ee-KAH-hoh-doh dehs KAH*
Does the rate include the service charge?	サービス料も入っていますか。 *SAH-bee-soo ryoh moh, HAH-eet-teh ee-mahs KAH*
Does the rate include breakfast?	料金は，朝食込みですか。 *RYOH-keen wah, choh-shoh-koo koh-MEE dehs KAH*
Is there a discount for children?	子供の割引きは，ありますか。 *koh-doh-moh noh wah-REE-bee-kee wah, ah-REE-mahs KAH*
Is there a charge for the baby?	赤ん坊にも，料金がかかりますか。 *ah-KAHM-boh nee-moh, RYOH-keen gah kah-KAH-ree-mahs KAH*
Do you have anything cheaper?	もうちょっと，安い部屋がありますか。 *MOH choht-toh, yah-SOO-ee heh-yah gah ah-REE-mahs KAH*
I'll be staying just tonight.	今晩だけ泊まります。 *KOHN-bahn dah-keh toh-MAH-ree-mahs*
a few days	数日 *SOO-jee-tsoo*
a week	一週間 *eesh-SHOO-kahn*
at least a week	少なくとも一週間 *soo-KOO-nah-koo-toh-moh eesh-SHOO-kahn*
I'm not sure yet how long I'm staying.	何日泊まるか，まだわかりません。 *NAHN nee-chee toh-mah-roo kah, MAH-dah wah-KAH ree-mah-sehn*
What floor is it on?	部屋は，何階ですか。 *heh-YAH wah, NAHN-kah-ee dehs KAH*
Can I get the room right now?	部屋は，今すぐとれますか。 *heh-YAH wah, EE-mah soo-goo toh-REH-mahs KAH*

Changing the Room

Could I get a different room?	部屋を，変えてもらえますか。 *heh-yah oh, kah-EH-teh moh-rah-eh-mahs KAH*

It's <u>too big</u>.	この部屋は、ちょっと<u>大き過ぎる</u>ようです。 *koh-NOH heh-yah wah, __ CHOHT-toh OH-kee-soo-gee-roo yoh dehs*
too small	小さ過ぎる *CHEE-sah-soo-gee-roo*
too dark	暗ら過ぎる *koo-RAH-soo-gee-roo*
too noisy	やかまし過ぎる *yah-KAH-mah-shee-soo-gee-roo*
Do you have a <u>better</u> room?	もう少しいい部屋が、ありますか。 *MOH SKOH-shee, EE heh-yah gah, ah-REE-mahs KAH*
larger	大きい *OH-kee*
smaller	小さい *CHEE-sah-ee*
quieter	静かな *SHEE-zoo-kah nah*
I'd like a room <u>with more light</u>.	もう少し<u>明るい</u>部屋が、欲しいのですが。 *MOH SKOH-shee <u>ah-KAH-roo-ee</u> heh-yah gah, hoh-SHEE noh dehs gah*
on a higher floor	上の階の *oo-EH noh KAH-ee noh*
on a lower floor	下の階の *SHTAH noh KAH-ee noh*
Do you have a room with a better view?	もう少し、ながめのいい部屋がありますか。 *MOH SKOH-shee, nah-GAH-meh noh EE heh-yah gah ah-REE-mahs KAH*

Hotel Information

Is room service available?	ルーム・サービスが、ありますか。 *ROO-moo sah-bee-soo gah, ah-ree-mahs KAH*
Is a masseur/ masseuse available?	あんまさんを、よべますか。 *AHN-mah sahn oh, yoh-BEH-mahs KAH*
Is a babysitter available?	子守りを、たのめますか。 *koh-MOH-ree oh, tah NOH mch-mahs KAH*
Is there a <u>restaurant</u> in the hotel?	ホテルに、<u>レストラン</u>がありますか。 *HOH-teh-roo nee, <u>REH-soo-toh-rahn</u> gah ah-ree-mahs KAH*

bar	バー *BAH*
coffee shop	コーヒー・ショップ *KOH-hee shohp-poo*
barbershop	床屋 *toh-KOH-yah*
beauty parlor	美容院 *bee-YOH-een*
pharmacy	薬局 *yahk-KYOH-koo*
newsstand	新聞売り場 *SHEEN-boon OO-ree-bah*
shopping arcade	ショッピング・アーケード *shohp-PEEN-goo ah-keh-doh*
Where is it?	どこに、ありますか。 *DOH-koh nee, ah-ree-mahs KAH*
Is an English-language interpreter available?	英語の通訳をたのめますか。 *EH-goh noh TSOO-yah-koo oh, tah-noh-meh-mahs KAH*
Is there a <u>gym</u>?	<u>ジム</u>は、ありますか。 *JEE-moo wah, ah-ree-mahs KAH*
health club	ヘルス・クラブ *heh-ROOS koo-rah-boo*
sauna	サウナ *SAH-oo-nah*
swimming pool	プール *POO-roo*
tennis court	テニスコート *teh-NEES koh-toh*
What time does it open?	何時にあきますか。 *NAHN-jee nee, ah-kee-mahs KAH*
Is there a charge?	料金は。 *RYOH-keen WAH*
Can I rent a typewriter?	タイプ・ライターを、借りられますか。 *tah-EE-poo rah-ee-tah oh, kah-REE-rah-reh-mahs KAH*
Where's the <u>elevator</u>?	<u>エレベーター</u>は、どこですか。 *eh-REH-beh-tah wah, DOH-koh dehs KAH*
telephone	電話 *dehn-wah*
dining room	食堂 *shoh-KOO-doh*
bathroom	トイレ *TOH-ee-reh*

| ladies' room | 女子用のトイレ *joh-SHEE yoh noh TOH-ee-reh* |
| men's room | 男子用のトイレ *DAHN-shee yoh noh TOH-ee-reh* |

In the Room

Electrical voltage is 100; American 110-volt small appliances can just be plugged in with no adapter.

Where do I control the air conditioner?	冷房の調節は，どこでしますか。 *REH-boh noh choh-seh-tsoo wah, DOH-koh deh shee-mahs KAH*
heater	暖房 *DAHN-boh*
Where can I plug in my electric razor?	電気カミソリの，差込みはどこですか。 *DEHN-kee kah-mee-soh-ree noh sah-SHEE-koh-mee wah, DOH-koh dehs KAH*
hair dryer	ヘアー・ドライヤー *heh-AH doh-rah-ee-yah*
Do you have an adapter plug?	差込み用のアダプターが，ありますか。 *sah-SHEE-koh-mee yoh noh ah-DAH-poo-tah gah, ah-ree-mahs KAH*
electrical transformer	変圧器 *HEHN-ah-tsoo-kee*
How does the shower work?	シャワーの使い方は。 *SHAH-wah noh tsoo-KAH-ee-kah-tah WAH*
I need a bellhop.	ボーイさんを，よこして下さい。 *boh-ee sahn oh, yoh-KOH-shteh koo-dah-sah-ee*
maid	メイド *meh-doh*
Please send breakfast to my room.	朝食を，部屋にとどけて下さい。 *CHOH-shoh-koo oh, heh-yah nee toh-DOH-keh-teh koo-dah-sah-ee*
some towels	タオル *TAH-oh-roo*
some soap	せっけん *sehk-KEHN*
some hangers	ハンガー *HAHN-gah*
a pillow	枕 *MAH-koo-rah*
a blanket	毛布 *MOH-foo*

some ice	氷 *koh-ree*
some ice water	アイス・ウォーター *ah-EE-soo woh-tah*
an ashtray	灰皿 *hah-EE-zah-rah*
some toilet paper	トイレット・ペーパー *toh-EE-reht-toh peh-pah*
a luggage rack	荷物の置き台 *NEE-moh-tsoo noh oh-KEE-dah-ee*
Who is it?	だれですか。 *DAH-reh dehs KAH*
Just a minute.	ちょっと待って下さい。 *CHOHT-toh MAHT-teh koo-dah-sah-ee*
Come in.	どうぞ。 *DOH-zoh*
Put it on the <u>table</u> please.	テーブルの上に，置いてください。 *teh-boo-roo noh oo-eh nee, oh-EE-teh koo-dah-sah-ee*
bed	ベッド *BEHD-doh*
I'd like <u>room service</u> please.	ルーム・サービスを，お願いします。 *ROO-moo sah-bee-soo oh, oh-NEH-gah-ee shee-mahs*
a masseur/ a mas-seuse	男のあんまさん／女のあんまさん *oh-TOH-koh noh ahn-mah sahn/ OHN-nah noh ahn-mah suhn*
a babysitter	子守り *koh-MOH-ree*
I'd like a 6 o'clock wakeup call, please.	あす六時に，モーニング・コールをお願いします。 *ah-soo roh-KOO-jee nee, MOH-neen-goo koh-roo oh oh-NEH-gah-ee shee-mahs*

Problems

There's no electricity.	電気が，つきません。 *DEHN-kee gah, tsoo-KEE-mah-sehn*
The <u>TV</u> doesn't work.	テレビが，つきません。 *TEH-reh-bee gah, tsoo-KEE mah-sehn*
radio	ラジオ *RAH-jee-oh*
electric fan	扇風機 *SEHN-poo-kee*

lamp	ランプ *RAHN-poo*
The air conditioning doesn't work.	冷房が、ききません。*reh-boh gah, kee-KEE-mah-sehn*
There's no heat.	暖房が、ききません。*dahn-boh gah, kee-KEE-mah-sehn*
There's no <u>running water</u>.	水が、出ません。*mee-zoo gah, deh-MAH-sehn*
hot water	お湯 *oh-yoo*
The toilet won't flush.	トイレの水が、流れません。*TOH-ee-reh noh mee-zoo gah, nah-GAH-reh-mah-sehn*
The toilet is stopped up.	トイレが、つまっています。*TOH-ee-reh gah, tsoo-MAHT-teh ee-mahs*
The sink is stopped up.	洗面台が、つまっています。*sehn-mehn-dah-ee gah, tsoo-MAHT-teh ee-mahs*
The bathtub won't drain properly.	（お）風呂の排水が、よくありません。*(oh)-FOO-roh noh hah-ee-soo-ee gah, YOH-koo ah-ree-mah-sehn*
I need a new lightbulb.	電球が、切れています。*DEHN-kyoo gah, KEE-reh-teh ee-mahs*
The <u>window</u> won't open.	窓が、あきません。*MAH-doh gah, ah-KEE-mah-sehn*
Venetian blind	ブラインド *boo-RAH-een-doh*
The <u>window</u> won't close.	窓が、しまりません。*MAH-doh gah, shee-MAH-ree-mah-sehn*
Venetian blind	ブラインド *boo-RAH-een-doh*
Can I get it fixed?	直してもらえますか。*nah-OH-shteh moh-RAH-eh-mahs KAH*
I've locked myself out.	鍵を部屋に置いたまま、戸をしめてしまいました。*kah-GEE oh heh-yah nee oh-EE-tah mah-mah, toh oh SHEE-meh-teh shee-mah-ee-mahsh-tah*
I've lost my key.	鍵を、なくしてしまいました。*kah-GEE oh, nah-KOOSH-teh shee-mah-ee-mahsh-tah*

These shoes aren't mine.	私のくつではありません。	*wah-TAHK-shee noh koo-TSOO deh-wah ah-ree-mah-sehn*
This laundry isn't mine.	私の洗たく物ではありません。	*wah-TAHK-shee noh SEHN-tah-koo moh-noh deh-wah ah-REE-mah-sehn*

ORDERING BREAKFAST

Most large hotels will have dining rooms where breakfast is served, or you may order breakfast sent up to your room. For more phrases dealing with meals, see the food section, p. 180.

I'd like _____.	_____を，ください。	_____ *oh, koo-DAH-sah-ee*
Do you have _____?	_____は，ありますか。	_____ *wah, ah-REE-mahs KAH*
May I have some more _____?	_____を，もう少しください。	_____ *oh, MOH SKOH-shee koo-DAH-sah-ee*
There isn't any _____.	_____がありません。	_____ *gah, ah-REE-mah-sehn*
Could you bring me _____.	_____を，ください。	_____ *oh, koo-DAH-sah-ee*

Fruit

Check the price before ordering fruit. It can be very expensive.

apple	りんご	*reen-goh*
orange	オレンジ	*oh-REHN-jee*
melon	メロン	*MEH-rohn*
Japanese pear	なし	*nah-SHEE*
strawberries	いちご	*ee-CHEE-goh*
pineapple	パイナップル	*pah-EE-nahp-poo-roo*
grapefruit	グレープ・フルーツ	*goo-REH-poo foo-ROO-tsoo*

Juice

As with fruit, check the price before ordering juice.

orange juice	オレンジジュース	*oh-REHN-jee joo-soo*
grapefruit juice	グレープ・フルーツ ジュース	*GREH-poo-foo-ROO-tsoo joo-soo*
tomato juice	トマトジュース	*toh-MAH-toh joo-soo*
pineapple juice	パイナップルジュース	*pah-EE-nahp-poo-roo joo-soo*
apple juice	りんごジュース	*reen-goh joo-soo*

Beverages

coffee	コーヒー	*koh-hee*
tea	紅茶	*koh-chah*
milk	ミルク／牛乳	*MEE-roo-koo/ gyoo-nyoo*
hot milk	あたたかい牛乳	*ah-TAH-tah-kah-ee gyoo-nyoo*
hot chocolate	ココア	*KOH-koh-ah*
iced tea	アイス・ティー	*ah-EES-tee*

Cereal

corn flakes	コーン・フレーク	*KOHN foo-reh-koo*
oatmeal	オートミール	*OH-toh MEE-roo*

Eggs

scrambled eggs	スクランブル・エッグ	*soo-KOO-rahn-boo-roo EHG-goo*
fried eggs	目玉焼き	*meh-DAH-mah yah-kee*
soft boiled eggs	半じゅくのたまご	*HAHN-joo-koo noh tah-MAH-goh*
omelet	オムレツ	*oh-MOO-reh-tsoo*

Meat

bacon	ベーコン	*BEH-kohn*
ham	ハム	*HAH-moo*
sausages	ソーセージ	*soh-SEH-jee*

Combinations

ham and eggs	ハム・エッグ	*hah-MOO ehg-goo*
bacon and eggs	ベーコン・エッグ	*BEH-kohn ehg-goo*
sausage and eggs	ソーセージとたまご	*soh-SEH-jee toh tah-MAH-goh*
ham omelet	ハムオムレツ	*hah-MOO OH-moo-reh-tsoo*
cheese omelet	チーズオムレツ	*CHEE-zoo OH-moo-reh-tsoo*

Other Hot Dishes

pancakes	ホット・ケーキ	*hoht-TOH keh-kee*
waffles	ワッフル	*WAHF-foo-roo*
French toast	フレンチ・トースト	*foo-REHN-chee TOH-soo-toh*

Bread

toast	トースト	*TOH-soo-toh*
rolls	ロール・パン	*ROH-roo pahn*
croissant	クロワッサン	*koo-ROH-wahs-sahn*
English muffins	マフィン	*MAH-feen*
Danish pastry	デーニッシュ／菓子パン	*DEH-neesh-shoo／kah-SHEE pahn*
doughnuts	ドーナツ	*DOH-nah-tsoo*

Accompaniments

jam	ジャム	*JAH-moo*
marmalade	マーマレード	*MAH-mah-reh-doh*

honey	はちみつ	*hah-CHEE-mee-tsoo*
syrup	シロップ	*SHEE-rohp-poo*

Special Requests

decaffeinated coffee	カフェイン抜きの コーヒー	*kah-FEH-een noo-kee noh KOH-hee*
skim milk	スキム・ミルク	*soo-KEE-moo mee-roo-koo*
lowfat milk	ローファット・ミルク	*ROH-faht-toh mee-roo-koo*
decaffeinated tea	カフェイン抜きの紅茶	*kah-FEH-een noo-kee noh koh-chah*
sugar substitute	ダイエットの甘味料	*DAH-ee-eht-toh noh kahn-mee ryoh*

I'd like it cooked without <u>salt</u>, please.	<u>塩</u>を使わないで，料理してください。 *shee-oh oh tsoo-KAH-wah-nah-ee deh, RYOH-ree-shteh koo-dah-sah-ee*
butter or oil	バターやオイル *BAH-tah yah OH-ee-roo*

DESK AND PHONE SERVICE

With the Desk Clerk

Could you keep this in your safe?	これを，金庫にあずかってもらえますか。 *koh-reh oh, KEEN-koh nee ah-ZOO-kaht-teh moh-rah-eh-mahs KAH*
I'd like to take my things out of your safe.	金庫にあずけた物を，出したいのですが。 *KEEN-koh nee ah-ZOO-keh-tah moh-noh oh, dahsh-TAH-ee noh dehs gah*
The key for Room 200 please.	200号室の，鍵をください。 *nee-HYAH-koo GOH shtsoo noh, kah-GEE oh koo-dah-sah-ee*
Are there any <u>messages</u> for me?	私あての，<u>メッセージ</u>がありますか。 *wah-TAHK-shee ah-teh noh, <u>MEHS-seh-jee</u> gah ah-REE-mahs KAH*

letters 手紙 *teh-GAH-mee*

With the Telephone Operator

I'd like an outside line. 市内を，お願いします。 *SHEE-nah-ee oh, oh-neh-gah-ee shee-mahs*

Hello. I'd like to make a long-distance call. もしもし，長距離電話をかけたいのですが。 *MOH-shee moh-shee. CHOH-kyoh-ree dehn-wah oh kah-KEH-tah-ee noh dehs gah*

The number is <u>Osaka 111–2222</u>. 番号は，<u>大阪111の2222</u>です。 *bahn-goh wah, <u>oh-sah-kah ee-CHEE ee-chee ee-chee noh, NEE nee nee nee</u> dehs*

Nagoya 333–4444. 名古屋333の4444 *NAH-goh-yah SAHN sahn sahn noh, YOHN yohn yohn yohn*

Hello, operator! I was cut off. もしもし，電話が切れてしまいました。 *MOH-shee moh-shee, dehn-wah gah KEE-reh-teh shee-mah-ee-mahsh-tah*

Could you try it again? もう一度，かけてもらえますか。 *moh ee-chee-doh, KAH-keh-teh moh-rah-eh-mahs KAH*

CHECKING OUT

I'm checking out <u>this morning</u>. <u>けさ</u>，たちます。 *<u>KEH-sah</u>, tah-chee-mahs*

soon もうじき *MOH-jee-kee*

around noon 昼ごろ *hee-ROO GOH-roh*

early tomorrow あす早く *ah-SOO HAH-yah-koo*

tomorrow morning あすの朝 *ah-SOO noh AH-sah*

Please have my bill ready. 勘定書を用意しておいてください。 *KAHN-joh gah-kee oh, YOH-ee shteh OH-ee-teh koo-dah-sah-ee*

Would you send someone to carry my luggage down?	荷物をおろすのに，だれかよこしてください。*NEE-moh-tsoo oh oh-ROH-soo noh nee, DAH-reh kah yoh-KOH-shteh koo-dah-sah-ee*
May I have my bill, please. My room is 600.	お勘定を，お願いします。部屋は，600号室です。*oh-KAHN-joh oh, oh-neh-gah-ee shee-mahs. heh-yah wah, rohp-PYAH-koo GOH shee-tsoo dehs*
I don't have much time. Could you hurry please?	あまり，時間がありません。いそいでもらえますか。*ah-mah-ree, jee-KAHN gah ah-REE-mah-sehn. ee-SOH-ee-deh moh-rah-eh-mahs KAH*
Does this include the tax and service charge?	サービス料と税金が，入っていますか。*SAH-bee-soo ryoh toh ZEH-keen gah, HAH-eet-teh ee-mahs KAH*
There seems to be an error in the bill.	勘定書に，間違いがあるようですが。*KAHN-joh gah-kee nee, mah-CHEE-gah-ee gah ah-roo yoh dehs gah*
Could you check it again?	すみませんが，もう一度確かめてください。*soo-MEE-mah-sehn gah, moh ee-chee-doh tahsh-KAH-meh-teh koo-dah-sah-ee*
Could you get me a taxi?	タクシーをよんでもらえますか。*TAHK-shee oh YOHN-deh moh-rah-eh-mahs KAH*
Can I check my baggage till noon?	荷物を，お昼まであずかってもらえますか。*NEE-moh-tsoo oh, oh-HEE-roo mah-deh ah-ZOO-kaht-teh moh-rah-eh mahs KAH*
evening	夕方 *YOO-gah-tah*

JAPANESE-STYLE LODGING

Ryokan: Japanese Inns

Staying at a **ryokan** is a good way to experience everyday Japanese customs firsthand. These inns offer traditional and authentic Japanese flavor, from the architecture and furnishings to the pace and style of life. You'll have everything you need to be comfortable, but the daily rituals of bathing, dressing, eating, and sleeping will be quite different from what you're used to. If you do decide to stay at a ryokan, there is a range in quality and price (as with Western-style hotels) from luxurious to simple. Some inns have private bathrooms, and some are used to dealing with Western guests. Dinner and breakfast are included in the room rate. There are about 9,000 ryokan in Japan, and about 2,500 of them are members of the Japan Ryokan Association (JRA), which ensures high standards of service and facilities. The Japan National Tourist Organization Tourist Information Centers (TICs) or a travel agency can help you choose one that's appropriate for your taste and budget.

Minshuku: Family Guest Houses

Minshuku are guest houses that take in travelers. They are often located in resort and vacation areas, and they charge reasonable rates. Because most are family-run operations, guests are usually treated as members of the family. This means no maid service, preparing your own bed (Japanese **futon**, or mattress on the floor) at night, and taking it up in the morning. You eat with the family—breakfast and dinner are included in the rate, and there's no special service. Your bill will be a good deal lower than at ryokan or hotels. There's no service charge, and no 10 percent tax. You can get more information on minshuku lodgings from the Japan Minshuku Association at the Japan Minshuku Center in Tokyo.

Language for Japanese-Style Accommodations

Most of the phrases in this section can be used for both ryokan and minshuku. In some cases, however, the phrase cannot be used for one or the other. For example, in a minshuku you would not say, "I'd like a suite." And in a ryokan you would not say, "Where is the futon (mattress and bedding)?" because the maid will make up the bed for you. When such a phrase occurs, there is an **R** for ryokan, or an **M** for minshuku, and the letter is crossed out. **M̶** means don't say this at a minshuku, and **R̶** means don't say this at a ryokan.

CHECKING IN

You remove your shoes when you arrive. Then you step up onto the floor proper, where you'll find slippers. This is the real beginning of your stay. The staff will usually be there to greet you.

Excuse me for bothering you. (The equivalent of "Hello" to announce your arrival.)

ごめんください。 *goh-MEHN koo-dah-sah-ee*

My name is ____, and I've made a reservation.

私は，____と申します。予約がしてあるはずですが。 *wah-TAHK-shee wah____ toh moh-shee-mahs. yoh-YAH-koo gah, shteh AH-roo hah-zoo dehs gah*

I don't have a reservation, but could I stay?

予約がないのですが，とめていただけますか。 *yoh-YAH-koo gah NAH-ee noh dehs gah, toh-MEH-teh ee-tah-dah-keh-mahs KAH*

I'm alone.

一人です。 *hee-TOH-ree dehs*

Two of us.

二人です。 *foo-TAH-ree dehs*

Three of us.

三人です。 *SAHN-neen dehs*

Four of us.

四人です。 *yoh-NEEN dehs*

☒ I'd like a <u>suite</u>.

次の間付きの部屋を，お願いします。 *tsoo-GEE noh mah tskee noh heh-YAH oh, oh-neh-gah-ee shee-mahs*

☒ a room with a private bathroom.

（お）風呂とトイレ付きの部屋 *(oh)-FOO-roh toh toh-EE-reh tskee noh heh-YAH*

☒ a room on the ground floor

一階の部屋 *eek-KAH-ee noh heh-YAH*

☒ a room on the second floor

二階の部屋 *nee-KAH-ee noh heh-YAH*

Rates

How much would it be for a night?

一泊，いかほどですか。 *eep-PAH-koo, ee-KAH-hoh-doh dehs KAH*

Ⓧ Does that include tax and service charge? 税金とサービス料が，入っています か。 *ZEH-keen toh SAH-bee-soo ryoh gah, HAH-eet-teh ee-mahs KAH*

Ⓧ Does that include dinner and breakfast? 二食付きですか。 *nee-SHOH-koo tskee dehs KAH*

Ⓧ Do you have a less expensive room? もう少し，安い部屋がありません か。 *moh skoh-shee, yah-SOO-ee heh-yah gah ah-ree-mah-sehn KAH*

I'd like to stay just tonight. 今晩だけ，お世話になりたいのです が。 *KOHN-bahn dah-keh, oh-SEH-wah nee nah-REE-tah-ee noh dehs gah*

two days 二日 *foots-KAH*

three days 三日 *meek-KAH*

In the Room

In the ryokan, the room maid will show you to your room. Since the floor is covered with tatami, or straw mats, be sure to remove your slippers before you enter. Once inside, you'll find a **yukata** (*yoo-KAH-tah*), or informal cotton kimono, for each guest. You can change into the yukata if you like (you can wear this anywhere at the ryokan, indoors and out). Then the maid brings you tea. Introduce yourself and others in your party, and mention how long you'll be staying. It is also customary to present the maid with a small tip (about 2,000 yen will cover your entire stay) at this time, although you may do it at your departure if you prefer. Place the money in an envelope or fold a sheet of paper around it before you give it to the maid, and you'll be doing it the Japanese way! At a minshuku, say the same thing, but with no tip.

How do you do? I'll be staying here (under your care) for two days or so. 二日ほど，お世話になります。どうぞ， よろしく。 *foots-KAH hoh-doh, oh-SEH-wah nee nah-ree-mahs. DOH-zoh, yoh-roh-shee-koo*

This is my wife. これは，家内です。 *koh-reh wah, KAH-nah-ee dehs*

husband 主人 *SHOO-jeen*

friend   友達 *toh-MOH-dah-chee*

At this time the maid will bring a register for you to sign. It will probably be in Japanese, so you will need help. Here's a list of the items the register might contain. Show it to the maid, and she can point to the equivalent items on the register.

Ryokan or Minshuku Register

passport number	旅券番号	*ryoh-KEHN bahn-goh*
name	名前	*nah-MAH-eh*
family name	姓	*SEH*
given name	名	*meh*
male	男	*oh-TOH-koh*
female	女	*OHN-nah*
date of birth	生年月日	*SEH-nehn gahp-pee*
nationality	国籍	*koh-KOO-seh-kee*
occupation	職業	*shoh-KOO-gyoh*
home address	住所	*JOO-shoh*
length of stay	滞在期間	*tah-ee-zah-ee KEE-kahn*
date	日付	*hee-ZOO-keh*
signature	署名	*shoh-MEH*

I can't read Japanese.	日本語が，読めません。 *nee-HOHN-goh gah, yoh-meh-mah-sehn*
Could you help me fill it out?	書くのを，手伝ってもらえますか。 *KAH-koo noh oh, teh-TSOO-daht-teh moh-rah-eh-mahs KAH*
What does it say?	何と，書いてありますか。 *NAHN toh, kah-ee-teh ah-ree-mahs KAH*

THE BATH

Ofuro? Literally, it means bath; practically, it can mean, "Do you want your bath now?" or "When would you like your bath?" or "Please take your bath now, because others are waiting." While this interest in your bath may seem unusual to foreigners, it is *very* Japanese, and for good reason. The Japanese bath is a ritual meant for relaxing and unwinding as much as for cleansing. At a ryokan, many people like to take a bath before dinner. The bath at the ryokan or the minshuku may be communal—that is, several people can use it at one time. If so, there will be separate facilities or separate times for men and women.

The law of the Japanese bath: NO SOAP INSIDE THE TUB. Rinse, soap, and scrub yourself outside—you'll find spigots, basins, and perhaps a small stool to sit on—then rinse off all the soap and enter the tub. It's deep, and the water is usually very hot. If you're alone, you may adjust the temperature by adding some cold water from the tap. But remember that you do not drain the water after you, that others will use the same water, and that Japanese like their bath water unimaginably hot. Now enjoy a nice, relaxing soak!

Where is the bath?	お風呂は，どこですか。 *oh-FOO-roh wah, DOH-koh dehs KAH*
Ⓜ Can I take a bath whenever I want?	お風呂は，いつでもはいれますか。 *oh-FOO-roh wah, ee-TSOO deh-moh hah-EE-reh-mahs KAH*
Ⓚ Is there a specific time for the bath?	お風呂の時間がありますか。 *oh-FOO-roh oh jee-KAHN gah ah-ree-mahs KAH*

The Toilet

The toilet is not located in the bath area, but in a room by itself, usually with a small sink, Leave your slippers outside the door, and put on those that you find just inside the door.

Where is the toilet?	お手洗いは，どこですか。 *oh-TEH-ah-rah-ee wah, DOH-koh dehs KAH*
Ⓜ Is there a toilet on this floor?	この階に，お手洗いがありますか。 *koh-NOH kah-ee nee, oh-TEH-ah-rah-ee gah ah-ree-mahs KAH*

MEALS

In most ryokan, your maid serves your meals in your room. In the minshuku, you eat with the family. The food is Japanese-style.

✘ What time is dinner?	晩ご飯は，何時でしょうか。	*BAHN goh-hahn wah, NAHN-jee deh-shoh kah*
breakfast	朝ご飯	*ah-SAH GOH-hahn*
✘ I'd like dinner at 6 o'clock.	夕食は，六時にお願いします。	*YOO-shoh-koo wah, roh-KOO-jee nee oh-neh-gah-ee shee-mahs*
breakfast	朝食	*CHOH-shoh-koo*
✘ Could I get a Western-style breakfast?	朝食は，洋式をお願いできますか。	*CHOH-shoh-koo wah, YOH-shkee oh-NEH-gah-ee deh-kee-mahs KAH*
✘ Could I have a knife and fork with my meals too?	食事には，ナイフとフォークもお願いします。	*shoh-KOO-jee nee-wah, NAH-ee-foo toh FOH-koo moh oh-neh-gah-ee shee-mahs*
✘ Where is the dining room?	食事の部屋は，どこでしょうか。	*shoh-KOO-jee noh heh-yah wah, DOH-koh deh-shoh kah*

Before and after the meal, whether at a ryokan or minshuku, there are certain ritual phrases to say aloud; they are expressions of thanks for the meal.

Before beginning to eat	いただきます。	*ee-TAH-dah-kee-mahs*
After the meal	ごちそうさまでした。	*goh-CHEE-soh-sah-mah dehsh-tah*

COMMUNICATING

The following phrases are used with the front desk staff of the ryokan, or with the people who run the minshuku. Some fulfill ritual requirements as well as providing information. It's customary, for example, to say, "I'm going out" when leaving, and "I'm back" when returning.

The minshuku proprietors:

the husband	御主人	*goh SHOO-jeen*
the wife	奥さん	*OHK-sahn*

🏠 Could you send the maid to my room?　係りの方を，部屋へお願いします。 *KAH-kah-ree noh kah-tah oh, heh-YAH eh oh-NEH-gah-ee shee-mahs*

🏠 May I have my shoes, please?　くつを，お願いします。 *KTSOO oh, oh-NEH-gah-ee shee-mahs*

I'm going out.　出かけてきます。 *deh-KAH-keh-teh kee-mahs*

I'll be back <u>soon</u>.　<u>すぐ</u>もどってきます。 *<u>SOO-goo</u> moh-DOHT-teh kee-mahs*

　by evening　夕方までに *ȲOO-gah-tah MAH-deh nee*

I'm back.　ただいま。 *tah-DAH-ee-mah*

CHECKING OUT

I enjoyed my stay very much.　大変お世話になりました。 *tah-ee-hehn oh-SEH-wah nee nah-REE-mahsh-tah*

It was wonderful. Thank you very much.　とても，素晴しかったです。どうも，ありがとう。 *toh-TEH-moh, soo-BAH-rahsh-kaht-<u>tah</u> dehs. D̄OH-moh, ah-REE-gah-toh.*

I'll come back again.　また来ます。 *mah-TAH kee-mahs*

YOUTH HOSTELS

There are two kinds of youth hostels in Japan: public or goverment-operated, and privately run. The latter are affiliated with Japan Youth Hostels Inc. (JYH). The Japan National Tourist Organization can provide you with information and listings of facilities.

Is there a youth hostel nearby?	近くに，ユースホステルがあります か。 *chee-KAH-koo nee, YOO-soo HOHS-teh-roo gah ah-ree-mahs KAH*
Can I stay here? I'm a member.	泊まれますか。私は，会員です。 *toh-MAH-reh-mahs KAH. wah-TAHK-shee wah, kah-ee een dehs*
Here's my membership card.	これが，私の会員証です。 *koh-reh gah, wah-TAHK-shee noh kah-ee-EEN shoh dehs*
When is meal time?	食事の時間は，何時ですか。 *shoh-KOO-jee noh jee-KAHN wah, NAHN-jee dehs KAH*
Where's the dining room?	食堂は，どこですか。 *shoh-KOO-doh wah, DOH-koh dehs KAH*
Can I cook for myself?	自炊できますか。 *jee-SOO-ee deh-kee-mahs KAH*
Is there a bath time?	お風呂の時間がありますか。 *oh-FOO-roh noh jee-kahn gah ah-REE-mahs KAH*
Can I use my sleeping bag?	スリーピング・バッグを使えます か。 *soo-REE-peen-goo BAHG-goo oh TSKAH-eh-mahs KAH*
Can I <u>rent</u> sleeping sheets?	敷布を，借りられますか。 *shee-KEE-foo oh, kah-REE rah-reh-mahs KAH*
buy	買えます *kah-EE-mahs*
Is there a curfew?	門限は，ありますか。 *MOHN-gehn wah, ah-REE-mahs KAH*
When is wakeup time?	起床時間は，何時ですか。 *kee-SHOH jee-kahn wah, NAHN-jee dehs KAH*
When is "lights out"?	消灯時間は，何時ですか。 *SHOH-toh jee-kahn wah, NAHN-jee dehs KAH*

TAXIS

Cruising taxis are plentiful in cities and large towns; there are also taxi stands at train stations, near hotels, and in certain downtown districts. Meters show the fare in digits; there's a 20 percent surcharge added from 11 P.M. until 5 A.M.; you don't tip the driver unless he does something special for you, like carrying luggage or waiting while you make a stop. Don't open or close the door—the driver operates it automatically.

Japanese taxis don't always take you right to your destination. The driver may not know exactly where it is, and if he does, he's not expected to venture far from a main road unless he chooses to. If you're going someplace well known, like a hotel or train station, there's no problem. Otherwise, tell the driver the main intersection or landmark near your destination (ask someone to write it in Japanese beforehand). Some drivers will help you from there; others will expect you to get out and find your own way from the main road.

How long will it take to Ginza by cab?	銀座まで、タクシーでどの位時間がかかりますか。 *GEEN-zah mah-deh, TAHK-shee deh doh-NOH koo-rah-ee jee-kahn gah kah-kah-ree-mahs KAH*
Tokyo Station	東京駅 *TOH-kyoh eh-kee*
the Imperial Hotel	帝国ホテル *TEH-koh-koo HOH-teh roo*
How much will it cost to go to Shinjuku by cab?	新宿まで、タクシーでいくらかかりますか。 *SHEEN-joo-koo mah-deh, TAHK-shee deh EE-koo-rah kah-kah-ree-mahs KAH*
Meiji Shrine	明治神宮 *MEH-jee jeen-goo*
How far is it?	距離は、どの位ありますか。 *KYOH-ree wah, doh-NOH koo-rah-ee ah-ree-mahs KAH*

Where can I get a taxi?	タクシーは，どこで乗れますか。 *TAHK-shee wah, DOH-koh deh noh-reh-mahs KAH*
Can I get a cab in the street around here?	この近くで，タクシーがひろえますか。*koh-noh chee-KAH-koo deh, TAHK-shee gah hee-ROH-eh-mahs KAH*
Would you call me a cab please?	タクシーを，よんでいただけますか。*TAHK-shee oh YOHN-deh ee-tah-dah-keh-mahs KAH*
Take me to the Kabuki Theater please.	歌舞伎座まで，お願いします。*kah-BOO-kee zah mah-deh, oh-NEH-gah-ee shee-mahs*
Haneda Airport	羽田空港 *hah-NEH-dah koo-koh*
I'd like to go near Roppongi intersection.	六本木の交差点のそばまで，行ってください。*rohp-POHN-gee noh KOH-sah-tehn noh soh-bah mah-deh, eet-TEH koo-dah-sah-ee*
Zojoji Temple in Shiba	芝の増上寺 *SHEE-bah noh ZOH-joh-jee*
Nomura Building in Shinjuku	新宿の野村ビル *SHEEN-joo-koo noh noh-MOO-rah bee-roo*
Do you know where this address is?	この住所がどこか，わかりますか。*koh-noh JOO-shoh gah DOH-koh kah, wah-KAH-ree-mahs KAH*
the American Embassy	アメリカ大使館 *ah-MEH-ree-kah tah-EE-shee-kahn*
Can I get there by one o'clock?	一時までに，着けますか。*ee-CHEE jee mah-deh nee, TSKEH-mahs KAH*
two	二 *NEE*
Could you go faster, please?	急いでもらえますか。*ee-SOH-ee-deh moh-rah-eh-mahs KAH*
There's no need to hurry.	急がなくても，けっこうです。*ee-SOH-gah-nah-koo-teh-moh, KEHK-koh dehs*
Go straight please.	まっすぐ，行ってください。*mahs-SOO-goo, eet-teh koo-dah-sah-ee*

Turn to the <u>right</u> at the next corner, please.	次の角を，<u>右</u>に曲がってください。 *tsoo-GEE noh kah-doh oh, <u>mee-GEE</u> nee mah-gaht-teh koo-dah-sah-ee*
left	左 *hee-DAH-ree*
Could you go a little farther please?	もう少し先まで，行ってもらえますか。 *MOH skoh-shee sah-KEE mah-deh, eet-teh moh-rah-eh-mahs KAH*
Would you mind going back a little?	少し，ひき返してもらえますか。 *SKOH-shee, hee-KEE-kah-eh-shteh moh-rah-eh-mahs KAH*
I think it's around here.	この辺のはずですが。 *koh-NOH hehn noh hah-zoo dehs gah*
Could you stop <u>just before</u> the next intersection?	次の交差点の<u>手前</u>でとめてください。 *tsoo-GEE noh koh-sah-tehn noh <u>teh-MAH-eh</u> deh, toh-meh-teh koo-dah-sah-ee*
right after	すぐ後 *SOO-goo ah-toh*
Around here is fine.	この辺で，けっこうです。 *koh-NOH hehn deh, KEHK-koh dehs*
Stop here please.	ここで，とめてください。 *koh-koh deh, toh-MEH-teh koo-dah-sah-ee*
Please wait here for a moment.	ここで，ちょっと待ってもらえますか。 *koh-koh deh, choht-toh MAHT-teh moh-rah eh-mahs KAH*
How much do I owe you?	いくらですか。 *EE-koo-rah dehs KAH*

SUBWAYS AND COMMUTER TRAINS

Most major Japanese cities have fast, clean, and efficient subway and commuter train systems. The latter are not quite the Western equivalent of commuter trains. They're actually a complex system of public and private trains crisscrossing and encircling the urban areas, and linking with the subways. In Tokyo, the Yamanote-sen is the line that encircles, or loops around, the city's downtown area; in Osaka, the loop line is called the Kanjo-sen.

Subway entrances are marked by these symbols:

You can use the subways and commuter trains easily if you have a map or guide, and there are many available. The station signs are in Roman letters, or romaji, so you'll be able to read them. The only difficulty you might have will be with the ticket machines at the entrance. Figuring out the cost of the ride can be complicated. But you can just buy the cheapest ticket in order to get in. Keep it until the end of your ride. Hand it to the ticket taker at the exit; he'll tell you how much you owe, and you can pay him.

subway	地下鉄	*chee-KAH-teh-tsoo*
commuter train	電車	*DEHN-shah*

Is there a subway in this city?
この市には，地下鉄がありますか。
koh-noh SHEE nee-wah, chee-KAH-teh-tsoo gah ah-ree-mahs KAH

Is there a <u>commuter train</u> map <u>in English</u>?
英語の，電車の地図がありますか。
EH-goh noh, DEHN-shah noh chee-zoo gah ah-ree-mahs KAH

subway 地下鉄 *chee-KAH-teh-tsoo*

Where can I get a commuter train map in English?
英語の電車の地図は，どこで買えますか。
EH-goh noh DEHN-shah noh chee-zoo wah, DOH-koh deh kah-eh-mahs KAH

When is the <u>morning</u> rush hour?
朝のラッシュ・アワーは，何時ごろですか。
AH-sah noh rahsh-SHOO ah-wah wah, NAHN-jee goh-roh dehs KAH

evening 夕方の *YOO-gah-tah noh*

When is the earliest train of the day?
一番電車は，何時ですか。
ee-CHEE-bahn dehn-shah wah, NAHN-jee dehs KAH

When does the last train depart?
最終電車は，何時に出ますか。
sah-EE-shoo dehn-shah wah, NAHN-jee nee deh-mahs KAH

Is there a <u>train</u> station nearby?
近くに，電車の駅がありますか。
chee-KAH-koo nee, DEHN-shah noh EH-kee gah ah-ree-mahs KAH

subway 地下鉄 *chee-KAH-teh-tsoo*

Could you tell me how to get to the nearest train station?	一番近い電車の駅への行き方を，教えてください。 *ee-CHEE-bahn chee-kah-ee DEHN-shah noh eh-kee eh-noh ee-kee-kah-tah oh, oh-SHEE-eh-teh koo-dah-sah-ee*
Where is the <u>Yama no te line</u> station?	山手線の駅は，どこですか。 *yah-MAH-noh-teh sehn noh EH-kee wah, DOH-koh dehs KAH*
Marunouchi line	丸の内線 *mah-ROO-noh-oo-chee sehn*
Ginza line	銀座線 *GEEN-zah sehn*
Toyoko line	東横線 *TOH-yoh-koh sehn*
Which line should I take to <u>Ginza</u>?	銀座に行くには，何線に乗ったらいいですか。 *GEEN-zah nee ee-KOO nee-wah, nah-NEE sehn nee noht-tah-rah ee dehs KAH*
Akasaka	赤坂 *ah-KAH-sah-kah*
Excuse me, could you help me?	すみませんが，ちょっと教えてください。 *soo-MEE-mah-sehn gah, CHOHT-toh oh-shee-eh-teh koo-dah-sah-ee*
I can't read the Japanese for the fare information.	日本語の料金案内が読めません。 *nee-HOHN-goh noh ryoh-keen AHN-nah-ee gah yoh-MEH-mah-sehn*
How much is the fare to <u>Asakusa</u>?	浅草まで，いくらですか。 *ah-SAH-koo-sah mah-deh EE-koo-rah dehs KAH*
Ueno	上野 *oo-EH-noh*
Where is the ticket machine?	切符の販売機は，どこですか。 *keep-POO noh hahn-bah-ee-kee wah, DOH-koh dehs KAH*
Which machine should I use?	どの販売機を使ったらいいですか。 *DOH-noh hahn-bah-ee-kee oh TSKAHT-tah-rah ee dehs KAH*
How many stations are there from here to <u>Shin-bashi</u>?	新橋は，いくつ目ですか。 *SHEEN-bah-shee wah, ee-KOO-tsoo-meh dehs KAH*

Roppongi	六本木 *rohp-POHN-gee*
Do I have to change?	乗りかえがありますか。 *noh-REE-kah-eh gah, ah-REE-mahs KAH*
At which station do I have to change?	乗りかえは，どの駅ですか。 *noh-REE-kah-eh wah, DOH-noh eh-kee dehs KAH*
Which line do I change to?	何線に，乗りかえますか。 *nah-NEE sehn nee, noh-REE-kah-eh mahs KAH*
Which track does the train leave from?	何番線から，出ますか。 *NAHN-bahn sehn kah-rah, deh-mahs KAH*
Where is the platform for the train to Shibuya?	渋谷行きのホームは，どこですか。 *shee-BOO-yah ee-kee noh hoh-moo wah, DOH-koh dehs KAH*
Yotsuya	四谷 *yoh-TSOO-yah*
Is this the right platform for the train to Harajuku?	原宿に行くには，このホームでいいですか。 *hah-RAH-joo-koo nee ee-koo nee-wah, koh-NOH hoh-moo deh EE dehs KAH*
Tora no mon	虎の門 *toh-RAH noh mohn*
Does the express stop at Nakano?	快速は，中野にとまりますか。 *kah-ee-soh-koo wah, nah-KAH-noh nee toh-MAH-ree-mahs KAH*
Ogikubo	萩窪 *oh-GEE-koo-boh*
Is this seat free?	この席は，あいていますか。 *koh-noh SEH-kee wah, ah-ee-teh ee-mahs KAH*
What's the next station?	次の駅は，どこですか。 *tsoo-GEE noh eh-kee wah, DOH-koh dehs KAH*
How many more stops to Omiya?	大宮まで，途中何回とまりますか。 *OH-mee-yah mah-deh, toh-choo NAHN-kah-ee toh-mah-ree-mahs KAH*
Hamamatsucho	浜松町 *hah MAH-muh-tsoo-choh*
Where is the east exit?	東口は，どこですか。 *hee-GAH-shee goo-chee wah, DOH-koh dehs KAH*
west	西 *nee SHEE*
north	北 *kee-TAH*

south	南 *mee-NAH-mee*
Where is the exit to the Sony Building?	ソニー・ビルへの出口は，どこです か。 *soh-NEE bee-roo eh noh DEH-goo-chee wah, DOH-koh dehs KAH*
Hibiya Park	日比谷公園 *hee-BEE-yah koh-ehn*
Where is the lost and found office?	遺失物係りは，どこですか。 *ee-SHEE-tsoo boo-tsoo gah-kah-ree wah, DOH-koh dehs KAH*
I've left my attache case on the train.	電車の中に，アタッシェ・ケースを 置き忘れてしまいました。 *DEHN-shah noh nah-kah nee, ah-TAHSH-sheh kehs oh oh-KEE-wah-soo-reh-teh shee-mah-ee-mahsh-tah*
package	荷物 *NEE-moh-tsoo*

MONORAIL

The monorail operates between Hamamatsucho in Tokyo and Haneda Airport. Some people find it a convenient way to get from town to their domestic flights.

Where do I get the monorail?	モノレールは，どこで乗れますか。 *moh-NOH-reh-roo wah, DOH-koh deh noh-reh-mahs KAH*
How long does it take to go to Haneda?	羽田まで，どの位時間がかかります か。 *hah-NEH-dah mah-deh, doh-NOH koo-rah-ee jee-kahn gah kah-kah-ree-mahs KAH*
How often does it run?	何分ごとに出ますか。 *NAHN-poon goh-toh nee deh-mahs KAH*
How much is the fare?	料金は，いくらですか。 *RYOH-keen wah, EE-koo-rah dehs KAH*

BUSES

If you travel by bus, it's a good idea to have someone write down your destination so you can show it to the driver, who may not understand English.

Where can I get a bus to Ginza?	銀座行きのバス停は、どこですか。 *GEEN-zah yoo-kee noh bah-SOO-teh wah, DOH-koh dehs KAH*
Where's the nearest bus stop for Shinjuku?	新宿行きの、最寄りのバス停はどこですか。 *SHEEN-joo-koo yoo-kee noh, moh-YOH-ree noh bah-SOO-teh wah DOH-koh dehs KAH*
Can I get a bus to Harajuku around here?	この近くで、原宿行きのバスに乗れますか。 *koh-NOH chee-kah-koo deh, hah-RAH-joo-koo yoo-kee noh BAH-soo nee noh-reh-mahs KAH*
Which bus do I take to go to Asakusa?	浅草行きのバスは、どれですか。 *ah-SAH-koo-sah yoo-kee noh BAH-soo wah, DOH-reh dehs KAH*
Where does this bus go?	このバスは、どこ行きですか。 *koh-NOH bah-soo wah, doh-KOH yoo-kee dehs KAH*
Does this bus go to Shibuya?	このバスは、渋谷に行きますか。 *koh-NOH bah-soo wah, shee-BOO-yah nee ee-kee-mahs KAH*
Does this bus stop at the Kabuki Theater?	このバスは、歌舞伎座でとまりますか。 *koh-NOH bah-soo wah, kah-BOO-kee-zah deh toh-MAH-ree-mahs KAH*
Where do I get off to go to the British Consulate?	イギリス領事館に行くには、どこで降りればいいですか。 *ee-GEE-ree-soo ryoh-jee-kahn nee ee-koo nee-wah, DOH-koh deh oh-ree-reh-bah EE dehs KAH*
Do I need to change buses to go to the National Theater?	国立劇場に行くには、乗りかえがありますか。 *koh-KOO-ree-tsoo geh-kee-joh nee ee-koo nee-wah, noh-REE-kah-eh gah ah-ree-mahs KAH*
How often does the bus for Tokyo Station come?	東京駅行きのバスは、何分おきに出ますか。 *TOH-kyoh-eh-kee yoo-kee noh BAH-soo wah, NAHN-poon oh-kee nee deh-mahs KAH*

When does the next bus to Ikebukuro come?	次の池袋行きのバスは，いつですか。 *tsoo-GEE noh ee-KEH-boo-koo-roh yoo-kee noh BAH-soo wah, EE-tsoo dehs KAH*
How long does it take from here to Akasaka?	ここから赤坂まで，どの位時間がかかりますか。 *koh-koh kah-rah ah-KAH-sah-kah mah-deh, doh-NOH koo-rah-ee jee-kahn gah kah-kah-ree-mahs KAH*
How many stops are there from here to Tokyo Tower?	東京タワーは，ここからいくつ目ですか。 *TOH-kyoh tah-wah wah, koh-KOH kah-rah ee-KOO-tsoo-meh dehs KAH*
How much will it be to Aoyama?	青山まで，いくらですか。 *ah-OH-yah-mah mah-deh, EE-koo-rah dehs KAH*
Do I have to pay the exact change?	料金は，きっかり払わなければなりませんか。 *RYOH-keen wah, keek-KAH-ree hah-RAH-wah-nah-keh-reh-bah nah-ree-mah-sehn KAH*
Can I get change?	おつりが，もらえますか。 *oh-TSOO-ree gah, moh-rah-eh-mahs KAH*
Where do I put the fare?	料金は，どこに入れますか。 *RYOH-keen wah, DOH-koh nee ee-reh-mahs KAH*
Could you tell me when to get off?	いつ降りるか，教えてもらえますか。 *EE-tsoo oh-ree-roo kah, oh-SHEE-eh-teh moh-rah-eh-mahs KAH*

SIGHTSEEING

Japan is so rich in things to see and do that your only problem will be limiting yourself to those you have time for. If your tastes run to the traditional, you'll find that the Japan of yesteryear is very much alive today. There are many places where the past is preserved—cities like Kyoto, for example. And in towns like Kanazawa and Kurashiki, you can see what feudal Japan was like.

Throughout Japan there are homes, temples, and shrines built according to traditional Japanese styles of architecture. And the centuries-old art forms are still intact: brush painting, flower arranging, ceramics, tea ceremony, and woodblock prints, among others. The stylized entertainment of theatrical arts like Kabuki, Noh, and Bunraku also reflect the preservation of traditional values. The old culture is everywhere.

Do you prefer things contemporary? Then high-tech Japan is for you: the excitement and vitality of the cities, the world of Japanese industry, the taste and purity of modern Japanese design. You'll find sightseeing easy in Japan. The country is well-equipped to accommodate tourists, and the Japanese like foreign visitors. They'll do everything they can to help you enjoy their country.

Inquiries

Are there English guidebooks for Tokyo?	東京のガイド・ブックが欲しいのですが，英語のがありますか。 *TOH-kyoh noh gah-EE-doh book-koo gah hoh-SHEE noh dehs gah, EH-goh noh gah ah-ree-mahs KAH*
Kyoto	京都 *KYOH-toh*
Which guidebook would you recommend?	どのガイド・ブックがいいか，教えてください。 *DOH-noh gah-ee-doh book-koo gah EE kah, oh-SHEE-eh-teh koo-dah-sah-ee*
Where can I buy the guidebook?	そのガイド・ブックは，どこで買えますか。 *soh-NOH gah-ee-doh book-koo wah, DOH-koh deh kah-eh-mahs KAH*
Could you tell me the points of interest here?	ここでの名所を，教えてください。 *koh-KOH deh noh MEH-shoh oh, oh-SHEE-eh-teh koo-dah-sah-ee*
there	そこ *soh-KOH*
I'm interested in antiques.	私は，こっとう品に興味があります。 *wah-TAHK shee wah, kohl-TOH heen nee KYOH-mee gah ah-ree-mahs*
architecture	建築 *KEHN-chee-koo*
art	美術 *BEE-joo-tsoo*

Buddhist temples	お寺 *oh-TEH-rah*
ceramics	陶磁器 *TOH-jee-kee*
crafts	工芸 *KOH-geh*
festivals	お祭り *oh-MAH-tsoo-ree*
folk art	民芸 *MEEN-geh*
furniture	家具 *KAH-goo*
historical sites	旧跡 *KYOO-seh-kee*
Japanese gardens	日本庭園 *nee-HOHN teh-ehn*
Japanese painting	日本画 *nee-HOHN gah*
pottery	陶器 *TOH-kee*
sculpture	彫刻 *CHOH-koh-koo*
Shinto shrines	神社 *JEEN-jah*

What would you recommend that I see <u>here</u>?
ここでは，どんなものを見ればいいでしょうか。 *koh-KOH deh-wah, DOHN-nah moh-noh oh MEE-reh-bah ee deh-shoh kah*

   in that city
　その都市 *soh-NOH toh-shee*

Is ____ worth going to see?
____ は，見に行く価値がありますか。 *____ wah, MEE nee ee-koo KAH-chee gah ah-ree-mahs KAH*

What are the main attractions there?
そこでは主に，何が見られますか。 *soh-KOH deh-wah OH-moh nee, NAH-nee gah mee-rah-reh mahs KAH*

Is it easy to get there?
そこには，簡単に行けますか。 *soh-KOH nee-wah, KAHN-tahn nee ee-keh-mahs KAH*

Where is <u>the tourist information center</u>?
<u>旅行案内所</u>は，どこですか。 *ryoh-KOH ahn-nah-ee joh wah, DOH-koh dehs KAH*

   the Japan National Tourist Organization Tourist Information Center (TIC)
　国際観光振興会 *kohk-SAH-ee kahn-koh SHEEN-koh kah-ee*

We have <u>a half day</u> free here.	ここでは，半日時間があります。 *koh-KOH deh-wah, <u>HAHN nee-chee</u> jee-kahn gah ah-ree-mahs*
a day	一日 *ee-CHEE nee-chee*
a few days	数日 *SOO jee-tsoo*
a week	一週間 *ees-SHOO-kahn*
We'd like to see the <u>aquarium</u>.	<u>水族館</u>を，見たいのですが。 *<u>soo-EE-zoh-koo kahn</u> oh, mee-TAH-ee noh dehs gah*
business district	ビジネス街 *bee-JEE-neh-soo gah-ee*
castle	お城 *oh-SHEE-roh*
downtown area	繁華街 *HAHN-kah gah-ee*
gardens	庭園 *TEH-ehn*
harbor	港 *mee-NAH-toh*
lake	湖 *mee-ZOO-oo-mee*
market	市場 *EE-chee-bah*
museum	博物館 *hah-KOO-boo-tsoo kahn*
old town	旧市街 *KYOO shee-gah-ee*
palace	宮殿 *KYOO-dehn*
park	公園 *KOH-ehn*
shrine	神社 *JEEN-jah*
stock exchange	証券取引所 *SHOH-kehn toh-ree-hee-kee joh*
temple	お寺 *oh-TEH-rah*
zoo	動物園 *DOH-boo-tsoo ehn*

Sightseeing Tours

Considering how difficult driving in Japan can be for foreigners, organized sightseeing tours are a convenient way to get around. The JNTO Tourist Information Centers (TIC) or any travel agency can help you find a suitable one. You can spend a few hours seeing some major points of interest, or a few days or weeks seeing much more. You can travel by bus, train, or plane, or a combination of all three. And you'll have competent, English-speaking guides.

Are there sightseeing buses in the city?	市内の，観光バスがありますか。 *SHEE-nah-ee noh, KAHN-koh bah-soo gah ah-ree-mahs KAH*
Are there sightseeing buses to <u>Hakone</u>?	箱根への，観光バスがありますか。 <u>*hah-KOH-neh*</u> *eh noh, KAHN-koh bah-soo gah ah-ree-mahs KAH*
Nara	奈良 *NAH-rah*
Are there <u>morning</u> tours?	午前の観光バスがありますか。 <u>*GOH-zehn*</u> *noh KAHN-koh bah-soo gah, ah-ree-mahs KAH*
afternoon	午後 *GOH-goh*
evening	夜 *YOH-roo*
all-day	一日 *ee-CHEE nee-chee*
two-day	二日 *foo-TSOO-kah*
three-day	三日 *meek-KAH*
Are there group tours to <u>Kyoto</u>?	京都への，グループツアーがありますか。 <u>*KYOH-toh*</u> *eh noh, goo-ROO-poo tsoo-ah gah ah-ree-mahs KAH*
Hokkaido	北海道 *hohk-KAH-ee-doh*
Shikoku	四国 *shee-KOH-koo*
Kyushu	九州 *KYOO-shoo*
What kind of transportation do you use?	どんな交通機関を使いますか。 *DOHN-nah koh-tsoo kee-kahn oh tsoo-KAH-ee-mahs KAH*
Are the meals and lodging included in the tour fare?	食事と宿泊は，ツアーの代金に入っていますか。 *shoh-KOO-jee toh shoo-KOO-hah-koo wah, TSOO-ah noh dah-ee-keen nee HAH-eet-teh ee-mahs KAH*
Are the meals Western or Japanese?	食事は，洋式ですか，それとも和式ですか。 *shoh-KOO-jee wah, YOH-shee-kee dehs KAH, soh-REH toh-moh wah-SHEE-kee dehs KAH*
Is the hotel Western style?	泊まるホテルは洋式ですか。 *toh-mah-roo HOH-teh-roo wah, YOH-shee-kee dehs KAH*

Is there a chance to stay at a Japanese inn?
旅館に泊まる機会がありますか。
ryoh-KAHN nee toh-mah-roo kee-KAH-ee gah, ah-ree-mahs KAH

Where does the tour go?
そのツアーでは，何がみられますか。
soh-NOH tsoo-ah deh-wah, NAH-nee gah mee-rah-reh-mahs KAH

How many hours does the tour take?
そのツアーは，何時間かかりますか。
soh-NOH tsoo-ah wah, NAHN-jee-kahn kah-kah-ree-mahs KAH

   how many days
何日間 *NAHN nee-chee kahn*

When does the tour start?
ツアーは，何時に始まりますか。
TSOO-ah wah, NAHN-jee nee hah-jee-mah-ree-mahs KAH

   finish
終ります *oh-wah-ree-mahs*

Where does the tour start?
ツアーは，どこからですか。
TSOO-ah wah, DOH-koh kah-rah deh-mahs KAH

At which hotels do you have pickup service?
どのホテルで，ピック・アップサービスがありますか。 *DOH-noh hoh-teh-roo deh, peek-KOO ahp-poo sah-bee-soo gah ah-ree-mahs KAH*

Can I join the tour at the ____ Hotel?
そのツアーには，____ホテルから乗れますか。 *soh-NOH tsoo-ah nee-wah, ____ hoh-teh-roo kah-rah noh-REH-mahs KAH*

Does the all-day tour stop for lunch some-where?
一日のツアーは，どこかでランチにとまりますか。 *ee-CHEE nee-chee noh tsoo-ah wah, DOH-koh-kah deh RAHN-chee nee toh-mah-ree-mahs KAH*

Is lunch included in the tour fare?
ランチは，ツアーの料金に入っていますか。 *RAHN-chee wah, TSOO-ah noh ryoh-keen nee HAH-eet-teh ee-mahs KAH*

Is there any free time for shopping?
ショッピングのために，自由時間がありますか。 *shohp-PEEN-goo noh tah-meh nee, jee-YOO jee-kahn gah ah-ree-mahs KAH*

How much is the fare for the tour?	そのツアーの料金はいくらですか。 *soh-NOH tsoo-ah noh ryoh-keen wah, EE-koo-rah dehs KAH*
I'd like one ticket for that tour.	そのツアーの券を、一枚ください。 *soh-NOH tsoo-ah noh kehn oh, ee-CHEE mah-ee koo-dah-sah-ee*
two tickets	券を、二枚 *kehn oh, NEE mah-ee*
three tickets	券を、三枚 *kehn oh, SAHN mah-ee*
four tickets	券を、四枚 *kehn oh, YOHN mah-ee*

Car With Driver

This is the Western equivalent of limousine service, but the car is not limousine-sized. It's a convenient way to get around, especially in places like Kyoto, where you may want to visit several temples or shrines on the outskirts of town. The "hire" car, as the Japanese call it, has the added advantage of the driver's knowing the sights.

If he speaks some English, he can be a helpful guide. It's not as expensive as you might think, especially if a few of you share the costs. Tip the driver 7 or 8 percent at the end of your excursion.

Is a limousine available for sightseeing?	観光に、ハイヤーをやとえますか。 *KAHN-koh nee, HAH-ee-yah oh yah-toh-eh-mahs KAH*
Is an English-speaking chauffeur available?	英語を　話せる運転手が、います か。 *EH-goh oh hah-nah-seh-roo OON-tehn-shoo gah, ee-mahs KAH*
Is the rate by meter?	料金は、メーター制ですか。 *RYOH-keen wah, MEH-tah seh dehs KAH*
by the hour	時間 *jee-KAHN*
by the half day	半日 *HAHN nee-chee*
by the day	一日 *ee-CHEE nee-chee*
How much is the hourly rate?	一時間の料金は、いくらですか。 *ee-CHEE jee-kahn noh ryoh keen wah, EE-koo-rah dehs KAH*
half-day	半日 *HAHN nee-chee*
daily	一日 *ee-CHEE nee-chee*

Where can I get a limousine?	ハイヤーは，どこでやとえますか。 *HAH-ee-yah wah, DOH-koh deh yah-toh-eh-mahs KAH*
Do I need to call?	電話をする必要が，ありますか。 *DEHN-wah oh soo-roo hee-TSOO-yoh gah, ah-ree-mahs KAH*

Tour Guides

Is a tour guide available?	観光ガイドがやとえますか。 *KAHN-koh gah-ee-doh gah, yah-toh-eh-mahs KAH*
Is there an English-speaking guide?	英語を話せるガイドがいますか。 *EH-goh oh hah-nah-seh-roo GAH-ee-doh gah, ee-mahs KAH*
How much does a guide charge <u>per hour</u>?	ガイドの料金は，<u>一時間</u>いくらですか。 *GAH-ee-doh noh RYOH-keen wah, ee-CHEE jee-kahn EE-koo-rah dehs KAH*
per day	一日 *ee-CHEE nee-chee*
I'd like an English-speaking guide for <u>a half day</u>.	英語が話せるガイドを，<u>半日</u>たのみたいのですが。 *EH-goh gah hah-nah-seh-roo GAH-ee-doh oh, <u>HAHN nee-chee</u> tah-NOH-mee-tah-ee noh dehs gah*
a day	一日 *ee-CHEE-nee-chee*
two days	二日 *foo-TSOO-kah*
How can I arrange for a guide?	ガイドは，どうやって手配できますか。 *GAH-ee-doh wah, DOH yaht-teh TEH-hah-ee deh-kee-mahs KAH*
Could you arrange for the guide for me?	ガイドを，手配してもらえますか。 *GAH-ee-doh oh, TEH-hah-ee shteh moh-rah-eh-mahs KAH*

Sightseeing on Your Own

If you want to get out and see things on your own, some preliminary inquiries can help. You can use these phrases with hotel staff, tourist information center personnel, or Japanese friends or acquaintances.

I'd like to look around <u>Kyoto</u> on my own.	自分で，京都を見てまわりいのです が。 *jee-BOON deh, KYOH-toh oh MEE-teh mah-wah-ree-tah-ee noh dehs gah*
here	ここ *koh-KOH*
What's the best way to spend <u>a day</u> sightseeing on my own?	自分で一日見物するには，どんな所 へ行けばいいでしょうか。 *jee-BOON deh ee-CHEE nee-chee kehn-boo-tsoo soo-roo nee-wah, DOHN-nah toh-koh-roh eh ee-KEH-bah ee deh-shoh kah*
two days	二日 *foo-TSOO-kah*
Could you tell me what sightseeing sequence I should follow?	どんな順序でまわればいいか，教え てください。 *DOHN-nah joon-joh deh mah-WAH-reh-bah ee kah, oh-SHEE-eh-teh koo-dah-sah-ee*
I'd like to see <u>traditional</u> architecture.	伝統的な建築を見たいのですが。 *DEHN-toh teh-kee nah kehn-chee-koo oh, mee-TAH-ee noh dehs gah*
typical	典型的 *TEHN-keh teh-kee*
modern	モダン *moh-DAHN*
I'd like to see a festival.	お祭りを，見たいのですが。 *oh-MAH-tsoo-ree oh, mee-TAH-ee noh dehs gah*
Is there a festival some-where <u>today</u>?	今日どこかで，お祭りがあります か。 *kyoh DOH-koh-kah deh, oh-MAH-tsoo-ree gah ah-ree-mahs KAH*
tomorrow	あした *ahsh-TAH*
this week	今週 *KOHN-shoo*
Where can I see ___ ?	___は，どこで見られますか。 ___ wah, DOH-koh deh mee-rah-reh-mahs KAH
Which museum would be best for seeing ___ ?	___を見るには，どの博物館が一番 いいですか。 ___ oh MEE-roo nee-wah, DOH-noh hah-KOO-boo-tsoo kahn gah ee-CHEE-bahn ee dehs KAH

I'd like to go to ____, ____, and ____.	____と, ____と, ____に行きたいのですが。 ____ toh, ____ toh, ____ nee ee-KEE-tah-ee noh dehs gah
Could you tell me how to go to ____?	____への行き方を, 教えてください。 ____ eh noh ee-KEE-kah-tah oh, oh-SHEE-eh-teh koo-dah-sah-ee
Can I get to ____ by train and bus?	____へは, 電車やバスを使って行けますか。 ____ eh wah, DEHN-shah yah BAH-soo oh tsoo-kaht-teh ee-KEH-mahs KAH
Which line do I take to go to ____?	____へ行くには, 何線に乗ればいいですか。 ____ eh ee-KOO nee-wah, nah-NEE sehn nee noh-reh-bah ee dehs KAH
Where can I get the ____ line?	____線は, どこで乗れますか。 ____ sehn wah, DOH-koh deh noh-reh-mahs KAH
How far is ____ from the station?	駅から____まで, 距離はどの位ありますか。 EH-kee kah-rah ____ mah-deh, KYOH-ree wah doh-NOH-koo-rah-ee ah-ree-mahs KAH
Can I get there from the station on foot?	駅からそこまで, 歩いて行けますか。 EH-kee kah-rah soh-KOH mah-deh, ah-ROO-ee-teh ee-keh-mahs KAH
Can I find it easily?	すぐ, 見つかりますか。 SOO-goo, mee-tsoo-kah-ree-mahs KAH
Can I walk from ____ to ____?	____から____まで, 歩いて行けますか。 ____ kah-rah ____ mah-deh, ah-ROO-ee-teh ee-keh-mahs KAH

While Sightseeing: Getting In

What time does it <u>open</u>?	何時に, あきますか。 NAHN-jee nee, ah-kee-mahs KAH
close	しまります shee-mah-ree-mahs
Is it open <u>on Saturdays</u>?	土曜日に, あいていますか。 doh-YOH-bee nee, ah-EE-teh ee-mahs KAH
on Sundays	日曜日 nee-CHEE-yoh-bee nee

now	今 *EE-mah*
Is it still open?	まだあいていますか。 *MAH-dah ah-EE-teh ee-mahs KAH*
How long does it stay open?	何時まで，あいていますか。 *NAHN-jee mah-deh, ah-EE-teh ee-mahs KAH*
Is there an admission fee?	入場料が，いりますか。 *NYOO-joh ryoh gah, ee-ree-mahs KAH*
How much is the admission?	入場料は，いくらですか。 *NYOO-joh ryoh wah, EE-koo-rah dehs KAH*
Is there a discount for <u>students</u>?	<u>学生</u>の割引が，ありますか。 *gah-KOO-seh noh wah-ree-bee-kee gah, ah-REE-mahs KAH*
senior citizens	年寄り *toh-SHEE-yoh-ree*
children	子供 *koh-DOH-moh*
What's the minimum age for the discount? (senior citizens)	割引は，何才からですか。 *wah-REE-bee-kee wah, NAHN-sah-ee kah-rah dehs KAH*
What's the age limit for the discount? (children)	割引は，何才までですか。 *wah-REE-bee-kee wah, NAHN-sah-ee mah-deh dehs KAH*
Am I allowed to take pictures inside?	中で，写真をとってもかまいませんか。 *NAH-kah deh, shah-SHEEN oh toht-teh-moh kah-MAH-ee-mah-sehn KAH*
Where is the <u>entrance</u>?	<u>入口</u>は，どこですか。 *ee-REE-goo-chee wah, DOH-koh dehs KAH*
gift shop	売店 *bah-EE-tehn*
exit	出口 *DEH-goo-chee*
Do you have an English <u>guidebook</u>?	英語の<u>ガイド・ブック</u>がありますか。 *EH-goh noh gah-EE-doh book-koo gah ah-ree-mahs KAH*
catalog	カタログ *kah-TAH-roh-goo*
How much is the <u>guidebook</u>?	<u>ガイド・ブック</u>は，いくらですか。 *gah-EE-doh book-koo wah, EE-koo-rah dehs KAH*
catalog	カタログ *kah-TAH-roh-goo*

Do I have to take off my shoes?	くつを，ぬがなければなりませんか。 *koo-TSOO oh, noo-GAH-nah-keh-reh-bah nah-ree-mah-sehn KAH*
Can I just look around?	勝手に，見てまわれますか。 *kaht-TEH nee, MEE-teh mah-wah-reh-mahs KAH*
Do I have to wait for a guided tour?	ガイドの案内を，待たなければなりませんか。 *GAH-ee-doh noh AHN-nah-ee oh, mah-TAH-nah-keh-reh-bah nah-ree-mah-sehn KAH*
How long do we have to wait?	どの位，待たなければなりませんか。 *doh-NOH koo-rah-ee, mah-TAH-nah-keh-reh-bah nah-ree-mah-sehn KAH*

Asking about the Sights

What is it?	それは，何ですか。 *soh-REH wah, NAHN dehs KAH*
that building	あの建物 *ah-noh tah-TEH-moh-noh*
that monument	あの記念碑 *ah-noh kee-NEHN hee*
How old is it?	それは，どの位古いものですか。 *soh-REH wah, doh-NOH koo-rah-ee foo-roo-ee moh-noh dehs KAH*
Is it original?	それは，もとからのものですか。 *soh-REH wah, moh-TOH kah-rah noh moh-noh dehs KAH*
Who was the architect?	建築家は，誰ですか。 *KEHN-chee-koo kah wah, DAH-reh dehs KAH*
artist	芸術家 *GEH-joo-tsoo kah*
craftsman	工芸家 *KOH-geh kah*
painter	画家 *gah-KAH*
sculptor	彫刻家 *CHOH-koh-koo kah*
Who made this?	これは，誰が作りましたか。 *koh-reh wah, DAH-reh gah tskoo-ree-mahsh-tah KAH*

What's the purpose of ____?	____の目的は，何ですか。 ____ noh moh-KOO-teh-kee wah, NAHN dehs KAH
How long did it take to complete?	完成までに，どの位時間がかかりましたか。 KAHN-seh mah-deh nee, doh-NOH koo-rah-ee jee-kahn gah kah-kah-ree-mahsh-tah KAH
Is it an everday object?	それは，毎日使われるものですか。 soh-reh wah, MAH-ee-nee-chee tsoo-KAH-wah-reh-roo moh-noh dehs KAH
a religious	宗教の目的で SHOO-kyoh noh moh-koo-teh-kee deh
a ceremonial	儀式で GEE-shee-kee deh
What was it used for?	それは，何のために使われましたか。 soh-reh wah, NAHN noh tah-meh nee tsoo-KAH-wah-reh-mahsh-tah KAH
What is it made of?	材料は，何ですか。 zah-EE-ryoh wah, NAHN dehs KAH
How was it made?	それは，どんな方法で作られましたか。 soh-reh wah, DOHN-nah hoh-hoh deh tsoo-KOO-rah-reh-mahsh-tah KAH

POINTS OF INTEREST

The high points of sightseeing in Japan include castles, gardens, hot springs, museums, palaces and imperial villas, shrines, and temples. Several in each category are listed so you can pronounce the names of some of the major attractions, The categories are not exclusive; that is , when you visit a temple, you may also find a garden and a museum there. And this list is by no means exhaustive.

Because Japanese festivals are especially colorful and unique, there's also a list, by month, of a few that you might enjoy. There are many more: no matter when you visit Japan, you can find a festival to attend.

Castles

Japanese castles are spectacular: Himeji Castle, one of the few remaining original ones, has a five-storied dungeon at the center, and some buildings are preserved as national treasures. Osaka Castle is famous for its stone walls. Dramatic Nijo Castle, built in 1603, was where the Tokugawa shogun stayed when he visited Kyoto.

Name	Location	Name	Pronunciation
Himeji Castle	Himeji	姫路城	*hee-MEH-jee joh*
Hiroshima Castle	Hiroshima	広島城	*hee-ROH-shee-mah joh*
Inuyama Castle	Inuyama	犬山城	*ee-NOO-yah-mah joh*
Kumamoto Castle	Kumamoto	熊本城	*koo-MAH-moh-toh joh*
Matsue Castle	Matsue	松江城	*mah-TSOO-eh joh*
Matsumoto Castle	Matsumoto	松本城	*mah-TSOO-moh-toh joh*
Matsuyama Castle	Matsuyama	松山城	*mah-TSOO-yah-mah joh*
Nagoya Castle	Nagoya	名古屋城	*nah-GOH-yah joh*
Nijo Castle	Kyoto	二条城	*nee-JOH joh*
Odawara Castle	Odawara	小田原城	*oh-DAH-wah-rah joh*
Osaka Castle	Osaka	大阪城	*OH-sah-kah joh*
Shimabara Castle	Shimabara	島原城	*shee-MAH-bah-rah joh*

Gardens

Japan is a garden-lover's dream. There are gardens of every size and shape, each one different from the next. Some 132 of them have been designated masterpieces to be preserved and maintained under the Valuable Cultural Properties Act of Japan. The first three on this list are widely known by the Japanese as the "big three" of Japanese gardens, although most would also admit that it's very difficult to choose a best or favorite one!

Name	Location	Name	Pronunciation
Kairakuen Garden	Mito	偕楽園	*kah-EE-rah-koo ehn*
Kenrokuen Garden	Kanazawa	兼六園	*KEHN-roh-koo ehn*
Korakuen Garden	Okayama	後楽園	*KOH-rah-koo ehn*
Korakuen Garden	Tokyo	後楽園	*KOH-rah-koo ehn*
Moss Garden	Kyoto	こけ寺	*koh-KEH deh-rah*
Rikugien Garden	Tokyo	六義園	*ree-KOO-gee ehn*
Ritsurin Garden	Takamatsu	栗林公園	*ree-TSOO-reen koh-ehn*
Rock Garden	Kyoto	竜安寺の石庭	*RYOH-ahn-jee noh seh-KEE-teh*
Shinjuku Gyoen Garden	Tokyo	新宿御園	*SHEEN-joo-koo gyoh-ehn*

Hot Springs

Two of the most famous hot springs are Noboribetsu in Hokkaido and Beppu in Oita Prefecture , Kyushu. The former features a Valley of Hell: columns of steam rise from the ground, which is part of an old crater. The latter also has a "hell" —in this case, boiling mud ponds.

Name	Location	Name	Pronunciation
Arima Hot Springs	Hyogo Prefecture	有馬温泉	*ah-REE-mah ohn-sehn*
Atami Hot Springs	Shizuoka Prefecture	熱海	*AH-tah-mee*
Beppu Hot Springs	Oita Prefecture	別府温泉	*behp-POO ohn-sehn*
Dogo Hot Springs	Ehime Prefecture	道後温泉	*DOH-goh ohn-sehn*
Hakone Hot Springs	Kanagawa Prefecture	箱根	*hah-KOH-neh*

Ibusuki Hot Springs	Kagoshima Prefecture	指宿温泉	*ee-BOO-soo-kee ohn-sehn*
Ito Hot Springs	Shizuoka Prefecture	伊東温泉	*ee-TOH ohn-sehn*
Jozankei Hot Springs	Hokkaido	定山渓温泉	*JOH-zahn-keh ohn-sehn*
Kinugawa Hot Springs	Tochigi Prefecture	鬼怒川温泉	*kee-NOO-gah-wah ohn-sehn*
Kusatsu Hot Springs	Gunma Prefecture	草津温泉	*koo-SAH-tsoo ohn-sehn*
Noboribetsu Hot Springs	Hokkaido	登別温泉	*noh-BOH-ree-beh-tsoo ohn-sehn*
Yugawara Hot Springs	Kanagawa Prefecture	湯河原温泉	*yoo-GAH-wah-rah ohn-sehn*
Yuzawa Hot Springs	Niigata Prefecture	湯沢温泉	*yoo-ZAH-wah ohn-sehn*

Museums

In Tokyo, be sure to see the Tokyo National Museum. Specializing in Japanese and Far Eastern ancient and medieval art, it houses over 85,000 objects. It's the largest museum in Japan. In Kyoto, the Kyoto National Museum is a must. It was established in 1868 as a repository for art objects and treasures from temples, shrines, and individual collections. There are now 10,000 objects. Also in Kyoto, don't miss the Kyoto Municipal Museum of Traditional Industry. Because most of Kyoto's traditional industry is handicrafts, there are outstanding displays of lacquer, bamboo, silk, paper, and ceramic objects. You can also see demonstrations of centuries-old production methods for these arts and crafts.

If you visit Kurashiki, one of the highlights is the Kurashiki Folkcraft Museum, renowned throughout Japan for its collection of craft objects used in daily life. The building itself is an old rice granary, symbolic of the town's historic role in the rice trade.

Name	Location	Name	Pronunciaton
Fujita Art Museum	Osaka	藤田美術館	*foo-JEE-tah bee-JOO-tsoo kahn*

Kobe City Museum	Kobe	神戸市立博物館	*KŌH-beh shee-ree-tsoo hah-KOO-boo-tsoo kahn*
Kyoto Municipal Museum of Traditional Industry	Kyoto	京都市伝統産業会館	*KYŌH-toh-shee DEHN-toh sahn-gyoh kah-ee-kahn*
Kyoto National Museum	Kyoto	京都国立博物館	*KYŌH-toh koh-koo-ree-tsoo hah-KOO-boo-tsoo kahn*
Kurashiki Folkcraft Museum	Kurashiki	倉敷民芸館	*koo-RAH-shee-kee MEEN-geh kahn*
Nara National Museum	Nara	奈良国立博物館	*NAH-rah koh-koo-ree-tsoo hah-KOO-boo-tsoo kahn*
National Museum of Western Art	Tokyo	国立西洋美術館	*koh-KOO-ree-tsoo seh-yoh bee-JOO-tsoo kahn*
Ohara Art Gallery	Kurashiki	大原美術館	*ŌH-hah-rah bee-JOO-tsoo kahn*
Osaka Japan Folk Art Museum	Osaka	大阪日本民芸館	*ŌH-sah-kah-neep-pohn MEEN-geh kahn*
Tokugawa Art Museum	Nagoya	徳川美術館	*toh-KOO-gah-wah bee-JOO-tsoo kahn*
Tokyo National Art Museum	Tokyo	東京国立博物館	*TŌH-kyoh koh-koo-ree-tsoo hah-KOO-boo-tsoo kahn*

Palaces and Imperial Villas

The Imperial Palace, with its gardens covering 250 acres in the heart of Tokyo, is where the imperial family resides. The Kyoto Imperial Palace was the residence from 1331 until 1868, when the family moved to Tokyo. Also in Kyoto, the Katsura Imperial Villa represents a high point of traditional Japanese architecture and landscape gardening. To visit the Kyoto Imperial Palace and the Katsura Imperial Villa (and the Shugakuin Imperial Villa as well), you must apply in advance for permission. Passes are issued by the Kyoto Office of the Imperial Household Agency. You must have your passport with you when you pick up your pass. For the palace pass, you apply in person shortly before your visit; for the villas, you apply in person, by phone, or by mail one month to one week in advance. You <u>must</u> be <u>in Japan</u> in order to apply.

Name	Location	Name	Pronunciation
Hama Imperial Villa	Tokyo	浜離宮	*hah-MAH-ree-kyoo*
Imperial Palace	Tokyo	皇居	*KOH-kyoh*
Katsura Imperial Villa	Kyoto	桂離宮	*kah-TSOO-rah ree-kyoo*
Kyoto Imperial Palace	Kyoto	京都御所	*KYOH-toh goh-shoh*
Shugakuin Imperial Villa	Kyoto	修学院離宮	*shoo-gah-KOO-een ree-kyoo*

Shrines

Japanese shrines are sacred Shinto places of worship. Shinto, the indigenous religion of Japan, is today as much a value system as a religion. In fact, most Japanese would say that they are Buddhists as well as Shintoists, and see no conflict or contradiction in this dual allegiance. Shinto embodies the deep Japanese respect for nature; the shrines are places of great natural beauty.

The shrines to visit include the Meiji Shrine in Tokyo, the Heian Shrine in Kyoto, the Toshogu Shrine in Nikko, and the Ise Shrine at Ise. The Ise Shrine is the most venerated of all Shinto shrines.

Name	Location	Name	Pronunciation
Atsuta Shrine	Nagoya	熱田神宮	*ah-TSOO-tah jeen-goo*
Dazaifu Shrine	Fukuoka	太宰府天満宮	*dah-ZAH-ee-foo tehn-mahn-goo*

Fushimi Inari Shrine	Kyoto	伏見稲荷神社	*foo-SHEE-mee ee-nah-ree jeen-jah*
Heian Shrine	Kyoto	平安神宮	*HEH-ahn jeen-goo*
Ikuta Shrine	Kobe	生田神社	*ee-KOO-tah jeen-jah*
Ise Shrine	Ise	伊勢神宮	*ee-SEH jeen-goo*
Itsukushima Shrine	Miyajima	厳島神社	*ee-TSOO-koo-shee-mah jeen-jah*
Izumo Grand Shrine	Izumo	出雲大社	*ee-ZOO-moh tah-ee-shah*
Kasuga Grand Shrine	Nara	春日大社	*kah-SOO-gah tah-ee-shah*
Kitano Shrine	Kyoto	北野天神	*kee-TAH-noh tehn-jeen*
Kotohira Shrine	Kotohira	琴平神社	*koh-TOH-hee-rah jeen-jah*
Meiji Shrine	Tokyo	明治神宮	*MEH-jee jeen-goo*
Sumiyoshi Shrine	Osaka	住吉神社	*soo-MEE-yoh-shee jeen-jah*
Toshogu Shrine	Nikko	東照宮	*TOH-shoh-goo*
Tsurugaoka Hachimangu Shrine	Kamakura	鶴岡八幡宮	*tsoo-ROO-gah-oh-kah hah-chee-mahn-goo*
Yasaka Shrine	Kyoto	八坂神社	*yah-SAH-kah jeen-jah*

TEMPLES

Japan's Buddhist temples are so varied that choosing from among them is especially difficult. Todaji, near Nara, is famous as the site of the world's largest bronze statue of Buddha. The building which houses it is the world's largest wooden structure. Horyuji, also in Nara, has about 40 buildings, each one of them designated either a National Treasure or an Important Cultural

Property. These buildings contain a fabulous collection of Japanese sculpture and art treasures.

Name	Location	Name	Pronunciation
Asakusa Kannon	Tokyo	浅草観音	*ah-SAH-koo-sah kahn-nohn*
Byodoin	Uji	平等院	*BYOH-doh-een*
Chuguji	Nara	中宮寺	*CHOO-goo-jee*
Chusonji	Hiraizumi	中尊寺	*CHOO-sohn-jee*
Daitokuji	Kyoto	大徳寺	*DAH-ee-toh-koo-jee*
Enryakuji	Hieisan	延暦寺	*EHN-ryah-koo-jee*
Ginkakuji	Kyoto	銀閣寺	*GEEN-kah-koo-jee*
Horyuji	Nara	法隆寺	*HOH-ryoo-jee*
Kinkakuji	Kyoto	金閣寺	*KEEN-kah-koo-jee*
Kiyomizudera	Kyoto	清水寺	*kee-YOH-mee-zoo-deh-rah*
Kofukuji	Nara	興福寺	*KOH-foo-koo-jee*
Koryuji	Kyoto	広隆寺	*KOH-ryoo-jee*
Kotokuji	Kamakura	高徳寺	*KOH-toh-koo-jee*
Nanzenji	Kyoto	南禅寺	*NAHN-zehn-jee*
Nishi Honganji	Kyoto	西本願寺	*nee-SHEE-hohn-gahn-jee*
Ryoanji	Kyoto	竜安寺	*RYOH-ahn-jee*
Saihoji	Kyoto	西芳寺	*SAH-ee-hoh-jee*
Sanjusangendo	Kyoto	三十三間堂	*SAHN-joo-sahn-gehn-doh*
Tenryuji	Kyoto	天龍寺	*TEHN-ryoo-jee*
Todaiji	Nara	東大寺	*TOH-dah-ee-jee*
Toji	Kyoto	東寺	*TOH-jee*
Toshodaiji	Nara	唐招提寺	*TOH-shoh-dah-ee-jee*
Yakushiji	Nara	薬師寺	*yah-KOO-shee-jee*

Festivals

Here are just a few of the multitude of festivals held throughout Japan each year. Check with local sources in Japan to find others you can attend during your visit.

Festival 祭

January 一月 (*ee-CHEE gah-tsoo*)

| 6 | 消防出初め式 | New Year Firemen's Parade (Tokyo) *shoh-boh deh-ZOH-meh sheekee* |
| 15 | 若草山の山焼き | Grass-Burning Festival on Wakaku-sayama Hill (Nara) *wah-KAH-koo-sah-yah-mah noh yah-MAH yah-kee* |

February 二月 (*nee GAH-tsoo*)

First Fri.–Sun.	札幌雪祭り	Snow Festival (Sapporo) *sahp-POH-roh yoo-KEE mah-tsoo-ree*
2, 3, or 4	節分	Bean-Throwing Ceremony (nationwide) *seh-TSOO boon*
2, 3, or 4	春日大社万燈籠	Lantern Festival of Kasuga Shrine (Nara) *kah-SOO-gah tah-ee-shah MAHN doh-roh*

March 三月 (*SAHN gah-tsoo*)

| 3 | 雛祭 | Doll Festival (nationwide) *hee-NAH mah-tsoo-ree* |
| 12 | 東大寺二月堂お水取り | Water-Drawing Ceremony of Todaiji (Nara) *TOH-* |

		dah-ee-jee nee-GAH-tsoo-doh oh-MEE-zoo toh-ree
April 四月 (*shee GAH-tsoo*)		
8	花祭	Buddha's Birthday, at Buddhist temples (nationwide) *hah-NAH mah-tsoo-ree*
16–17	二荒山神社の弥生祭	Yayoi Festival of Futarasan Shrine (Nikko) *foo-TAH-rah-sahn jeen-jah noh yah-YOH-ee mah-tsoo-ree*
May 五月 (*GOH gah-tsoo*)		
3–5	博多どんたく	Hakata Dontaku Parade (Hakata) *hah-KAH-tah dohn-tah-koo*
Second Sat. and Sun., odd-numbered years	神田祭	Festival of Kanda Myojin Shrine (Tokyo) *KAHN-dah mah-tsoo-ree*
Third Sat. and Sun.	三社祭	Festival of Asakusa Shrine (Tokyo) *SAHN-jah mah-tsoo-ree*
15	葵祭	Hollyhock Festival of Shimogamo and Kamigamo Shrines (Kyoto) *ah-OH-ee mah-tsoo-ree*
17–18	東照宮春祭り	Grand Festival of Toshogu Shrine (Nikko) *TOH-shoh-goo hah-ROO mah-tsoo-ree*
June 六月 (*roh-KOO gah-tsoo*)		
14	住吉の御田植	Rice-Planting Fes-

		tival at Sumiyoshi Shrine (Osaka) *soo-MEE-yoh-shee noh OHN-tah-oo-eh*
July 七月 (*shee-CHEE gah-tsoo*)		
7	**七夕**	Star Festival (nationwide) *tah-NAH-bah-tah*
13–16	**お盆**	Bon Festival (nationwide) *oh-BOHN*
mid–July	**管絃祭**	Music Festival of Itsukushima Shrine (Miyajima) *KAHN-gehn sah-ee*
16–24	**祇園祭**	Gion Festival of Yasaka Shrine (Kyoto) *gee-OHN mah-tsoo-ree*
24–25	**天神祭**	Tenjin Festival of Tenmangu Shrine (Osaka) *TEHN-jeen mah-tsoo-ree*
August 八月 (*hah-CHEE gah-tsoo*)		
3–7	**ねぶた**	Float Festival of Aomori (Aomori) *neh-BOO-tah*
5–7	**かんとう**	Bamboo Pole and Lantern Balancing Festival (Akita) *KAHN-toh*
6–8	**七夕**	Star Festival (Sendai) *tah-NAH-bah-tah*
12–15	**阿波踊**	Awa Odori Folk Dance (Tokushima City) *ah-WAH oh-doh-ree*

| 16 | 大文字焼き | Daimonji Bonfire on Mount Nyoigatake (Kyoto) *dah-EE-mohn-jee yah-kee* |

September 九月 (*KOO gah-tsoo*)

| 16 | 流鏑馬 | Horseback Archery of Tsurugaoka Hachimangu Shrine (Kamakura) *yah-BOO-sah-meh* |

October 十月 (*JOO gah-tsoo*)

7–9	おくんち	Okunchi Festival of Suwa Shrine (Nagasaki) *oh-KOON-chee*
11–13	お会式	Oeshiki Festival of Honmonji Temple (Tokyo) *oh-EH-shee-kee*
17	東照宮秋祭り	Autumn Festival of Toshogu Shrine (Nikko) *TOH-shoh-goo ah-KEE mah-tsoo-ree*
22	時代祭	Festival of the Ages, Heian Shrine (Kyoto) *jee-DAH-ee mah-tsoo-ree*

November 十一月 (*JOO-ee-chee gah-tsoo*)

| 3 | 大名行列 | Feudal Lord's Procession (Hakone) *dah-EE-myoh gyoh-reh-tsoo* |
| 15 | 七五三 | Children's Shrine-Visiting Day [for 3-year-old boys and girls, 5-year-old boys, and 7-year-old girls] (nationwide) *shee-CHEE goh sahn* |

December 十二月 (*JOO-nee gah-tsoo*)

17	御祭	On Matsuri of Kasuga Shrine (Nara) *OHN mah-tsoo-ree*
mid-December	年の市	Year-End Market at Asakusa Kannon Temple (Tokyo) *toh-SHEE noh ee-chee*

RELIGIOUS SERVICES

Although the predominant religions in Japan are Buddhism and Shintoism, there are Christian, Jewish, Muslim, and other places of worship. In the large cities, you may find not only your religious denomination, but also services in your language. If not, these phrases will help.

Where can I find a directory of churches?	教会のリストがありますか。 *KYOH-kah-ee noh REES-toh gah ah-ree-mahs KAH*
Is there a <u>Catholic church</u> near here?	近くに，<u>カトリック教の教会</u>がありますか。 *chee-KAH-koo nee, kah-TOH-reek-koo kyoh noh kyoh-kah-ee gah ah-ree-mahs KAH*
Protestant church	プロテスタントの教会 *poo-ROH-teh-soo-tahn-toh noh kyoh-kah-ee*
synagogue	ユダヤ教の寺院 *yoo-DAH-yah-kyoh noh jee-een*
mosque	回教の寺院 *KAH-ee-kyoh noh jee-een*
Buddhist temple	お寺 *oh-TEH-rah*
What time is the service?	礼拝は，何時に始まりますか。 *REH-hah-ee wah, NAHN-jee nee hah-jee-mah-ree-mahs KAH*
I'd like to speak to a <u>priest</u>.	神父 さんと話したいのですが。 *SHEEN-poo sahn toh hah-NAH-shtah-ee noh dehs gah*

minister	牧師さん *boh-KOO-shee sahn*
rabbi	ラビ *RAH-bee*
I'd like to attend services here today.	今日，ここの礼拝に出席したいのですが。 *kyoh, koh-KOH noh reh-hah-ee nee shoos-SEH-kee shtah-ee noh dehs gah*
I enjoyed the services very much.	素晴しい礼拝式でした。 *soo-BAH-rah-shee reh-hah-ee shee-kee deh-shtah*
Are there any other activities here <u>today</u>?	<u>今日</u>ここで，ほかに何かありますか。 *kyoh koh-KOH deh, hoh-kah nee NAH-nee-kah ah-ree-mahs KAH*
this week	今週 *kohn-shoo*
this month	今月 *kohn-geh-tsoo*
I'd like to come back again.	また来たいです。 *mah-TAH kee-tah-ee dehs*
Thank you. Goodbye.	ありがとうございました。さようなら。 *ah-REE-gah-toh goh-zah-ee-mah-shtah. sah-YOH-nah-rah.*
I'll see you again.	また，おめにかかります。 *mah-TAH, oh-meh nee kah-kah-ree-mahs*

PLANNING TRIPS

During your stay you may want to plan some longer excursions. Tourists can get around Japan by plane, train or boat.

TRANS

There are few porters available in Japanese train stations, and there are many staircases to climb. You'll do well to travel light!

Super Express or Bullet Trains

| Shinkansen | 新幹線 | *SHEEN-kahn-sehn* |

The Japanese bullet trains, or Shinkansen as they're known in Japan, are world-famous for speed, safety, and comfort. Now there are three Shinkansen lines; each line has two different kinds of trains, a faster one that makes fewer stops, and a slower one that makes more stops. The two kinds of trains have special names for each line, as you can see on the chart. You specify the one you want when buying your ticket.

TOKAIDO-SANYO SHINKANSEN

Route	Tokyo Station, Tokyo—Hakata
Fewer stops	Hikari trains
More stops	Kodama trains

TOHOKU SHINKANSEN

Route	Ueno Station, Tokyo—Morioka
Fewer stops	Yamabiko trains
More stops	Aoba trains

JOETSU SHINKANSEN

Route	Ueno Station, Tokyo—Niigata
Fewer stops	Asahi trains
More stops	Toki trains

Other Types of Trains

Limited express	特急	*tohk-KYOO*
Ordinary express	急行	*KYOO-koh*
Local trains	普通	*foo-TSOO*

Fares and Classes

You need a basic fare ticket for all train travel. And if you travel by Shinkansen, limited express, or ordinary express, you pay a supplementary fare as well. There are three classes of seats on these trains: Green Car (first class), reserved seats, and unreserved seats. Green Car and reserved seats also cost extra. Before you depart for Japan, you might want to inquire at your local Japan Air Lines office about the money-saving Japan Railpass.

Green Car	グリーン車	*GREEN shah*
reserved seats	指定席	*shee-TEH-seh-kee*
unreserved seats	自由席	*jee-YOO-seh-kee*

Inquiries

Is there a timetable in English?	英語の時刻表が，ありますか。	*EH-goh noh jee-KOHK hyoh gah, ah-ree mahs KAH*
Where can I get a time-table in English?	英語の時刻表は，どこでもらえますか。	*EH-goh noh jee-KOHK-hyoh wah, DOH-koh deh moh-rah-eh-mahs KAH*
Which line do I take to go to <u>Kyoto</u>?	京都行きは，何線ですか。	*KYOH-toh yoo-kee wah, nah-NEE sehn dehs KAH*
Hakone	箱根	*hah-KOH-neh*
Which station does the train for <u>Kamakura</u> leave from?	鎌倉行きの列車は，どの駅から出ますか。	*kah-MAH-koo-rah yoo-kee noh rehsh-shah wah, DOH-noh eh-kee kah-rah deh-mahs KAH*
Aomori	青森	*ah-OH-moh-ree*
Niigata	新潟	*NEE-gah-tah*
Where can I buy a ticket for the <u>Shinkansen</u>?	新幹線の切符は，どこで買えますか。	*SHEEN-kahn-sehn noh keep-poo wah, DOH-koh deh kah-eh-mahs KAH*

JNR	国鉄 *koh-KOO-teh-tsoo*
Can I buy a ticket in advance?	前売り券が、買えますか。*mah-EH oo-ree kehn gah, kah-EH-mahs KAH*
Can I buy a ticket on the day of the trip?	当日券は、ありますか。*TOH-jee-tsoo kehn wah, ah-REE-mahs KAH*
Where is the ticket window/ counter?	切符売り場は、どこですか。*Keep-POO OO-ree-bah wah, DOH-koh dehs KAH*
ticket window/ counter for Shinkansen reservations	緑の窓口 *MEE-doh-ree noh mah-DOH-goo-chee*
Shinkansen ticket window/ counter for today's trains	新幹線の当日券の窓口 *SHEEN-kahn-sehn noh TOH-jee-tsoo kehn noh mah-DOH-goo-chee*
Where is the window/ counter for reserved tickets?	前売り券の窓口は、どこですか。*mah-EH-oo-ree-kehn noh mah-DOH-goo-chee wah, DOH-koh dehs KAH*

Train Information

Where is the information center?	案内所は、どこですか。*AHN-nah-ee joh wah, DOH-koh dehs KAH*
I'd like to go to Hakata.	博多に行きたいのですが。*hah-KAH-tah nee ee-kee-TAH-ee noh dehs gah*
Sapporo	札幌 *sahp-POH-roh*
Can I stop over?	途中下車が、できますか。*toh-CHOO geh-shah gah, deh-kee-mahs KAH*
Can I get to Hiroshima by way of Nagoya?	名古屋経由で、広島へ行けますか。*nah-GOH-yah keh-yoo deh, hee-ROH-shee-mah eh ee-keh-mahs KAH*
Kobe	神戸 *KOH-beh*
Is there a sleeping car on the train?	寝台車が、ついていますか。*SHEEN-dah-ee shah gah, TSOO-ee-teh ee-mahs KAH*
dining car	食堂車 *shoh-KOO-doh shah*

Are there <u>limited express</u> trains to Nagoya?	名古屋へは，特急がありますか。 *NAH-goh-yah eh wah, tohk-KYOO gah ah-ree-mahs KAH*
ordinary express	急行 *KYOO-koh*
Is there a through train to <u>Nara</u>?	奈良への，直通列車がありますか。 *NAH-rah eh noh, choh-KOO-tsoo rehsh-shah gah ah-ree-mahs KAH*
Ise	伊勢 *EE-seh*
Do I have to change trains?	乗りかえがありますか。 *noh-REE-kah-eh gah ah-REE-mahs KAH*
Where do I have to change trains?	どこで，乗りかえですか。 *DOH-koh deh, noh-REE-kah-eh dehs KAH*
Is there a convenient connecting train for <u>Yonago</u>?	米子へは，便利な接続列車があります か。 *yoh-NAH-goh eh wah, BEHN-ree nah seh-TSOO-zoh-koo rehsh-shah gah ah-REE-mahs KAH*
Hida Takayama	飛騨高山 *HEE-dah tah-KAH-yah-mah*
How long do I have to wait?	どの位待たなければなりませんか。 *doh-NOH koo-rah-ee mah-TAH-nah-keh-reh-bah nah-ree-mah-sehn KAH*
Does the Kodama stop at <u>Atami</u>?	こだまは，熱海にとまりますか。 *koh-DAH-mah wah, AH-tah-mee nee toh-mah-ree-mahs KAH*
Kyoto	京都 *KYOH-toh*
Does the Hikari stop at <u>Odawara</u>?	ひかりは，小田原にとまりますか。 *hee-KAH-ree wah, oh-DAH-wah-rah nee toh-mah-ree-mahs KAH*
Kurashiki	倉敷 *koo-RAH-shee-kee*
When is the <u>earliest</u> train of the day for Nikko?	日光行きの始発は，何時ですか。 *neek-KOH yoo-kee noh shee-HAH-tsoo wah, NAHN-jee dehs KAH*
last	最終 *sah-EE-shoo*
What's the difference in cost between the limited express and ordinary express?	特急と急行の料金の差は，いくらで すか。 *tohk-KYOO toh KYOO-koh noh RYOH-keen noh sah wah, EE-koo-rah dehs KAH*

Buying Tickets

When traveling on intercity trains in Japan, you should buy your tickets in advance. Trains are popular, and choice seats fill up fast. Check with a travel agency, and get the train and class you want. You can, of course, buy tickets at the station as well.

I'd like a <u>one-way ticket</u> to Kyoto.

京都への，片道を一枚ください。
KYOH-toh eh noh, kah-TAH-mee-chee oh ee-CHEE mah-ee koo-dah-sah-ee

round-trip ticket

往復 *oh-foo-koo*

ticket for a reserved seat

座席指定券 *zah-SEH-kee SHTEH kehn*

first-class ticket

グリーン車の券／一等の券 *goo-REEN shah noh kehn／eet-TOH noh kehn*

I'd like two tickets to Kyoto for <u>today</u>.

今日の，京都行きを二枚ください。
KYOH noh, KYOH-toh yoo-kee oh, NEE mah-eh koo-dah-sah-ee

tomorrow

あした *ah-SHTAH*

the day after tomorrow.

あさって *ah-SAHT-teh*

Is there a discount for a child?

子供の割引が，ありますか。 *koh-DOH-moh noh wah-REE-bee-kee gah, ah-ree-mahs KAH*

We'd like <u>unreserved</u> <u>seats</u>.

自由席を，お願いします。 *jee-YOO seh-kee oh, oh-neh-gah-ee shee-mahs*

reserved seats

指定席 *SHTEH seh-kee*

first class seats

グリーン車の席 *GREEN shah noh seh-kee*

the sleeping car

寝台車 *SHEEN-dah-ee shah*

Can I get a seat by the <u>window</u>?

窓ぎわの席が，ありますか。 *mah-DOH gee-wah noh seh-kee gah, ah-ree-mahs KAH*

aisle

通路がわ *TSOO-roh gah-wah*

How much is the fare?

料金は，いくらですか。 *RYOH-keen wah, EE-koo-rah dehs KAH*

| Does that include the limited express charge? | それは，特急券も含んでいますか。 *soh-reh wah, tohk-KYOO kehn moh foo-KOON-deh ee-mahs KAH* |
| ordinary express | 急行 *KYOO-koh* |

Waiting for the Train

Where's the newsstand?	新聞売り場は，どこですか。 *SHEEN-boon oo-ree-bah wah, DOH-koh dehs KAH*
restaurant	食堂 *shoh-KOO-doh*
toilet	トイレ *TOH-ee-reh*
waiting room	待合室 *mah-CHEE-ah-ee-shee-tsoo*
Where can I find a porter?	赤帽は，どこにいますか。 *ah-KAH-boh wah, DOH-koh nee ee-mahs KAH*
Excuse me, could you help with my baggage?	すみませんが，荷物を運んでください。 *soo-MEE-mah-sehn gah, NEE-moh-tsoo oh hah-kohn-deh koo-dah-sah-ee*
Put it down here, please.	ここで，けっこうです。 *koh-KOH deh, KEHK-koh dehs*
How much do I owe you?	いかほどですか。 *ee-KAH-hoh-doh dehs KAH*
Where is the track for the Shinkansen?	新幹線乗り場は，どこですか。 *SHEEN-kahn-sehn NO A-ree-bah wah, DOH-koh dehs KAH*
track 10	10番線 *JOO-bahn sehn*
the track for Hikari 3	ひかり3号のホーム *hee-KAH-ree SAHN goh noh hoh-moo*
Which track does the train for Hakata leave from?	博多行きの列車は，何番線から出ますか。 *hah-KAH-tah yoo-kee noh rehsh-shah wah, NAHN-bahn sehn kah-rah deh-mahs KAH*
Which track does the train from Hakata arrive at?	博多からの列車は，何番線に着きますか。 *hah-KAH-tah kah-rah noh rehsh-shah wah, NAHN-bahn sehn nee TSKEE mahs KAH*

What time does the <u>train</u> for Atami leave?	熱海行きの列車は，何時に出ますか。 *ah-TAH-mee yoo-kee noh <u>rehsh-shah</u> wah, NAHN-jee nee deh-mahs KAH*
next train	次の列車 *tsoo-GEE noh rehsh-shah*
Is this the platform for the train to <u>Ueno</u>?	上野行きの列車のホームは，ここですか。 *<u>oo-EH-noh</u> yoo-kee noh rehsh-shah noh HOH-moo wah, koh-KOH dehs KAH*
Aomori	青森 *ah-OH-moh-ree*
Will the train for <u>Nagano</u> leave on time?	長野行きの列車は，時間通りにでますか <u>nah-GAH-noh</u> yoo-kee noh rehsh-shah wah, jee-KAHN doh-ree nee deh-mahs KAH*
Kanazawa	金沢 *kah-NAH-zah-wah*

On the Train

Is this seat free?	この席は，あいていますか。 *koh-noh SEH-kee wah, ah-ee-teh ee-mahs KAH*
I think that's my seat.	それは，私の席だと思いますが。 *soh-reh wah, wah-TAHK-shee noh SEH-kee dah toh oh-moh-ee-mahs gah*
Where's the <u>dining car</u>?	食堂車は，何号車ですか。 *<u>shoh-KOO-doh shah</u> wah, NAHN-goh shah dehs KAH*
buffet car	ビュッフェ車 *byoof-FEH shah*
sleeping car	寝台車 *SHEEN-dah-ee shah*
telephone	電話 *DEHN-wah*
Can I change to first class?	グリーン車／一等に，かえられますか。 *GREEN shah／eet-TOH nee, kah-EH-rah-reh-mahs KAH*
Where are we now?	今，どの辺ですか。 *EE-mah, doh-NOH hehn dehs KAH*
What time do we arrive at Kyoto?	京都には，何時に着きますか。 *KYOH-toh nee-wah, NAHN-jee nee tskee-mahs KAH*

Food: Ekiben

Ekiben (literally, station box lunch) is one of the best features of riding Japanese trains. Also called **obento**, the Japanese-style meals come in many varieties: There are choices of food, and containers of many shapes and sizes, some reusable — you can keep them if you like! Buy obento at the station before the trip, or on the train from vendors. For the adventuresome, there's an additional choice. At some stations along the way, obento vendors wait for the train. Passengers jump off, purchase a box lunch, and board the train again, all within two or three minutes. You can get good local specialties that way, but you must know beforehand exactly how many minutes the train will stop.

What's the next stop?	次の停車駅は，どこですか。	*tsoo-GEE noh teh-shah eh-kee wah, DOH-koh dehs KAH*
How long does the train stop there?	停車時間は，どの位ですか。	*TEH-shah jee-kahn wah, doh-NOH koo-rah-ee dehs KAH*
Is there enough time to go buy a box lunch?	お弁当を買いに行く時間が，ありますか。	*oh-BEHN-toh oh kah-ee nee ee-koo jee-KAHN gah, ah-ree mahs KAH*

Food: Vendors

Although many trains have dining cars and buffet cars, you can eat at your seat if you prefer. Vendors come through quite often, and they sell a variety of foods, from the delicious Japanese box lunches (obento), to sandwiches and other snack foods.

Excuse me. Do you have <u>beer</u>?	ちょっと，すみません。ビールが，ありますか。	*CHOHT-toh, soo-MEE-mah-sehn <u>BEE</u>-roo gah, ah-ree-mahs KAH*
candy	キャンデー	*KYAHN-deh*
chocolate	チョコレート	*choh-KOH-reh-toh*
cigarettes	たばこ	*tah-BAH-koh*
coffee	コーヒー	*KOH-hee*
cola	コーラ	*KOH-rah*

ice cream	アイスクリーム	*ah-EES-koo-ree-moo*
Japanese tea	お茶	*oh-CHAH*
Japanese box lunch	お弁当	*oh-BEHN-toh*
juice	ジュース	*JOO-soo*
mandarin oranges	みかん	*MEE-kahn*
nuts	ナッツ	*NAHT-tsoo*
peanuts	ピーナッツ	*PEE-naht-tsoo*
pudding	プリン	*POO-reen*
rice crackers	（お）せんべい	*(oh)-SEHM-beh*
sake	お酒	*oh-SAH-keh*
sandwiches	サンドイッチ	*SAHN-doh-eet-chee*
tea	紅茶	*KOH-chah*
whiskey	ウイスキー	*oo-EES-kee*

What kind of <u>cigarettes</u> do you have?
どんな<u>たばこ</u>が，ありますか。 *DOHN-nah <u>tah-BAH-koh</u> gah, ah-ree-mahs KAH*

juice
ジュース *JOO-soo*

box lunches
お弁当 *oh-BEHN-toh*

What is that?
それは，何ですか。 *soh-reh wah, NAHN dehs KAH*

Give me a beer, please.
ビールをください。 *BEE-roo oh, koo-dah-sah-ee*

Give me Japanese tea and a box lunch, please.
お茶とお弁当をください。 *oh-CHAH toh oh-BEHN-toh oh koo-dah-sah-ee*

How much is it?
いくらですか。 *EE-koo-rah dehs KAH*

Lost and Found

Where is the lost lost and found office?
遺失物取扱所は，どこですか。 *ee-SHEE-tsoo boo-tsoo toh-REE-ah-tsoo-kah-ee joh wah, DOH-koh dehs KAH*

I've lost my <u>camera</u>.	カメラを，なくしてしまいました。 *KAH-meh-rah oh, nah-KOO-shteh shee-mah-ee-mahsh-tah*
travelers' checks	トラベラー・チェック *toh-RAH-beh-rah chehk-koo*
passport	パスポート *pah-SOO-poh-toh*

AIR TRAVEL

Three principal airlines operate within Japan: Japan Air Lines (JAL), All Nippon Airways (ANA), and Toa Domestic Airlines (TDA). Although most airlines personnel know at least some English, the Japanese phrases can be helpful, especially at local airports.

When traveling on domestic flights, don't count on food being served. You might get coffee, tea, soft drinks, or a snack, but full meal service is not customary. Check first, so you can eat before your flight if you're hungry.

Inquiries

Is there a flight to <u>Sendai</u>?	仙台への飛行機が，ありますか。 *SEHN-dah-ee eh noh hee-KOH-kee gah, ah-ree-mahs KAH*
Beppu	別府 *behp-POO*
Is it a <u>nonstop</u> flight?	それは，<u>ノン・ストップ</u>ですか。 *soh-reh wah, nohn-STOHP-poo dehs KAH*
direct	直行便 *chohk-KOH been*
Where does it stop over?	途中で，どこにとまりますか。 *toh-CHOO deh, DOH-koh nee toh-mah-ree-mahs KAH*
Is there a daily flight to <u>Toyama</u>?	富山への便は，毎日ありますか。 *TOH-yah-mah eh noh been wah, MAH-ee-nee-chee ah-REE-mahs KAH*
Takamatsu	高松 *tah-KAH-mah-tsoo*

Is that a Japan Air Lines flight?

それは，日航の便ですか。 *soh-reh wah, neek-KOH noh been dehs KAH*

All Nippon Airways

全日空 *ZEHN-neek-koo*

Toa Domestic Airlines

東亜航空 *TOH-ah koh-koo*

Which day of the week does the flight to Okayama leave?

岡山行きの便は，何曜日に出ますか。 *oh-KAH-yah-mah yoo-kee noh been wah, nah-NEE yoh-bee nee deh-mahs KAH*

Kumamoto

熊本 *koo-MAH-moh-toh*

What type of aircraft do they use for that flight?

その便には，どんな飛行機を使いますか。 *soh-NOH been nee-wah, DOHN-nah hee-KOH-kee oh tsoo-kah-ee-mahs KAH*

Is there a connecting flight to Oita?

大分への乗りつぎ便が，ありますか。 *OH-ee-tah eh noh noh-REE-tsoo-gee been gah ah-ree-mahs KAH*

Kochi

高知 *KOH-chee*

Is there meal service in flight?

食事のサービスが，ありますか。 *shoh-KOO-jee noh SAH-bee-soo gah, ah-ree-mahs KAH*

Should I buy my air ticket in advance?

航空券は，前もって買っておくべきですか。 *KOH-koo kehn wah, mah-EH moht-teh kaht-TEH oh-koo beh-kee dehs KAH*

Can I get a ticket at the airport the day of the trip?

当日，空港で券が買えますか。 *toh-jee-tsoo, koo-koh deh KEHN gah kah-EH-mahs KAH*

Buying Tickets

Can I get a ticket to Okinawa for today?

今日の沖縄行きの券が，ありますか。 *KYOH noh oh-KEE-nah-wah yoo-kee noh kehn gah, ah-REE-mahs KAH*

tomorrow

あした *ah-SHTAH*

the day after tomorrow

あさって *ah-SAHT-teh*

I'd like a <u>one-way</u> ticket to Osaka.	大阪行きの，<u>片道</u>をください。 $\overline{OH}$-sah-kah yoo-kee noh, kah-TAH-mee-chee oh koo-dah-sah-ee
round trip	往復 $\overline{OH}$-foo-koo
<u>Two</u> tickets to Sapporo, please.	札幌行きの券を，<u>二枚</u>ください。 sahp-POH-roh yoo-kee noh KEHN oh, NEE-mah-ee koo-dah-sah-ee
three	三枚 SAHN-mah-ee
four	四枚 yoh-MAH-ee
Is there a <u>morning</u> flight to Kagoshima?	鹿児島行きの，<u>朝</u>の便があります か。 kah-GOH-shee-mah yoo-kee noh, AH-sah noh been gah ah-ree-mahs KAH
afternoon	昼間 hee-ROO-mah
evening	夜 YOH-roo
I'd like a ticket to Osaka on <u>August 10</u>.	<u>八月十日</u>の大阪行きの券を，お願い します。 hah-CHEE-gah-tsoo TOH-kah noh $\overline{OH}$-sah-kah yoo-kee noh kehn oh, oh-neh-gah-ee shee-mahs
September 20	九月二十日 KOO-gah-tsoo hah-TSKAH
October 30	十月三十日 $\overline{JOO}$-gah-tsoo SAHN-joo nee-chee
When is the next available flight to Osaka?	次に乗れる大阪行きの便は，何時で すか。 tsoo-GEE nee noh-reh-roo $\overline{OH}$-sah-kah yoo-kee noh been wah NAHN-jee dehs KAH
Is there <u>an earlier</u> flight than that?	それより<u>早い</u>便が，ありますか。 soh-REH yoh-ree hah-YAH-ee been gah, ah-ree-mahs KAH
a later	おそい oh-SOH-ee
What's the air fare to <u>Nagasaki</u>?	<u>長崎</u>まで，いくらかかりますか。 nah-GAH-sah-kee mah-deh EE-koo-rah kah-kah-ree-mahs KAH
Hiroshima	広島 hee-ROH-shee-mah

What's the flying time to <u>Okinawa</u>?	沖縄までの飛行時間は、どの位ですか。 *oh-KEE-nah-wah mah-deh noh hee-KOH jee-kahn wah, doh-NOH koo-rah-ee dehs KAH*
Hakodate	函館 *hah-KOH-dah-teh*
Is there a limit on the number of bags?	荷物の数には、制限がありますか。 *NEE-moh-tsoo noh kah-zoo nee-wah, SEH-gehn gah ah-ree-mahs KAH*
When do I have to check in?	何時にチェック・インしなければなりませんか。 *NAHN-jee nee chehk-KOO-een shee-NAH-keh-reh-bah nah-ree-mah-sehn KAH*
Do I need to reconfirm the reservation?	予約の再確認は、必要ですか。 *yoh-YAH-koo noh sah-EE-kah-koo-neen wah, hee-TSOO-yoh dehs KAH*

Information about the Airport

Where is the airport?	空港は、どこにありますか。 *koo-koh wah, DOH-koh nee ah-ree-mahs KAH*
Is the airport far?	空港まで、遠いですか。 *koo-koh mah-deh, TOH-ee dehs KAH*
How can I get to the airport?	空港へは、どう行ったらいいですか。 *koo-koh eh-wah, DOH eet-tah-rah EE dehs KAH*
Is there a <u>train</u> to the airport?	空港へは、<u>電車</u>がありますか。 *koo-koh eh-wah, DEHN-shah gah ah-ree-mahs KAH*
bus	バス *BAH-soo*
hotel bus	ホテルのバス *HOH-teh-roo noh bah-soo*
subway	地下鉄 *chee-KAH-teh-tsoo*
How much does the <u>train</u> to the airport cost?	空港まで、<u>電車</u>はいくらかかりますか。 *koo-koh mah-deh, dehn-shah wah EE-koo-rah kah-kah-ree-mahs KAH*
taxi	タクシー *TAHK-shee*

How long does the <u>taxi</u> take to the airport?	空港まで，タクシーでどの位時間が かかりますか。 *koo-koh mah-deh, TAHK-shee deh doh-NOH koo-rah-ee jee-kahn gah kah-kah-ree-mahs KAH*
bus	バス *BAH-soo*

At the Airport

I'd like to check in this suitcase.	このスーツ・ケースをチェック・イ ンします。 *koh-noh SOO-tsoo KEH-soo oh chehk-KOO-een shee-mahs*
This is carry-on.	これは，機内持込み品です。 *koh-reh wah, KEE-nah-ee moh-chee-KOH-mee-heen dehs*
ls a seat in the no-smoking section available?	禁煙席は，ありますか。 *KEEN-ehn seh-kee wah, ah-REE-mahs KAH*
Can I get a seat by the <u>window</u>?	<u>窓ぎわの席</u>を，もらえますか。 *<u>mah-DOH gee-wah</u> noh seh-kee oh, moh-RAH-eh-mahs KAH*
aisle	<u>道路がわ</u> *TSOO-roh gah-wah*
When is the departure?	何時発ですか。 *NAHN-jee hah-tsoo dehs KAH*
What's the departure gate?	出発ゲートは，何番ですか。 *shoop-PAH-tsoo geh-toh wah, NAHN-bahn dehs KAH*
What's the arrival time?	何時着ですか。 *NAHN-jee chah-koo dehs KAH*

International Air Travel

I'd like a ticket to <u>Hong Kong</u>.	<u>香港</u>への券をください。 *<u>HOHN-kohn</u> eh noh KEHN oh koo-dah-sah-ee*
Manila	マニラ *MAH-nee-rah*
When is the first available flight to <u>Jakarta</u>?	次に乗れる<u>ジャカルタ</u>行きの便は， いつですか。 *lsoo-GEE nee noh-reh-roo <u>jah-KAH-roo-tah</u> yoo-kee noh been wah, EE-tsoo deh-mahs KAH*
Bangkok	バンコック *BAHN-kohk-koo*

Is there a direct flight to <u>Seoul</u> from this airport?	この空港から，<u>ソウルへの直行便が</u>ありますか。 *koh-NOH-koo-koh kah-rah, <u>SOH-oo-roo</u> eh noh chohk-KOH been gah ah-ree-mahs KAH*
Guam	ガム島 *gah-MOO-toh*
What's the air fare to <u>Peking</u>?	<u>北京</u>まで，いくらですか。 <u>*PEH-keen*</u> *mah-deh, EE-koo-rah dehs KAH*
Kuala Lumpur	クアラルンプール *koo-AH-rah-roon-poo-roo*
How long does the flight take?	飛行時間は，何時間ですか。 *hee-KOH jee-kahn wah, NAHN jee-kahn dehs KAH*
Is that a <u>lunch</u> flight?	この便では，<u>ランチ</u>が出ますか。 *koh-NOH been deh-wah, <u>RAHN-chee</u> gah deh-mahs KAH*
dinner	ディナー *DEE-nah*
When is the <u>departure</u> time?	出発の時間は，何時ですか。 *shoop-PAH-tsoo noh jee-kahn wah, NAHN-jee dehs KAH*
arrival	到着 *TOH-chah-koo*

BOAT TRAVEL: STEAMSHIP, FERRY, HYDROFOIL, HOVERCRAFT

Is there a cruise ship on the Inland Sea?	瀬戸内海に，遊覧船がありますか。 *seh-TOH-nah-ee-kah-ee nee, YOO-rahn-sehn gah ah-ree-mahs KAH*
Can I go to <u>Hokkaido</u> by ship?	北海道に，船で行けますか。 *hokh-KAH-ee-doh nee, FOO-neh deh ee-keh-mahs KAH*
Okinawa	沖縄 *oh-KEE-nah-wah*
What type of ship is it?	どんな種類の船ですか。 *DOHN-nah shoo-roo-ee noh FOO-neh dehs KAH*
When does the next <u>ship</u> leave?	次の船は，いつ出ますか。 *tsoo-GEE noh foo-neh wah, EE-tsoo deh-mahs KAH*
ferry	連絡船 *REHN-rahk-sehn*
hydrofoil	水中翼船 *soo-EE-choo yohk-sehn*
hovercraft	ホーバー・クラフト *HOH-bah koo-rahf-toh*
Where is the <u>harbor</u>?	港は，どこですか。 *mee-NAH-toh wah, DOH-koh dehs KAH*
ticket office	切符売り場 *keep-POO oo-ree-bah*
pier	埠頭 *foo-TOH*
How long does the <u>crossing</u> take?	渡るには，どの位時間がかかりますか。 *wah-TAH-roo nee-wah, doh-NOH koo-rah-ee jee-kahn gah kah-KAH-ree-mahs KAH*
cruise	航海 *KOH-kah-ee*
When do we board?	乗船時間は，何時ですか。 *JOH-sehn jee-kahn wah, NAHN-jee dehs KAH*
Do we stop at any ports?	途中で，ほかの港にとまりますか。 *toh-CHOO deh, hoh-KAH noh mee-nah-toh nee toh-MAH-ree-mahs KAH*

How long do we remain in port?	その港では，どの位停船しますか。 *soh-NOH mee-nah-toh deh-wah, doh-NOH koo-rah-ee teh-sehn shee-mahs KAH*
I'd like a <u>first class</u> ticket.	一等の券をください。 *eet-TOH noh KEHN oh koo-dah-sah-ee*
second class	二等 *nee-TOH*
Are meals served on board?	船で，食事が出ますか。 *FOO-neh deh, shoh-KOO-jee gah deh-mahs KAH*
Can we buy something to eat on board?	船で，何か食べ物が買えますか。 *FOO-neh deh, NAH-nee kah tah-BEH-moh-noh gah kah-eh mahs KAH*
I don't feel well.	気分が，すぐれません。 *KEE-boon gah, soo-GOO-reh-mah-sehn*
Do you have something for seasickness?	何か，船酔いの薬がありますか。 *NAH-nee kah, foo-NAH-yoh-ee noh ksoo-ree gah ah-ree-mahs KAH*
Do we have time to go ashore at this port?	この港では，上陸する時間がありますか。 *koh-NOH mee-nah-toh deh-wah, JOH-ree-koo soo-roo jee-KAHN gah ah-ree-mahs KAH*
What time do we have to be back on board?	何時までに，船にもどってこなければなりませんか。 *NAHN-jee mah-deh nee, FOO-neh nee moh-DOHT-teh koh-nah-keh-reh-bah nah-ree-mah-sehn KAH*
When do we arrive at <u>Sado</u>?	佐渡には，何時に着きますか。 *SAH-doh nee-wah, NAHN-jee nee tsoo-kee-mahs KAH*
Beppu	別府 *behp-POO*

A FEW ITINERARIES

If you want to sightsee, here are a few suggestions: some in-Tokyo tours, some side trips from Tokyo, and one to Kyoto and Nara. For the convenience of a package tour, make arrangements with a travel agency. On your own, you can get to any of these places by public transportation, by car, or a combination of the two.

TOKYO

Meiji Shrine

The Meiji Shrine is one of the grandest in Japan. It's easy to reach, located right near Harajuku station. Walk through the entrance, a huge torii gate made of 1,700-year-old cedar trees, then along the pebbled path to the Iris Garden; in June, there are 100 varieties in full bloom! There's a teahouse nearby, and small pavilions with traditional thatched roofs. Stroll through the thickly wooded gardens, then back along the pebbled path, until you come to the main shrine buildings, or **honden**. There you may see couples with newborn babies, come for naming and blessing by the priests. During the New Year holiday week, festive crowds come to pay their respects.

When you leave, walk down the wide boulevard known as Omote Sando. It's a trendy area of small coffee shops, boutiques, restaurants, craft shops, and other amusements. You can easily spend several hours there.

Do I have a chance to see a Shinto ceremony at the shrine?	神社で，神道の儀式を見る機会がありますか。 *JEEN-jah deh, SHEEN-toh noh gee-shee-kee oh MEE-roo kee-kah-ee gah ah-ree-mahs KAH*
What's the meaning of rinsing the mouth and washing the hands?	口をすすいだり，手を洗ったりする意味は，何ですか。 *koo-CHEE oh soo-soo-ee-dah-ree, TEH oh ah-RAHT-tah-ree soo-roo ee-mee wah, NAHN dehs KAH*
Who comes here to pray?	だれが，お祈りにきますか。 *DAH-reh gah, oh-ee-noh-ree nee kee-mahs KAH*
What's the proper way to pray?	正しいお祈りのしかたが，ありますか。 *tah-DAH-shee oh-EE-noh-ree noh shee-kah-tah gah, ah-REE-mahs-KAH*
Are you supposed to throw money when you pray?	お祈りするとき，おさいせんをあげるべきですか。 *oh-EE-noh-ree soo-roo-toh-kee, oh-SAH-ee-sehn oh ah-GEH-roo beh-kee dehs KAH*

| May I try a fortune? | おみくじをひいてみてもいいです か。 *oh-MEE-koo-jee oh hee-teh-mee-teh-moh, EE dehs KAH* |

Imperial Palace, National Diet, Ginza

Begin at the Imperial Palace, located in the heart of Tokyo; depending on where you're staying, you might be able to walk from your hotel. The palace itself is open to visitors only at the New Year and on the Emperor's birthday. But you can visit the East Garden, Imperial Palace Plaza, and the Nijubashi Bridge, all popular with Tokyoites. From there, walk to the National Diet Building, the home of Japan's legislature, in Kasumigaseki, where you'll find other government buildings too.

From Kasumigaseki, you can go to Ginza, the most famous shopping area in Japan. At the center of the Ginza district is the Chuo-dori, the largest street, which runs northeast to southwest. The intersection of Chuo-dori and Harumi-dori is a good starting point. Elegant galleries, boutiques, department stores, and restaurants line the streets. Be sure to explore the narrow streets that run parallel to the main roads. These side streets and alleys contain tiny shops, restaurants, coffee houses, bars, and other amusements. You can spend several hours or several days wandering through Ginza, and there will still be more to see next time!

| Is this the main residence for the Emperor and his family? | これが，天皇と御家族の主なお住い ですか。 *koh-REH gah, TEHN-noh toh goh-KAH-zoh-koo noh OH-moh nah oh-SOO-mah-ee dehs KAH* |

| How big is the palace area? | 皇居の広さは，どの位ですか。 *KOH-kyoh noh hee-roh-sah wah, doh-NOH koo-rah-ee dehs KAH* |

| Have all the Emperors lived here? | 歴代の天皇は，みんなここに住みま したか。 *reh-KEE-dah-ee noh tehn-noh wah, MEEN-nah koh-koh nee soo-mee-mah-shtah KAH* |

| When was it built? | いつ建造されましたか。 *EE-tsoo kehn-zoh sah-reh-mah-shtah KAH* |

| Is the Diet in session now? | いま国会は審議中ですか。 *ee-mah kohk-KAH-ee wah, SHEEN-gee choo dehs KAH* |

Can I go inside?	中に入れますか。 *NAH-kah nee, hah-EE-rch-mahs KAH*
Is there a guided tour of the Diet Building?	議事堂見学の，ガイド付きツアーがありますか。 *gee-JEE-doh kehn-gah-koo noh, gah-EE-doh tsoo-kee TSOO-ah gah ah-ree-mahs KAH*
Is Ginza more expensive than other shopping areas?	銀座は，他のショッピング街とくらべて，高いですか。 *GEEN-zah wah, hoh-KAH noh shohp-PEEN-goo gah-ee toh koo-rah-beh-teh, tah-KAH-ee dehs KAH*
Are the stores open at night too?	お店は，夜もあいていますか。 *oh-MEE-seh wah, yoh-roo-moh ah-EE-teh ee-mahs KAH*
Is the Kabuki Theater within walking distance from Ginza?	歌舞伎座は，銀座から歩いていけますか。 *kah-BOO-kee-zah wah, GEEN-zah kah-rah ah-ROO-ee-teh ee-keh-mahs KAH*
Tsukiji Fish Market	築地の魚市場 *tsoo-KEE-jee noh oo-OH ee-chee-bah*

Asakusa and Ueno

The main attraction in the Asakusa area is the Asakusa Kannon Temple. You'll see a huge paper lantern at the Kaminarimon (gate). Through the gate, a long arcade leads up to the temple. Known as Nakamise, this colorful arcade is lined with small shops open to the walkway. They sell traditional Japanese sweets and rice crackers, clothing, toys, and other souvenirs. The temple itself dates back to 645. Kannon is the goddess of mercy, and many visitors pray for relief from physical ailments at a huge incense brazier close to the entrance. After you leave the temple, you might look at some more shops in the arcade and then have lunch at a nearby restaurant. The Asakusa Kannon Temple area is not far from the Tokyo National Museum in Ueno, a must on your tour, and is also accessible to the Ueno Zoo, where you can see the pandas.

| Is this area an old part of Tokyo? | この辺は，昔の東京の下町ですか。 *koh-NOH hehn wah, moo-KAH-shee noh toh-kyoh noh SHTAH-mah-chee dehs KAH* |

Is it always crowded?	いつも、こんでいますか。 *EE-tsoo moh, KOHN-deh ee-mahs KAH*
Why are the people rubbing the smoke from the incense onto their bodies?	（お）線香の煙を、体にこすりつけるのはなぜですか。 *(oh)-SEHN-koh noh keh-moo-ree oh, kah-rah-dah nee koh-SOO-ree-tskeh-roo noh wah NAH-zeh dehs KAH*
Do you think I should go to the Tokyo National Museum?	国立博物館へは、行くべきですか。 *koh-KOO-ree-tsoo hah-koo-boo-tsoo-kahn eh wah, ee-KOO beh-kee dehs KAH*
What type of collection are they exhibiting now?	今どんなものを、展示していますか。 *ee-mah DOHN-nah moh-noh oh, TEHN-jee shteh ee-mahs KAH*
How late is it open?	何時まであいていますか。 *NAHN-jee mah-deh ah-ee-teh ee-mahs KAH*
How long does a quick look around the zoo take?	動物園をいそいで見てまわるのに、どの位時間がかかりますか。 *DOH-boo-tsoo ehn oh ee-SOH-ee-deh MEE-teh mah-wah-roo noh nee, doh-NOH koo-rah-ee jee-kahn gah kah-kah-ree-mahs KAH*
Can I see pandas at the zoo?	パンダを見ることが、できますか。 *PAHN-dah oh MEE-roo koh-toh gah, deh-KEE-mahs KAH*

DAY TRIPS FROM TOKYO

Kamakura and Yokohama

Spend a morning visiting Kamakura, on Japan's Pacific coast. You can get there in about an hour by bus, train, or car. Once the seat of Japan's feudal government, Kamakura offers many attractions in a quiet, peaceful setting. The highlight is the Daibutsu, a 700-year-old bronze statue of Buddha, the second largest in Japan. Near the Kamakura station is the Tsurugaoka Hachimangu Shrine, which has two museums on its grounds. Also well worth seeing are Engakuji and Kenchoji, both ranked among the five outstanding Zen temples in Kamakura. You can have lunch at one of Kamakura's fine small restaurants, and then on your way back to Tokyo stop at the port city of Yokohama, about a half hour from Kamakura, and roughly halfway between Kamakura and Tokyo. Visit the Sankei-en Garden, which contains many historic buildings, then go to Yamashita Park for a panoramic view of the city and harbor. Walk to nearby Chinatown, where you can wander through the exotic streets at your leisure, visiting the small shops, sampling Chinese delicacies, and perhaps having dinner at one of the superb restaurants before you return to Tokyo.

When was Kamakura the capital?	鎌倉が首都だったのは，いつごろですか。 *kah-MAH-koo-rah gah SHOO-toh daht-tah noh wah, ee-TSOO-goh-roh dehs KAH*
How tall is the Great Buddha?	大仏の高さは，どの位ですか。 *dah-EE-boo-tsoo noh TAH-kah-sah wah, doh-NOH koo-rah-ee dehs KAH*
What is the Tsurugaoka Hachimangu Shrine dedicated to?	鶴岡八幡宮には，何がまつってありますか。 *tsoo-ROO-gah-oh-kah hah-chee-mahn-goo nee-wah, NAH-nee gah mah-TSOOT-teh ah-ree-mahs KAH*
What are the special handicrafts in Kamakura?	鎌倉には，何か手工芸品がありますか。 *kah-MAH-koo-rah nee wah, NAH-nee kah shoo-KOH-geh heen gah ah-ree-mahs KAH*
Where is the shopping/restaurant area in Yokohama?	横浜のショッピング／レストラン街は，どこですか。 *yoh-KOH-hah-mah noh shohp-PEEN-goo/ reh-SOO-toh-rahn gah-ee wah, DOH-koh dehs KAH*
What type of Chinese food do they have?	どんな種類の中華料理が，ありますか。 *DOHN-nah shoo-roo-ee noh CHOO-kah ryoh-ree gah, ah-ree-mahs KAH*
Which one is a Cantonese style restaurant?	どれが，広東料理のレストランですか。 *DOH-reh gah, KAHN-tohn ryoh-ree noh rehs-toh-rahn dehs KAH*
Peking	北京 *peh-KEEN*
Shanghai	上海 *SHAHN-hah-ee*
Szechuan	四川 *shee-SEHN*

Hakone and Mount Fuji

Hakone can be reached by train from Tokyo's Shinjuku station in about an hour and a half, or by bus or car. It's the center of the Fuji-Hakone-Izu National Park, an area of hot springs, pine forests, scenic mountain slopes, and places of historic interest. Nearby Mount Fuji, the venerated 12,388-foot high (3,776 meters) dormant volcano with the perfect cone shape, can be seen from many places in and near Hakone. One of the best viewing spots is beautiful Lake Ashi, which on a clear day shows Mount Fuji's inverted reflection. There are sightseeing boats on the lake. Have lunch at one of the fine hotels in Hakone (perhaps lakeside), and then take a cable-car or funicular railway for spectacular views along the slopes of Mount Sounzan. There's a good open-air museum for sculpture nearby. Among the many other attractions in Hakone are the Owakudani and Kowakidani valleys, where sulphurous fumes rise from rock crevices. You might also want to take a bus trip partway up Mount Fuji before your return to Tokyo. This one-day excursion can easily extend to several days if you have the time — or you could return to Hakone someday.

Do you think I can see Mount Fuji today?	今日は，富士山が見えるでしょうか。 KYOH wah, FOO-jee-sahn gah mee-EH-roo deh shoh kah
Is it difficult to climb Mount Fuji?	富士山に登るのは，難しいですか。 FOO-jee-sahn nee noh-BOH-roo noh wah, moo-ZOO-kah-shee dehs KAH
What are the local hand-icrafts in Hakone?	箱根には，何か手工芸品がありますか。 hah-KOH-neh nee-wah, NAH-nee kah shoo-KOH-geh heen gah ah-ree-mahs KAH
Do I need a jacket or sweater in Hakone?	箱根では，ジャケットやセーターがいりますか。 hah-KOH-neh deh-wah, jah-KEHT-toh yah SEH-tah gah ee-REE-mahs KAH
Can you swim in the lakes?	湖では，泳げますか。 mee-ZOO-oo-mee deh-wah, oh-YOH-geh-mahs KAH
Is it possible to try a hot spring bath?	温泉に，入ってみることができますか。 OHN-sehn nee, HAH-eet-teh mee-roo koh-toh gah deh-KEE-mahs KAH

Nikko

Nikko is two hours by train from Tokyo, in a northerly direction. It's known for great scenic beauty, with gentle mountain slopes, cedar trees, lakes, rivers, streams, and waterfalls. When you arrive, go directly to the Toshogu Shrine, which was built in 1636 as the mausoleum of Ieyasu, founder of the Tokugawa shogunate. Many consider it an architectural masterpiece. Toshogu is located in a complex of shrines, temples, and museums, and you can get one ticket to admit you to all of them. Begin with Toshogu, for it will require some time to see everything. Proceed down the Omote–Sando, and pass through the carved and decorated Yomeimon gate to the treasures inside. You could spend all day here, seeing the various buildings in the complex. But if you have time, go by bus or taxi along the 48 hairpin curves on the road that climbs to Lake Chuzenji, 10 miles to the west. Kegon Falls, 328 feet high, is spectacular. The scenery is worth the side trip.

Is Ieyasu in the novel <u>Shogun</u>?	家康は，小説の「ショーグン」に出てきますか。 *ee-EH-yah-soo wah, shoh-seh-tsoo noh SHOH-goon nee DEH-teh kee-mahs KAH*
Is the Toshogu Shrine still owned by the Tokugawa family?	東照宮は，今でも徳川家のものですか。 *TOH-shoh-goo wah, EE-mah deh-moh toh-KOO-gah-wah keh noh moh-noh dehs KAH*
Are the colors original?	色は，もとのままですか。 *ee-ROH wah, MOH-toh noh mah-MAH dehs KAH*
Is Lake Chuzenji good for fishing?	中禅寺湖は，つりにはいいところですか。 *CHOO-zehn-jee-koh wah, tsoo-REE nee-wah, EE toh-koh-roh dehs KAH*

TRIPS OF TWO DAYS OR MORE

Kyoto and Nara

If you have more than a day to spend outside Tokyo (ideally more than two days), visit Kyoto and Nara. Kyoto is easy to reach by plane, train (there are many Shinkansen daily), bus, or car. The plane trip is about 55 minutes, and the train about 3 hours. The capital of Japan from 794 to 1868, Kyoto is still considered by many to be the true repository of traditional Japanese culture. The main attractions are centuries-old temples, shrines, and gardens. There are approximately 400 Shinto shrines and 1,650 Buddhist temples located along thousand-year old streets and paths. Once you arrive, you can obtain detailed walking tour maps from the Tourist Information Center, or you can arrange with a travel agency for a guided tour.

From Kyoto, Nara is about a 35-minute train ride. Although Nara is much smaller than Kyoto, its history is even older. Many temples contain Buddhist antiquities and other priceless treasures. The famous Deer Park is a 15-minute walk east of the Kintetsu Nara station. Over 1,000 tame deer roam the park. Also within walking distance is Todaiji , a temple famous for the world's largest bronze statue of Buddha. Walk to Kofukuji, a five-story pagoda, and then to the Nara National Museum. If you have time, stop and see the Kasuga Grand Shrine and Shin-Yakushiji, another temple, before returning to Kyoto.

ENTERTAINMENT AND DIVERSIONS

Japan has a wide variety of amusements that visitors are sure to enjoy. You'll find films, plays, dance, music, sports — all the entertainment and recreation you're used to, plus some that may be new to you, like traditional Japanese theatrical productions, martial arts, and sports.

Schedules

For current schedules of events, you can find weekly English-language publications in most hotels, at JNTO Tourist Information Centers, at travel agencies, and in many restaurants and shops that deal with visitors. You can also get this sort of information in the English-language newspapers such as The Japan Times, the Asahi Evening News, The Daily Yomiuri, the Mainichi Daily News, the Tokyo Weekender, the Tokyo Journal, the Tour Companion, and the TCJ Companion.

Where can I find English schedules for current entertainment?	今やっている催し物の英語のスケジュールは、どこを見ればわかりますか。 *EE-mah yaht-teh-ee-roo moh-YOH-shee-moh-noh noh eh-goh noh SKEH-joo-roo wah, DOH-koh oh mee-reh-bah wah-KAH-ree-mahs KAH*
Where can I buy an English-language newspaper?	英語の新聞は、どこで売っていますか。 *EH-goh noh sheen-boon wah, DOH-koh deh oot-teh ee-mahs KAH*

Tickets

Tickets for most theatrical and many sporting events can be purchased in advance at ticket bureaus known as Play Guides. There are Play Guides at convenient locations in downtown areas, and also in some department stores. Clerks at the Play Guide bureaus are more likely to speak English than those at the box offices. Be sure to purchase your tickets before the day of the event; Play Guides can't sell you tickets on the same day as the performance (but box offices can).

Is there a Play Guide nearby? 近くに, プレーガイドがあります か。 *chee-KAH-koo nee, poo-REH gah-ee-doh gah ah-ree-mahs KAH*

Where's the Play Guide? プレーガイドは, どこにあります か。 *poo-REH gah-ee-doh wah, DOH-koh nee ah-ree-mahs KAH*

FILMS AND THEATER

Foreign-made films are shown with their original sound tracks and Japanese titles. Japanese films, of course, have Japanese sound tracks, but you might enjoy them just the same: a good samurai adventure film is always exciting! For theater fans, there are good stage productions in Tokyo and other Japanese cities.

Let's go to the movies. 映画に, 行きましょう。 *EH-gah nee, ee-KEE-mah-shoh*

   theater 観劇 *KAHN-geh-kee*

I'd like to go see a film. 映画を, 見たいのですが。 *EH-gah oh, mee-TAH-ee noh dehs gah*

   play 演劇 *EHN-geh-kee*

Are there any good films in town? どこかで, おもしろい映画をやって いますか。 *DOH-koh-kah deh, oh-MOH-shee-roh-ee eh-gah oh yaht-teh ee-mahs KAH*

   plays 演劇 *ehn-geh-kee*

Could you recommend one? 一つ, 推薦してもらえますか。 *hee-TOH-tsoo, soo-EE-sehn shteh moh-rah-eh-mahs KAH*

Where's the movie theater? 映画館は, どこですか。 *EH-gah kahn wah, DOH-koh dehs KAH*

   theater 劇場 *geh-KEE joh*

What's the title of the film? 映画の題名は, 何ですか。 *EH-gah noh dah-ee-meh wah, NAHN-dehs KAH*

   play 劇 *GEH-kee*

Who's the <u>director of the film</u>?	映画監督は，だれですか。 $\overline{EH}$-gah kahn-toh-koo wah, DAH-reh dehs KAH
director of the play	演出家 EHN-shoo-tsoo kah
Who's playing the lead?	だれが，主演していますか。 DAH-reh gah, shoo-EHN shteh ee-mahs KAH
Is it a <u>comedy</u>?	それは，喜劇ですか。 soh-REH wah, <u>KEE-geh-kee</u> dehs KAH
historical drama	時代物 jee-DAH-ee moh-noh
musical	ミュージカル $MY\overline{OO}$-jee-kah-roo
mystery	ミステリー MEE-soo-teh-$\overline{ree}$
romance	恋愛物 REHN-ah-ee moh-noh
science fiction film	サイエンス・フィクション sah-EE-ehn-soo fee-koo-shohn
thriller/ horror movie	スリラー SOO-ree-$\overline{rah}$
tragedy	悲劇 HEE-geh-kee
Western	西部劇 $\overline{SEH}$-boo geh-kee
war film	戦争映画 SEHN-soh eh-gah
Is it a <u>Japanese</u> film?	それは，日本の映画ですか。 soh-REH wah, <u>nee-HOHN noh</u> eh-gah dehs KAH
an American	アメリカの ah-MEH-ree-kah noh
a British	イギリスの ee-GEE-rees noh
Do they show it in the original language?	原語で，上演しますか。 GEHN-goh deh, joh-eh shee-mahs KAH
Is it dubbed in Japanese?	日本語に，吹き替えられていますか。 nee-HOHN-goh nee, foo-kee-KAH-eh-rah-reh-teh ee-mahs KAH
Does it have English subtitles?	英語の字幕が，ありますか。 $\overline{EH}$-goh noh jee-mah-koo gah, ah-ree-mahs KAH
Is it a first-run film?	それは，封切りの映画ですか。 soh-REH wah, $\overline{FOO}$-kee-ree noh eh-gah dehs KAH

Is the film black and white, or color?	映画は白黒ですか，それともカラーですか。 *eh-gah wah shee-ROH-koo-roh dehs KAH, soh-reh-toh-moh KAH-rah dehs KAH*
What kind of story is it?	どんな筋ですか。 *DOHN-nah soo-jee dehs KAH*
Are the performers Americans or Japanese?	出演者はアメリカ人ですか，それとも日本人ですか。 *shoo-TSOO-ehn shah wah ah-MEH-ree-kah-jeen dehs KAH, soh-reh-toh-moh nee-HOHN-jeen dehs KAH*
Do they speak English or Japanese?	出演者は英語を話しますか，それとも日本語を話しますか。 *shoo-TSOO-ehn shah wah EH-goh oh hah-nah-shee-mahs KAH, soh-reh-toh-moh nee-HOHN-goh oh hah-nah-shee-mahs KAH*
Is there a Broadway show being performed now?	今，ブロードウェーからのショーを，やっていますか。 *EE-mah, boo-ROH-doh-weh kah-rah noh shoh oh, yaht-TEH ee-mahs KAH*
What time does the first show begin?	最初のショーは，何時に始まりますか。 *sah-EE-shoh noh shoh wah, NAHN-jee nee hah-jee-mah-ree-mahs KAH*
last	最後 *SAH-ee-goh*
What time does the show end?	ショーは，何時に終りますか。 *SHOH wah, NAHN-jee nee oh-wah-ree-mahs KAH*
What time does the performance begin?	開演は，何時ですか。 *kah-EE-ehn wah, NAHN-jee dehs KAH*
end	終演 *SHOO ehn*
How long will it run?	いつまで，やっていますか。 *EE-tsoo mah-deh, yaht-TEH ee-mahs KAH*
Is there a matinee?	マチネーは，ありますか。 *MAH-chee-neh wah, ah-ree-mahs KAH*
Where can I buy a ticket?	券は，どこで買えますか。 *KEHN wah, DOH-koh deh kah-eh-mahs KAH*

Where's the box office?	切符売り場は，どこですか。 *keep-POO OO-ree-bah wah, DOH-koh dehs KAH*
Do you have any tickets left for <u>tonight</u>?	今晩の切符が，まだありますか。 <u>*KOHN bahn*</u> *noh keep-poo gah, MAH-dah ah-ree-mahs KAH*
the next show	次のショー *tsoo-GEE noh shoh*
I'd like to buy <u>a ticket</u> for tonight.	今晩の券を，一枚ください。 *KOHN bahn noh* <u>*kehn oh, ee-CHEE mah-ee*</u> *koo-dah-sah-ee*
two tickets	券を，二枚 *kehn oh, NEE mah-ee*
three tickets	券を，三枚 *kehn oh, SAHN mah-ee*
four tickets	券を，四枚 *kehn oh, YOHN mah-ee*
I'd like to buy a ticket for <u>tomorrow</u> night.	あしたの晩の券を，一枚ください。 <u>*ah-SHTAH noh*</u> *bahn noh kehn oh, ee-CHEE mah-ee koo-dah-sah-ee*
Friday	金曜日の *KEEN-yoh bee noh*
Saturday	土曜日の *doh-YOH bee noh*
Sunday	日曜日の *nee-CHEE-yoh bee noh*
Monday	月曜日の *geh-TSOO-yoh bee noh*
Tuesday	火曜日の *kah-YOH bee noh*
Wednesday	水曜日の *soo-EE-yoh bee noh*
Thursday	木曜日の *moh-KOO-yoh bee noh*
Do yoou have seats in the <u>orchestra</u>?	舞台に近い席が，ありますか。 <u>*BOO-tah-ee nee chee-KAH-ee*</u> *seh-kee gah, ah-ree-mahs KAH*
balcony	二階の *nee-KAH-ee noh*
mezzanine	中二階の *CHOO-nee-kah-ee noh*
Do you have better seats than that?	それよりいい席がありますか。 *soh-REH yoh-ree EE seh-kee gah, ah-ree-mahs KAH*
Do you have seats a little more <u>forward</u>?	もう少し前の席が，ありますか。 *MOH skoh-shee* <u>*MAH-eh*</u> *noh seh-kee gah, ah-ree-mahs KAH*

to the rear	うしろ *oo-SHEE-roh*
toward the center	中央寄り *CHOO-oh yoh-ree*
Is there a cloakroom?	コートをあずける場所があります か。 *KOH-toh oh ah-ZOO-keh-roo bah-shoh gah, ah-ree-mahs KAH*
Is there a program in English?	英語のプログラムが，ありますか。 *EH-goh noh poo-ROH-goo-rah-moo gah, ah-ree-mahs KAH*
Please show me to my seat.	私の席まで，案内してください。 *wah-TAHK-shee noh seh-kee mah-deh, AHN-nah-ee shteh koo-dah-sah-ee*

CONCERTS, OPERA, AND BALLET

I'd like to attend <u>a ballet</u>.	<u>バレー</u>を見に行きたいのですが。 <u>*BAH-reh*</u> *oh MEE nee ee-kee-tah-ee noh dehs gah*
a concert	コンサートを聞きに *kohn-SAH-toh oh kee-KEE nee*
an opera	オペラを見に *OH-peh-rah oh mee nee*
Do I need to dress formally?	正装の必要が，ありますか。 *SEH-soh noh hee-tsoo-yoh gah, ah-ree-mahs KAH*
What shall I wear?	何を着たらいいでしょうか。 *NAH-nee oh kee-tah-rah EE deh-shoh kah*
I prefer <u>chamber music</u>.	<u>室内楽</u>が，好みです。 *shee-TSOO-nah-ee gah-koo gah, KOH-noh-mee dehs*
classical music	クラシック・ミュージック *koo-RAH-sheek-koo myoo-jeek-koo*
concertos	協奏曲 *KYOH-soh kyoh-koo*
country music	カントリー・ミュージック *KAHN-toh-ree myoo-jeek-koo*
folk songs	フォーク・ソング *FOH-koo sohn-goo*

jazz	ジャズ *JYAH-zoo*
modern music	モダン・ミュージック *moh-DAHN myoo-jeek-koo*
popular songs	ポピュラー・ソング *poh-PYOO-rah sohn-goo*
rock'n'roll	ロックン・ロール *rohk-KOON roh-roo*
symphonies	シンフォニー *SHEEN-foh-nee*
classical ballet	古典バレー *koh-TEHN bah-reh*
modern ballet	モダンバレー *moh-DAHN bah-reh*
modern dance	モダン・ダンス *moh-DAHN dahns*
Where's the <u>concert hall</u>?	コンサート・ホールは，どこにあります か。 *kohn-SAH-toh hoh-roo wah, DOH-koh nee ah-ree-mahs KAH*
opera house	オペラ劇場 *oh-PEH-rah geh-kee-joh*
ballet theater	バレー劇場 *bah-REH geh-kee-joh*
Is it nearby?	それは，近くにありますか。 *soh-REH wah, chee-KAH-koo nee ah-ree-mahs KAH*
Is a <u>ballet</u> being performed now?	今，バレーをやっていますか。 *EE-mah, BAH-reh oh yaht-teh ee-mahs KAH*
an opera	オペラ *OH-peh-rah*
a concert	コンサート *kohn-SAH-toh*
Which <u>ballet company</u> is performing?	どのバレー団が，上演しています か。 *DOH-noh bah-REH dahn gah, joh-ehn shteh ee-mahs KAH*
opera company	歌劇団 *kah-GEH-kee dahn*
Which <u>orchestra</u> is playing?	どの管弦楽団が，演奏しています か。 *DOH-noh kahn-gehn-gah-koo dahn gah, ehn-soh shteh ee-mahs KAH*
symphony orchestra	交響楽団 *koh-kyoh-gah-koo dahn*
band	楽団 *gah-koo dahn*
group	グループ *goo-roo-poo*

Is that a Japanese <u>ballet company</u>?	それは，日本の<u>バレー団</u>ですか。 *soh-REH wah, nee-HOHN noh bah-reh dahn dehs KAH*
opera company	歌劇団 *kah-geh-kee dahn*
orchestra	管弦楽団 *kahn-gehn-gah-koo dahn*
Is that a foreign <u>ballet company</u>?	それは，外国の<u>バレー団</u>ですか。 *soh-REH wah, gah-EE-koh-koo noh bah-reh dahn dehs KAH*
opera company	歌劇団 *kah-geh-kee dahn*
orchestra	管弦楽団 *kahn-gehn-gah-koo dahn*
Which country do they come from?	どの国から来ましたか。 *DOH-noh koo-nee kah-rah kee-MAH-shtah KAH*
What are they <u>performing</u>?	何を<u>上演</u>していますか。 *NAH-nee oh joh-ehn shteh ee-mahs KAH*
playing	演奏 *ehn-soh*
Who's <u>conducting</u>?	だれが，<u>指揮して</u>いますか。 *DAH-reh gah, shee-KEE shteh ee-mahs KAH*
dancing	おどって *oh-DOHT-teh*
playing	演奏して *ehn-soh shteh*
singing	歌って *oo-TAHT-teh*
Who is the <u>composer</u>?	作曲家はだれですか。 *sahk-KYOH-koo kah wah, DAH-reh dehs KAH*
lead dancer	主演のダンサー *shoo-EHN noh dahn-sah*
lead singer	主演の歌手 *shoo-EHN noh kah-shoo*
pianist	ピアニスト *pee-AH-nee-stoh*
violinist	バイオリニスト *bah-EE-oh-ree-nee-stoh*
What time does tonight's performance start?	今晩の公演は，何時に始まりますか。 *KOHN-bahn noh koh-ehn wah, NAHN-jee nee hah-jee-mah-ree-mahs KAH*
Are tonight's tickets <u>sold out</u>?	今晩の券は，売り切れですか。 *KOHN-bahn noh kehn wah, oo-REE-kee-reh dehs KAH*

still available	まだあります *MAH-dah ah-ree-mahs*
Should I get tickets in advance?	前売券を、買うべきですか。 *mah-EH oo-ree kehn oh, kah-OO beh-kee dehs KAH*
What are the least expensive seats?	一番安い券は、いくらですか。 *ee-CHEE-bahn yah-soo-ee kehn wah, EE-koo-rah dehs KAH*
I'd like to get good seats.	いい席が、欲しいのですが。 *EE seh-kee gah, hoh-SHEE noh dehs gah*
How much are the front-row seats?	前列の席は、いくらですか。 *ZEHN-reh-tsoo noh seh-kee wah, EE-koo-rah dehs KAH*
I'll take any seats available.	あれば、どの席でもいいからください。 *AH-reh-bah, DOH-noh seh-kee deh-moh ee kah-rah koo-DAH-sah-ee*
Could you show me where our seats are on the chart?	座席表で、席がどこか教えてください。 *zah-SEH-kee hyoh deh, seh-kee gah DOH-koh kah oh-SHEE-eh-teh koo-dah-sah-ee*
Can I see well from there?	そこから、よく見えますか。 *soh-KOH kah-rah, yoh-koo mee-EH-mahs KAH*
hear	聞こえます *kee-KOH-eh-mahs*
Is there an intermission?	途中で、休憩がありますか。 *toh-CHOO deh, KYOO-keh gah ah-ree-mahs KAH*

BUNRAKU, KABUKI, AND NOH

Bunraku, Kabuki, and Noh are the three major forms of traditional Japanese theater. They originated many centuries ago. Although the performances are in Japanese, English-language programs are usually available, so you can follow the story. The performance lasts longer than you may expect: A five-hour show is not unusual, and some Kabuki productions last up to ten hours! If the performance lasts through a meal time, you can buy a box lunch from vendors at the theater, and eat right at your seat. It's standard practice, not considered rude. You don't have to stay for the entire event — just leave whenever you like.

Bunraku is a kind of Japanese puppet theater dating from the seventeenth century. It features a special type of accompaniment: samisen music, and a reciter who sings or chants both the story line and the lines for each character in the play. The puppets are unique; each is between three and five feet high, with eyes and mouths that open and close, even eyebrows that move. Each is manipulated by three puppeteers wearing black hoods that cover their heads and faces.

Kabuki is perhaps the most popular of these classical amusements. The only one of the three where the actors speak (or chant) their own parts, Kabuki features highly stylized delivery and movement, stunning costumes and makeup, and male actors only. There are three basic types of drama: one deals with warriors and nobles, one with the common people, and another incorporates dance. Kabuki is performed on a revolving stage, with a runway extending into the audience. Except for certain plays, music, played on classical Japanese instruments, is a key element of Kabuki.

Noh is highly stylized dance-drama, originally performed at Shinto religious festivals. The actors wear elaborate, elegant costumes, but no makeup. Instead they wear masks representing different types of people; the actors have to develop the characters through movements, not facial expressions. The plays are performed on a square stage with no curtain. The orchestra sits at the rear. There are drums of different sizes, and a special Noh flute. The main characters express themselves through dance. All speaking is done by a special chorus that sings or chants the narration and the lines. Noh often reminds Westerners of classical Greek drama.

In which city can I see <u>Bunraku</u>?	文楽は，どの都市で見られますか。 *BOON-rah-koo wah, DOH-noh toh-shee deh mee-rah-reh-mahs KAH*
Kabuki	歌舞伎 *kah-BOO-kee*
Noh	能 *NŌH*
Is <u>Bunraku</u> being performed in Tokyo now?	今東京で，<u>文楽</u>が上演されています か。*EE-mah toh-kyoh deh, <u>BOON-</u>*

		rah-koo gah JŌH-ehn sah-reh-teh ee-mahs KAH
Kabuki	歌舞伎	*kah-BOO-kee*
Noh	能	*NŌH*
Is Kabuki being performed in <u>Osaka</u> now?	今<u>大阪</u>で、歌舞伎が上演されていますか。	*EE-mah <u>oh-sah-kah</u> deh, kah-BOO-kee gah JŌH-ehn sah-reh-teh ee-mahs KAH*
Kyoto	京都	*kyoh-toh*
What kind of play are they performing?	出し物は何ですか。	*dah-SHEE-moh-noh wah, NAHN dehs KAH*
When does it <u>start</u>?	何時に始まりますか。	*NAHN-jee nee hah-jee-mah-ree-mahs KAH*
<u>finish</u>	終ります	*oh-wah-ree-mahs*
How long does the performance last?	上演は、どの位続きますか。	*JŌH-ehn wah, doh-NOH koo-rah-ee tsoo-zoo-kee-mahs KAH*
Is there a place to eat during the intermission?	幕間に、何か食べる場所がありますか。	*mah-KOO-ah-ee nee, NAH-nee-kah tah-BEH-roo bah-shoh gah ah-ree-mahs KAH*
Is there a matinee?	昼の興行が、ありますか。	*hee-ROO noh koh-gyoh gah, ah-ree-mahs KAH*
Are advance tickets necessary?	予約券が、必要ですか。	*yoh-YAH-koo kehn gah, hee-tsoo-yoh dehs KAH*
Where can I buy the tickets?	券は、どこで買えますか。	*KEHN wah, DOH-koh deh kah-eh-mahs KAH*
How much will it be?	券は、いくらでしょうか。	*KEHN wah, EE-koo-rah deh-shoh kah*
Do they have a program in English?	英語のプログラムが、ありますか。	*EH-goh noh poo-roh-GOO-rah-moo gah, ah-ree-mahs KAH*

Bunraku

puppets	人形	*NEEN-gyoh*
puppeteers	人形つかい	*NEEN-gyoh tsoo-kah-ee*

| ballad–drama | 浄瑠璃 | $\overline{JOH}$-roo-ree |
| reciter | 浄瑠璃語り | $\overline{JOH}$-roo-ree gah-tah-ree |

Kabuki

actor playing a female role	女形	OHN-nah gah-tah
actor playing a good male character	立役	tah-CHEE yah-koo
actor playing a bad male character	敵役	kah-TAH-kee yah-koo
runway	花道	hah-NAH mee-chee
revolving stage	回り舞台	mah-WAH-ree boo-tah-ee
quick change of cos-tume	早変り	hah-YAH gah-wah-ree

Noh

Noh stage	能舞台	$\overline{NOH}$ boo-tah-ee
Noh masks	能面	$\overline{NOH}$ mehn
Noh singing	謡曲	$\overline{YOH}$ kyoh-koo
main character	シテ	shee-TEH
assisting character	ワキ	wah-KEE

FLOWER ARRANGEMENT AND TEA CEREMONY

Flower arrangement, or **ikebana**, originally emphasized natural materials — flowers, leaves, grasses, and branches — and the way they were used to express harmony with nature. The fundamental traditions continue: the arrangement of the main branches or sprays signify sky, earth, and mankind. Today some avant-garde schools use artificial materials as well as natural ones.

The formal art of the **tea ceremony** was perfected in the fifteenth century. A deeply esthetic experience, the tea ceremony has precise rituals of form and etiquette for host and guests. They include the tea room itself, the selection of the tea bowls, the making and serving of the tea, and the appreciation of the hospitality. Tea is a basic part of Japanese life. The custom of serving tea to family or guests in the home may be considered an informal extension of the ritual tea ceremony.

You can see flower arrangement or tea ceremony demonstrations; you might even want to attend a few classes. The arrangements can be made easily. Check the notices in the English-language media, or consult with your travel agent, a JNTO Tourist Information Center, or the hotel staff.

Where can I go to see flower arrangement?	華道を見るには，どこへ行けばいいですか。 *KAH-doh oh mee-roo nee-wah, DOH-koh eh ee-keh-bah ee dehs KAH*
tea ceremony	茶道 *SAH-dōh*
Which school is giving a demonstration?	どの流派が，実演しますか。 *DOH-noh ryoo-hah gah, jee-TSOO-ehn shee-mahs KAH*
Can I participate in the tea ceremony demonstration?	お茶の実演に，参加できますか。 *oh-CHAH noh jee-tsoo-ehn nee, SAHN-kah deh-kee-mahs KAH*
flower arrangement	おはな *oh-HAH-nah*
Do they have demonstrations every day?	実演は，毎日ありますか。 *jee-TSOO-ehn wah, MAH-ee-nee-chee ah-ree-mahs KAH*
Which day of the week do they have demonstrations?	実演は，何曜日にありますか。 *jee-TSOO-ehn wah, nah-NEE yoh-bee nee ah-ree-mahs KAH*
What time does the demonstration start?	実演は，何時に始まりますか。 *jee-TSOO-ehn wah, NAHN-jee nee hah-jee-mah-ree-mahs KAH*
How long does the demonstration last?	実演は，どの位続きますか。 *jee-TSOO-ehn wah, doh-NOH koo-rah-ee tsoo-zoo-kee-mahs KAH*
Can I also get a brief lesson?	簡単なおけいこを，受けることもできますか。 *kahn-tahn nah oh-KEH-koh oh, oo-KEH-roo koh-toh moh deh-kee-mahs KAH*

Do I need to make a reservation in advance?	前もって，予約の必要があります か。	*mah-EH moht-teh, yoh-YAH-koo noh hee-tsoo-yoh gah ah-ree-mahs KAH*
How far in advance do I have to make a reservation?	どの位前に，予約しなければなりま せんか。	*doh-NOH koo-rah-ee mah-eh nee, yoh-YAH-koo shee-nah-keh-reh-bah nah-ree-mah-sehn KAH*
Is there an admission fee?	見学料が，ありますか。	*KEHN-gah-koo ryoh gah, ah-ree-mahs KAH*
How much will it be?	見学料は，いくらですか。	*KEHN-gah-koo ryoh wah, EE-koo-rah dehs KAH*

Flower Arrangement

headmaster	家元	*ee-EH moh-toh*
container	容器	*YOH-kee*
bowl	鉢	*hah-CHEE*
basin	水盤	*soo-EE-bahn*
cut	切り取る	*kee-REE toh-roo*
prune	せん定する	*SEHN-teh soo-roo*
bend	曲げる	*mah-GEH-roo*
asymmetrical	非対称的な	*HEE tah-ee-shoh teh-kee nah*

Tea Ceremony

powdered tea	抹茶	*maht-CHAH*
tea bowl	茶碗	*chah WAHN*
tea utensils	茶道具	*chah DOH-goo*
tea whisk	茶筅	*chah SEHN*
tea cannister (ceramic)	茶入れ	*chah EE-reh*
tea cannister (lacquered wood)	なつめ	*nah-TSOO-meh*
tea ladle	茶杓	*chah SHAH-koo*

tea napkin (host's)	茶巾	*chah keen*
tea napkin (guests')	ふくさ	*foo-KOO-sah*
tea kettle	茶釜	*chah-GAH-mah*
tea urn	茶つぼ	*CHAH tsoo-boh*
tea etiquette	点前	*tah-TEH mah-eh*

RADIO AND TELEVISION

The American military radio station, the Far East Network (FEN), broadcasts in English round the clock, with brief newscasts on the hour. For more extensive news coverage, sports, and commentary, tune in NHK, the government broadcasting corporation, which has a brief daily news program in English.

Many foreigners enjoy Japanese TV, even without understanding the language. You can see traditional Japanese entertainment such as Kabuki, Western and Japanese sports events, game shows and musical revues, even soap operas. There are also reruns of popular American series and sitcoms. Some hotels have multiplex systems or cable, which show the programs in the original language. Occasionally you can see an English-language program on Japanese networks.

NIGHTLIFE

Japanese cities offer the usual variety of after-hours diversion, with one important difference: the costs can be astronomical. To avoid unpleasant surprises when your check arrives, you should know beforehand what kind of place it is. While some bars, clubs, cabarets, and discos are reasonable and affordable for most foreign visitors, many are not. A few drinks, a dish of peanuts or rice crackers, and some conversation with a hostess could add up to the yen equivalent of hundreds of dollars. Not all Japanese nightspots welcome foreigners; some might not admit you unless you're with a Japanese. Such places are usually frequented exclusively by expense-account customers, and the staff might not speak English.

Before you set out for an evening on the town— or for a drink or two anywhere other than your hotel bar— ask a Japanese friend or acquaintance, or check with your hotel staff or a Tourist Information Center, to get information on the kind of place you're looking for. DO NOT CHOOSE A BAR, NIGHTCLUB, OR CABARET ON YOUR OWN. And remember that appearances can be misleading. A modest-looking place could turn out to be extremely expensive. ASK FIRST!

This section contains phrases useful for various kinds of nightlife. For ordering once inside, refer to the FOOD AND DRINK section, p. 180, which gives complete listings for beverages and snacks.

Bars

I'd like to go to a bar.	バーに，行きたいのですが。 *BAH nee, ee-KEE-tah-ee noh dehs gah*
Is there <u>an inexpensive</u> bar nearby?	近くに，安いバーがありますか。 *chee-KAH-koo nee, yah-SOO-ee bah gah ah-ree-mahs KAH*
a quiet	静かな *SHEE-zoo-kah nah*
a pleasant	楽しい *tah-NOH-shee*
Do you know of a bar <u>with nice atmosphere</u>?	いい雰囲気のバーを，ごぞんじですか。 *EE foon-ee-kee noh BAH oh, goh-ZOHN-jee dehs KAH*
with no hostesses	ホステスのいない *HOH-soo-tehs noh ee-nah-ee*
with a nice reputation	評判のいい *HYOH-bahn noh ee*
with clearly listed prices	値段のはっきりした *neh-DAHN noh hahk-kee-ree shtah*
Where is a bar that's popular among <u>young people</u>?	若い人に人気のあるバーは，どこにありますか。 *wah-KAH-ee hee-toh nee NEEN-kee noh ah-roo BAH wah, DOH-koh nee ah-ree-mahs KAH*
students	学生 *gahk-SEH*
women	女性 *joh-SEH*
office workers	サラリーマン *sah-RAH-ree-mahn*

Is there a bar I can go to without worrying about the bill?

（お）勘定を心配しないで行けるバーが，ありますか。 *(oh)-KAHN-joh oh SHEEN-pah-ee shee-nah-ee deh ee-keh-roo BAH gah, ah-ree-mahs KAH*

Would you suggest which bar I should go to?

どのバーに行ったらいいか，教えてください。 *DOH-noh bah nee eet-TAH-rah ee kah, oh-SHEE-eh-teh koo-dah-sah-ee*

Do you have a bar you go to often?

行きつけのバーが，ありますか。 *ee-KEE-tskeh noh BAH gah, ah-ree-mahs KAH*

Do they have a minimum charge?

最低料金が，ありますか。 *sah-EE-teh ryoh-keen gah, ah-ree-mahs KAH*

Do I have to buy drinks for the hostesses?

ホステスの飲み代を，払わなければなりませんか。 *HOH-soo-tehs noh noh-MEE-dah-ee oh, hah-RAH-wah-nah-keh-reh-bah nah-ree-mah-sehn KAH*

Are strangers welcome there?

ふりの客でも，かまいませんか。 *foo-REE noh kyah-koo deh-moh, kah-MAH-ee-mah-sehn KAH*

How much will it be for a bottle of beer there?

そこでは，ビール一本いくら位でしょうか。 *soh-KOH deh-wah, BEE-roo eep-pohn ee-KOO-rah goo-rah-ee deh-shoh kah*

a shot of whiskey

ウイスキー一杯 *oo-EES-kee eep-pah-ee*

Do you think 5,000 yen per person is enough?

そこでは，一人五千円あればたりますか。 *soh-KOH deh-wah, hee-TOH-ree goh SEHN ehn ah-reh-bah tah-ree-mahs KAH*

10,000 yen

一万円 *ee-CHEE mahn ehn*

15,000 yen

一万五千円 *ee-CHEE mahn goh sehn ehn*

20,000 yen

二万円 *nee MAHN ehn*

Nightclubs and Cabarets

I'd like to visit a night-club. | ナイト・クラブへ，行ってみたいのですが。 *nah-EE-toh koo-rah-boo eh, eet-TEH mee-tah-ee noh dehs gah*

 cabaret | キャバレー *KYAH-bah-reh*

Are the nightclubs and cabarets extremely expensive? | ナイト・クラブとキャバレーは，とても高いですか。 *nah-EE-toh koo-rah-boo toh KYAH-bah-reh wah, toht-TEH-moh tah-kah-ee dehs KAH*

For example, how much does it cost per person? | たとえば，一人当りいくらかかりますか。 *tah-TOH-eh-bah, hee-TOH-ree ah-tah-ree EE-koo-rah kah-kah-ree-mahs KAH*

Do you know the best night club/ cabaret? | 一番いいナイト・クラブ／キャバレーをごぞんじですか。 *ee-CHEE bahn ee nah-EE-toh koo-rah-boo/ KYAH-bah-reh oh goh-ZOHN-jee dehs KAH*

 a cozy | 居心地のいい *ee-GOH-koh-chee noh ee*

 an inexpensive | 安い *yah-SOO-ee*

 a nice | いい *ee*

 a posh | 豪華な *GOH-kah nah*

 a small | 小さい *CHEE-sah-ee*

Could you recommend a reasonable nightclub? | 手ごろな値段のナイト・クラブを，教えてくれませんか。 *teh-GOH-roh nah neh-dahn noh nah-EE-toh koo-rah-boo oh, oh-SHEE-eh-teh koo-reh-mah-sehn KAH*

 cabaret | キャバレー *KYAH-bah-reh*

Do I need to make a reservation? | 予約の必要が，ありますか。 *yoh-YAH-koo noh hee-tsoo-yoh gah, ah-ree-mahs KAH*

Do they have a cover charge? | カバー・チャージがありますか。 *kah-BAH chah-jee gah, ah-ree-mahs KAH*

How much is the <u>hostess fee</u>?	<u>ホステス料</u>は，いくらですか。 *hoh-SOO-tehs ryoh* wah, *EE-koo-rah* dehs KAH
cover charge	カバー・チャージ *kah-BAH chah-jee*
Is the hostess fee by the hour?	ホステス料は，時間制ですか。 *hoh-SOO-tehs ryoh* wah, *jee-KAHN seh* dehs KAH
Are couples welcome?	カップルでも，歓迎されますか。 *KAHP-poo-roo deh-moh, KAHN-geh sah-reh-mahs KAH*
Do they have a floor show?	フロアー・ショーが，ありますか。 *foo-ROH-ah shoh gah, ah-ree-mahs KAH*
What kind of a floor show do they have?	どんな種類のフロア・ショーですか。 *DOHN-nah shoo-roo-ee noh, foo-ROH-ah shoh dehs KAH*
What time does the floor show start?	フロア・ショーは，何時に始まりますか。 *foo-ROH-ah shoh wah, NAHN-jee nee hah-jee-mah-ree-mahs KAH*
Do they have a good dance band?	おどるのに，いいバンドが入っていますか。 *oh-DOH-roo noh nee, EE bahn-doh gah HAH-eet-teh ee-mahs KAH*
What kind of music does the band play?	バンドは，どんな曲を演奏しますか。 *bahn-doh wah, DOHN-nah kyoh-koo oh ehn-soh shee-mahs KAH*
Can I have dinner there too?	そこで，食事もできますか。 *soh-KOH deh, shoh-KOO-jee moh deh-kee-mahs KAH*
What kind of clothes do I need to wear?	どんな服装を，するべきですか。 *DOHN-nah foo-koo-soh oh, soo-roo beh-kee dehs KAH*

Snack Bars

Japanese bars and nightclubs close relatively early — 11 to 11:30 P.M. in most cases. For those who prefer to continue their evening on the town, there are the so-called snack bars. Despite the name, these are also drinking places. The difference is that because they're called snack bars and they serve food, they're allowed to stay open late.

Is there <u>a nice</u> snack bar nearby?	近くに、いいスナック・バーがありますか。 *chee-KAH-koo nee, <u>EE</u> soo-nahk-koo bah gah ah-ree-mahs KAH*
an interesting	おもしろい *oh-MOH-shee-roh-ee*
an inexpensive	安い *yah-SOO-ee*
a quiet	静かな *SHEE-zoo-kah nah*
Where is it?	それは、どこにありますか。 *soh-reh wah, DOH-koh nee ah-ree-mahs KAH*
What's the name of the snack bar?	そのスナック・バーの名前は何ですか。 *soh-noh soo-NAHK-koo bah noh nah-mah-eh wah, NAHN dehs KAH*
What time does it open?	何時に開きますか。 *NAHN-jee nee, ah-kee-mahs KAH*
Is it open now?	今、開いていますか。 *EE-mah, ah-EE-teh ee-mahs KAH*
How late is it open?	何時まで開いていますか。 *NAHN-jee mah-deh, ah-EE-teh ee-mahs KAH*
What kind of <u>drinks</u> do they serve?	どんな飲み物がありますか。 *DOHN-nah <u>noh-mee-moh-noh</u> gah ah-ree-mahs KAH*
food	食べ物 *tah-beh-moh-noh*
Do I need to order food?	食べ物を、注文する必要がありますか。 *tah-BEH-moh-noh oh, choo-mohn soo-roo hee-TSOO-<u>yoh</u> gah ah-ree-mahs KAH*
Is it okay to just have drinks?	飲むだけで、いいですか。 *NOH-moo dah-keh deh, ee dehs KAH*
Is the price reasonable?	値段は、手ごろですか。 *neh-DAHN wah, teh-GOH-roh dehs KAH*

Beer Halls and Beer Gardens

Beer halls and beer gardens are good places to go to eat and drink at reasonable prices. They're popular with Japanese who

want to relax after work. The beer halls are open all year round,
and the beer gardens are open during the summer, many on the
roofs of department stores or office buildings.

What time do they <u>open</u>?	何時にあきますか。	*NAHN-jee nee ah-kee-mahs KAH*
close	しまります	*shee-mah-ree-mahs*
Are they open at lunch-time?	ランチ・タイムにも，あいていますか。	*RAHN-chee tah-ee-moo nee-moh, ah-ee-teh ee-mahs KAH*
Do they serve only beer?	あるのは，ビールだけですか。	*AH-roo noh wah, BEE-roo dah-keh dehs KAH*
Do they serve other drinks besides beer?	ビールのほかに，何か飲み物がありますか。	*BEE-roo noh hoh-kah nee, NAH-nee-kah noh-MEE-moh-noh gah ah-ree-mahs KAH*
Is there <u>ale</u>?	エールがありますか。	*EH-roo gah ah-ree-mahs KAH*
dark beer	黒ビール	*koo-ROH bee-roo*
draft beer	生ビール	*nah-MAH bee-roo*
lager beer	普通のビール	*foo-TSOO noh bee-roo*
light beer	ライト・ビール	*rah-EE-toh bee-roo*
stout	スタウト	*soo-TAH-oo-toh*
Do they have <u>imported</u> beer?	外国のビールが，ありますか。	*gah-EE-koh-koo noh bee-roo gah, ah-ree-mahs KAH*
American	アメリカの	*ah-MEH-ree-kah noh*
Australian	オーストラリアの	*OH-soo-toh-rah-ree-ah noh*
British	イギリスの	*ee-GEE-ree-soo noh*
German	ドイツの	*DOH-ee-tsoo noh*
Do they serve food?	何か，食べ物がありますか。	*NAH-nee-kah, tah-BEH-moh-noh gah ah-ree-mahs KAH?*

Can I have a light meal?	軽い食事が，できますか。 *kah-ROO-ee shoh-koo-jee gah, deh-KEE-mahs KAH*
Do they serve dinner?	ディナーが，ありますか。 *DEE-nah gah, ah-ree-mahs KAH*
What kind of food do they have?	どんな食べ物が，ありますか。 *DOHN-nah tah-beh-moh-noh gah, ah-ree-mahs KAH*
Do they have entertainment?	ショーが，ありますか。 *SHOH gah, ah-ree-mahs KAH*
What kind of entertainment do they have?	どんなショーが，ありますか。 *DOHN-nah shoh gah, ah-ree-mahs KAH*

Discotheques

I feel like dancing in a disco.	ディスコで，おどりたいのですが。 *DEES-koh deh, oh-DOH-ree-tah-ee noh dehs gah*
Is there a good disco nearby?	近くに，いいディスコがありますか。 *chee-KAH-koo nee, EE dees-koh gah ah-ree-mahs KAH*
Which discos are very popular now?	今とてもはやっているディスコは，どれですか。 *EE-mah toh-teh-moh hah-YAHT-teh-ee-roo DEES-koh wah, DOH-reh dehs KAH*
Could you recommend one?	一つ，推薦してもらえますか。 *hee-TOH-tsoo, soo-EE-sehn shteh moh-rah-eh-mahs KAH*
What's the name of it?	名前は，何ですか。 *nah-MAH-eh wah, NAHN dehs KAH*
Where is it?	それは，どこにありますか。 *soh-REH wah, DOH-koh nee ah-ree-mahs KAH*
What time does it open?	何時に，あきますか。 *NAHN-jee nee, ah-kee-mahs KAH*
How late does it stay open?	何時まで，あいていますか。 *NAHN-jee mah-deh, ah-ee-teh ee-mahs KAH*

Is there an admission charge?	入場料が, ありますか。 *NYOO-joh ryoh gah, ah-ree-mahs KAH*
How much is the admission?	入場料は, いくらですか。 *NYOO-joh ryoh wah, EE-koo-rah dehs KAH*
How much does a drink cost?	飲み物は, 一杯いくらしますか。 *noh-MEE-moh-noh wah, eep-pah-ee EE-koo-rah shee-mahs KAH*
Is the music recorded?	音楽は, レコードでですか。 *OHN-gah-koo wah, reh-KOH-doh deh dehs KAH*
Do they have live music?	生の音楽が, ありますか。 *NAH-mah noh ohn-gah-koo gah, ah-ree-mahs KAH*

GAMES

You can play cards or chess in Japan, but they're not as popular as in Western countries. If you're a video game fan, you'll find the latest versions in Japanese video arcades. If you want to relax the Japanese way, try _their_ games. Here are phrases for a few.

Pachinko

Pachinko is a vertical pinball game played in parlors all over Japan. You can't miss the places: Just follow the blaring music and the sound of thousands of tiny steel balls crashing against each other. Enter and you'll see scores of people, each sitting on a stool in front of a machine, turning the trajectory knob with singular concentration, and staring straight ahead. Addicts tell of the old days before automatic knobs, when you launched each ball with a thumb-operated lever. What do you get for your efforts? Cash in your winning balls for prizes such as chocolate, cigarettes, socks, cooking oil, mandarin oranges, razors, dolls, and other of life's necessities.

| Do you play pachinko? | パチンコをしますか。 *pah-CHEEN-koh oh shee-mahs KAH* |
| I'd like to try pachinko. | パチンコを, やってみたいです。 *pah-CHEEN-koh oh, yaht-teh mee-tah-ee dehs* |

Could you take me to a pachinko parlor?	パチンコ屋へ，連れていってくれませんか。 *pah-CHEEN-koh yah eh, tsoo-REH-teh EET-teh koo-reh-mah-sehn KAH*
Where do I buy pachinko balls?	玉は，どこで買いますか。 *tah-MAH wah, DOH-koh deh kah-ee-mahs KAH*
How much should I spend for the balls?	玉は，いくら買ったらいいですか。 *tah-MAH wah, EE-koo-rah kaht-tah-rah ee dehs KAH*
Which machine should I use?	どの機械を使ったらいいですか。 *DOH-noh kee-kah-ee oh tsoo-KAHT-tah-rah ee dehs KAH*
Is there a knack to shooting the balls?	玉の打ち方に，こつがありますか。 *tah-MAH noh oo-chee-kah-tah nee, koh-TSOO gah ah-ree-mahs KAH*
How many balls do I need to win a prize?	景品をもらうには，玉がいくつ必要ですか。 *KEH-heen oh moh-rah-oo nee-wah, tah-mah gah EE-koo-tsoo hee-tsoo-yoh dehs KAH*
What kind of prizes do they have?	どんな景品がありますか。 *DOHN-nah keh-heen gah ah-ree-mahs KAH*
Where can I exchange the balls for prizes?	どこで，玉を景品にかえますか。 *DOH-koh deh, tah-MAH oh keh-heen nee kah-eh-mahs KAH*

Go and Shogi

These are two of Japan's oldest traditional board games. **Shogi** is similar to chess, but the opponent's captured pieces can be used. **Go** is a territorial game, played with flat, round black and white stones. It's been in Japan for about 1300 years, and originally came from China. You probably won't master the fine points of go and shogi in a short time, but you can learn the basics, and then continue to play back home.

Do you <u>play go</u>?	<u>碁を打ち</u>ますか。 *goh oh oo-CHEE mahs KAH*
play shogi	将棋をさします *shoh-gee oh sah-SHEE mahs*

I <u>don't know</u> how to play go.	碁の打ち方を知りません。 *goh noh oo-CHEE-kah-tah oh <u>shee-REE-mah-sehn</u>*
know	知っています *sheet-TEH ee-mahs*
I <u>don't know</u> how to play shogi.	将棋のさし方を知りません。 *shoh-gee noh sah-SHEE-kah-tah oh <u>shee-REE-mah-sehn</u>*
know	知っています *sheet-TEH ee-mahs*
Could you play <u>go</u> with me?	碁のお相手を，お願いできますか。 *goh noh oh-AH-ee-teh oh, oh-NEH-gah-ee deh-kee-mahs KAH*
shogi	将棋 *shoh-gee*
Could you teach me <u>how to play go</u>.	碁の打ち方を，教えてもらえますか。 *goh noh oo-CHEE-kah-tah oh, oh-SHEE-eh-teh moh-rah-eh-mahs KAH*
how to play shogi	将棋のさし方 *shoh-gee noh sah-SHEE-kah-tah*
Is it difficult to learn <u>go</u>?	碁を習うのは，難しいですか。 *goh oh nah-RAH-oo noh wah, moo-ZOO-kah-shee dehs KAH*
shogi	将棋 *shoh-gee*
Do you have a <u>go board and stones</u>?	碁盤と碁石を，お持ちですか。 *goh-BAHN toh goh EE-shee oh, oh-MOH-chee dehs KAH*
shogi board and pieces	将棋盤と駒 *SHOH-gee-bahn toh koh-mah*
How do you decide the winner and loser?	勝ち負けは，どうやって決めますか。 *kah-CHEE mah-keh wah, DOH-yaht-teh kee-meh-mahs KAH*
How do you capture your opponent's <u>stones</u>?	相手の石は，どうやって取りますか。 *ah-EE-teh noh ee-shee wah, DOH-yaht-teh toh-ree mahs KAH*
pieces	駒 *koh-mah*

Mahjong

A dominolike game of Chinese origin, **mahjong** has gone through cycles of popularity in the West, but it is still well-liked in Japan.

Do you play mahjong?	マージャンをしますか。 *mah-jahn oh shee-mahs KAH*
I <u>don't know</u> how to play mahjong.	マージャンのしかたを、<u>知りません</u>。 *mah-jahn noh shee-kah-tah oh, shee-REE-mah-sehn*
know	知っています *sheet-TEH ee-mahs*
I'd like to play mahjong.	マージャンを、したいのですが。 *mah-jahn oh, shee-TAH-ee noh dehs gah*
Do you think you can get two more people?	もう二人、集めることができると思いますか。 *moh foo-TAH-ree, ah-TSOO-meh-roo koh-toh gah deh-KEE-roo toh oh-moh-ee-mahs KAH*
I'd like to learn how to play mahjong.	マージャンのしかたを、習いたいのですが。 *mah-jahn noh shee-KAH-tah oh, nah-RAH-ee-tah-ee noh dehs gah*
Is it difficult to learn mahjong?	マージャンを習うのは、難しいですか。 *mah-jahn oh nah-RAH-oo noh wah, moo-ZOO-kah-shee dehs KAH*
Do you have a mahjong set?	マージャンのセットを、お持ちですか。 *mah-jahn noh SEHT-toh oh, oh-MOH-chee dehs KAH*
What are the basic rules of mahjong?	マージャンの、基本的なルールは何ですか。 *mah-jahn noh, kee-HOHN teh-kee nah roo-roo wah NAHN dehs KAH*

SPECTATOR SPORTS

If you enjoy spectator sports, you'll find a lot to watch in Japan. The big two are **sumo**, the most popular of the traditional Japanese sports, and baseball.

Sumo

Professional sumo, or traditional Japanese wrestling, has a centuries-old history. There are six major tournaments a year, three in Tokyo's Kuramae Kokugikan Sumo Hall in January, May, and September, and the others in March at Osaka, in July at Nagoya, and in November at Fukuoka. Each tournament lasts 15 days, and is televised every day from 4 to 6 P.M. The sumo events are colorful: They last from early morning until late afternoon, with spectators usually arriving by early afternoon to catch the main events. The 250 to 300-pound wrestlers provide a lot of drama with their topknots and loincloths, ceremonial aprons, and costumed retainers. Just before the match, the wrestlers throw salt into the ring, in an old Shinto purification ritual. The match itself is usually over in seconds: It lasts just long enough for one wrestler to throw his opponent out of the ring or make any part of his body except the feet touch the ground.

I'm interested in sumo.	相撲に，興味があります。 *soo-MOH nee, KYOH-mee gah ah-ree-mahs*
Is there a sumo tournament going on now?	今，相撲をやっていますか。 *EE-mah, soo-MOH oh yaht-teh ee-mahs KAH*
Where is the sumo tournament now?	今，相撲はどこでやっていますか。 *EE-mah, soo-MOH wah DOH-koh deh yaht-teh ee-mahs KAH*
When is the next sumo tournament?	次の場所は，いつですか。 *tsoo-GEE noh bah-shoh wah, EE-tsoo dehs KAH*
where	どこであります *DOH-koh deh ah-ree-mahs*
Which day of the 15-day sumo tournament is today?	今日は，場所の何日目ですか。 *KYOH wah, bah-shoh noh NAHN nee-chee meh dehs KAH*
Which channel has live sumo broadcasts?	相撲の生中継があるのは，何チャンネルですか。 *soo-MOH noh nah-MAH choo-keh gah ah-roo noh wah, NAHN chahn-neh-roo dehs KAH*
I'd like to go to see sumo.	相撲を，見に行きたいのですが。 *soo-MOH oh, MEE nee ee-kee-tah-ee noh dehs gah*

Is it difficult to buy sumo tickets?	相撲の券を買うのは，難しいですか。 *soo-MOH noh kehn oh kah-oo noh wah, moo-ZOO-kah-shee dehs KAH*
Where can I buy tickets?	相撲の券は，どこで買えますか。 *soo-MOH noh kehn wah, DOH-koh deh kah-eh-mahs KAH*
Can I buy sumo tickets at the Play Guide?	相撲の券は，プレーガイドで買えますか。 *soo-MOH noh kehn wah, poo-REH gah-ee-doh deh kah-eh-mahs KAH*
I'd like good seats for sumo.	相撲の，いい席が欲しいのですが。 *soo-MOH noh, EE seh-kee gah hoh-SHEE noh dehs gah*
How much does a good seat cost?	いい席は，いくらしますか。 *EE seh-kee wah, EE-koo-rah shee-mahs KAH*
When do the sumo matches start?	取り組みは，何時に始まりますか。 *toh-REE-koo-mee wah, NAHN-jee nee hah-jee-mah-ree-mahs KAH*
end	終ります *oh-wah-ree-mahs*
When do the matches with the senior wrestlers start?	幕内力士の取り組みは，いつ始まりますか。 *mah-KOO-oo-chee ree-kee-shee noh toh-REE-koo-mee wah, EE-tsoo hah-jee-mah-ree-mahs KAH*
How many matches with the senior wrestlers are there?	幕内力士の取り組みは，いくつありますか。 *mah-KOO-oo-chee ree-kee-shee noh toh-REE-koo-mee wah, EE-koo-tsoo ah-ree-mahs KAH*
Where is the sumo hall?	相撲は，どこでありますか。 *soo-MOH wah, DOH-koh deh ah-ree-mahs KAH*
What's the best time to get there?	そこへは，何時頃行くのが一番いいですか。 *soh-KOH eh wah, NAHN-jee goh-roh ee-koo noh gah ee-chee-bahn EE dehs KAH*
Can I get something to eat and drink there?	そこでは，食べ物や飲み物が買えますか。 *soh-KOH deh-wah, tah-BEH-moh-noh yah noh-MEE-moh-noh gah kah-EH-mahs KAH*

sumo wrestler	力士	*ree-KEE-shee*
sumo match	取り組み	*toh-REE-koo-mee*
judge	行司	*gyoh-jee*
ring	土俵	*doh-hyoh*
grand champion	横綱	*yoh-KOH-zoo-nah*

What's that wrestler's name?	あの力士の名前は，何ですか。 *ah-noh ree-KEE-shee noh nah-mah-eh wah, NAHN dehs KAH*
How much does he weigh?	体重は，どの位ありますか。 *tah-EE-joo wah, doh-NOH koo-rah-ee ah-ree-mahs KAH*
How tall is he?	背の高さは，どの位ですか。 *SEH noh tah-kah-sah wah, doh-NOH koo-rah-ee dehs KAH*

Baseball

Baseball is so popular in Japan that even high school tournaments attract huge crowds and TV audiences. There are two professional leagues, the Central and the Pacific, each composed of six teams. The playoff at the end of the season is called the Japan Series. Each major league team can have two foreign ballplayers, and each farm team, one. If you go to see a pro game, you might recognize some of the players!

I like to watch baseball.	野球を見るのが好きです。 *yah-KYOO oh mee-roo noh gah SKEE dehs*
Is this the baseball season?	野球は，今シーズン中ですか。 *yah-KYOO wah, ee-mah SHEE-zoon choo dehs KAH*
Are they <u>professional</u> ball games?	プロ野球の試合ですか。 *poo-ROH yah-kyoo noh shee-ah-ee dehs KAH*
college	大学 *dah-EE-gah-koo*
high school	高校 *KOH-koh*
Do you have a professional ball team in this city?	この都市には，プロ野球のチームがありますか。 *koh-NUH toh-shee nee-wah, poo-ROH yah-kyoo noh CHEE-moo gah ah-ree-mahs KAH*

Is there a professional ball game <u>today</u>?	今日，プロ野球の試合があります か。 *kyoh, poo-ROH yah-kyoo noh shee-ah-ee gah ah-ree-mahs KAH*
tomorrow	あした *ahsh-TAH*
this weekend	この週末 *koh-NOH shoo-mah-tsoo*
Is the game televised?	試合は，テレビ中継されますか。 *shee-AH-ee wah, teh-REH-bee choo-keh sah-reh-mahs KAH*
Which channel will broadcast the game?	野球の試合を放送するのは，どのチャ ンネルですか。 *yah-KYOO noh shee-ah-ee oh hoh-soh soo-roo noh wah, DOH-noh chahn-neh-roo dehs KAH*
I'd like to go see the game.	野球の試合を，見に行きたいです。 *yah-KYOO noh shee-ah-ee oh, MEE nee ee-kee-tah-ee dehs*
Where is the ballpark?	野球場は，どこにありますか。 *yah-KYOO joh wah, DOH-koh nee ah-ree-mahs KAH*
Which teams are playing?	どのチームが，試合しますか。 *DOH-noh chee-moo gah, shee-ah-ee shee-mahs KAH*
Is it a day or a night game?	試合は，昼間の試合ですか，ナイター ですか。 *shee-AH-ee wah, hee-ROO-mah noh shee-ah-ee dehs KAH, NAH-ee-tah dehs KAH*
What time does the game start?	試合は，何時に始まりますか。 *shee-AH-ee wah, NAHN-jee nee hah-jee-mah-ree-mahs KAH*
Where can I buy base-ball tickets?	野球の券は，どこで買えますか。 *yah-KYOO noh kehn wah, DOH-koh deh kah-eh-mahs KAH*
Can I buy baseball tick-ets at a Play Guide?	プレーガイドで，野球の券が買えま すか。 *poo-REH gah-ee-doh deh, yah-KYOO noh kehn gah kah-eh-mahs KAH*
Can I buy the tickets at the ballpark on the day of the game?	試合の日に，野球場で券が買えます か。 *shee-AH-ee noh hee nee, yah-KYOO joh deh KEHN gah kah-eh-mahs KAH*

I'd like seats <u>behind home plate</u>.	ネット裏の席をください。 *neht-TOH oo-rah noh seh-kee oh koo-dah-sah-ee*
on the first base side	一塁側の内野 *ee-CHEE roo-ee gah-wah noh nah-ee-yah*
on the third base side	三塁側の内野 *SAHN roo-ee gah-wah noh nah-ee-yah*
along left field	左翼の外野 *SAH-yoh-koo noh gah-ee-yah*
along right field	右翼の外野 *OO-yoh-koo noh gah-ee-yah*

Judo, Karate, and Kendo

Is there a <u>judo</u> demonstration?	柔道の実演がありますか。 *JOO-doh noh jee-TSOO-ehn gah ah-ree-mahs KAH*
karate	空手 *kah-RAH-teh*
kendo	剣道 *KEHN-doh*
Where is it?	それは、どこでありますか。 *soh-REH wah, DOH-koh deh ah-ree-mahs KAH*
Where can I see a <u>judo</u> practice?	柔道のけい古は、どこでみられますか。 *JOO-doh noh keh-koh wah, DOH-koh deh mee-rah-reh-mahs KAH*
karate	空手 *kah-RAH-teh*
kendo	剣道 *KEHN-doh*
What day of the week can I see the <u>demonstration</u>?	実演は、何曜日にありますか。 *jee-TSOO-ehn wah, nah-NEE yoh-bee nee ah-ree-mahs KAH*
practice	けい古 *KEH-koh*
What time does the <u>demonstration</u> begin?	実演は、何時に始まりますか。 *jee-TSOO-ehn wah, NAHN-jee nee hah-jee-mah-ree-mahs KAH*
practice	けい古 *KEH-koh*
What time does it end?	何時に終りますか。 *NAHN-jee nee oh-wah-ree-mahs KAH*

Is there an admission fee?	入場料が，ありますか。	*NYOO-joh ryoh gah, ah-ree-mahs KAH*
Can I participate in the practice?	けい古に参加できますか。	*KEH-koh nee, sahn-kah deh-kee-mahs KAH*
Is there a judo tournament being held now?	今，柔道のトーナメントが行われていますか。	*ee-mah, JOO-doh noh TOH-nah-mehn-toh gah oh-koh-nah-wah-reh-teh ee-mahs KAH*
karate	空手	*kah-RAH-teh*
kendo	剣道	*KEHN-doh*
What kind of tournament is it?	どんな種類のトーナメントですか。	*DOHN-nah shoo-roo-ee noh toh-nah-mehn-toh dehs KAH*
Where is the tournament held?	トーナメントは，どこでありますか。	*TOH-nah-mehn-toh wah, DOH-koh deh ah-ree-mahs KAH*
Where can I buy a ticket?	入場券は，どこで買えますか。	*NYOO-joh kehn wah, DOH-koh deh kah-eh-mahs KAH*
judo/ karate/ kendo suit	柔道／空手／剣道着	*JOO-doh/ kah-RAH-teh/ KEHN-doh gee*
bamboo sword	竹刀	*SHEE-nah-ee*
face guard	面	*mehn*
arm guard	小手	*koh-teh*
instructor	師範	*SHEE-hahn*
match	試合	*shee-ah-ee*
win	勝ち	*kah-CHEE*
loss	負け	*mah-KEH*
draw	引きわけ	*hee-KEE-wah-keh*
Which grade black belt does the player have?	あの選手は，何段ですか。	*ah-noh SEHN-shoo wah, NAHN dahn dehs KAH*

Soccer

Although there is no professional soccer in Japan, you can see good games played by university or company teams.

Is this the soccer season?	サッカーは，今シーズン中ですか。 *SAHK-kah wah, ee-mah SHEE-zoon choo dehs KAH*
Is there a soccer match today?	今日，サッカーの試合がありますか。*kyoh, SAHK-kah noh shee-ah-ee gah ah-ree-mahs KAH*
tomorrow	あした *ah-shtah*
this weekend	この週末 *koh-NOH shoo-mah-tsoo*
Is the soccer game televised?	試合は，テレビ中継されますか。 *shee-AH-ee wah, teh-REH-bee choo-keh sah-reh-mahs KAH*
Which channel will broadcast the soccer match?	サッカーの試合を放送するのは，どのチャンネルですか。 *SAHK-kah noh shee-ah-ee oh hoh-soh soo-roo noh wah, DOH-noh chahn-neh-roo dehs KAH*
I'd like to go to a soccer game.	サッカーの試合を，見にいきたいです。 *SAHK-kah noh shee-ah-ee oh, MEE nee ee-kee-tah-ee dehs*
Where is the soccer stadium?	サッカーの競技場は，どこにありますか。 *SAHK-kah noh kyoh-gee joh wah, DOH-koh nee ah-ree-mahs KAH*
Which teams are playing?	どのチームが，試合しますか。 *DOH-noh chee-moo gah, shee-ah-ee shee-mahs KAH*
What time does the game start?	試合は，何時に始まりますか。 *shee-AH-ee wah, NAHN-jee nee hah-jee-mah-ree-mahs KAH*
Where can I buy soccer tickets?	サッカーの券は，どこで買えますか。 *SAHK-kah noh kehn wah, DOH-koh deh kah-eh-mahs KAH*
Can I buy soccer tickets at a Play Guide?	プレーガイドで，サッカーの券が買えますか。 *poo-REH gah-ee-doh deh, SAHK-kah noh kehn gah kah-eh-mahs KAH*

Can I buy tickets at the soccer stadium on the day of the game?

試合の日に，競技場で券が買えますか。 shee-AH-ee noh hee nee, kyoh-gee joh deh KEHN gah kah-eh-mahs KAH

PARTICIPATORY SPORTS

Bicycling

Where can I rent a bike?

自転車は，どこで借りられますか。 jee-TEHN-shah wah, DOH-koh deh kah-ree-rah-reh-mahs KAH

Can I rent a ten-speed bike?

十段変速の自転車が，借りられますか。 JOO-dahn hehn-soh-koo noh jee-TEHN-shah gah, kah-ree-rah-reh-mahs KAH

How much is the <u>fee</u>?

料金は，いくらですか。 RYOH-keen wah, EE-koo-rah dehs KAH

deposit

保証金 hoh-SHOH keen

Is the fee by the hour?

料金は，時間制ですか。 RYOH-keen wah, jee-KAHN seh dehs KAH

Does the law require a helmet?

ヘルメットをかぶる法律がありますか。 heh-ROO-meht-toh oh kah-BOO-roo hoh-ree-tsoo gah, ah-ree-mahs KAH

Is there a bicycling course nearby?

近くに，サイクリング・コースがありますか。 chee-KAH-koo nee, sah-EE-koo-reen-goo koh-soo gah ah-ree-mahs KAH

Golf

Although golf is extremely popular in Japan, it's not easy to go out for a casual game. The courses are crowded, and even at a public course, you have to make reservations in advance. Japanese courses are well tended, and many offer spectacular scenery. Play tends to be slow. Allow two to two and a half hours for nine holes.

Do you play golf?

ゴルフをしますか。 GOH-roo-foo oh shee-mahs KAH

Where do you play golf?

ゴルフは，どこでしますか。 GOH-roo-foo wah, DOH-koh deh shee-mahs KAH

Could you tell me where I can play golf?	ゴルフはどこでできるか、教えてもらえますか。 *GOH-roo-foo wah DOH-koh deh deh-KEE-roo kah, oh-SHEE-eh-teh moh-rah-eh-mahs KAH*
Is there a public golf course?	公共のゴルフ・コースが、ありますか。 *koh-kyoh noh goh-ROO-foo koh-soo gah, ah-ree-mahs KAH*
Is there a hotel with a golf course?	ゴルフ・コースのあるホテルが、ありますか。 *goh-ROO-foo koh-soo noh ah-roo HOH-teh-roo gah, ah-ree-mahs KAH*
If I call today for a reservation, when can I play golf?	今日予約を申し込んだら、いつゴルフができますか。 *kyoh yoh-YAH-koo oh moh-shee-kohn-dah-rah, EE-tsoo goh-roo-foo gah deh-kee-mahs KAH*
How much is the greens fee?	グリーン・フィーは、いくらですか。 *goo-REEN fee wah, EE-koo-rah dehs KAH*
Do I have to hire a caddy?	キャディーを、やとわなければなりませんか。 *KYAH-dee oh, yah-TOH-wah-nah-keh-reh-bah nah-ree-mah-sehn KAH*
How much does the caddy cost per round?	キャディーは、一ラウンドいくらしますか。 *KYAH-dee wah, ee-CHEE rah-oon-doh EE-koo-rah shee-mahs KAH*
Can I rent <u>golf clubs</u>?	ゴルフ・クラブが、借りられますか。 *goh-ROO-foo koo-rah-boo gah, kah-ree-rah-reh-mahs KAH*
a golf cart	ゴルフ・カート *goh-ROO-foo kah-toh*
Is it <u>a difficult</u> course?	コースは、難しいですか。 *KOH-soo wah, moo-ZOO-kah-shee dehs KAH*
an easy	やさしい *yah-SAH-shee*
What's par?	パーは、いくつですか。 *PAH wah, EE-koo-tsoo dehs KAH*

Can I use the clubhouse facilities?	クラブ・ハウスの，施設を使えますか。 *koo-RAH-boo hah-oo-soo noh, SHEE-seh-tsoo oh tsoo-kah-eh-mahs KAH*

Tennis

There aren't many public tennis courts, and private clubs are expensive to join. For visitors in Japan, the hotel courts are a good alternative.

I love to play tennis.	テニスをするのが，大好きです。 *TEH-nees oh soo-roo noh gah, DAH-ee-skee dehs*
Do you play tennis?	テニスをしますか。 *TEH-nees oh shee-mahs KAH*
Where do you play tennis?	テニスは，どこでしますか。 *TEH-nees wah, DOH-koh deh shee-mahs KAH*
Could you tell me where I can play tennis?	どこでテニスができるか，教えてください。 *DOH-koh deh teh-nees gah deh-KEE-roo kah, oh-SHEE-eh-teh koo-dah-sah-ee*
Is there a public tennis court?	公共のテニス・コートが，あ{ります}か。 *koh-kyoh noh teh-NEES koh-toh gah, ah-ree-mahs KAH*
Is there a hotel with a tennis court?	テニス・コートのあるホテルが，あ{り}ますか。 *teh-NEES koh-toh noh ah-roo HOH-teh-roo gah, ah-ree-mahs KAH*
Is the hotel tennis court for guests only?	ホテルのテニス・コートは，泊り客専用ですか。 *HOH-teh-roo noh teh-NEES koh-toh wah, toh-MAH-ree kyah-koo sehn-yoh dehs KAH*
Can guests use the hotel tennis court free?	泊り客は，ホテルのテニス・コートをただで使えますか。 *toh-MAH-ree kyah-koo wah, hoh-teh-roo noh teh-NEES koh-toh oh TAH-dah deh tsoo-kah-eh-mahs KAH*

Is there a discount for hotel guests?	泊り客の，料金割引きがあります か。 toh-MAH-ree kyah-kyoo noh, RYOH-keen wah-ree-bee-kee gah ah-ree-mahs KAH
Is it difficult to make a reservation for a <u>public tennis court</u>?	<u>公共のテニス・コート</u>を予約するの は，難しいですか。 <u>KOH-kyoh noh teh-NEES koh-toh</u> oh yoh-YAH-koo soo-roo noh wah, moo-ZOO-kah-shee dehs KAH
hotel tennis court	ホテルのテニス・コート HOH-teh-roo noh teh-NEES koh-toh
Is the fee by <u>the hour</u>?	料金は，時間制ですか。 RYOH-keen wah, <u>jee-KAHN</u> seh dehs KAH
the half day	半日 HAHN nee-chee
Can I rent a racket?	ラケットが，借りられますか。 rah-KEHT-toh gah, kah-ree-rah-reh-mahs KAH

Swimming

Japan has good beaches, but they're crowded — don't expect to enjoy the sun and sand in solitude. Pools are crowded too. Your hotel pool may be your best bet if you're a swimming enthusiast.

I like swimming.	泳ぐのが好きです。 oh-YOH-goo noh gah SKEE dehs
Do you like swimming?	泳ぐのが好きですか。 oh-YOH-goo noh gah SKEE dehs KAH
Where do you go swimming?	どこへ泳ぎに行きますか。 DOH-koh eh, oh-yoh-gee nee ee-kee-mahs KAH
Could you tell me where I can swim?	どこで泳げるか，教えてください。 DOH-koh deh oh-yoh-geh-roo kah, oh-SHEE-eh-teh koo-dah-sah-ee
Is there a swimming pool nearby?	近くに，プールがありますか。 chee-KAH-koo nee, POO-roo gah ah-ree-mahs KAH
Is it a public swimming pool?	それは，公共のプールですか。 soh REH wah, koh-kyoh noh poo-roo dehs KAH

Is there a hotel with a swimming pool?	プールのあるホテルがありますか。 *POO-roo noh ah-roo hoh-teh-roo gah, ah-ree-mahs KAH*
Can hotel guests swim free of charge?	泊り客は、ただで泳げますか。 *toh-MAH-ree kyah-koo wah, TAH-dah deh oh-yoh-geh-mahs KAH*
Is the hotel swimming pool for guests only?	ホテルのプールは、泊り客専用ですか。 *HOH-teh-roo noh poo-roo wah, toh-MAH-ree kyah-koo sehn-yoh dehs KAH*
How much is the charge?	料金は、いくらですか。 *RYOH-keen wah, EE-koo-rah dehs KAH*
What hours are the swimming pool open?	プールは、何時から何時まであいていますか。 *POO-roo wah, NAHN-jee kah-rah NAHN-jee mah-deh ah-ee-teh ee-mahs KAH*
Is there a <u>nice</u> beach around here?	近くに、いい海岸がありますか。 *chee-KAH-koo nee, EE kah-ee-gahn gah ah-ree-mahs KAH*
beautiful	きれいな *KEE-reh nah*
Where is the closest beach?	一番近い海岸は、どこにありますか。 *ee-CHEE-bahn chee-kah-ee kah-ee-gahn wah, DOH-koh nee ah-ree-mahs KAH*
How can I get there?	そこへは、どう行けばいいですか。 *soh-KOH eh wah, DOH ee-keh-bah ee dehs KAH*
Is there a <u>train</u> that goes there?	そこまで、電車がありますか。 *soh-KOH mah-deh, DEHN-shah gah ah-ree-mahs KAH*
bus	バス *BAH-soo*
How long does it take to get there?	そこまで、どの位時間がかかりますか。 *soh-KOH mah-deh, doh-NOH koo-rah-ee jee-kahn gah kah-kah-ree-mahs KAH*
Is the water <u>cold</u>?	水は、冷たいですか。 *mee-ZOO wah, tsoo-MEH-tah-ee dehs KAH*
clean	きれい *KEE-reh*

calm	静か *SHEE-zoo-kah*
Is the beach sandy?	海岸は，砂浜ですか。 *kah-ee-gahn wah, soo-NAH-hah-mah dehs KAH*
Are there big waves?	大きい波が，ありますか。 *OH-kee nah-mee gah, ah-ree-mahs KAH*
Is it safe for children?	子供にも，安全ですか。 *koh-DOH-moh nee-moh, AHN-zehn dehs KAH*
Are there lifeguards on duty?	見張りが，出ていますか。 *mee-HAH-ree gah, DEH-teh-ee-mahs KAH*
Are there <u>jellyfish</u>?	<u>くらげ</u>がいますか。 *koo-RAH-geh gah ee-mahs KAH*
sharks	さめ *sah-MEH*
Can I rent <u>an air mattress</u>?	<u>エアー・マットレス</u>が借りられますか。 *eh-AH maht-toh-rehs gah, kah-REE-rah-reh-mahs KAH*
a beach chair	ビーチ・チェアー *BEE-chee cheh-ah*
a beach towel	ビーチ・タオル *BEE-chee tah-oh-roo*
a beach umbrella	ビーチ・パラソル *BEE-chee PAH-rah-soh-roo*
a boat	ボート *BOH-toh*
a motor boat	モーター・ボート *MOH-tah boh-toh*
a sailboat	ヨット *YOHT-toh*
a swimming tube	浮き袋 *oo-KEE-boo-koo-roh*
skin diving equipment	スキン・ダイビング用具 *soo-KEEN dah-ee-been-goo yoh-goo*
water skis	水上スキー *soo-EE-joh skee*
How much is it per hour?	一時間，いくらですか。 *ee-CHEE jee-kahn, EE-koo-rah dehs KAH*
Do you want a deposit?	保証金が，いりますか。 *hoh-SHOH keen gah, ee-ree-mahs KAH*
How much is the deposit?	保証金は，いくらですか。 *hoh-SHOH keen wah, EE-koo-rah dehs KAH*

Skiing

Japan has excellent ski areas, both on Honshu and Hokkaido, the site of the 1972 Winter Olympics near Sapporo. Transportation to the ski areas is usually by bus or train (or to Hokkaido, by plane); it's wise to book travel reservations ahead of time.

Do you like skiing?	スキーが好きですか。 *SKEE gah SKEE dehs KAH*
Where do you go for skiing?	どこへ、スキーをしに行きますか。 *DOH-koh eh, SKEE oh shee nee ee-kee-mahs KAH*
Is this the ski season?	今は、スキー・シーズンですか。 *EE-mah wah, SKEE shee-zoon dehs KAH*
Where can I ski now?	今、どこでスキーができますか。 *ee-mah, DOH-koh deh SKEE gah deh-kee-mahs KAH*
Where is a nearby ski resort?	近くのスキー場は、どこにあります か。 *chee-KAH-koo noh skee joh wah, DOH-koh nee ah-ree-mahs KAH*
How can I get there?	そこまで、どう行けばいいですか。 *soh-KOH mah-deh, DOH ee-keh-bah ee dehs KAH*
Is there a <u>train</u> that goes there?	そこへ行く汽車がありますか。 *soh-KOH eh ee-koo kee-SHAH gah ah-ree-mahs KAH*
bus	バス *BAH-soo*
How long does it take to get there?	そこまで、どの位時間がかかります か。 *soh-KOH mah-deh, doh-NOH koo-rah-ee jee-kahn gah kah-kah-ree-mahs KAH*
Is the ski resort crowded?	スキー場は、こんでいますか。 *SKEE joh wah, KOHN-deh ee-mahs KAH*
Is the ski slope <u>difficult</u>?	ゲレンデは、難しいですか。 *geh-REHN-deh wah, moo-ZOO-kah-shee dehs KAH*
steep	急 *KYOO*

How is the snow quality?	雪質は，どうですか。 *yoo-KEE shee-tsoo wah, DOH dehs KAH*
Is the snow <u>powdery</u>?	雪は，粉雪ですか。 *yoo-KEE wah, koh-NAH yoo-kee dehs KAH*
wet	湿っています *shee-MEHT-teh ee-mahs*
How much is the snow accumulation?	雪積は，どの位ですか。 *seh-KEE seh-tsoo wah, doh-NOH koo-rah-ee dehs KAH*
Do they have a <u>ski lift</u>?	リフトがありますか。 *REE-foo-toh gah ah-ree-mahs KAH*
ropeway	ロープ・ウェー *ROH-poo-weh*
cable car	ゴンドラ *GOHN-doh-rah*
How long do I have to wait?	どの位，待たなければなりませんか。 *doh-NOH koo-rah-ee, mah-TAH-nah-keh-reh-bah nah-ree-mah-sehn KAH*
Should I make a re–servation for a <u>hotel</u>?	ホテルの予約は，するべきですか。 *HOH-teh-roo noh yoh-YAH-koo wah, soo-ROO-beh-kee dehs KAH*

ryokan	旅館 *ryoh-KAHN*
minshuku	民宿 *MEEN-shoo-koo*
Can I rent ski equipment at the ski resort?	スキー場で，スキー用具が借りられますか。 *SKEE joh deh, SKEE yoh-goo gah kah-ree-rah-reh-mahs KAH*
Can I rent <u>skis</u>?	<u>スキー</u>が，借りられますか。 <u>*SKEE*</u> *gah, kah-ree-rah-reh mahs KAH*
ski shoes	スキーぐつ *SKEE goo-tsoo*
poles	ストック *soo-TOHK-koo*

Fishing

Do you like fishing?	釣が好きですか。 *tsoo-REE gah skee dehs KAH*
Where do you go fishing?	どこへ，釣に行きますか。 *DOH-koh eh, tsoo-ree nee ee-kee-mahs KAH*
Where is a nearby fishing spot?	近くの釣場は，どこにありますか。 *chee-KAH-koo noh tsoo-ree bah wah, DOH-koh nee ah-ree-mahs KAH*
How can I get there?	そこまで，どう行けばいいですか。 *soh-KOH mah-deh, DOH ee-keh-bah ee dehs KAH*
How long does it take to get there?	そこまで，どの位時間がかかりますか。 *soh-KOH mah-deh, doh-NOH koo-rah-ee jee-kahn gah kah-kah-ree-mahs KAH*
I like <u>river</u> fishing.	<u>川</u>釣りが好きです。 <u>*kah-WAH*</u> *zoo-ree gah SKEE dehs*
sea	海 *oo-MEE*
surf	磯 *ee-SOH*
offshore	沖 *oh-KEE*
What can you catch now?	今，何が釣れますか。 *EE-mah, NAH-nee gah tsoo-reh-mahs KAH*
What kind of fishing equipment do you use?	どんな釣道具を使いますか。 *DOHN-nah tsoo-ree doh-goo oh tskah-ee-mahs KAH*

Where can I rent <u>fishing equipment</u>?	釣道具は，どこで借りられますか。 *tsoo-REE doh-goo wah, DOH-koh deh kah-ree-rah-reh-mahs KAH*
a fishing boat	釣船 *tsoo-REE boo-neh*
Where can I buy fishing gear?	釣道具は，どこで買えますか。 *tsoo-REE doh-goo wah, DOH-koh deh kah-eh-mahs KAH*
Where can I join a chartered fishing boat?	釣船には，どこで乗れますか。 *tsoo-REE boo-neh nee-wah, DOH-koh deh noh-reh-mahs KAH*
What time does the fishing boat <u>leave</u>?	釣船は，何時に<u>出ます</u>か。 *tsoo-REE boo-neh wah, NAHN-jee nee <u>deh-mahs</u> KAH*
return	もどります *moh-doh-ree-mahs*
Do I need to make a reservation?	予約の必要が，ありますか。 *yoh-YAH-koo noh hee-tsoo-yoh gah, ah-ree-mahs KAH*
What's the charge?	料金は，いくらですか。 *RYOH-keen wah, EE-koo-rah dehs KAH*
Do I need to take my own food and drinks?	食べ物と飲み物は，持参する必要がありますか。 *tah-BEH-moh-noh toh noh-MEE-moh-noh wah, jee-SAHN soo-roo hee-tsoo-yoh gah ah-ree-mahs KAH*
Can I buy bait?	えさは買えますか。 *eh-SAH wah kah-eh-mahs KAH*
What kind of bait is it?	どんな種類のえさですか。 *DOHN-nah shoo-roo-ee noh eh-SAH dehs KAH*
Is there a fishing rights charge?	入漁料がありますか。 *NYOO-gyoh ryoh gah ah-ree-mahs KAH*

CAMPING AND COUNTRYSIDE

Although camping is not as widespread in Japan as in some other countries, you can find some fine campsites. The best source of information is the JNTO Tourist Information Centers.

Where is the Tourist Information Center?	観光案内所は，どこにありますか。 *KAHN-koh ahn-nah-ee joh wah, DOH-koh nee ah-ree-mahs KAH*
Is there a camping site near here?	近くに，キャンプ場がありますか。 *chee-KAH-koo nee, KYAHN-poo joh gah ah-ree-mahs KAH*
I like camping at <u>a lake</u>.	<u>湖</u>のそばのキャンプ場が，好きです。 *<u>mee-ZOO-oo-mee</u> noh soh-bah noh kyahn-poo joh gah, SKEE dehs*
a mountain	山 *yah-MAH*
the seashore	海岸 *kah-ee-gahn*
Could you recommend a site?	どのキャンプ場がいいか，教えてください。 *DOH-noh kyahn-poo joh gah ee kah, oh-SHEE-eh-teh koo-dah-sah-ee*
Could you tell me how to get there?	そこまで，どう行けばいいでしょうか。 *soh-KOH mah-deh, DOH ee-keh-bah ee deh-shoh kah*
Where is it on the map?	そこは，地図のどこにありますか。 *soh-KOH wah, chee-zoo noh DOH-koh nee ah-ree-mahs KAH*
Do I need to make a reservation?	予約の必要がありますか。 *yoh-YAH-koo noh hee-TSOO-yoh gah ah-ree-mahs KAH*
Can I camp for the night?	一晩，キャンプできますか。 *hee-TOH-bahn, kyahn-poo deh-kee-mahs KAH*
Where can I spend the night?	どこに泊まれますか。 *DOH-koh nee toh-mah-reh mahs KAH*
Is there <u>drinking water</u>?	<u>飲み水</u>が，ありますか。 *noh-MEE mee-zoo gah, ah-ree-mahs KAH*
running water	水道 *soo-EE-doh*
gas	ガス *GAH-soo*
electricity	電気 *DEHN-kee*
a children's play- ground	子供の遊び場 *koh-DOH-moh noh ah-soh-bee-bah*
a grocery	食料品店 *shoh-KOO-ryoh-heen tehn*

Are there <u>toilets</u>?	トイレがありますか。 *TOH-ee-reh gah ah-ree-mahs KAH*
baths	お風呂 *oh-FOO-roh*
showers	シャワー *SHAH-wah*
tents	テント *TEHN-toh*
cooking facilities	料理の設備 *RYOH-ree noh seh-tsoo-bee*
Can I rent <u>a sleeping bag</u>?	スリーピング・バッグが借りられますか。 *soo-REE-peen-goo bahg-goo gah, kah-REE-rah-reh mahs KAH*
a blanket	毛布 *MOH-foo*
cooking utensils	炊事用具 *soo-EE-jee yoh-goo*
a lamp	ランプ *RAHN-poo*
a tent	テント *TEHN-toh*
I intend staying <u>a day</u>.	一日滞在の予定です。 *ee-CHEE nee-chee tah-ee-zah-ee noh yoh-teh dehs*
two days	二日 *foo-TSOO-kah*
three days	三日 *meek-KAH*
How much is the charge per person per day?	料金は、一人一日いくらですか。 *RYOH-keen wah, hee-TOH-ree ee-chee-nee-chee EE-koo-rah dehs KAH*
Can I play <u>tennis</u> there?	そこで、テニスができますか。 *soh-koh deh, TEH-nees gah deh-kee-mahs KAH*
basketball	バスケットボール *bah-SOO-keht-toh boh-roo*
badminton	バドミントン *bah-DOH-meen-tohn*
ping pong	ピンポン *PEEN-pohn*
volleyball	バレー・ボール *bah-REH boh-roo*
Can I go <u>fishing</u>?	釣りに行けますか。 *tsoo-REE nee ee-keh-mahs KAH*
swimming	泳ぎ *oh-YOH-gee*
bicycling	サイクリング *SAH-ee-koo-reen-goo*

Is there a hiking trail nearby?	近くに，ハイキング・コースがありますか。 *chee-KAH-koo nee, hah-EE-keen-goo koh-soo gah ah-ree-mahs KAH*
Is there a map for the hiking trail?	ハイキング・コースの地図がありますか。 *hah-EE-keen-goo koh-soo noh CHEE-zoo gah ah-ree-mahs KAH*
What a beautiful landscape!	素晴しい景色ですねえ。 *soo-BAH-rah-shee keh-shee-kee dehs neh*
Look at the barn. (*male speaker*)	あの納屋を，見てごらん。 *ah-noh NAH-yah oh, MEE-teh goh-rahn*
Look at the barn. (*female speaker*)	あの納屋を，見てごらんなさい。 *ah-noh NAH-yah oh, MEE-teh goh-rahn nah-sah-ee*

birds	鳥 *toh-REE*
bridge	橋 *hah-SHEE*
cottage	小屋 *koh-YAH*
farm	畑 *hah-TAH-keh*
fields	野原 *NOH-hah-rah*
flowers	花 *hah-NAH*
forest	森 *moh-REE*
hill	丘 *oh-KAH*
lake	湖 *mee-ZOO-oo-mee*
mountains	山 *yah-MAH*
ocean	海 *OO-mee*
plants	草 *koo-SAH*
pond	池 *ee-KEH*
rice paddy	水田 *soo-EE-dehn*
river	川 *kah-WAH*
shrine	神社 *JEEN-jah*
stream	小川 *oh-GAH-wah*
temple	お寺 *oh-TEH-rah*
thatch roof	わらぶき屋根 *wah-RAH-boo-kee yah-neh*

trees	木 *KEE*
valley	谷 *tah-NEE*
view	ながめ *nah-GAH-meh*
village	村 *moo-RAH*
waterfall	滝 *tah-KEE*
Where does this path/road lead to?	この道は，どこへ行きますか。 *koh-NOH mee-chee wah, DOH-koh eh ee-kee-mahs KAH*
How far away is ____?	____まで，どの位距離がありますか。 *____ mah-deh, doh-NOH koo-rah-ee kyoh-ree gah ah-ree-mahs KAH*
How long does it take to get to ____?	____まで，どの位時間がかかりますか。 *____ mah-deh, doh-NOH koo-rah-ee jee-kahn gah kah-kah-ree-mahs KAH*
I'm lost.	道に，迷ってしまいました。 *mee-CHEE nee, mah-YOHT-teh shee-mah-ee-mah-shtah*
Can you tell me the way to ____?	____への行き方を，教えてください。 *____ eh noh ee-KEE-kah-tah oh, oh-SHEE-eh-teh koo-dah-sah-ee*

FOOD AND DRINK

Dining is one of the most pleasurable aspects of visiting Japan.
You have a choice of good Western-style restaurants, and an
almost endless variety of Japanese food to explore. If you crave
American fast food, you can even get that. You won't go hungry in
Japan!

Japanese-style eating is unlike Western style. You use
chopsticks, the food is different, and table manners are different as
well. Therefore, we have separate sections for the two styles.

Tipping

You don't need to tip anyone in Japanese restaurants. A service
charge will be added to your bill, so enjoy your meal and the
customary good service. No one expects anything more from you.

Towels

Whenever and wherever you drink or dine in Japan, you'll begin
with a refreshing hot or cold damp towel for your hands and face.

hot or cold towel   おしぼり   *oh-SHEE-boh-ree*

JAPANESE RESTAURANTS

Japanese cuisine is characterized by freshness, presentation,
and variety. Some restaurants offer a selection of different kinds
of dishes. Others specialize in one type of food or style of cooking,
often prepared in front of you at your table or on a grill. Many
(though not all) Japanese eateries display replicas of their offerings
outside the front door in glass cases. The dishes look quite real and
may tempt you to enter. It makes ordering easy: just point to what
you want. You can't do this everywhere, but sometimes it works
quite well!

Here are some of the most popular Japanese dishes:

sushi   すし   *SOO-shee*

Small blocks of vinegared rice, topped with pieces of raw fish
or other seafood, and hot Japanese horseradish. These and

other ingredients may also be rolled in seaweed, or combined in a bowl or lacquer box. Sushi is eaten with soy sauce.

tempura　　　　天ぷら　　　　*TEHM-poo-rah*

Batter-fried seafood and vegetables, served with a dipping sauce containing grated radish.

yakitori　　　　焼き鳥　　　　*yah-KEE-toh-ree*

Grilled chicken and vegetables on small skewers.

sukiyaki　　　　すき焼　　　　*SKEE-yah-kee*

Beef and vegetables cooked in a seasoned sauce, then dipped into a lightly-beaten raw egg.

shabu shabu　　しゃぶしゃぶ　　*shah-BOO-shah-boo*

Thinly-sliced beef and vegetables cooked in a hot broth, eaten with dfferent dipping sauces.

sashimi　　　　刺身　　　　*sah-SHEE-mee*

Fresh, sliced fish or shellfish, eaten raw, dipped in soy sauce and hot Japanese horseradish. (Some items, like shrimp, may be cooked; others, like mackerel, may be pickled or smoked.)

yosenabe　　　よせなべ　　　*yoh-SEH-nah-beh*

Seafood, chicken, and vegetables cooked in broth, eaten with several kinds of dipping sauce, and perhaps Japanese noodles.

teppanyaki　　鉄板焼き　　　*tehp-PAHN yah-kee*

Beef, chicken, seafood, and vegetables cooked on a grill in front of you and served with various sauces.

kushikatsu　　串かつ　　　　*koo-SHEE kah-tsoo*

Pork, chicken, seafood, and vegetables, skewered on bamboo sticks, breaded, and deep fried, then eaten with salt, hot mustard, and sauces.

tonkatsu　　　トンカツ　　　*TOHN-kah-tsoo*

Pork cutlets, breaded, deep fried, and eaten with a special sauce and thinly shredded cabbage.

soba and udon　そば／うどん　　*SOH-bah／oo-DOHN*

Japanese noodles, served in hot or cold broth, or with dipping sauce.

ramen　　　　　　ラーメン　　　　　*RAH-mehn*

Chinese noodles, served in hot broth or chilled.

Some Special Cuisines

Here are some kinds of cooking you may encounter or seek out during your stay in Japan.

kaiseki ryori　　　懐石料理　　　　*kah-EE-seh-kee ryoh-ree*

Originally part of the tea ceremony, now a succession of many small dishes served in a formal style. The ingredients change with the seasons, and may include fowl and seafood, but no meat.

shojin ryori　　　精進料理　　　*SHOH-jeen ryoh-ree*

Originally Buddhist temple food, made up of vegetarian ingredients only.

kyodo ryori　　　郷土料理　　　*KYOH-doh ryoh-ree*

Local or regional specialties — this may consist of one dish or an entire meal that typifies the cooking of a particular area.

robata yaki　　　ろばた焼き　　　*roh-BAH-tah-yah-kee*

Literally "fireside cooking," these meals were originally served to travelers. Now they feature country-style service, food, and atmosphere.

fugu ryori　　　ふぐ料理　　　*foo-GOO ryoh-ree*

Meals featuring blowfish, from which the poisonous organs have been removed by licensed chefs.

unagi ryori　　　うなぎ料理　　　*oo-NAH-gee ryoh-ree*

Meals featuring eel.

tofu ryori　　　豆腐料理　　　*TOH-foo ryoh-ree*

Meals featuring beancurd.

General Inquiries

I'd like to have yakitori.　焼き鳥が，食べたいのですが。*yah-KEE-toh-ree gah, tah-beh-TAH-ee noh dehs gah*

Is these a ramen restaurant neaby?	近くに，ラーメン屋がありますか。 *chee-KAH-koo nee, RAH-mehn yah gah ah-ree-mahs KAH*
I'd like to go to a sushi restaurant.	すし屋へ行きたいのですが。 *soo-SHEE yah eh, ee-kee-TAH-ee noh dehs gah*
Would you recommend a <u>good</u> sushi restaurant?	いいすし屋を，教えてください。 *EE soo-SHEE yah oh, oh-SHEE-eh-teh koo-dah-sah-ee*
the best	一番いい *ee-CHEE-bahn ee*
an inexpensive	高くない *tah-KAH-koo-nah-ee*
a nearby	近くの *chee-KAH-koo noh*
How much will it cost per person?	大体一人，いくら位ですか。 *dah-ee-tah-ee hee-TOH-ree, ee-KOO-rah goo-rah-ee dehs KAH*

Arriving

At many Japanese restaurants you have a choice of where to sit: counter, table, private room, or a Japanese room. Some of the best cooking is done behind a counter. If you're sitting right there you get each morsel the moment it's prepared or cooked. At a sushi or tempura restaurant, it's the best place to sit. A Japanese room is private, but you remove your shoes (with *no* exceptions) before entering, and you sit on cushions on the tatami floor, in front of a low dining table. You may request your desired seating arrangements when you make a reservation, or when you arrive at the restaurant.

Good afternoon./ Good evening.	こんにちは／こんばんは *KOHN-nee-chee-wah/ KOHN-bahn-wah*
My name is ___. I have a reservation at 6.	私は___ですが，六時に予約してあります。 *wah-TAHK-shee wah ___ dehs gah, roh-KOO-jee nee yoh-yah-koo shee-teh ah-ree-mahs*
Is a <u>counter</u> available?	<u>カウンター</u>は，あいていますか。 *kah-OON-tah wah, ah-ee-teh ee-mahs KAH*
table	テーブル *TEH-boo-roo*

private room	個室 *koh-shee-TSOO*
Japanese room	お座敷 *oh-ZAH-shkee*
We'll wait till a counter is available.	カウンターがあくまで，待ちます。 *kah-OON-tah gah ah-koo mah-deh, mah-CHEE-mahs*
How long do we have to wait?	どの位，待たねばなりませんか。 *doh-NOH koo-rah-ee, mah-tah-neh-bah nah-ree-mah-sehn KAH*
Either a counter or a table is fine.	カウンターでも、テーブルでも，かまいません。 *kah-OON-tah deh-moh, TEH-boo-roo deh-moh, kah-mah-ee-mah-sehn*
Could you seat us now?	今、すわれますか。 *EE-mah, soo-WAH-reh-mahs KAH*

At the Table

You'll probably order certain kinds of drinks at a Japanese restaurant: sake (hot, cold, or on the rocks), beer, and Japanese whiskey for starters or during the meal, Japanese tea toward the end (or at the start if you prefer). You might not be able to get cocktails or mixed drinks.

Is there a menu in English?	英語のメニューが，ありますか。 *EH-goh no MEH-nyoo gah, ah-ree-mahs KAH*
No drinks, thank you.	飲み物は，けっこうです。 *noh-MEE-moh-noh wah, KEHK-koh dehs*
Japanese tea, please.	お茶を，ください。 *oh-CHAH oh, koo-dah-sah-ee*
water	水 *mee-ZOO*
What kinds of drinks do you serve?	どんな飲み物がありますか。 *DOHN-nah noh-MEE-moh-noh gah, ah-ree-mahs KAH*
Bring us sake, please.	お酒を，ください。 *oh-SAH-keh oh, koo-dah-sah-ee*
beer	ビール *BEE-roo*
whiskey	ウイスキー *oo-EE-skee*

Give us one <u>large bottle</u> of beer, please.	ビールは，<u>大びん</u>を一本ください。 *BEE-roo wah, <u>OH-been</u> oh EEP-pohn koo-dah-sah-ee*
medium size bottle	中びん *CHOO-been*
small bottle	小びん *koh-BEEN*
Give us two large bottles of beer, please.	ビールは，大びんを<u>二本</u>ください。 *BEE-roo wah, OH-been oh <u>NEE-hohn</u> koo-dah-sah-ee*
three	三本 *SAHN-bohn*
four	四本 *YOHN-hohn*
five	五本 *goh-HOHN*
Give me <u>whiskey and water</u>, please.	<u>水割り</u>をください。 *mee-ZOO-wah-ree oh koo-dah-sah-ee*
whiskey and soda	ハイボール *hah-EE-boh-roo*
wiskey on the rocks	オン・ザ・ロック *OHN zah rohk-koo*
Give us two bottles of <u>hot sake</u>, please.	あつかんを，二本ください。 *ah-TSOO-kahn oh, NEE-hohn koo-dah-sah-ee*
cold sake	ひや *HEE-yah*
Do you have nonalcoholic drinks?	アルコール分のない飲み物が，ありますか。 *ah-ROO-koh-roo boon noh nah-ee noh-MEE-moh-noh gah, ah-ree-mahs KAH*
Could you bring something to eat with drinks?	何か，おつまみを持ってきてください。 *NAH-nee kah, oh-TSOO-mah-mee oh moht-TEH kee-teh koo-dah-sah-ee*
What kinds of appetizers do you have?	どんなつきだしが，ありますか。 *DOHN-nah TSKEE-dah-shee gah, ah-ree-mahs KAH*
Could you bring us something good?	何か，適当な物を持ってきてください。 *NAH-nee kah, teh-KEE-toh nah moh-noh oh, moht-TEH kee-teh koo-dah-sah-ee*
Do you have a set meal/ table d'hote?	セット・コース／定食が，ありますか。 *seht-TOH KOH-soo/ TEH-shoh-koo gah, ah-ree-mahs KAH*

What's good today?	今日 は，何 が おいしいです か。 *KYOH wah, NAH-nee gah oh-ee-shee dehs KAH*
Do you serve anything special for this region?	何か，この土地の，特産物がありますか。 *NAH-nee kah koh-NOH toh-chee noh, toh-KOO-sahn-boo-tsoo gah ah-ree-mahs KAH*
Is it <u>raw</u>?	それは，<u>なま</u>ですか。 *soh-reh wah, NAH-mah dehs KAH*
cooked	料理してあります *RYOH-ree shteh ah-ree-mahs*
hot (spicy)	からい で す *kah-RAH-ee dehs*
salty	塩からいです *shee-OH-kah-rah-ee dehs*
How is it cooked?	それは，どんな風に料理しますか。 *soh-reh wah, DOHN-nah foo nee RYOH-ree shee-mahs KAH*
I'll have this.	これを，お願いします。 *koh-REH oh, oh-neh-gah-ee shee-mahs*
Can you make an assorted dish?	盛り合せを，お願いできますか。 *moh-REE-ah-wah-seh oh, oh-neh-gah-ee deh-kee-mahs KAH*

Some Basic Foods

（お）豆腐	*(oh)-TOH-foo*	bean curd
みそしる	*mee-SOH shee-roo*	bean paste soup
吸い物	*soo-EE-moh-noh*	clear soup
わさび	*wah-SAH-bee*	Japanese horse-radish
唐辛子	*TOH-gah-rah-shee*	Japanese hot pepper
（お）つけ物	*(oh)-TSKEH-moh-noh*	Japanese pickles
酒／お酒	*sah-KEH/ oh-SAH-keh*	Japanese rice wine
お茶	*oh-CHAH*	Japanese tea
緑茶	*ryoh-KOO-chah*	green tea
ほうじ茶	*HOH-jee-chah*	roasted tea

梅干	oo-MEH boh-shee	pickled plums
たくあん	tah-KOO-ahn	pickled radish
ご飯	GOH-hahn	cooked rice
米	koh-MEH	uncooked rice
のり	noh-REE	seaweed
しょう油	SHOH-yoo	soy sauce

EATING THE JAPANESE WAY: A FEW POINTERS

Menus are not always provided. Some restaurants just serve what they have that day. Others might bring a succession of items served in a set order. Just tell them when you've had enough.

Prices are not always listed. This may mean it's a very expensive place, or that prices vary from day to day, as in a sushi shop. To avoid any surprises with your check, inquire about the price range beforehand.

Desserts are not traditional with Japanese meals, but you can usually get fresh fruit or sweet bean paste. Some places serve ice cream or sherbet as well.

Japanese noodles may be slurped noisily — it's quite proper, and may even indicate you're enjoying the flavor.

Soy sauce is not poured on white rice. The rice is served in individual rice bowls, which may be held in the left hand. Dip food morsels, one at a time, in soy sauce, and then eat together with the rice.

Soup is served in individual lacquer bowls, without spoons. Sip directly from the bowl, with an assist from chopsticks if there are vegetables or other bits of food in it.

Chopsticks are easy! Rest one at the base of the thumb and index finger and between the ends of the ring and middle finger. That chopstick remains stationary. Grasp the other between the ends of the thumb and the first two fingers, and enjoy your food.

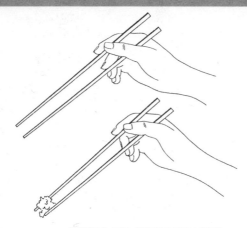

KINDS OF RESTAURANTS

At a Sushi Restaurant

If you sit at the counter, you usually order sushi one kind at a time (two bite-size pieces). At a table, you might order an assorted sushi tray, or other sushi specialties.

raw fish	刺身 *sah-SHEE-mee*
I'd like <u>assorted sashimi and rice in a box</u>.	ちらしを，ください。 *chee-RAH-shee oh, koo-dah-sah-ee*
assorted sushi rolled in seaweed.	のり巻きの盛り合せ *noh-REE-mah-kee noh moh-REE-ah-wah-seh*
tuna on rice in a large bowl	鉄火丼 *tehk-KAH DOHN-boo-ree*
assorted sushi	すしの盛り合せ *SOO-shee noh moh-REE-ah-wah-seh*
I'd like the <u>regular</u> kind.	並のを，ください。 *nah-MEH noh oh, koo-dah-sah-ee*
deluxe	上 *JOH*
super deluxe	特上 *toh-KOO joh*

What's good today?	今日 は，何 が おいしいです か。	*KYOH wah, NAH-nee gah oh-ee-shee dehs KAH*
I'd like to start with assorted sashimi.	始めに，刺身の盛り合せをお願いします。	*hah-JEE-meh nee, sah-SHEE-mee noh moh-REE-ah-wah-seh oh oh-neh-gah-ee shee-mahs*
What is it?	これは，何ですか。	*koh-reh wah, NAHN dehs KAH*
This one please.	これを，ください。	*koh-REH oh, koo-dah-sah-ee*

Some of the names of the seafood used in sushi sound exotic to foreign visitors. Try them: you may like them. For those who don't care for fish, there's always omelet sushi!

I'll have <u>abalone</u> please.	あわびを，ください。	*AH-wah-bee oh, koo-dah-sah-ee*
ark shell	赤貝	*ah-KAH-gah-ee*
ark shell lip	赤貝のひも	*ah-KAH-gah-ee noh hee-MOH*
clam	はまぐり	*hah-MAH-goo-ree*
cockle	とり貝	*toh-REE-gah-ee*
conger eel	あなご	*ah-NAH-goh*
crab	かに	*kah-NEE*
cuttlefish	もんごういか	*MOHN-goh ee-kah*
flounder	平目	*hee-RAH-meh*
herring roe	数の子	*kah-ZOO-noh-koh*
horse clam	みる貝	*mee-ROO-gah-ee*
horse mackerel	あじ	*AH-jee*
mackerel	さば	*sah-BAH*
mantis shrimp	しゃこ	*SHAH-koh*
marlin	かじき	*kah-JEE-kee*
octopus	たこ	*TAH-koh*
omelet	たまご	*tah-MAH-goh*
porgy	鯛	*TAH-ee*

salmon roe	いくら	*ee-KOO-rah*
sea bass	すずき	*soo-ZOO-kee*
sea urchin	うに	*OO-nee*
shrimp	えび	*eh-BEE*
skipjack tuna	かつお	*kah-TSOO-oh*
squid	いか	*ee-KAH*
tuna	まぐろ	*mah-GOO-roh*
medium fatty tuna	中とろ	*CHOH toh-roh*
fatty tuna	大とろ	*OH toh-roh*
yellowtail	はまち	*hah-MAH-chee*
young gizzard shad	こはだ	*koh-HAH-dah*

Do you have eel?　うなぎは，ありますか。 *oo-NAH-gee wah, ah-ree-mahs KAH*

swordfish　　まかじき *mah-KAH-jee-kee*

trout　　ます *mah-SOO*

Could you roll flounder, please?　平目を，巻いてください。 *hee-RAH-meh oh, mah-ee-teh koo-DAH-sah-ee*

omelet　　たまご *tah-MAH-goh*

sea bass　　すずき *soo-ZOO-kee*

yellowtail　　はまち *hah-MAH-chee*

Tuna roll, please.　鉄火巻きを，ください。 *tehk-KAH mah-kee oh, koo-DAH-sah-ee*

cucumber　　かっぱ *kahp-PAH*

pickled radish　　たくあん *tah-KOO-ahn*

Could you make me a hand roll of tuna, please?　鉄火の手巻きを，お願いします。 *tehk-KAH noh teh-MAH-kee oh, oh-neh-gah-ee shee-mahs*

pickled plum　　梅干 *oo-MEH-boh-shee*

pickled radish　　たくあん *tah-KOO-ahn*

cucumber　　かっぱ *kahp-PAH*

Would you put a little <u>less</u> Japanese horse radish, please?	わさびを，<u>少なめ</u>にしてもらえますか。 *wah-SAH-bee oh, SKOO-nah-meh nee shee-teh moh-rah-eh-mahs KAH*
more	多め *OH-meh*
Another <u>sake</u>, please.	お酒を，もう一本お願いします。 *oh-SAH-keh oh, moh eep-pohn oh-NEH-gah-ee shee-mahs*
beer	ビール *BEE-roo*
May I have some more <u>ginger</u>?	しょうがを，もう少しお願いします。 *SHOH-gah oh, moh skoh-shee oh-NEH-gah-ee shee-mahs*
tea	お茶 *oh-CHAH*
I'm close to the end.	そろそろ，終りにします。 *SOH-roh-soh-roh, oh-WAH-ree nee shee-mahs*
This is my last order.	最後に，これをください。 *SAH-ee-goh nee, koh-REH oh koo-dah-sah-ee*
I've had plenty.	十分，いただきました。 *JOO-boon, ee-TAH-dah-kee-mah-shtah*
It was really delicious.	とっても，おいしかったです。 *toht-TEH-moh, oh-EE-shee-kaht-tah dehs*
Thank you very much for a wonderful meal.	どうも，ごちそうさまでした。 *DOH-moh, goh-chee-SOH sah-mah deh-shtah*
May I have the check please?	お会計を，お願いします。 *oh-KAH-ee-keh oh, oh-NEH-gah-ee shee-mahs*

At a Tempura Restaurant

If you sit at a counter, you'll receive your tempura from the chef piece by piece as it is cooked. There's often a set order for the items, but you may request more of those you like. If you sit at a table, you'll get a selection of other tempura specialties.

Do you have a <u>set menu</u>?	セット・コースは，ありますか。 *seht-TOH KOH-soo wah, ah-ree-mahs KAH*
assorted tempura	てんぷらの盛り合せ *TEHM-poo-rah noh moh-REE-ah wah-seh*
a bowl of tempura on rice	天丼 *TEHN-dohn*

vegetable tempura.	精進あげ	*SHOH-jeen ah-geh*
I'll have asparagus please.	アスパラガスを、ください。	*ah-SOO-pah-rah-gahs oh, koo-dah-sah-ee*
beefsteak plant	しそ	*shee-SOH*
burdock	ごぼう	*goh-BOH*
carrot	にんじん	*NEEN-jeen*
chicken	とり	*toh-REE*
broccoli	ブロッコリ	*boo-ROHK-koh-ree*
cauliflower	カリフラワー	*kah-REE-foo-rah-wah*
eggplant	なす	*NAH-soo*
ginko nuts	ぎんなん	*GEEN-nahn*
green pepper	ピーマン	*PEE-mahn*
Japanese green pepper	ししとう	*shee-SHEE toh*
lotus root	はす	*hah-SOO*
mushroom	マッシュルーム	*mahsh-SHOO-roo-moo*
okra	オクラ	*oh-KOO-rah*
onion	玉ねぎ	*tah-MAH-neh-gee*
pork	ぶた	*boo-TAH*
pumpkin	かぼちゃ	*kah-BOH-chah*
scallops	貝柱	*kah-EE-bah-shee-rah*
shiitake mushroom	しいたけ	*SHEE-tah-keh*
shrimp	えび	*eh-BEE*
smelt	きす	*kee-SOO*
squid	いか	*ee-KAH*
string beans	さやえんどう	*sah-YAH-ehn-doh*
sweet potato	さつまいも	*sah-TSOO-mah-ee-moh*
trefoil	みつば	*mee-TSOO-bah*
zucchini	ズッキーニ	*zook-KEE-nee*

I'll have <u>crab</u> next, please.	次に，<u>かに</u>をください。 *tsoo-GEE nee, kah-NEE oh koo-dah-sah-ee*
eggplant	なす *NAH-soo*
I'll have <u>green pepper</u> again, please.	又，<u>ピーマン</u>をください。 *mah-TAH, PEE-mahn oh koo-dah-sah-ee*
scallops	貝柱 *kah-EE-bah-shee-rah*
Could you give me some more <u>tempura dipping sauce</u>?	<u>天つゆ</u>を，もう少しお願いします。 *TEHN tsoo-yoo oh, moh skoh-shee oh-NEH-gah-ee shee-mahs*
grated radish	大根おろし *dah-ee-kohn-OH-roh-shee*
lemon	レモン *REH-mohn*
salt	塩 *shee-OH*
I'm ready for rice and miso soup.	そろそろ，ご飯とおみおつけをお願いします。 *SOH-roh-soh-roh, GOH-hahn toh oh-MEE-oh-tskeh oh oh-neh-gah-ee shee-mahs*
I've had enough, thank you.	もう，けっこうです。 *moh, KEHK-koh dehs*
Thank you for a wonderful meal.	どうも，ごちそうさまでした。 *DOH-moh, goh-CHEE-soh sah-mah deh-shtah*
May I have the check, please?	お会計を，お願いします。 *oh-KAH-ee-keh oh, oh-NEH-gah-ee shee-mahs*

At a Sukiyaki or Shabu Shabu Restaurant

In these restaurants, you sit at a table, and the food is cooked right there, in a flat pan for sukiyaki, and a deeper one for shabu shabu. The waitress may ask if you want to cook for yourself, or she may cook and serve you.

We don't know how to cook it.	料理のしかたが，わかりません。 *RYOH-ree noh shkah-tah gah, wah-KAH-ree-mah-sehn*
Would you cook it for us?	料理してもらえますか。 *RYOH-ree shteh moh-RAH-eh-mahs KAH*

We'd like one more order of <u>meat</u>.	肉を，もう一人前お願いします。 *nee-KOO oh, moh ee-CHEE-neen mah-ee oh-neh-gah-ee shee-mahs*
vegetables	野菜 *yah-SAH-ee*
Can you give me some more <u>shabu shabu dipping sauce</u>?	しゃぶしゃぶのたれを，もう少しお願いします。 <u>*shah-BOO-shah-boo noh tah-REH oh, moh skoh-shee oh-NEH-gah-ee shee-mahs*</u>
rice	ご飯 *GOH-hahn*
I've had plenty.	たくさん，いただきました。 *tahk-SAHN, ee-TAH-dah-kee mah-shtah*
Thank you very much for cooking for us.	お世話様でした。 *oh-SEH-wah sah-mah deh-shtah*
It was delicious.	とても，おいしかったです。 *toh-TEH-moh, oh-EE-shee-kaht-tah dehs*

At a Yakitori Restaurant

Yakitori can be expensive or inexpensive, depending on where you go. You can even get yakitori at an open-front street stall, buying a few skewers on the run!

Do you have <u>lunch courses</u>?	ランチのコースが，ありますか。 <u>*RAHN-chee noh koh-soo*</u> gah, ah-ree-mahs KAH
dinner courses	ディナーのコース *DEE-nah noh koh-soo*
assorted yakitori	焼き鳥の盛り合せ *yah-KEE-toh-ree noh moh-REE-ah-wah-seh*
I'll have <u>chicken liver</u>, please.	レバを，ください。 <u>*REH-bah*</u> oh, koo-dah-sah-ee
chicken wing	とりの手羽 *toh-REE noh teh-BAH*
chicken meat ball	つくね *TSKOO-neh*
dark meat	しょにく *shoh-NEE-koo*
duck liver	鴨レバ *kah-MOH REH-bah*
ginko nuts	ぎんなん *GEEN-nahn*
green pepper	ピーマン *PEE-mahn*

hearts	ハツ *HAH-tsoo*
Japanese green pepper	ししとう *shee-SHEE-toh*
leek	長ねぎ *nah-GAH-neh-gee*
loin of duck	鴨ロースト *kah-MOH ROHS-toh*
minced chicken in mushrooms	つみれ *tsoo-MEE-reh*
tree mushroom	しめじ *SHEE-meh-jee*
white meat	ささ身 *sah-SAH-mee*

At a Japanese Coffee Shop

kissaten   喫茶店   *kees-SAH-tehn*

The kissaten is a coffee shop (sometimes referred to as a tea room) where you can get Western-style snacks and light food, Japanese-style light food, or both, depending on the place. A unique feature of most kissaten is the breakfast special, literally "morning service" in Japanese. This is popular with people rushing to work without breakfast. The kissaten are places where you can sit and drink your coffee or tea undisturbed as long as you like.

I'd like to sit at a table.	テーブルを，お願いします。 *TEH-boo-roo oh, oh-NEH-gah-ee shee-mahs*
the counter	カウンター *kah-OON-tah*
Do you have a menu?	メニューが，ありますか。 *MEH-nyoo gah, ah-ree-mahs KAH*
Do you have a breakfast special?	モーニング・サービスが，ありますか。 *moh-neen-goo SAH-bee-soo gah, ah-ree-mahs KAH*
What do I get for the breakfast special?	モーニング・サービスには，何がつきますか。 *moh-neen-goo SAH-bee-soo nee-wah, NAH-nee gah tskee-mahs KAH*
I'd like to order a breakfast special.	モーニング・サービスをお願いします。 *moh-neen-goo SAH-bee-soo oh, oh-NEH-gah-ee shee-mahs*

Something Different

ryotei　　　　　　料亭　　　　　　*ryoh-TEH*

The **ryotei** is a traditional Japanese restaurant in a building all
its own, usually in a garden. You dine in private Japanese-style
rooms, with waitresses at your table throughout the meal to assist
you. Food is served in many small courses, on exquisite ceramics
and lacquer. If requested, geisha may entertain. It's an elegant,
extremely expensive way to dine. Many ryotei require an
introduction from another customer before giving you a reservation. A good way to experience the ryotei is with a Japanese friend
— or host!

WESTERN AND INTERNATIONAL RESTAURANTS

There is good Western food in Japan, and a full range of
possibilities from elegant and expensive restaurants to simple and
inexpensive ones.

General Inquiries

Is there a restaurant nearby?	近くに、レストランがありますか。 *chee-KAH-koo nee, REHS-toh-rahn gah ah-ree-mahs KAH*
Is there a restaurant that is <u>still</u> open?	<u>まだ</u>、あいているレストランがあります か。 <u>*MAH-dah*</u>*, ah-ee-teh-ee-roo REHS-toh-rahn gah, ah-ree-mahs KAH*
already	もう <u>*MOH*</u>
Is there a <u>MacDonald's</u> around here?	この辺に、<u>マクドナルド</u>があります か。 *koh-NOH hehn nee,* <u>*mah-KOO doh-nah-roo-doh*</u> *gah ah-ree-mahs KAH*
Kentucky Fried Chicken	ケンタッキー・フライドチキン *KEHN-tahk-kee foo-RAH-ee-doh CHEE-keen*
Shakey's	シェーキー *SHEH-kee*
Mr. Donut	ミスター・ドーナッツ *MEES-tah DOH-naht-tsoo*

Baskin-Robbins	31アイスクリーム *SAH-tee-wahn ah-EES-koo-ree-moo*
Do you know a good restaurant?	いいレストランを，知っていますか。 *EE REHS-toh-rahn oh, sheet-TEH ee-mahs KAH*
an inexpensive	安い *yah-SOO-ee*
a quiet	静かな *SHEE-zoo-kah nah*
the nearest	一番近い *ee-CHEE-bahn chee-KAH-ee*
the best	一番いい *ee-CHEE-bahn ee*
Can you recommend a nice restaurant?	いいレストランを，教えてください。 *EE REHS-toh-rahn oh, oh-SHEE-eh-teh koo-dah-sah-ee*
small	小さい *CHEE-sah-ee*
fancy	しゃれた *shah-REH-tah*
first class	一流の *ee-CHEE ryoo noh*
I'd like to have American food.	アメリカ料理が，食べたいのですが。 *ah-MEH-ree-kah ryoh-ree gah, tah-BEH-tah-ee noh dehs gah*
Chinese	中華 *CHOO-kah*
French	フランス *foo-RAHN-soo*
German	ドイツ *doh-EE-tsoo*
Indian	インド *EEN-doh*
Italian	イタリア *ee-TAH-ree-ah*
Korean	韓国 *KAHN-koh-koo*
Scandinavian	スカンジナビア *soo-KAHN-jee-nah-bee-ah*
Spanish	スペイン *soo-PEH-een*
How much would it be per person?	大体一人，いくら位ですか。 *dah-ee-tah-ee hee-TOH-ree, ee-KOO-rah goo-rah-ee dehs KAH*

Do they take credit cards?	クレジット・カードが，使えますか。 *koo-REH-jeet-toh KAH-doh gah, TSKAH-eh-mahs KAH*
Are they open for <u>lunch</u>?	昼食に，あいていますか。 *choo-shoh-koo nee, ah-EE-teh ee-mahs KAH*
dinner	夕食 *yoo-shoh-koo*
breakfast	朝食 *choh-shoh-koo*
What are their hours?	営業時間は。 *eh-gyoh JEE-kahn WAH*
Do you have the telephone number?	そこの電話番号を，御存知ですか。 *soh-KOH noh dehn-wah bahn-goh oh, goh-ZOHN-jee dehs KAH*

Making Reservations

Do I need to make a reservation?	予約が，必要ですか。 *yoh-YAH-koo gah, hee-TSOO-yoh dehs KAH*
Do you take reservations?	予約を，受け付けますか。 *yoh-YAH-koo oh, oo-KEH-tskeh-mahs KAH*
I'd like to make a reservation for <u>dinner tonight</u>.	今晩のディナーの，予約をしたいのですが。 *KOHN-bahn noh DEE-nah noh, yoh-YAH-koo oh shtah-ee noh dehs gah*
lunch today	今日のランチ *KYOH noh RAHN-chee*
lunch tomorrow	あしたのランチ *ah-SHTAH noh RAHN-chee*
dinner tomorrow	あしたのディナー *ah-SHTAH noh DEE-nah*
<u>Two people</u> at 12, please.	十二時に，二人お願いします。 *joo-nee-jee nee, foo-TAH-ree oh-NEH-gah-ee shee-mahs*
Three people	三人 *SAHN-neen*
Four people	四人 *yoh-NEEN*
Five people	五人 *goh-NEEN*
Six people	六人 *roh-KOO-neen*
Seven people	七人 *nah-NAH-neen*
Eight people	八人 *hah-CHEE-neen*

Two people at <u>12:30</u>, please.	十二時半に，二人お願いします。 *joo-nee-jee HAHN nee, foo-TAH-ree oh-neh-gah-ee-shee-mahs*
1:00	一時 *ee-CHEE-jee*
1:30	一時半 *ee-CHEE-jee HAHN*
2:00	二時 *NEE-jee*
6:00	六時 *roh-KOO-jee*
6:30	六時半 *roh-KOO-jee HAHN*
7:00	七時 *shee-CHEE-jee*
7:30	七時半 *shee-CHEE-jee HAHN*
8:00	八時 *hah-CHEE-jee*
My name is ____.	私の名前は，____です。 *wah-TAHK-shee noh nah-MAH-eh wah, ____ dehs*

Arriving

Good afternoon./ Good evening.	こんにちは／こんばんは。 *KOHN-nee-chee-wah/ KOHN-bahn-wah*
I have a reservation for 8 o'clock. My name is ____.	八時に，予約してあります。名前は，____です。 *hah-CHEE-jee nee, yoh-YAH-koo shteh ah-ree-mahs. nah-MAH-eh, wah ____ dehs.*
I'd like a table for four.	四人ですが，テーブルがありますか。 *yoh-NEEN dehs gah, teh-boo-roo gah ah-REE-mahs KAH*
We'd like to sit at the counter.	カウンターを，お願いします。 *kah-OON-tah oh, oh-neh-gah-ee shee-mahs*
Can we get a table now?	今，テーブルをもらえますか。 *EE-mah, teh-boo-roo oh moh-RAH-eh-mahs KAH*
Do we have to wait?	待たなければなりませんか。 *mah-TAH-nah-keh-reh-bah nah-ree-mah-sehn KAH*
How long do we have to wait?	どの位待たなければなりませんか。 *doh-NOH koo-rah-ee mah-TAH-nah-keh-reh-bah nah-ree-mah-sehn KAH*

At the Table

No drinks, thank you.	飲み物は，けっこうです。 *noh-MEE-moh-noh wah, KEHK-koh dehs*
Give us a menu, please.	メニューをください。 *MEH-nyoo oh koo-dah-sah-ee*
We'd like to order drinks first.	始めに，飲み物をお願いします。 *hah-JEE-meh nee, noh-MEE-moh-noh oh oh-neh-gah-ee shee-mahs*
I'd like some <u>peanuts</u>.	<u>ピーナッツ</u>を，お願いします。 *<u>PEE-naht-tsoo</u> oh, oh-NEH-gah-ee shee-mahs*
potato chips	ポテト・チップ *poh-TEH-toh CHEEP-poo*

Questions

What's the specialty of the house?	ここの自慢料理は，なんですか。 *koh-KOH noh jee-mahn RYOH-ree wah, NAHN dehs KAH*
Is there a special today?	今日のスペシャルが，ありますか。 *KYOH noh SPEH-shah-roo gah, ah-ree-mahs KAH*
Do you have a fixed-price <u>lunch</u>?	<u>ランチ</u>のコースが，ありますか。 *<u>RAHN-chee</u> noh KOH-soo gah, ah-ree-mahs KAH*
dinner	ディナー *DEE-nah*
What's good today?	今日は，何がおいしいですか。 *KYOH wah, NAH-nee gah oh-ee-shee dehs KAH*
What would you recommend?	おすすめ品が，ありますか。 *oh-SOO-soo-meh heen gah, ah-REE-mahs KAH*
Can we order now?	今，注文できますか。 *EE-mah, choo-mohn deh-KEE-mahs KAH*
We'll take some more time before ordering.	注文には，もう少し時間がかかります。 *choo-mohn nee-wah, MOH skoh-shee jee-KAHN gah kah-kah-ree-mahs*
Could you bring some bread and butter?	パンとバターを，お願いします。 *PAHN toh BAH-tah oh, oh-NEH-gah-ee shee-mahs*

Water, please.	水を，ください。 *mee-ZOO oh, koo-dah-sah-ee*

Ordering

I'd like ____.	____を，ください。 ____ *oh, koo-dah-sah-ee*
I'll have ____.	____に，します。 ____ *nee, shee-mahs*
I don't think I want ____	____は，けっこうです。 ____ *wah, KEHK-koh dehs*
Do you have ____?	____が，ありますか。 ____ *gah, ah-ree-mahs KAH*
I'd like to have some ____ first.	始めに，____をお願いします。 *hah-JEE-meh nee,* ____ *oh oh-NEH-gah-ee shee-mahs*
I'd like to have ____, ____, and ____.	____と，____と，____を，ください。 ____ *toh,* ____ *toh,* ____ *oh, koo-dah-sah-ee*
I'd like to have <u>two orders</u> of ____.	____を，<u>二人前</u>ください。 ____ *oh nee-NEEN mah-eh koo-dah-sah-ee*
three orders	三人前 *SAHN-neen mah-eh*
four orders	四人前 *yoh-NEEN mah-eh*
Bring me ____ later.	____は，あとでお願いします。 ____ *wah, AH-toh deh oh-NEH-gah-ee shee-mahs*
May I change A to B?	**A**を**B**に，かえられますか。 *A oh B nee, kah-EH-rah-reh-mahs KAH*
I like my steak <u>rare</u>.	ステーキは，<u>レア</u>をお願いします。 *STEH-kee wah, <u>REH-ah</u> oh oh-NEH-gah-ee shee-mahs*
medium	ミディアム *MEE-dee-ah-moo*
well-done	よく焼けたの *YOH-koo yah-KEH-tah noh*
I'd like it cooked without <u>salt</u>.	<u>塩</u>を使わないで，料理してください。 *<u>shee-OH</u> oh TSKAH-wah-nah-ee deh, RYOH-ree shteh-koo-dah-sah-ee*

butter or oil	バターや油	*BAH-tah yah ah-BOO-rah*
MSG	化学調味料	*kah-GAH-koo choh-mee ryoh*
Does it take long?	時間が，かかりますか。	*jee-KAHN gah, kah-KAH-ree-mahs-KAH*

DRINKS

Alcoholic

Do you have Japanese beer?	日本のビールが，ありますか。	*nee-HOHN noh BEE-roo gah, ah-ree-mahs KAH*
wine	ワイン	*WAH-een*
whiskey	ウイスキー	*oo-EE-skee*
I want it straight, please.	ストレートで，ください。	*STOH-reh-toh deh, koo-dah-sah-ee*
Make it double, please.	ダブルで，ください。	*DAH-boo-roo deh, koo-dah-sah-ee*
With lemon please.	レモンを，入れてください。	*REH-mohn oh, ee-REH-teh koo-dah-sah-ee*
lemon peel	レモンの皮	*REH-mohn noh kah-wah*
an olive	オリーブ	*oh-REE-boo*
onion	オニオン	*OH-nee-ohn*
aperitif	アペリチフ	*ah-PEH-ree-chee-foo*
bourbon	バーボン	*BAH-bohn*
bourbon and soda	バーボンのハイボール	*BAH-bohn noh hah-ee BOH-roo*
bourbon and water	バーボンの水割り	*BAH-bohn noh mee-ZOO wah-ree*
bourbon on the rocks	バーボンのオンザ・ロック	*BAH-bohn noh ohn zah ROHK-koo*
straight bourbon	バーボンのストレート	*BAH-bohn noh STOH-reh-toh*

beer	ビール	*BEE-roo*
dark beer	黒ビール	*koo-ROH BEE-roo*
draught beer	生ビール	*nah-MAH BEE-roo*
light beer	ライト・ビール	*rah-EE-toh BEE-roo*
Bloody Mary	ブラディー・マリー	*boo-RAH-dee mah-ree*
brandy	ブランデー	*boo-RAHN-deh*
Campari	カンパリ	*KAHN-pah-ree*
cognac	コニャック	*koh-NYAHK-koo*
Dubonnet	デュボネ	*dyoo-BOH-neh*
gin	ジン	*JEEN*
gin and tonic	ジン・トニック	*JEEN toh-neek-koo*
gin fizz	ジン・フィーズ	*JEEN FEE-zoo*
gin on the rocks	ジンのオン・ザ・ロック	*JEEN noh ohn zah ROHK-koo*
Mai Tai	マイタイ	*mah-EE TAH-ee*
Manhattan	マンハッタン	*MAHN-HAHT-tahn*
Margarita	マーガリータ	*MAH-gah-ree-tah*
Martini	マティーニ	*mah-TEE-nee*
port	ポート・ワイン	*poh-toh wah-een*
rum	ラム	*RAH-moo*
rum and coke	ラム・コーク	*rah-MOO koh-koo*
Screwdriver	スクリュー・ドライバー	*SKOO-ryoo doh-rah-ee-bah*
scotch	スコッチ	*SKOHT-chee*
scotch and soda	スコッチのハイボール	*SKOHT-chee noh hah-ee BOH-roo*
scotch and water	スコッチの水割り	*SKOHT-chee noh mee-ZOO wah-ree*
scotch on the rocks	スコッチのオン・ザ・ロック	*SKOHT-chee noh ohn zah ROHK-koo*

straight scotch	スコッチのストレート	*SKOHT-chee noh STOH-reh-toh*
sherry	シェリー	*SHEH-ree*
sweet vermouth	スイート・ベルモット	*soo-EE-toh beh-roo-moht-toh*
vermouth	ベルモット	*beh-ROO-moht-toh*
vodka	ウォッカ	*WOHK-kah*
vodka and tonic	ウォッカ・トニック	*wohk-KAH toh-neek-koo*
vodka on the rocks	ウォッカのオン・ザ・ロック	*WOHK-kah noh ohn zah ROHK-koo*

Nonalcoholic

Is the juice fresh?	ジュースは，新鮮ですか。	*JOO-soo wah, SHEEN-sehn dehs KAH*
Do you have diet soda?	何か，ダイエットの飲み物が，ありますか。	*NAH-nee kah, DAH-ee-eht-toh noh noh-MEE-moh-noh gah, ah-ree-mahs KAH*
club soda	炭酸／プレイン・ソーダ	*TAHN-sahn/ poo-REH-een soh-dah*
Coca Cola	コカコーラ	*koh-KAH-koh-rah*
iced coffee	アイス・コーヒー	*ah-EES koh-hee*
diet soda	ダイエットの飲み物	*DAH-ee-eht-toh noh noh-MEE-moh-noh*
fruit juice	フルーツ・ジュース	*foo-ROO-tsoo joo-soo*
apple juice	りんごジュース	*REEN-goh joo-soo*
grape juice	グレープ・ジュース	*goo-REH-poo joo-soo*
grapefruit juice	グレープ・フルーツ・ジュース	*goo-REH-poo foo-roo-tsoo joo-soo*
orange juice	オレンジ・ジュース	*oh-REHN-jee joo-soo*
pineapple juice	パイナップル・ジュース	*pah-EE-nahp-poo-roo joo-soo*
tomato juice	トマト・ジュース	*toh-MAH-toh joo-soo*

ginger ale	ジンジャエール	*jeen-jah EH-roo*
lemonade	レモネード	*reh-MOH-neh-doh*
milk	ミルク	*MEE-roo-koo*
mineral water	ミネラル・ウォーター	*mee-NEH-rah-roo woh-tah*
Pepsi Cola	ペプシ・コーラ	*peh-POO-shee koh-rah*
Sprite	スプライト	*soo-POO-rah-ee-toh*
tea	紅茶	*KOH-chah*
tea with lemon	レモン・ティー	*reh-MOHN tee*
tea with milk	ミルク・ティー	*mee-ROO-koo tee*
iced tea	アイス・ティー	*ah-EES tee*
tonic water	トニック・ウォーター	*toh-NEEK-koo woh-tah*

Ordering Wine

Do you have a wine list?	ワイン・リストを，見せてください。 *wah-EEN REES-toh oh, MEE-seh-teh koo-dah-sah-ee*
Do you have French wine?	**フランスのワインが，ありますか。** *foo-RAHN-soo noh WAH-een gah, ah-ree-mahs KAH*
American	アメリカ *ah-MEH-ree-kah*
Italian	イタリア *ee-TAH-ree-ah*
Japanese	日本 *nee-HOHN*
We'll have white wine.	**ホワイト・ワインにします。** *hoh-WAH-ee-toh WAH-een nee shee-mahs*
red wine	レッド・ワイン *rehd-DOH WAH-een*
rosé	ロゼー *roh-ZEH*
Do you have anything dry?	ドライなワインは，ありますか。 *doh-RAH-ee nah WAH-een wah, ah-ree-mahs KAH*

Is it dry?	それは，ドライですか。 *soh-reh wah, doh-RAH-ee dehs KAH*
Do you have a house wine?	この店の，特別のワインがありますか。 *koh-noh mee-SEH noh, toh-KOO-beh-tsoo noh WAH-een gah ah-ree-mahs KAH*
Do you recommend anything in particular?	何か，特別のおすすめ品がありますか。 *NAH-nee kah, toh-KOO-beh-tsoo noh oh-SOO-soo-meh heen gah ah-ree-mahs KAH*
Where is it from?	どこのですか。 *DOH-koh noh dehs KAH*
What's the name of it?	名前は，何ですか。 *nah-MAH-eh wah, NAHN dehs KAH*
What's the vintage?	何年物ですか。 *NAHN-nehn moh-noh dehs KAH*
How much is a bottle of ____?	____は，一本いくらですか。 *____ wah, EEP-pohn EE-koo-rah dehs KAH*
I'll try this.	これを，試してみます。 *koh-reh oh, tah-MEH-shteh mee-mahs*
Can we order by the glass?	グラスで，注文できますか。 *GOO-rah-soo deh, choo-mohn deh-KEE-mahs KAH*
I'd like <u>a glass of white wine</u>.	<u>ホワイト・ワインを一杯</u>ください。 *<u>hoh-WAH-ee-toh WAH-een oh EEP-pah-ee</u> koo-dah-sah-ee*
a glass of red wine	<u>レッド・ワインを一杯</u> *rehd-DOH WAH-een oh EEP-pah-ee*
Bring me <u>a bottle</u>, please.	<u>一本</u>，お願いします。 *<u>EEP-pohn</u>, oh-neh-gah-ee shee-mahs*
a half bottle	ハーフ・ボトル *HAH-foo boh-toh-roo*

FOOD
Appetizers

| アンチョビ | *AHN-choh-bee* | anchovies |
| アンティパスト | *AHN-tee-pahs-toh* | antipasto |

アスパラガス	*ah-SOO-pah-rah-gahs*	asparagus
キャビア	*KYAH-bee-ah*	caviar
セロリとオリーブ	*SEH-roh-ree toh oh-REE-boo*	celery and olives
チーズ	*CHEE-zoo*	cheese
生はまぐり	*nah-MAH hah-mah-goo-ree*	clams on the half-shell
かに	*kah-NEE*	crabmeat
新鮮な果物のフルーツ・カップ	*sheen-sehn nah koo-DAH-moh-noh noh foo-ROO-tsoo KAHP-poo*	fresh fruit cup
ハム	*HAH-moo*	ham
にしん	*NEE-sheen*	herring
伊勢エビ	*ee-SEH-eh-bee*	lobster
マッシュルーム／シャンピニオン	*mahsh-SHOO-roo-moo／SHAHN-pee-nee-ohn*	mushrooms
メロン	*MEH-rohn*	melon
生がき	*nah-MAH gah-kee*	oysters on the half-shell
パテ	*PAH-teh*	pate
生ハム	*nah-MAH hah-moo*	prosciutto
生ハムとメロン	*nah-MAH hah-moo toh MEH-rohn*	prosciutto and melon
サラミ・ソーセージ	*sah-RAH-mee soh-seh-jee*	salami
サーディン／いわし	*SAH-deen／ee-WAH-shee*	sardines
ソーセージ	*soh-SEH-jee*	sausage
えびのカクテル	*eh-BEE noh KAHK-teh-roo*	shrimp cocktail
スモークド・サーモン	*SMOII-koo-doh SAH-mohn*	smoked salmon
エスカルゴ	*eh-soo-kah-roo-goh*	snails

Soup

チキン・スープ	chee-KEEN soo-poo	chicken soup
クラム・チャウダー	koo-RAH-moo CHAH-oo-dah	clam chowder
コンソメ	KOHN-soh-meh	consomme
コーン・スープ	KOHN SOO-poo	corn soup
クリーム・スープ	koo-REE-moo SOO-poo	cream soup
フィッシュ・スープ	feesh-SHOO SOO-poo	fish soup
ガーリック・スープ	GAH-reek-koo SOO-poo	garlic soup
ヌードル・スープ	NOO-doh-roo SOO-poo	noodle soup
オニオン・スープ	oh-NEE-ohn SOO-poo	onion soup
トマト・スープ	toh-MAH-toh SOO-poo	tomato soup
ベジタブル・スープ	beh-JEE-tah-boo-roo SOO-poo	vegetable soup
ビシソア	bee-SHEE-soh-ah	vichyssoise

Salad and Dressing

シーザー・サラダ	SHEE-zah sah-rah-dah	Caesar salad
グリーン・サラダ	goo-REEN sah-rah-dah	green salad
トマト・サラダ	toh-MAH-toh sah-rah-dah	tomato salad
ミックス・サラダ	meek-KOOS sah-rah-dah	tossed salad
ブルー・チーズのドレッシング	boo-ROO CHEE-zoo noh doh-REHSH-sheen-goo	blue cheese dressing
レストラン特製のドレッシング	REHS-toh-rahn toh-KOO-seh noh doh-REHSH-sheen-goo	house dressing

| イタリアン・ドレッシング | *ee-TAH-ree-ahn doh-REHSH-sheen-goo* | Italian dressing |
| サラダ油とす | *sah-RAH-dah-yoo toh SOO* | oil and vinegar |

Main Course Dishes

For the main course, you must choose among some of the best seafood, fowl, and meat you've ever tasted. Japan has fish and shellfish in abundance. You've probably heard of the famous beer-fed Kobe beef cattle. The Japanese prize their beef highly; some restaurants offer a choice of beef from different parts of the country. Here are some cooking instructions for your entrees.

I'd like it <u>baked</u>.	それは，<u>天火で焼いて</u>ください。 *soh-reh wah, <u>TEHN-pee deh yah-ee-teh</u> koo-dah-sah-ee*
boiled	ゆでて *YOO-deh-teh*
broiled	直火で焼いて *jee-KEE-bee deh yah-EE-teh*
fried	油であげて *ah-BOO-rah deh ah-geh-teh*
grilled	焼網で焼いて *yah-KEE-ah-mee deh yah-ee-teh*
roasted	ローストにして *ROH-stoh nee shteh*
sauteed	ソテーにして *soh-TEH nee shteh*
rare	レアにして *REH-ah nee shteh*
medium	ミディアムにして *MEE-dee-ah-moo nee shteh*
well-done	よく焼いて *YOH-koo yah-ee-teh*

Fish and Shellfish

あわび	*AH-wah-bee*	abalone
はまぐり	*hah-MAH-goo-ree*	clams
たら	*TAH-rah*	cod
かに	*kah-NEE*	crab

平目	*hee-RAH-meh*	flounder
おひょう	*oh-HYOH*	halibut
にしん	*NEE-sheen*	herring
伊勢エビ／ロブスター	*ee-SEH eh-bee／ROH-boo-stah*	lobster
さば	*sah-BAH*	mackerel
ムール貝	*MOO-roo gah-ee*	mussels
かき	*KAH-kee*	oysters
鯛	*TAH-ee*	porgy
車えび	*koo-ROO-mah eh-bee*	prawns
にじます	*nee-JEE mahs*	rainbow trout
さけ	*SAH-keh*	salmon
いわし	*ee-WAH-shee*	sardines
貝柱	*kah-EE-bah-shee-rah*	scallops
すずき	*soo-ZOO-kee*	sea bass
えび	*eh-BEE*	shrimp
きす	*kee-SOO*	smelt
したびらめ	*SHTAH-bee-rah-meh*	sole
さわら	*sah-WAH-rah*	Spanish mackerel
まかじき	*mah-KAH-jee-kee*	swordfish
ます	*mah-SOO*	trout
まぐろ	*mah-GOO-roh*	tuna
はまち／ぶり	*hah-MAH-chee／BOO-ree*	yellowtail

Fowl

にわとり	*nee-WAH-toh-ree*	chicken
おんどり	*OHN-doh-ree*	capon
とりのささ身	*toh-ree noh sah-SAH-mee*	chicken breast (boneless)

とりのもも肉	*toh-ree noh moh-MOH nee-koo*	chicken thigh
あひる	*ah-HEE-roo*	duck
まがも	*mah-GAH-moh*	mallard
山うずら	*yah-MAH OO-zoo-rah*	partridge
ひなばと	*hee-NAH-bah-toh*	squab
うずら	*oo-ZOO-rah*	quail
うさぎ	*oo-SAH-gee*	rabbit
七面鳥	*shee-CHEE-mehn-choh*	turkey

Meat

ベーコン	*BEH-kohn*	bacon
牛肉	*gyoo nee-koo*	beef
ビフテキ	*bee-FOO-teh-kee*	beefsteak
シャトー・ブリアン	*shah-TOH BOO-ree-ahn*	chateaubriand
冷肉とチーズの盛り合せ	*reh-nee-koo toh CHEE-zoo noh moh-REE-ah-wah-seh*	cold cuts
コーン・ビーフ	*KOHN-bee-foo*	corned beef
ひれ肉	*hee-REH nee-koo*	filet
ヒレミニオン	*hee-REH MEE-nee-ohn*	filet mignon
牛のひき肉	*GYOO noh hee-KEE nee-koo*	ground beef
豚のひき肉	*boo-TAH noh hee-KEE nee-koo*	ground pork
ハム	*HAH-moo*	ham
ハンバーグ・ステーキ	*hahn-bah-goo soo-TEH-kee*	hamburger steak
じん臓	*JEEN-zoh*	kidneys

子羊	koh-HEE-tsoo-jee	lamb
ラム・チョップ	rah-MOO chohp-poo	lamb chop
子羊の足	koh-HEE-tsoo-jee noh ah-shee	leg of lamb
肝臓／レバー	KAHN-zoh/ REH-bah	liver
ミート・ボール／肉だんご	MEE-toh-BOH-roo/ nee-KOO-dahn-goh	meatballs
ミニッツ・ステーキ	mee-NEET-tsoo soo-TEH-kee	minute steak
羊肉	yoh nee-koo	mutton
オックス・テール	ohk-KOO-soo teh-roo	ox tail
ペパー・ステーキ	peh-PAH soo-teh-kee	pepper steak
豚肉	boo-TAH nee-koo	pork
ポーク・チョップ	POH-koo CHOHP-poo	pork chop
ロースト・ビーフ	ROH-soo-toh bee-foo	roast beef
ロースト・ポーク	ROH-soo-toh poh-koo	roast pork
ソーセージ	soh-SEH-jee	sausage
サーロイン／ロース	SAH-roh-een/ ROH-soo	sirloin
ステーキ	soo-TEH-kee	steak
シチュー肉	shee-CHOO nee-koo	stew meat
骨付きのステーキ	hoh-NEH tskee noh soo-TEH-kee	T-bone steak
テンダロイン	TEHN-dah-roh-een	tenderloin
タン	TAHN	tongue
トルヌードー	toh-ROO-noo-doh	tournedos
子牛	koh-OO-shee	veal

Vegetables

ブロッコリ	*boo-ROHK-koh-ree*	broccoli
芽キャベツ	*meh KYAH-beh-tsoo*	brussels sprouts
キャベツ	*KYAH-beh-tsoo*	cabbage
人参	*NEEN-jeen*	carrot
カリフラワー	*kah-REE-foo-rah-wah*	cauliflower
セロリ	*SEH-roh-ree*	celery
コーン／とうもろこし	*KOHN/ TOH-moh-roh-koh-shee*	corn
きゅうり	*KYOO-ree*	cucumber
なす	*NAH-soo*	eggplant
エンダイブ	*EHN-dah-ee-boo*	endive
ガーリック／にんにく	*GAH-reek-koo/ NEEN-nee-koo*	garlic
ピーマン	*PEE-mahn*	green pepper
長ねぎ	*nah-GAH-neh-gee*	leek
レタス	*REH-tah-soo*	lettuce
玉ねぎ	*tah-MAH-neh-gee*	onion
パセリ	*pah-SEH-ree*	parsley
ポテト／じゃがいも	*POH-teh-toh/ jah-GAH-ee-moh*	potato
ラディッシュ／二十日大根	*RAH-deesh-shoo/ hah-TSOO-kah DAH-ee-kohn*	radish
赤いピーマン	*ah-KAH-ee PEE-mahn*	red pepper
細ねぎ	*hoh-SOH-neh-gee*	spring onion
ほうれん草	*hoh-rehn-soh*	spinach
さやえんどう	*sah-YAH ehn-doh*	string beans
トマト	*TOH-mah-toh*	tomato
かぶ	*kah-BOO*	turnip
クレソン	*koo-REH-sohn*	watercress

Bread

Not all restaurants provide bread as a matter of course. You may have to ask for it. You may be asked if you want bread or rice. It's an either-or question, as if the two are so similar you wouldn't want both. And if you're asked, you <u>will</u> get one or the other, not both!

We'd like some bread, please.	パンを，お願いします。	*PAHN oh oh-NEH-gah-ee shee-mahs*	
クロワッサン	*koo-ROH-wahs-sahn*	croissant
フランス・パン	*foo-RAHN-soo pahn*	French bread
ガーリック・トースト	*GAH-reek-koo TOH-soo-toh*	garlic toast
イタリア・パン	*ee-TAH-ree-ah pahn*	Italian bread
ロールパン	*ROH-roo pahn*	rolls
黒パン	*koo-ROH pahn*	rye
トースト	*TOH-soo-toh*	toast
白パン	*shee-ROH pahn*	white bread

Pasta, Rice, and Potatoes

You're going to see and hear different words for rice in Japan. In restaurants where Western food is served, rice is **raisu,** served on a plate. In Japanese-style meals, rice is **gohan,** served in a bowl. It is the same rice!

ベークド・ポテト	*BEH-koo-doh POH-teh-toh*	baked potato
ゆでたじゃがいも	*YOO-deh-tah jah-GAH-ee-moh*	boiled potato
フレンチ・フライ	*foo-REHN-chee FOO-rah-ee*	French fries
マカロニ	*mah-KAH-roh-nee*	macaroni
マッシュ・ポテト	*mahsh-SHOO poh-teh-toh*	mashed potatoes
ライス	*RAH-ee-soo*	rice
スパゲッティー	*soo-PAH-geht-tee*	spaghetti

Accompaniments

butter	バター	*BAH-tah*
cream	ミルク	*MEE-roo-koo*
honey	はちみつ	*hah-CHEE-mee-tsoo*
horseradish	ホースラディッシュ／西洋わさび	*HOH-soo RAH-deesh-shoo/ seh-yoh WAH-sah-bee*
jam	ジャム	*JAH-moo*
ketchup	ケチャップ	*keh-CHAHP-poo*
lemon	レモン	*REH-mohn*
margarine	マーガリン	*MAH-gah-reen*
marmalade	マーマレード	*MAH-mah-reh-doh*
mayonnaise	マヨネーズ	*mah-YOH-neh-zoo*
mustard	マスタード／からし	*mah-SOO-tah-doh/ kah-RAH-shee*
oil	油／オイル	*ah-BOO-rah/ OH-ee-roo*
olive oil	オリーブ・オイル	*oh-REE-boo oo-ee-roo*
paprika	パプリカ	*pah-POO-ree-kah*
pepper	こしょう	*koh-SHOH*
salt	塩	*shee-OH*
sugar	砂糖	*sah-TOH*
syrup	シロップ	*SHEE-rohp-poo*
Tabasco	タバスコ	*tah-BAHS-koh*
vinegar	す	*SOO*
Worcestershire sauce	ウースター・ソース	*OO-soo-tah SOH-soo*

Cheese

Cheese is relatively new to the Japanese diet. There is, however, a variety of excellent cheeses available, some imported, and some made in Japan. Not all Japanese are familiar with the names of different kinds of cheese. Ask for what you want—it may be there even if it isn't known by name. Asking to see a cheese tray usually gets you the whole assortment.

What kind of cheese do you have?	チーズは，どんな種類がありますか。 *CHEE-zoo wah, DOHN-nah shoo-roo-ee gah ah-ree-mahs KAH*
Do you have a cheese tray?	チーズを盛った，お盆がありますか。 *CHEE-zoo oh moht-TAH, oh-bohn gah ah-ree-mahs KAH*
Can I see them (the cheeses)?	チーズを，みせてもらえますか。 *CHEE-zoo oh, MEE-seh-teh moh-rah-eh-mahs KAH*
Give me some <u>blue cheese</u>, please.	<u>ブルー・チーズ</u>をください *<u>boo-ROO CHEE-zoo</u> oh koo-DAH-sah-ee*
Brie	ブリー *boo-REE*
Camembert	カマンベール *kah-MAHN-beh-roo*
Cheddar cheese	チェダー *CHEH-dah*
Edam cheese	エダム *EH-dah-moo*
Swiss cheese	スイス・チーズ *soo-EE-soo CHEE-zoo*
Please bring some crackers, too.	クラッカーも，お願いします。 *koo-RAHK-kah moh, oh-NEH-gah-ee shee-mahs*

Fruit

Excellent fresh fruit is available throughout Japan, though often expensive. Check the price before ordering.

りんご	*REEN-goh*	apple
バナナ	*BAH-nah-nah*	banana
さくらんぼ／チェリー	*sah-KOO-rahn-boh/CHEH-ree*	cherries
いちじく	*ee-CHEE-jee-koo*	fig
ぶどう	*boo-DOH*	grapes
グレープ・フルーツ	*goo-REH-poo foo-ROO-tsoo*	grapefruit

キーウィー	_KEE-wee_	kiwi
びわ	_BEE-wah_	loquat
メロン	_MEH-rohn_	melon
ネクタリン	_neh-KOO-tah-reen_	nectarine
オレンジ	_oh-REHN-jee_	orange
パパイヤ	_pah-PAH-ee-yah_	papaya
桃	_moh-MOH_	peach
洋なし	_YOH nah-shee_	pear
なし	_nah-SHEE_	Japanese pear
柿	_kah-KEE_	persimmon
パイナップル	_pah-EE-nahp-poo-roo_	pineapple
プラム／すもも	_POO-rah-moo／ soo-MOH-moh_	plum
いちご	_ee-CHEE-goh_	strawberries
みかん	_MEE-kahn_	tangerine
西瓜	_soo-EE-kah_	watermelon

Nuts

アーモンド	_ah-mohn-doh_	almonds
くり	_koo-REE_	chestnuts
マカデミア・ナッツ	_mah-KAH-dah-mee-ah NAHT-tsoo_	Macadamia nuts
ピーナッツ	_PEE-naht-tsoo_	peanuts
くるみ	_koo-ROO-mee_	walnuts

Desserts

ケーキ	_KEH-kee_	cake
チーズ・ケーキ	_CHEE-zoo keh-kee_	cheesecake
チョコレート・ケーキ	_choh-KOH-reh-toh keh-kee_	chocolate cake
レヤ・ケーキ	_reh-YAH keh-kee_	layer cake

いちごのショート・ケーキ	*ee-CHEE-goh noh SHOH-toh keh-kee*	strawberry short-cake
クッキー	*KOOK-kee*	cookies
カスタード	*kahs-TAH-doh*	custard
フルーツ・カップ	*foo-ROOTS kahp-poo*	fruit compote
アイスクリーム	*ah-EES-koo-ree-moo*	ice cream
コーヒー・アイスクリーム	*KOH-hee ah-EES-koo-ree-moo*	coffee ice cream
チョコレート・サンデー	*choh-KOH-reh-toh sahn-deh*	chocolate sundae
ホット・ファッジ・サンデー	*hoht-TOH fahj-jee sahn-deh*	hot fudge sundae
ピーチ・メルバ	*PEE-chee MEH-roo-bah*	peach melba
ストロベリー・サンデー	*STOH-roh-beh-ree SAHN-deh*	strawberry sundae
バニラ・アイスクリーム	*bah-NEE-rah ah-EES-koo-ree-moo*	vanilla ice cream
ムース	*MOO-soo*	mousse
チョコレート・ムース	*choh-KOH-reh-toh MOO-soo*	chocolate mousse
ペーストリー	*PEH-soo-toh-ree*	pastry
チェスナッツ・タート	*chehs-naht-tsoo TAH-toh*	chestnut tart
シュークリーム	*SHOO-koo-ree-moo*	cream puff
エクレア	*eh-KOO-reh-ah*	eclair
フルーツ・タート	*foo-ROOTS TAH-toh*	fruit tart
ペティ・フォー／小型ケーキ	*peh-TEE foh／koh-GAH-tah KEH-kee*	petit four
パイ	*PAH-ee*	pie
アップル・パイ	*ahp-POO-roo PAH-ee*	apple pie

レモン・メレンゲ	*reh-MOHN meh-REHN-geh*	lemon meringue
プリン	*POO-reen*	pudding
シャーベット	*SHAH-beht-toh*	sherbet
メロン・シャーベット	*meh-ROHN SHAH-beht-toh*	melon sherbet
オレンジ・シャーベット	*oh-REHN-jee SHAH-beht-toh*	orange sherbet
パイナップル・シャーベット	*pah-EE-nahp-poo-roo SHAH-beht-toh*	pineapple sherbet
スフレ	*SOO-foo-reh*	soufflé
チョコレート・スフレ	*choh-KOH-reh-toh SOO-foo-reh*	chocolate soufflé
グレープ・フルーツ・スフレ	*goo-REH-poo foo-roots SOO-foo-reh*	grapefruit soufflé

Additional Requests

Waiter/ waitress!	ちょっと，すみませんが。 *CHOHT-toh soo-MEE-mah-sehn gah*
Could you bring me <u>a knife</u> please?	<u>ナイフ</u>を，持ってきてください。 *NAH-ee-foo oh, moht-TEH kee-teh koo-dah-sah-ee*
a fork	フォーク *FOH-koo*
a spoon	スプーン *SPOON*
a teaspoon	小さじ *koh-SAH-jee*
a tablespoon	大さじ *OH-sah-jee*
a glass	コップ *kohp-POO*
a cup	コーヒー茶わん *KOH-hee jah-wahn*
a saucer	受け皿 *oo-KEH-zah-rah*
a plate	お皿 *oh-SAH-rah*
a bowl	ボール *BOH-roo*
a napkin	ナプキン *NAH-poo-keen*
some toothpicks	ようじ *YOH-jee*

an ashtray	灰皿 *hah-EE-zah-rah*
Could you bring me some more <u>water</u> please?	<u>水</u>を，もう少しください。 *mee-ZOO oh, moh SKOH-shee koo-dah-sah-ee*
bread	パン *PAHN*
butter	バター *BAH-tah*
wine	ワイン *WAH-een*
Could you bring me <u>another bottle of wine</u> please?	<u>ワインをもう一本</u>，お願いします。 *WAH-een oh moh EEP-pohn, oh-NEH-gah-ee shee-mahs*
another glass of wine	ワインをもう一杯 *WAH-een oh moh EEP-pah-ee*
another order of this	これをもう一人前 *koh-reh oh moh ee-CHEE-neen mah-ee*
Show me the menu again, please.	メニューを，もう一度みせてください。 *MEH-nyoo oh, moh ee-chee-doh MEE-seh-teh koo-dah-sah-ee*

Complaints

It's not what I ordered.	これは，注文したのと違います。 *koh-REH wah, choo-mohn shtah noh toh chee-GAH-ee-mahs*
The meat is too rare.	肉が生すぎます。 *nee-koo gah, nah-MAH soo-gee mahs*
The meat is too well done.	肉が焼けすぎです。 *nee-koo gah, yah-KEE-soo-gee dehs*
This is undercooked.	これは，まだ料理できていません。 *koh-REH wah, mah-dah RYOH-ree deh-kee-teh ee-MAH-sehn*
This is overcooked.	これは，料理のしすぎです。 *koh-REH wah, RYOH-ree noh shee-SOO-gee dehs*
This isn't <u>hot</u>.	これは，熱くありません。 *koh-REH wah, ah-TSOO-koo ah-ree-mah-sehn*
cold	冷めたく *tsoo-MEH-tah-koo*
fresh	新鮮では *SHEEN-sehn deh-wah*

Would you get the manager, please?	マネージャーを，よんでください。 *mah-NEH-jah oh, YOHN-deh koo-dah-sah-ee*

The Check

Check, please.	チェック／（お）勘定を，お願いします。 *CHEHK-koo/ (oh)-KAHN-joh oh, oh-NEH-gah-ee shee-mahs*
Separate checks, please.	（お）勘定は，別々にお願いします。 *(oh)-KAHN-joh wah, beh-TSOO-beh-tsoo nee oh-NEH-gah-ee shee-mahs*
Do you take <u>credit cards</u>?	<u>クレジット・カード</u>が，使えますか。 *koo-REH-jeet-toh KAH-doh gah, tsoo-KAH-eh-mahs KAH*
traveler's checks	トラベラー・チェック *toh-RAH-beh-rah CHEHK-koo*
Which credit cards do you take?	どのクレジット・カードが，使えますか。 *DOH-noh koo-REH-jeet-toh KAH-doh gah, tsoo-KAH-eh-mahs KAH*
Are the tax and service charge included?	税金とサービス料が，入っていますか。 *zeh-keen toh SAH-bee-soo ryoh gah, HAH-eet-teh ee-mahs KAH*
Is this correct?	これは，正確ですか。 *koh-reh wah, SEH-kah-koo dehs KAH*
I don't think the bill is right.	（お）勘定に，間違いがあるようですが。 *(oh)-KAHN-joh nee, mah-CHEE-gah-ee gah ah-roo yoh dehs gah*
What are these charges for?	この代金は，何のためですか。 *koh-noh DAH-ee-keen wah, NAHN noh tah-meh dehs KAH*
I didn't order this.	これは，注文しませんでした。 *koh-REH wah, choo-mohn shee-MAH-sehn deh-shtah*
May I have a receipt, please?	領収書を，お願いします。 *RYOH-shoo-shoh oh, oh-NEH-gah-ee shee-mahs*

LIGHT FOOD AND SNACKS

biscuits	ビスケット	*bee-SOO-keht-toh*
cake	ケーキ	*KEH-kee*
candy	キャンデー	*KYAHN-dee*
cocoa	ココア	*KOH-koh-ah*
coffee	コーヒー	*KOH-hee*
coke	コカコーラ	*koh-KAH-koh-rah*
cookies	クッキー	*KOOK-kee*
crackers	クラッカー	*koo-RAHK-kah*
French toast	フレンチ・トースト	*foo-REHN-chee TOH-soo-toh*
fried eggs	目玉焼き	*meh-DAH-mah-yah-kee*
fruit	果物	*koo-DAH-moh-noh*
ham	ハム	*HAH-moo*
hamburger	ハンバーガー	*HAHN-bah-gah*
hard boiled eggs	ゆでたまご	*yoo-DEH-tah-mah-goh*
sandwich	サンドイッチ	*sahn-doh-EET-chee*
toast	トースト	*TOH-soo-toh*
waffles	ワッフル	*WAHF-foo-roo*

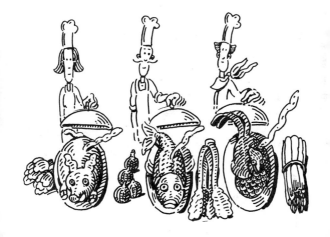

MEETING PEOPLE

As you travel around seeing the sights, you'll have many opportunities to meet Japanese people. Although as a rule Japanese prefer formal introductions, sightseeing does provide various situations where you can strike up a casual conversation. You may have questions about the places you're visiting, and Japanese are by nature hospitable; most would try to assist you. This section will help you get the conversation started — and to continue it if it seems appropriate! You can use these phrases with local Japanese people, and with those from out of town too. Japanese enjoy sightseeing; you'll probably meet a lot of Japanese tourists. For more information on Japanese customs in social situations, see p. 19, The Land and the People.

CONVERSATION STARTERS: WITH LOCAL PEOPLE

Do you live <u>here</u>?	ここに，お住いですか。 *koh-KOH nee, oh-soo-mah-ee dehs KAH*
in Tokyo	東京に *TOH-kyoh nee*
in Osaka	大阪に *OH-sah-kah nee*
in Kyoto	京都に *KYOH-toh nee*
I've always wanted to come here.	ここに来たいと，いつも思っていました。 *koh-koh nee kee-TAH-ee toh, EE-tsoo-moh oh-MOHT-teh ee-mah-shtah*
It's a wonderful place.	すばらしい所ですねえ。 *soo-BAH-rah-shee toh-koh-roh dehs neh*
I've really been enjoying it here.	ここを，とっても楽しんでいます。 *koh-KOH oh, toht-teh-moh tah-NOH-sheen-deh ee-mahs*
I've been to ____, ____, and ____.	今まで，____と，____と，____へ行きました。 *ee-MAH mah-deh, ____ toh, ____ toh, ____ eh ee-KEE-mahsh-tah*

I'm planning to go to ___, ___, and ___.

これから，___と，___と，___へ
行く予定です。 *koh-REH kah-rah,*
___ toh, ___ toh, ___ eh ee-KOO-
yoh-teh dehs

What do you think about my itinerary here?

私の旅行計画について，どう思いま
すか。 *wah-TAHK-shee noh ryoh-KOH*
keh-kah-koo nee tsoo-ee-teh, DOH oh-
moh-ee-mahs KAH

Is there anything not on my itinerary that you would recommend?

私の旅程以外に，どこか行くべき所
がありますか。 *wah-TAHK-shee noh*
ryoh-TEH ee-gah-ee nee, DOH-koh kah
ee-KOO-beh-kee toh-koh-roh gah ah-
ree-mahs KAH

Could you explain a lit-tle about ___?

___について，少し説明してもらえ
ますか。 *___ nee tsoo-ee-teh, SKOH-*
shee seh-TSOO-meh shteh moh-rah-eh-
mahs KAH

Would you recommend a nice place to eat?

食事にいい場所を，教えてもらえま
すか。 *shoh-KOO-jee nee EE bah-shoh*
oh, oh-SHEE-eh-teh moh-rah-eh-mahs
KAH

Where's a good place for souvenir shopping?

おみやげを買うには，どこがいいで
しょうか。 *oh-MEE-yah-geh oh kah-oo*
nee-wah, DOH-koh gah ee deh-shoh kah

CONVERSATION STARTERS: WITH OUT-OF-TOWN PEOPLE

Do you live here?

ここに，お住いですか。 *koh-KOH*
nee, oh-soo-mah-ee dehs KAH

Are you here for sight-seeing, or on business?

ここは観光ですか，それともお仕事
ですか。 *koh-koh wah, KAHN-koh*
dehs KAH, soh-REH-toh-moh oh-
SHEE-goh-toh dehs KAH

When did you come here?

ここへは，いつ来たのですか。 *koh-*
KOH eh wah, EE-tsoo kee-tah noh dehs
KAH

How do you like it here?	ここは，気に入りましたか。 *koh-KOH wah, kee NEE ee-ree-mah-shtah KAH*
What have you seen here?	今までに，何を見ましたか。 *ee-MAH mah-deh nee, NAH-nee oh mee-mah-shtah KAH*
I've been to ___, ___, and ___.	私は___と，___と，___を見ました。 *wah-TAHK-shee wah, ___ toh, ___ toh, ___ oh mee-MAH-shtah*
Have you been to ___?	___へは，行きましたか。 *___ eh wah, ee-KEE-mah-shtah KAH*
I recommend that you go to ___.	___へは，ぜひ行ったほうがいいですよ。 *___ eh wah, ZEH-hee eet-tah hoh gah EE dehs yoh*
I ate at ___, and it was wonderful.	___で食べましたが，とてもすばらしかったです。 *___ deh tah-BEH-mah-shtah gah, toh-TEH-moh soo-BAH-rah-shee-kaht-tah dehs*
Are you with a <u>tour group</u>?	観光旅行のグループと一緒ですか。 *KAHN-koh ryoh-koh noh goo-ROO-poo toh, ees-SHOH dehs KAH*
your <u>family</u>	御家族 *goh KAH-zoh-koo*
a <u>friend</u>	お友達 *oh-TOH-moh-dah-chee*
Are you on your own?	お一人ですか。 *oh-HEE-toh-ree dehs KAH*
How long will you be staying here?	ここには，もう何日滞在の予定ですか。 *koh-KOH nee wah, moh NAHN-nee-chee tah-ee-zah-ee noh yoh-teh dehs KAH*
Where are you staying?	どちらに，お泊りですか。 *DOH-chee-rah nee, oh-toh-mah-ree dehs KAH*
Where are you from?	お住いは，どちらですか。 *oh-SOO-mah-ee wah, DOH-chee-rah dehs KAH*
I hear it's nice there.	いい所だそうですねえ。 *EE toh-koh-roh dah soh dehs neh*

What's ____ famous for?

____では，何が有名ですか。____
deh-wah, NAH-nee gah yoo-meh dehs KAH

What's the special local food in ____?

____特産の食べ物は何ですか。____
toh-KOO-sahn noh tah-beh-moh-noh wah NAHN dehs KAH

What's a good <u>hotel</u> to stay at in ____?

____で泊まるには，どのホテルがいいですか。____ *deh toh-MAH-roo nee-wah, DOH-noh* <u>hoh-teh-roo</u> *gah ee dehs KAH*

　Japanese inn

旅館 *ryoh-KAHN*

Could you tell me a good place to eat?

食事にいい所を，教えてください。
shoh-KOO-jee nee ee toh-koh-roh oh, oh-SHEE-eh-teh koo-dah-sah-ee

Follow-up

What do you think of ____?

____については，どう思いますか。
____ *nee tsoo-ee-teh wah, DOH oh-moh-ee-mahs KAH*

Do you like ____?

____は，好きですか。____ *wah, SKEE dehs KAH*

I think ____ is very <u>beautiful</u>.

____は，とても<u>きれいだ</u>と思います。____ *wah, toh-TEH-moh* <u>KEE-reh dah</u> *toh oh-moh-ee-mahs*

　interesting

おもしろい *oh-MOH-shee-roh-ee*

　magnificent

立派だ *reep-PAH dah*

　wonderful

すばらしい *soo-BAH-rah-shee*

By the way, let me introduce myself.

ところで，自己紹介させてください。*toh-KOH-roh deh, jee-KOH shoh-kah-ee sah-seh-teh koo-DAH-sah-ee*

My name is ____.

私の名前は，____です。*wah-TAHK-shee noh nah-mah-eh wah,* ____ *dehs*

I'm here <u>alone</u>.

<u>一人で</u>，来ています。<u>*hee-TOH-ree deh*</u>, *kee-TEH ee-mahs*

　with my wife

家内と *KAH-nah-ee toh*

with my husband	主人と *SHOO-jeen toh*
with my friend	友達と *toh-MOH-dah-chee toh*
with my colleague	同僚と *DŌH-ryoh toh*
I'm a <u>student</u>.	私は，<u>学生</u>です。 *wah-TAHK-shee wah, <u>gah-KOO-seh</u> dehs*
businessman	ビジネスマン *bee-JEE-neh-soo mahn*
doctor	医者 *ee-SHAH*
lawyer	弁護士 *BEHN-goh-shee*
I'm from <u>the United States</u>.	<u>アメリカ</u>から，来ました *ah-MEH-ree-<u>kah</u> kah-rah, kee-MAH-shtah*
Canada	カナダ *KAH-nah-dah*
Italy	イタリア *ee-TAH-ree-ah*
I live in <u>New York</u>.	<u>ニューヨーク</u>に，住んでいます。 <u>*NYOO-yoh-koo*</u> *nee, SOON-deh ee-mahs*
Hong Kong	香港 *hohn-KOHN*
Cairo	カイロ *KAH-ee-roh*
I'm here for <u>sightseeing</u>.	<u>観光</u>で来ています。 <u>*KAHN-koh*</u> *deh kee-TEH ee-mahs*
business	仕事 *shee-GOH-toh*
I've been in Japan for <u>two days</u>.	日本に来てから，<u>二日</u>になります。 *nee-HOHN nee kee-TEH-kah-rah, <u>foo-TSOO-kah</u> nee nah-ree-mahs*
three days	三日 *meek-KAH*
four days	四日 *yohk-KAH*
one week	一週間 *ees-SHOO kahn*
I came here <u>today</u>.	ここへは，<u>今日</u>着きました。 *koh-KOH eh wah, <u>KYOH</u> tskee-mah-shtah*
yesterday	昨日 *kee-NOH*
two days ago	おととい *oh-TOH-toh-ee*
three days ago	さきおととい *sah-KEE oh-toh-toh-ee*

It's my first time in Japan.	日本は，初めてです。 *nee-HOHN wah, hah-JEE-meh-teh* dehs
Sapporo	札幌 *sahp-POH-roh*
Beppu	別府 *behp-POO*
I'll stay here overnight.	ここには，一晩泊まります。 *koh-KOH nee-wah, hee-TOH-bahn toh-mah-ree-mahs*
for a few days	数日 *SOO nee-chee*
for a week	一週間 *ees-SHOO kahn*
I'm staying at the ____ hotel.	私は，____ ホテルに泊まっています。 *wah-TAHK-shee wah, ____ hoh-teh-roo nee toh-MAHT-teh ee-mahs*
I'm single.	私は，独身です。 *wah-TAHK-shee wah, doh-KOO-sheen dehs*
married	結婚しています *kehk-KOHN shteh ee-mahs*
I have a family.	私には，家族があります。 *wah-TAHK-shee nee-wah, KAH-zoh-koo gah ah-ree-mahs*
I have no children.	子供は，いません。 *koh-DOH-moh wah, ee-MAH-sehn*
I have one child (ren).	子供が，一人います。 *koh-DOH-moh gah, hee-TOH-ree ee-mahs*
two	二人 *foo-TAH-ree*
three	三人 *SAHN-neen*
These are pictures of my family.	これが，私の家族の写真です。 *koh-REH gah, wah-TAHK-shee noh KAH-zoh-koo noh shah-SHEEN dehs*
Would you like to see them?	ごらんになりますか。 *goh-RAHN nee nah-ree-mahs KAH*
Are you a student?	学生さんですか。 *gah-KOO-seh sahn dehs KAH*
What are you studying?	何を勉強していますか。 *NAH-nee oh behn-kyoh shteh ee-mahs KAH*
What do you do?	お仕事は，何ですか。 *oh-SHEE-goh-toh wah, NAHN dehs KAH*

Are you <u>single</u>?	独身ですか。 *doh-KOO-sheen dehs KAH*
married	結婚しています *kehk-KOHN shteh ee-mahs*
Do you have any children?	お子さんが，いますか。 *oh-KOH-sahn gah, ee-mahs KAH*
How many children do you have?	お子さんは，何人ですか。 *oh-KOH-sahn wah, NAHN-neen dehs KAH*
How old are they?	お子さんは，おいくつですか。 *oh-KOH-sahn wah, oh-EE-koo-tsoo dehs KAH*
Is your <u>family</u> here?	御家族は，ここにおいでですか。 *goh-KAH-zoh-koo wah, koh-koh nee oh-EE-deh dehs KAH*
wife	奥さん *OHK-sahn*
husband	御主人 *goh-SHOO-jeen*
Do you have any pictures of your <u>family</u>?	御家族の写真を，お持ちですか。 *goh-KAH-zoh-koo noh shah-sheen oh, oh-MOH-chee dehs KAH*
children	お子さん *oh-KOH-sahn*

Taking Pictures

Would you like me to take a picture for you?	写真を，おとりしましょうか。 *shah-SHEEN oh, oh-TOH-ree shee-mah-shoh KAH*
May I take your picture?	あなたの写真をとっても，よろしいですか。 *ah-NAH-tah noh shah-SHEEN oh toht-teh-moh, yoh-ROH-shee dehs KAH*
Stand here.	そこに立ってください。 *soh-KOH nee TAHT-teh koo-dah-sah-ee*
Don't move.	動かないで。 *oo-GOH-kah-nah-ee deh*
Smile	笑って。 *wah-RAHT-teh*
That's it.	はい，終りました。 *hah-ee, oh-WAH-ree-mah-shtah*

Would you take a picture of me, please?	写真をとってもらえますか。 *shah-sheen oh TOHT-teh moh-rah-eh-mahs KAH*
Thank you.	どうも，ありがとうございました。 *DOH-moh, ah-REE-gah-toh goh-zah-ee-mah-shtah*

SAYING GOODBYE

Nice talking to you.	お話しできて，楽しかったです。 *oh-HAH-nah-shee deh-kee-teh, tah-NOH-shee-kaht-tah dehs*
I hope I'll see you again.	また，おめにかかれるといいですね。 *mah-TAH, oh-MEH nee kah-kah-reh-roo toh EE dehs neh*

GETTING TOGETHER

Could I see you again?	また，おめにかかれますか。 *mah-TAH, oh-MEH nee kah-kah-reh-mahs KAH*
Here's my name, hotel, telephone number, and extension.	これが，私の名前，ホテル，電話番号，内線です。 *koh-REH gah, wah-TAHK-shee noh nah-MAH-eh, HOH-teh-roo, DEHN-wah bahn-goh, nah-EE-sehn dehs*
Will you call me if you have time?	時間があったら，電話をしてくれますか。 *jee-KAHN gah aht-tah-rah, DEHN-wah oh shteh koo-reh-mahs KAH*
Could you give me your telephone number?	あなたの電話番号をいただけますか。 *ah-NAH-tah noh DEHN-wah bahn-goh oh ee-TAH-dah-keh-mahs KAH*
May I call you?	電話しても，かまいませんか。 *DEHN-wah shteh-moh, kah-MAH-ee-mah-sehn KAH*

Are you doing anything <u>this afternoon</u>?	今日の午後は，何か予定があります か。 _KYOH noh goh-goh wah, NAH-nee kah yoh-TEH gah ah-ree-mahs KAH_
this evening	今晩 _KOHN-bahn_
tomorrow	あした _ah-SHTAH_
Are you free this evening?	今晩，おひまですか。 _KOHN-bahn, oh-HEE-mah dehs KAH_
What about <u>dinner</u> together?	夕食を，一緒にいかがですか。 _YOO-shoh-koo oh, ees-shoh nee ee-KAH-gah dehs KAH_
drinks	お酒 _oh-SAH-keh_
sightseeing	見物 _KEHN-boo-tsoo_
I'd like to invite you for <u>cocktails</u>.	カクテルに，お招きしたいのです が。 _KAH-koo-teh-roo nee, oh-MAH-neh-kee shee-tah-ee noh dehs gah_
dinner	夕食 _YOO-shoh-koo_
a show	ショー _SHOH_
I hope you can come.	来ていただければ，うれしいのです が。 _kee-TEH ee-tah-dah-keh-reh-bah, oo-REH-shee-noh dehs gah_
Where shall I meet you?	どこで，お会いしましょうか。 _DOH-koh deh, oh-AH-ee shee-mah-shoh KAH_
Shall I meet you at <u>my hotel lobby</u>?	私のホテルのロビーで，お会いしま しょうか。 _wah-TAHK-shee noh HOH-teh-roo noh roh-bee deh, oh-AH-ee shee-mah-shoh KAH_
your hotel lobby	あなたのホテルのロビー _ah-NAH-tah noh HOH-teh-roo noh roh-bee_
the restaurant	レストラン _REHS-toh-rahn_
the cocktail lounge	カクテル・ラウンジ _kah-KOO-teh-roo rah-oon-jee_
the theater	劇場 _geh-KEE-joh_
Shall I come to pick you up?	おむかえに，行きましょうか。 _oh-MOO-kah-eh nee, ee-kee-mah-shoh KAH_

What time shall we meet?	何時に，お会いしましょうか。 *NAHN-jee nee, oh-AH-ee shee-mah-shoh KAH*
Is <u>six</u> convenient for you?	六時は，都合がいいですか。 *roh-<u>KOO</u> jee wah, tsoo-GOH gah ee dehs <u>KAH</u>*
six-thirty	六時半 *roh-KOO-jee hahn*
seven	七時 *shee-CHEE jee*
See you then.	では，のちほど。 *DEH-wah, noh-CHEE hoh-doh*

SHOPPING

How often have you read or heard that Japan is a "shoppers' paradise"? It's true. Not only can you buy familiar items that you need, now you can explore the Japanese decorative arts firsthand. During your shopping expeditions, remember that bargaining is not generally practiced in Japan.

I'd like to go shopping today.	今日，買い物に行きたいのですが。 *kyoh, kah-EE-moh-noh nee ee-kee-TAH-ee noh dehs gah*
Where can I find a good ____?	いい____は，どこにありますか。 *ee ____ wah, DOH-koh nee ah-ree-mahs KAH*

antique shop	骨董屋 *koht-TOH yah*
art gallery	画廊 *guh-ROH*
bakery	パン屋 *PAHN yah*
barber shop	床屋 *toh-KOH yah*
beauty parlor	美容院 *bee-YOH een*
bookstore	本屋 *HOHN yah*
camera shop	カメラ屋 *kah-MEH-rah yah*
ceramics store	瀬戸物屋 *seh-TOH-moh-noh yah*
clothing store	洋服屋 *YOH-foo-koo yah*
men's clothing store	紳士服の店 *SHEEN-shee foo-koo noh mee-seh*
women's clothing store	婦人服の店 *foo-JEEN foo-koo noh mee-seh*
confectionery	お菓子屋 *oh-KAH-shee yah*
cosmetics shop	化粧品店 *keh-SHOH heen tehn*
department store	デパート *deh-PAH-toh*
drugstore	ドラッグ・ストアー *doh-RAHG-goo stoh-ah*
electrical appliance store	電気器具店 *DEHN-kee kee-goo tehn*

fish market	魚屋	*sah-KAH-nah yah*
florist	花屋	*hah-NAH-yah*
folkware shop	民芸品店	*MEEN-geh-heen tehn*
grocery store	食料品店	*shoh-KOO-ryoh heen tehn*
handicrafts shop	工芸品店	*KOH-geh-heen tehn*
jewelry store	宝石店	*HOH-seh-kee tehn*
kimono store	呉服屋	*goh-FOO-koo yah*
liquor store	酒屋	*sah-KAH yah*
newsstand	新聞売り場	*SHEEN-boon oo-ree-bah*
optician	眼鏡屋	*meh-GAH-neh yah*
pharmacy	薬屋	*koo-SOO-ree yah*
photographer	写真屋	*shah-SHEEN yah*
photography shop	カメラ屋	*kah-MEH-rah yah*
record store	レコード屋	*reh-KOH-doh yah*
shoe store	くつ屋	*koo-TSOO yah*
souvenir shop	おみやげ屋	*oh-MEE-yah-geh yah*
sporting goods store	運動具店	*OON-doh-goo tehn*
stationery store	文房具店	*BOON-boh-goo tehn*
supermarket	スーパー	*SOO-pah*
tailor	仕立て屋	*shee-TAH-teh yah*
tobacco shop	たばこ屋	*tah-BAH-koh yah*
toiletries shop	化粧品店	*keh-SHOH-heen tehn*
toy store	おもちゃ屋	*oh-MOH-chah yah*
travel agency	旅行代理店	*ryoh-KOH dah-ee-ree tehn*
video equipment shop	ビデオ装置の店	*bee-DEH-oh soh-chee noh mee-seh*
watch and clock store	時計屋	*toh-KEH yuh*
woodblock print shop	版画屋	*HAHN-gah yah*

INQUIRIES ABOUT SHOPPING

Where's the nearest ____?	一番近い____は，どこにあります か。 ee-CHEE-bahn chee-kah-ee ____ wah, DOH-koh nee ah-ree-mahs KAH
Which ____ do you recommend?	どの____がいいでしょうか。 DOH-noh ____ gah ee deh-shoh kah
Where do they sell ____?	____は，どこで売っていますか。 ____ wah, DOH-koh deh oot-teh ee-mahs KAH
Where's the main shopping area?	主なショッピング街は，どこにあり ますか。 OH-moh nah shohp-PEEN-goo gah-ee wah, DOH-koh nee ah-ree-mahs KAH
I'd like to go to a shopping arcade.	ショッピング・アーケードに，行き たいのですが。 shohp-PEEN-goo ah-keh-doh nee, ee-KEE-tah-ee noh dehs gah
Is it far?	そこは，遠いですか。 soh-KOH wah, TOH-ee dehs KAH
Can you tell me how to get there?	そこまで，どうやって行けばいいで すか。 soh-KOH mah-deh, DOH-yaht-teh ee-keh-bah ee dehs KAH
Where's a good place to window shop?	ウィンドー・ショッピングには， どこに行ったらいいですか。 WEEN-doh shohp-peen-goo nee-wah, DOH-koh nee eet-TAH-rah ee dehs KAH

THE CLERK

Here are some things that you'll hear while you're shopping. If you're not quite sure what's being said, you can ask the clerk to point to the phrase in the book.

Welcome.	いらっしゃいませ。 ee-RAHS-shah-ee mah-seh

What are you looking for?	何か，おさがしですか。 *NAH-nee kah, oh-SAH-gah-shee dehs KAH*
What <u>color</u> do you want?	どんな色をお好みですか。 *DOHN-nah <u>ee-roh</u> oh oh-koh-noh-mee dehs KAH*
size	サイズ *sah-ee-zoo*
I'm sorry. We don't have it/ any.	あいにく，ございません。 *ah-EE-nee-koo, goh-ZAH-ee-mah-sehn*
Would you like us to order it for you?	御注文いたしましょうか。 *goh-CHOO-mohn ee-tah-shee-mah-shoh KAH*
Please write your name and phone number.	お名前とお電話番号を，お願いします。 *oh-NAH-mah-eh toh oh-DEHN-wah bahn-goh oh, oh-neh-gah-ee shee-mahs*
It should be here <u>in a few days.</u>	<u>数日中に</u>，来ると思います。 *<u>SOO-jee-tsoo-choo</u> nee, KOO-roo toh oh-moh-ee-mahs*
next week	来週 *rah-EE-shoo*
We'll call you when it's here.	来ましたら，お電話いたします。 *kee-MAH-shtah-rah, oh-DEHN-wah ee-tah-shee-mahs*
That will be ____ yen, please.	____円，ちょうだいいたします。 *__ ehn, choh-dah-ee ee-TAH-shee-mahs*
I'm sorry; we don't accept credit cards.	申し訳ありませんが，クレジット・カードは受け付けておりません。 *MOH-shee-wah-keh ah-ree-mah-sehn gah, koo-REH-jeet-toh kah-doh wah oo-KEH-tsoo-keh-teh oh-ree-mah-sehn*
We accept <u>Diners Club</u>.	<u>ダイナース・クラブ</u>を，受け付けております。 *<u>dah-EE-nah-soo koo-rah-boo</u> oh, oo-KEH-tskeh-teh oh-ree-mahs*
American Express	アメリカン・エクスプレス *ah-MEH-ree-kahn eh-KOO-soo-poo-rehs*
Visa	ビザ *BEE-zah*
MasterCard	マスター・カード *mah-soo-TAH kah-doh*

Here's your receipt.	領収書をどうぞ。 *RYOH-shoo shoh oh doh-zoh*
Thank you.	ありがとうございました。 *ah-REE-gah-toh goh-zah-ee-mah-shtah*
Come again.	また，おこしください。 *mah-TAH, oh-koh-shee koo-dah-sah-ee*

IN THE STORE

Excuse me.	すみませんが。 *soo-MEE-mah-sehn gah*
Can you help me?	ちょっと，お願いします。 *CHOHT-toh, oh-neh-gah-ee shee-mahs*
I'd like to see some ____.	____を，見せてもらえますか。 *____ oh, MEE-seh-teh moh-rah-eh-mahs KAH*
Do you have any ____?	____は，ありますか。 *____ wah, ah-ree-mahs KAH*
I'm just looking, thank you.	ちょっと，見ているだけです。 *CHOHT-toh, MEE-teh ee-roo dah-KEH dehs*
I'd like something for a <u>child</u>.	何か，子供のものが欲しいのですが。 *NAH-nee kah, koh-DOH-moh noh moh-noh gah hoh-SHEE noh dehs gah*
a 5-year-old boy	五才の男の子 *GOH-sah-ee noh oh-TOH-koh noh koh*
a 10-year-old girl	十才の女の子 *JOOS-sah-ee noh OHN-nah noh koh*
I'd like to see <u>that one</u>.	あれを見たいのですが。 *ah-REH oh mee-tah-ee noh dehs gah*
this one	これ *koh-REH*
the one in the window	あのショー・ウィンドーにあるの *ah-noh SHOH ween-doh nee ah-roo noh*

I'd like to replace this ____.	この____を，買いかえたいのですが。 koh-noh ____ oh, kah-EE-kah-eh-tah-ee noh dehs gah
I'm interested in something <u>inexpensive</u>.	高くないものが欲しいのですが。 tah-KAH-koo-nah-ee moh-noh gah hoh-SHEE noh dehs gah
handmade	手作りの teh-ZOO-koo-ree noh
Japanese	日本の nee-HOHN noh
Do you have any others?	ほかに，何かありますか。 hoh-kah nee, NAH-nee kah ah-ree-mahs KAH
I'd like a <u>big</u> one.	大きいのが，欲しいのですが。 OH-kee noh gah, hoh-SHEE noh dehs gah
small	小さい CHEE-sah-ee
cheap	安い yah-SOO-ee
better	もっといい MOHT-toh ee
good	いい EE
How much is <u>it</u>?	これは，いくらですか。 koh-REH wah, EE-koo-rah dehs KAH
that one	それ soh-REH
Could you write it down?	値段を，紙に書いてくれませんか。 neh-DAHN oh, kah-mee nee KAH-ee-teh koo-reh-mah-sehn KAH
I want to spend about ____ yen.	予算は，やく____円です。 yoh-SAHN wah, yah-koo ____ ehn dehs
Do you have something <u>less expensive</u>?	もう少し安いのが，ありますか。 MOH-skoh-shee yah-SOO-ee noh gah, ah-ree-mahs KAH
more expensive	もう少し高い MOH skoh-shee tah-KAH-ee
I'll take it/ this.	それを，ください。 soh-REH oh, koo-dah-sah-ee
May I use a <u>credit card</u>?	クレジット・カードが，使えますか。 koo-REH-jeet-toh kah-doh gah, tsoo-KAH-eh-mahs KAH

travelers check	トラベラー・チェック *toh-RAH-beh-rah chehk-koo*
Which cards do you take?	どのカードが、使えますか。 *DOH-noh kah-doh gah, tsoo-KAH-eh-mahs KAH*
May I have a receipt, please.	領収書を、お願いします。 *RYOH-shoo shoh oh, oh-NEH-gah-ee shee-mahs*
Could you send it to my hotel?	ホテルに、届けてもらえますか。 *HOH-teh-roo nee, toh-DOH-keh-teh moh-rah-eh-mahs KAH*
Could you send it to this address?	この住所に、送ってもらえますか。 *koh-NOH joo-shoh nee, oh-KOOT-teh moh-rah-eh-mahs KAH*
Could you ship it overseas for me?	海外に、郵送してもらえますか。 *KAH-ee-gah-ee nee, YOO-soh shee-teh moh-rah-eh-mahs KAH*
How much would it cost?	郵送料は、いくらですか。 *YOO-soh ryoh wah, EE-koo-rah dehs KAH*
I'd also like to see ___.	___も、見たいのですが。 *___ moh, mee-TAH-ee noh dehs gah*
That's all, thank you.	これで、けっこうです。 *koh-reh deh, KEHK-koh dehs*
I'd like to <u>exchange</u> this.	この品を、<u>交換</u>したいのですが。 *koh-NOH shee-nah oh, <u>KOH-kahn</u> shee- tah-ee noh dehs gah*
return	返品 *HEHN-peen*
May I have a refund, please?	払い戻ししてもらえますか。 *hah-RAH-ee moh-doh-shee-teh moh-rah-eh-mahs KAH*
Here's my receipt.	これが、領収書です。 *koh-REH gah, ryoh-shoo shoh dehs*
Thank you for your help.	助けてもらって、たすかりました。 *tahs-KEH-teh moh-raht-teh, tahs-KAH-ree-mah-shtah*

DEPARTMENT STORES

Japanese department stores carry all the things you would expect, and a lot more as well. The folkware or **mingei** sections have crafts from all over Japan: handmade dolls, toys, pottery, paper crafts, bamboo baskets, lacquer trays, bowls, chopsticks, handmade and dyed fabrics, and more. You'll also find typical Japanese craft items in the housewares section — in a range from everyday pottery to expensive lacquerware. Such items usually come in sets of five, not six or eight as in Western countries.

Don't miss the food section; the entire basement floor is devoted to fresh and packaged foods, both Japanese and Western style.

Where's the <u>men's clothing</u> department?	紳士服売り場は，どこにあります か。 *SHEEN-shee foo-koo oo-ree-bah wah, DOH-koh nee ah-ree-mahs KAH*
women's clothing	婦人服 *foo-JEEN foo-koo*
children's clothing	子供服 *koh-DOH-moh foo-koo*
shoe	くつ *koo-TSOO*
housewares	家庭用品の *kah-TEH yoh-heen noh*
china	瀬戸物 *seh-TOH-moh-noh*
jewelry	宝石 *HOH-seh-kee*
notions	小間物 *koh-MAH-moh-noh*
furniture	家具 *kah-GOO*
luggage	旅行かばん／スーツ・ケース *ryoh-KOH kah-bahn/ SOO-tsoo keh-soo*
handicrafts	手工芸品 *shoo-KOH-geh heen*
Japanese food	日本食品の *nee-HOHN shoh-koo-heen noh*
Western food	西洋食品の *SEH-yoh shoh-koo-heen noh*
kimono	呉服 *goh-FOO-koo*
Where's the <u>ladies' room</u>?	女性用のトイレは，どこにあります か。 *joh-SEH yoh noh toh-ee-reh wah, DOH-koh nee ah-ree-mahs KAH*

men's room	男性用のトイレ *DAHN-seh yoh noh toh-ee-reh*
elevator	エレベーター *eh-REH-beh-tah*
escalator	エスカレーター *eh-SOO-kah-reh-tah*
snack bar	スナック *soo-NAHK-koo*
coffee shop	喫茶室 *kees-SAH shee-tsoo*
restaurant	レストラン *REHS-toh-rahn*
telephone	電話 *DEHN-wah*
water fountain	水飲み場 *mee-ZOO noh-mee-bah*
information desk	案内所 *AHN-nah-ee joh*

BOOKS

Bookstores, newsstands and stationery stores are usually separate in Japan, although some bookstores do sell newspapers. At bookstores and newsstands in large tourist hotels you can find some American and European newspapers, and also weekly news magazines, usually international or Far East editions. You can also buy English-language newspapers written and published in Japan; these are available at most newsstands throughout the country. If you don't see them , ask the vendor. Many bookstores have good selections of books in English.

Do you have books in English?	英語の本が，ありますか。 *EH-goh noh hohn gah, ah-ree-mahs KAH*
French	フランス語 *foo-RAHN-soo-goh*
Italian	イタリア語 *ee-TAH-ree-ah-goh*
German	ドイツ語 *doh-EE-tsoo-goh*
Where are the books in English?	英語の本は，どこにありますか。 *EH-goh noh hohn wah, DOH-koh nee ah-ree-mahs KAH*
I want a guidebook.	ガイド・ブックが欲しいのですが。 *gah-EE-doh book-koo gah, hoh-SHEE noh dehs gah*

a map of this city	この都市の地図 *koh-NOH toh-shee noh chee-zoo*
a map of Japan	日本の地図 *nee-HOHN noh chee-zoo*
a pocket dictionary	ポケット版の辞書 *poh-KEHT-toh bahn noh jee-shoh*
an English-Japanese dictionary	英和辞典 $\overline{EH}$-*wah jee-tehn*
a book for learning Japanese	日本語を習うための本 *nee-HOHN-goh oh nah-RAH-oo tah-meh noh hohn*
Where can I find detective stories?	探偵小説は，どこにありますか。 *TAHN-teh shoh-seh-tsoo wah, DOH-koh nee ah-ree-mahs KAH*
history books	歴史の本 *reh-KEE-shee noh hohn*
novels	小説 *SHOH-seh-tsoo*
short story books	短編小説 *TAHN-pehn shoh-seh-tsoo*
Do you have English translations of Japanese classics?	日本の古典の，英訳がありますか。 *nee-HOHN noh koh-tehn noh, $\overline{EH}$-yah-koo gah ah-ree-mahs KAH*
modern Japanese novels	近代日本小説 *KEEN-dah-ee nee-HOHN shoh-seh-tsoo*
current Japanese novels	現代日本小説 *GEHN-dah-ee nee-HOHN shoh-seh-tsoo*
Do you have English translations of Yukio Mishima's books?	三島由起夫の本の，英訳がありますか。 *mee-SHEE-mah yoo-kee-oh noh hohn noh, $\overline{EH}$-yah-koo gah ah-ree-mahs KAH*
Yasunari Kawabata's	川端康成の *kah-WAH-bah-tah yah-soo-nah-ree noh*
Junichiro Tanizaki's	谷崎潤一郎の *tah-NEE-zah-kee joon-ee-chee-roh noh*
I'm looking for a copy of ____.	____を，さがしているのですが。 ____ *oh, sah-GAH-shteh ee-roo noh dehs gah*
The title of the book is ____.	本の題名は，____です。 *HOHN noh dah-ee-meh wah,* ____ *dehs*

The author of the book is ___.	著者は，___です。 *CHOH-shah wah, ___ dehs*
I don't know the title/author.	本の題名／著者は，知りません。 *HOHN noh dah-ee-meh̄/ CHOH-shah wah, shee-ree-mah-sehn*
I'll take these books.	この本を，お願いします。 *koh-NOH hohn oh, oh-NEH-gah-ee shee-mahs*

CLOTHING

Shopping for clothing in Japan yields basic styles as well as designs, patterns, and fabrics unavailable anywhere else. Most Japanese designers have boutiques in the department stores and elsewhere; some feature lines of clothing more affordable than you may expect, both high fashion items and simple, well-made sportswear. And don't overlook traditional Japanese clothing. A silk or cotton kimono, either antique or modern, makes a stylish gift — perhaps for yourself!

Items

Could you please show me some belts.	ベルトを，見せてください。 *beh-ROO-toh oh, MEE-seh-teh koo-dah-sah-ee*
blouses	ブラウス *boo-RAH-oo-soo*
bras	ブラジャー *boo-RAH-jah̄*
dresses	ドレス *DOH-reh-soo*
evening gowns	イブニング・ドレス *ee-BOO-neen-goo doh-reh-soo*
gloves	手袋 *teh-BOO-koo-roh*
handkerchiefs	ハンカチ *HAHN-kah-chee*
hats	帽子 *BOH-shee*
jackets	上着／ジャケット *oo-WAH-gee/ JAH-keht-toh*

jeans	ブルー・ジーン／ジーンズ boo-ROO jeen／JEEN-zoo
overcoats	オーバー OH-bah
pants	スラックス soo-RAHK-ksoo
pantyhose	パンティー・ストッキング pahn-tee STOHK-keen-goo
raincoats	レイン・コート reh-EEN-koh-toh
robes	化粧着 keh-SHOH gee
scarves	スカーフ SKAH-foo
shirts	ワイシャツ wah-EE-shah-tsoo
shorts (briefs)	ブリーフ boo-REE-foo
skirts	スカート SKAH-toh
slips	スリップ SREEP-poo
slippers	スリッパ SREEP-pah
socks	くつ下／ソックス koo-TSOO-shtah／SOHK-koo-soo
stockings	ストッキング STOHK-keen-goo
suits	スーツ SOO-tsoo
sweaters	セーター SEH-tah
cardigans	カーディガン KAH-dee-gahn
swim suits	水着 mee-ZOO-gee
tee shirts	ティー・シャツ TEE shah-tsoo
ties	ネクタイ NEHK-tah-ee
undershirts	アンダー・シャツ／肌着 AHN-dah shah-tsoo／hah-DAH gee
underwear	下着 SHTAH-gee
wallets	さいふ sah-EE-foo
warmup suits	トレーニング・ウェア toh-REH-neen-goo weh-ah
Is there a special sale today?	今日は，特売がありますか。 KYOH wah, toh-KOO-bah-ee gah ah-ree-mahs KAH

I'd like the ___ with long/ short sleeves.	長／半そでの___が，欲しいのですが。 *nah-GAH/ HAHN soh-deh noh ___ gah, hoh-SHEE noh dehs gah*
Do you have anything <u>else</u>?	何か，ほかのがありますか。 *NAH-nee kah, hoh-KAH noh gah ah-ree-mahs KAH*
larger	もっと大きい *moht-toh OH-kee*
smaller	もっと小さい *moht-toh CHEE-sah-ee*
cheaper	もっと安い *moht-toh yah-SOO-ee*
of better quality	もっと上等な *moht-toh JOH-toh nah*
longer	もっと長い *moht-toh nah-GAH-ee*
shorter	もっと短い *moht-toh mee-JEE-kah-ee*
I'd prefer a different <u>color</u>.	ほかの色のがいいのですが。 *hoh-KAH noh ee-roh noh gah ee noh dehs gah*
style	スタイル *STAH-ee-roo*
I want something in <u>black</u>.	何か，黒いのがありますか。 *nah-nee kah, koo-ROH-ee noh gah ah-REE-mahs KAH*
blue	青い *ah-OH-ee*
brown	茶色い *chah-EE-roh-ee*
gray	グレー *goo-REH*
green	グリーン *goo-REEN*
pink	ピンク *PEEN-koo*
purple	紫色 *moo-RAH-sah-kee ee-roh*
red	赤い *ah-KAH-ee*
white	白い *shee-ROH-ee*
yellow	黄色い *KEE-roh-ee*
I'd like a <u>solid color</u>.	無地のをください。 *MOO-jee noh oh koo-dah-sah-ee*
a print	プリント *poo-REEN-toh*

stripes	しま模様 *shee-MAH moh-yoh*
a plaid	格子じま *KOH-shee jee-mah*
checks	チェック／市松模様 *CHEHK-koo/ ee-CHEE-mah-tsoo moh-yoh*

I'd like a darker color.　もう少し，地味なのがありますか。
MOH skoh-shee, jee-MEE nah-noh gah ah-ree-mahs KAH

Do you have anything to match this?　これに合うものがありますか。 *koh-REH nee AH-oo moh-noh gah, ah-ree-mahs KAH*

Do you have something in <u>cotton</u>?　何か，<u>木綿</u>のものがありますか。 *nah-nee kah, <u>moh-MEHN</u> noh moh-noh gah ah-ree-mahs KAH*

wool	ウール *OO-roo*
silk	絹／シルク *KEE-noo/ SHEE-roo-koo*
linen	麻／リンネル *ah-SAH/ REEN-neh-roo*
polyester	ポリエステル *poh-REE-ehs-teh-roo*
leather	皮 *kah-WAH*
vinyl	ビニール *bee-NEE-roo*
nylon	ナイロン *NAH-ee-rohn*

Sizes

You should try on Japanese clothing before you buy it. Although you can find a good fit in most items, some may be short-waisted for Westerners, and some sleeves may also be short. For women, dress sizes run in odd numbers 7, 9, 13, and so forth, and are not too different from American sizes. Men's suit sizes are roughly the centimeter equivalent of American suit sizes (multiplying the inches by 2.5 instead of the usual 2.54 centimeters).

MEN

Suits, Coats

American	36	38	40	42	44	46
British	36	38	40	42	44	46
Continental	46	48	50	52	54	56
Japanese	90	95	100	105	110	115

Shirts

American	14 14½	15 15½	16 16½	17 17½
British	14 14½	15 15½	16 16½	17 17½
Continental	36 37	38 39	40 41	42 43
Japanese	36 37	38 39	40 41	42 43

WOMEN

Dresses, Blouses, Sportswear, Lingerie

American	6	8	10	12	14	16
British	8	10	12	14	16	18
Continental	34	36	38	40	42	44
Japanese	5/7	7/9	9/11	11/13	13/15	15/17
	S	S	M	ML	LL	LL

Pantyhose, Tights

American	A	B	C/D	plus E	plus F
British	small	medium	large	extra large	extra large
Continental	1	2	3	4	5
Japanese	S	M	L	BL	BLL

Please take my measurements.	私のサイズを，計ってください。 *wah-TAHK-shee noh sah-ee-zoo oh hah-KAHT-teh koo-dah-sah-ee*
I don't know the Japanese sizes.	日本のサイズを，知りません。 *nee-HOHN noh sah-ee-zoo oh, shee-REE-mah-sehn*
My size is <u>small</u>.	私のサイズは，<u>小</u>です。 *wah-TAHK-shee noh sah-ee-zoo wah, <u>SHOH</u> dehs*

medium	中 *CHOO*
large	大 *DAH-ee*
May I try it on?	試着してもいいですか。 *shee-CHAH-koo shee-teh-moh EE dehs KAH*
Where's the dressing room?	試着室はどこですか。 *shee-CHAH-koo shee-tsoo wah DOH-koh dehs KAH*
Do you have a mirror?	鏡がありますか。 *kah-GAH-mee gah ah-ree-mahs KAH*
It's too <u>long</u>.	<u>長</u>すぎます。 *nah-GAH soo-gee mahs*
short	短か *mee-JEE-kah*
tight	きつ *kee-TSOO*
loose	ゆる *yoo-ROO*
Can you alter it?	直してもらえますか。 *nah-OH-shteh moh-rah-eh mahs KAH*
The zipper doesn't work.	チャックが、こわれています。 *CHAHK-koo gah, koh-WAH-reh-teh ee-mahs*
There's a button missing.	ボタンが、なくなっています。 *boh-TAHN gah, nah-KOO naht-teh ee-mahs*
It doesn't fit me.	これは、合いません。 *koh-reh wah, ah-EE-mah-sehn*
It fits very well.	これは、ぴったりです。 *koh-reh wah, peet-TAH-ree dehs*
I'll take it.	これを、ください。 *koh-REH oh, koo-dah-sah-ee*

Shoes

It is not easy to find Japanese shoes that fit Western feet. There is one standard width, EE, and large sizes are hard to find; this is true for both men's and women's shoes. Size charts tend to be inconsistent; it's best to let the salesperson measure your feet.

I'd like to see a pair of <u>shoes</u>.	<u>くつ</u>を、見たいのですが。 *koo-TSOO oh, mee-TAH-ee noh dehs gah*

boots	ブーツ *BOO-tsoo*
casual shoes	普段ばきのくつ *foo-DAHN bah-kee noh koo-tsoo*
dressy shoes	改まったときのくつ *ah-RAH-tah-maht-tah toh-kee noh koo-tsoo*
high-heeled shoes	ハイヒール *hah-EE hee-roo*
low-heeled shoes	ローヒール *ROH hee-roo*
running shoes	ランニング・シューズ *RAHN-neen-goo shoo-zoo*
sandals	サンダル *SAHN-dah-roo*
sneakers	運動ぐつ／スニーカー *OON-doh goo-tsoo／soo-NEE-kah*
tennis shoes	テニス・シューズ *teh-NEE-soo shoo-zoo*

There's a pair in the window that I like.	ショー・ウインドーに好きなのがあります。 *SHOH ween-doh nee, SKEE nah noh gah ah-ree-mahs*
Do they come in <u>another color</u>?	これには、<u>ほかの色</u>のもあります か。 *koh-REH nee-wah, hoh-KAH noh ee-roh noh-moh ah-ree-mahs KAH*
calf	子牛の皮 *koh-OO-shee noh kah-wah*
suede	スウェード *soo-WEH-doh*
patent leather	エナメル *eh-NAH-meh-roo*
Can you measure my size?	私のサイズを、計ってもらえます か。 *wah-TAHK-shee noh sah-ee-zoo oh, hah-KAHT-teh moh-rah-eh-mahs KAH*
These are too <u>narrow</u>.	これは、<u>せま</u>すぎます。 *koh-REH wah, <u>seh-MAH</u> soo-gee mahs*
wide	広 *hee-ROH*
loose	ゆる *yoo-ROO*
tight	きつ *kee-TSOO*

They fit fine.	これは，ぴったりです。 *koh-REH wah, peet-TAH-ree dehs*
I'll take them.	これを，ください *koh-reh oh, koo-DAH-sah-ee*
Do you have shoelaces here?	くつひもは，売っていますか。 *koo-TSOO hee-moh wah, oot-teh ee-mahs KAH*

ELECTRICAL APPLIANCES

For a look at the latest in electrical appliances and electronic equipment, visit Tokyo's Akihabara wholesale-retail district. It's the biggest discount center in Japan. While fixed prices are standard almost everywhere else, in Akihabara shops offer large discounts, and bargaining is commonplace, even expected. Save the bargaining phrases listed here for Akihabara or shops clearly marked discount — no others!

Where can I buy electrical applicances?	電気製品は，どこで買えますか。 *DEHN-kee seh-heen wah, DOH-koh deh kah-eh-mahs KAH*
How can I get to Akihabara?	秋葉原へは，どうやって行けますか。 *ah-KEE-hah-bah-rah eh wah, DOH-yaht-teh ee-keh-mahs KAH*
I want to buy a battery.	電池を買いたいのですが。 *DEHN-chee oh kah-ee-tah-ee noh dehs gah*
a blender	ミキサー *MEE-kee-sah*
a cassette recorder	カセットレコーダー *kah-SEHT-toh reh-koh-dah*
an electric razor	電気カミソリ *DEHN-kee kah-mee-soh-ree*
a hair dryer	ヘアー・ドライヤー *heh-AH doh-rah-ee-yah*
a microcassette recorder	マイクロ・カセットレコーダー *mah-EE-koo-roh kah-seht-toh reh-koh-dah*

a miniature TV	超小型テレビ *CHOH koh-gah-tah teh-reh-bee*
a minicalculator	ポケット型計算器／ポケット電卓 *poh-KEHT-toh gah-tah keh-sahn kee／poh-KEHT-toh dehn-tah-koo*
a personal stereo cassette recorder／player	ミニステレオカセットレコーダー／プレーヤー *mee-nee STEH-reh-oh kah-seht-toh reh-KOH-dah／poo-REH-yah*
a personal AM-FM stereo cassette player	ミニエーエムエフエムステレオカセットプレーヤー *mee-nee EH-eh-moo eh-FOO-eh-moo STEH-reh-oh kah-seht-toh poo-reh-yah*
a portable component stereo system	携帯コンポステレオ装置 *keh-tah-ee KOHM-poh steh-reh-oh soh-chee*
a portable radio	ポータブルラジオ *POH-tah-boo-roo rah-jee-oh*
a record player	レコードプレーヤー *reh-KOH-doh poo-reh-yah*
a tape recorder	テープレコーダー *TEH-poo reh-koh-dah*
a television set	テレビ *TEH-reh-bee*
a wrist TV	腕時計式テレビ *oo-DEH doh-keh-shkee teh-reh-bee*
What voltage does this take?	これには，何ボルトが必要ですか。 *koh-REH nee-wah, NAHN boh-roo-toh gah hee-tsoo-yoh dehs KAH*
Do you have one suitable for <u>American</u> voltage?	<u>アメリカ</u>のボルトに合うのがありますか。 *ah-MEH-ree-kah noh boh-roo-toh nee AH-oo noh gah ah-ree-mahs KAH*
South American	南米 *NAHN beh*
European	ヨーロッパ *YOH-rohp-pah*
Is there a <u>110</u> volt one?	<u>110</u>ボルトのが，ありますか。 *hyah-KOO joo BOH-roo-toh noh gah, ah-ree mahs KAH*
220	220 *nee-HYAH-koo nee joo*

100 volts	*hyah-KOO boh-roo-toh*
110 volts	*hyah-KOO joo boh-roo-toh*
220 volts	*nee-HYAH-koo nee joo boh-roo-toh*

This is out of order/broken.	これは，こわれています。	*koh-reh wah, koh-WAH-reh-teh ee-mahs*
How much is this?	これは，いくらですか。	*koh-reh wah, EE-koo-rah dehs KAH*
It's rather expensive.	ちょっと高いですねえ。	*CHOHT-toh tah-KAH-ee dehs neh*
It's more than I expected.	思ったより，高いですねえ。	*oh-MOHT-tah yoh-ree, tah-KAH-ee dehs neh*
That's not a final price, is it?	それは，最終の値段ではないでしょ。	*soh-reh wah, sah-EE-shoo noh neh-dahn deh-wah NAH-ee deh-shoh*
Can't you come down a little?	もうちょっと，安くなりませんか。	*MOH choht-toh, yah-SOO-koo nah-ree-mah-sehn KAH*
How about ____ yen?	____円では，どうですか。	*____ ehn deh-wah, DOH dehs KAH*

FOOD AND HOUSEHOLD ITEMS

See page 180 and the dictionaries (page 361) for more food words.

I'd like ____.	____，ください。	*____, koo-DAH-sah-ee*
a bag of sugar	砂糖を一袋	*sah-TOH oh hee-TOH hoo-koo-roh*
a bar of chocolate	チョコレートを一枚	*choh-KOH-reh-toh oh ee-CHEE mah-ee*

a bottle of ketchup	ケチャップを一本 *keh-CHAHP-poo oh EEP-pohn*
a bottle of juice	ジュースを一本 *JOOS oh EEP-pohn*
a box of candy	キャンデーを一箱 *KYAHN-dee oh hee-TOH hah-koh*
a box of cereal	シリアルを一箱 *SHEE-ree-ah-roo oh hee-TOH hah-koh*
a box of chocolate	チョコレートを一箱 *choh-KOH-reh-toh oh hee-TOH hah-koh*
a box of crackers	クラッカーを一箱 *koo-RAHK-kah oh hee-TOH hah-koh*
a box of eggs	たまごを一箱 *tah-MAH-goh oh hee-TOH hah-koh*
a box of raisins	干しぶどうを一箱 *hoh-SHEE boo-doh oh hee-TOH hah-koh*
a can of nuts	ナッツをひとかん *NAHT-tsoo oh hee-TOH kahn*
a can of tuna	まぐろのかんづめをひとかん *mah-GOO-roh noh KAHN-zoo-meh oh hee-TOH kahn*
a half kilo* of cheese	チーズを五百グラム *CHEE-zoo oh goh HYAH-koo GOO-rah-moo*
a half kilo of tanger-ines	みかんを五百グラム *MEE-kahn oh goh-HYAH-koo GOO-rah-moo*
a jar of instant coffee	インスタント・コーヒーをひとびん *EEN-stahn-toh koh-hee oh hee-TOH been*
a jar of jam	ジャムをひとびん *JAH-moo oh hee-TOH been*
a jar of mayonnaise	マヨネーズをひとびん *mah-YOH-neh-zoo oh hee-TOH been*
a jar of pepper	こしょうをひとびん *koh-SHOH oh hee-TOH been*
a jar of salt	塩をひとびん *shee-OH oh hee-TOH been*

a kilo of apples	りんごを一キロ *REEN-goh oh EEK-kee-roh*
a kilo of bananas	バナナを一キロ *BAH-nah-nah oh EEK-kee-roh*
a kilo of ham	ハムを一キロ *HAH-moo oh EEK-kee-roh*
a liter of milk	ミルクを一リットル *MEE-roo-koo oh ee-CHEE reet-toh-roo*
a loaf of bread	パンを一本 *PAHN oh EEP-pohn*
a package of candy	キャンデーを一袋 *KYAHN-dee oh hee-TOH hoo-koo-roh*

Note: Common measurements for purchasing food are a kilo or fractions thereof, and 100, 200, and 500 grams. See also the pages on numbers p. 15-17, and p. 358.

METRIC WEIGHTS AND MEASURES

Solid Measures
(approximate measurements only)

OUNCES	GRAMS	GRAMS	OUNCES
$\frac{1}{4}$	7	10	$\frac{1}{3}$
$\frac{1}{2}$	14	100	$3\frac{1}{2}$
$\frac{3}{4}$	21	300	$10\frac{1}{2}$
1	28	500	18
POUNDS	KILO-GRAMS	KILO-GRAMS	POUNDS
1	$\frac{1}{2}$	1	$2\frac{1}{4}$
5	$2\frac{1}{4}$	3	$6\frac{1}{2}$
10	$4\frac{1}{2}$	5	11
20	9	10	22
50	23	50	110
100	45	100	220

Liquid Measures
(approximate measurements only)

OUNCES	MILLI-LITERS	MILLI-LITERS	OUNCES
1	30	10	$\frac{1}{3}$
6	175	50	$1\frac{1}{2}$
12	350	100	$3\frac{1}{2}$
16	475	150	5
GAL-LONS	LITERS	LITERS	GAL-LONS
1	$3\frac{3}{4}$	1	$\frac{1}{4}$ (1 quart)
5	19	5	$1\frac{1}{3}$
10	38	10	$2\frac{1}{2}$

JEWELRY

I'd like to see a bracelet.	ブレスレットを見せてください。 _boo-REH-soo-reht-toh_ oh, _MEE-seh-teh koo-dah-sah-ee_
a brooch	ブローチ _boo-ROH-chee_
a chain	チェーン／鎖 _chehn_／ _koo-SAH-ree_
some cufflinks	カフス・ボタン _kah-FOO-soo boh-tahn_
some earrings	イヤリング _ee-YAH-reen-goo_
some earrings for pierced ears	ピアスのイヤリング _PEE-ah-soo noh ee-yah-reen-goo_
a necklace	ネックレス _NEHK-koo-reh-soo_
a pendant	ペンダント _PEHN-dahn-toh_
a pin	飾りピン _kah-ZAH-ree peen_
a ring	指輪 _yoo-BEE-wah_
a wristwatch	腕時計 _oo-DEH doh-keh_
Is this gold?	それは金ですか。 _soh-reh wah KEEN dehs KAH_
platinum	プラチナ _poo-RAH-chee-nah_
silver	銀 _GEEN_
stainless steel	ステンレス _STEHN-rehs_
How many karats is it?	それは，何金ですか。 _soh-reh wah, NAHN-keen dehs KAH_
Is it solid gold?	それは，純金ですか。 _soh-reh wah, JOON keen dehs KAH_
Is it gold plated?	それは，金メッキですか。 _soh-reh wah, KEEN mehk-kee dehs KAH_
What kind of stone is that?	その石は，何ですか。 _soh-NOH ee-shee wah, NAHN dehs KAH_
I want an amethyst.	アメジストが，欲しいのですが。 _ah-MEH-jees-toh gah, hoh-shee noh dehs gah_

an aquamarine	アクア・マリン *ah-KOO-ah mah-reen*
coral	さんご *SAHN-goh*
a diamond	ダイヤ *dah-EE-yah*
an emerald	エメラルド *eh-MEH-rah-roo-doh*
ivory	象牙 *ZOH-geh*
jade	ひすい *hee-SOO-ee*
onyx	しまめのう *shee-MAH meh-noh*
pearls	真珠／パール *SHEEN-joo/ PAH-roo*
cultured pearls	養殖真珠 *YOH-shoh-koo sheen-joo*
a ruby	ルビー *ROO-bee*
a sapphire	サファイア *sah-FAH-ee-ah*
a topaz	トパーズ *TOH-pah-zoo*
turquoise	トルコ石 *toh-ROO-koh ee-shee*
How much is it?	それは，いくらですか。 *soh-reh wah, EE-koo-rah dehs KAH*
Are these Japanese pearls?	これは，日本の真珠ですか。 *koh-REH wah, nee-HOHN noh sheen-joo dehs KAH*
Are they fresh water or sea water pearls?	これは淡水産の真珠ですか，海の真珠ですか。 *koh-reh wah TAHN-soo-ee sahn noh sheen-joo dehs KAH, OO-mee noh sheen-joo dehs KAH*
The luster is wonderful.	素晴しい光沢です。 *soo-BAH-rah-shee koh-tah-koo dehs*
I prefer a baroque/ round shape.	変った／丸い形の方が，好きなんですが。 *kah-WAHT-tah/ mah-ROO-ee kah-tah-chee noh hoh gah, SKEE nahn-dehs gah*
Can you tell me how to care for them?	手入れのしかたを，教えてください。 *teh-EE-reh noh shee-kah-tah oh, oh-SHEE-eh-teh koo-dah-sah-ee*

Clocks and Watches

I'd like a wristwatch.	腕時計が，欲しいのですが。 *oo-DEH doh-keh gah, hoh-SHEE noh dehs gah*
I want a digital watch.	デジタルの時計が，欲しい です。 *DEH-jee-tah-roo noh toh-keh gah, hoh-SHEE dehs*
quartz	クオーツ *koo-OH-tsoo*
I want a watch with a calendar function.	カレンダー付きの時計が欲しいで す。 *kah-REHN-dah tsoo-kee noh toh-keh gah, hoh-SHEE dehs*
an electronic alarm	アラーム／ベル *ah-RAH-moo/ beh-ROO*
a calculator	計算器 *KEH-sahn kee*
I'd like a clock.	時計が，欲しいのですが。 *toh-KEH gah, hoh-shee noh dehs gah*
I want an alarm clock.	目覚し時計が欲しいです。 *meh-ZAH-mah-shee doh-keh gah hoh-SHEE dehs*
a travel alarm	旅行用の目覚し *ryoh-KOH yoh noh meh-ZAH-mah-shee*

MUSIC, RECORDS, AND TAPES

Is there a record shop around here?	近くに，レコード屋がありますか。 *chee-KAH-koo nee, reh-KOH-doh yah gah ah-ree-mahs KAH*
Do you sell cartridges?	カートリッジを，売っていますか。 *KAH-toh-reej-jee oh, oot-TEH ee-mahs KAH*
cassettes	カセット *kah-SEHT-toh*
8-track cartridges	エイトカートリッジテープ *eh-EE-toh kah-toh-reej-jee teh-poo*
needles	レコード針 *reh-KOH-doh bah-ree*
records	レコード *reh-KOH-doh*
tapes	録音テープ *roh-KOO-ohn teh-poo*

Do you have <u>an LP</u> album?	エルピーのアルバムがありますか。 *eh-ROO pee noh ah-roo-bah-moo gah ah-ree-mahs KAH*
a 33 RPM	33回転盤 *SAHN-joo sahn kah-ee-tehn bahn*
a 45 RPM	45回転盤 *YOHN-joo goh kah-ee-tehn bahn*
Where is the <u>American music</u> section?	アメリカの音楽は，どこにあります か。*ah-MEH-ree-kah noh ohn-gah-koo wah, DOH-koh nee ah-ree-mahs KAH*
classical music	クラシック *koo-RAHS-sheek-koo*
jazz	ジャズ *JAH-zoo*
latest hits	最近のヒット曲 *sah-EE-keen noh heet-TOH kyoh-koo*
opera	オペラ *OH-peh-rah*
pop music	ポピュラー・ソング *poh-PYOO-rah sohn-goo*
Can I listen to this re- cord?	このレコードを，聞かせてもらえま すか。*koh-NOH reh-koh-doh oh, kee-KAH-seh-teh moh-rah-eh-mahs KAH*
Do you have any re- cords/ tapes by ____ ?	____のレコード／テープが，ありま すか。 *____ noh reh-koh-doh/ teh-poo gah, ah-ree-mahs KAH*

NEWSPAPERS AND MAGAZINES

Do you carry news- papers/ magazines in English?	英語の新聞／雑誌が，ありますか。 *EH-goh-noh sheen-boon/ zahs-shee gah, ah-ree-mahs KAH*
I'd like an English- language newspaper.	英語の新聞が，欲しいのですが。 *EH-goh noh sheen-boon gah hoh-SHEE noh dehs gah*
May I see what you have, please?	何があるか，見せてください。 *NAH-nee-gah ah-roo kah, MEE-seh-teh koo-dah-sah-ee*

Do you have <u>news maga-zines</u>?	ニュース関係の雑誌がありますか。 *NYOO-soo kahn-keh noh zahs-SHEE gah ah-ree-mahs KAH*
picture postcards	絵葉書 *eh HAH-gah-kee*
stamps	切手 *keet-TEH*
I'd like these.	これをください。 *koh-REH oh koo-dah-sah-ee*
How much are they?	いくらですか。 *EE-koo-rah dehs KAH*

PHOTOGRAPHIC SUPPLIES

Where is there a camera shop?	カメラ屋は，どこにありますか。 *kah-MEH-rah yah wah, DOH-koh nee ah-ree-mahs KAH*
Do you develop film here?	フィルムの現像をしますか。 *foo-EE-roo-moo noh gehn-zoh oh shee-mahs KAH*
How much does it cost to develop a roll?	フィルム一本の，現像焼付代はいくらですか。 *foo-ee-roo-moo EEP-pohn noh, gehn-zoh yah-kee-tsoo-keh dah-ee wah EE-koo-rah dehs KAH*
I have one roll.	フィルムが一本あります。 *foo-EE-roo-moo gah EEP-pohn ah-ree-mahs*
two rolls	二本 *NEE hohn*
I want one print of each.	焼き付けは，一枚ずつお願いします。 *yah-KEE-tsoo-keh wah, ee-CHEE mah-ee zoo-tsoo oh-neh-gah-ee shee-mahs*
I want an enlargement.	引き伸しをしてください。 *hee-KEE-noh-bah-shee oh shteh koo-dah-sah-ee*
I want a print with a glossy finish.	つやのある仕上げにしてください。 *tsoo-YAH noh ah-roo shee-AH-geh nee shteh koo-dah-sah-ee*
matte	つや消しの *tsoo-YAH keh-shee noh*
I want a roll of color film.	カラーフィルムを，一本ください。 *kah-RAH foo-ee-roo-moo oh, EEP-pohn koo-dah-sah-ee*
black and white	白黒の *shee-ROH koo-roh noh*
I want a roll of film for slides.	スライド用のフィルムを，一本ください。 *soo-RAH-ee-doh yoh noh foo-ee-roo-moo oh, EEP-pohn koo-dah-sah-ee*
I want a film pack, number ____.	＿＿番のフィルムを，一箱ください。 *____ bahn noh foo-ee-roo-moo oh, hee-TOH hah-koh koo-dah-sah-ee*

I'd like some film for this camera.	このカメラ用のフイルムをください。 *koh-noh kah-MEH-rah yoh noh foo-ee-roo-moo oh koo-dah-sah-ee*
I'd like 20 exposures.	二十枚どりのフイルムをください。 *nee-JOO mah-ee doh-ree noh foo-ee-roo-moo oh koo-dah-sah-ee*
36 exposures	三十六枚どりのフイルム *sahn-joo roh-KOO mah-ee doh-ree noh foo-ee-roo-moo*
indoor type	室内用のフイルム *shee-TSOO-nah-ee yoh noh foo-ee-roo-moo*
outdoor type	屋外用のフイルム *oh-KOO-gah-ee yoh noh foo-ee-roo-moo*
Do you have film with ASA/ DIN __?	エー・エス・エー／ディー・アイ・エヌが＿＿の，フイルムがありますか。 *EH eh-soo eh/ dee ah-ee eh-noo gah ___ noh, foo-EE-roo-moo gah ah-ree-mahs KAH*
I'd like to buy a camera.	カメラを買いたいのですが。 *KAH-meh-rah oh, kah-ee-TAH-ee noh dehs gah*
I'd like to buy an expensive/ inexpensive camera.	高級／高くないカメラを，買いたいのですが。 *KOH-kyoo/ tah-KAH-koo-nah-ee kah-meh-rah oh, kah-ee-TAH-ee noh dehs gah*
I want an exposure meter.	露出計が欲しいのですが。 *roh-SHOO-tsoo keh gah hoh-SHEE noh dehs gah*
some flash bulbs	フラッシュ・バルブ *foo-RAHS-shoo bah-roo-boo*
a filter	フィルター *fee-roo-tah*
a lens	レンズ *rehn-zoo*
a lens cap	レンズ・キャップ *REHN-zoo kyahp-poo*
a lens cleaner	レンズ・クリーナー *REHN-zoo koo-ree-nah*
a telescopic lens	望遠レンズ *BOH-ehn rehn-zoo*

a tripod	三脚 $\overline{SAHN}$-kyah-koo
a wide angle lens	広角レンズ $\overline{KOH}$-kah-koo rehn-zoo
a zoom lens	ズーム・レンズ $\overline{ZOO}$-moo rehn-zoo

GIFT SHOPS: JAPANESE

Allow yourself time to browse in Japanese-style gift shops.
You're sure to see something you like. Japanese shopkeepers will
wrap purchases beautifully, whether they're intended as gifts or
not!

I'd like a nice gift.	いいおみやげを買いたいです。 $\overline{EE}$ oh-mee-yah-geh oh, kah-EE-tah-ee dehs
a small gift	小さなおみやげ $\overline{CHEE}$-sah-nah oh-mee-yah-geh
a souvenir	おみやげ／記念の品 oh-MEE-yah-geh/ kee-NEHN noh shee-nah
It's for ___.	___に，あげます。 ___ nee, ah-geh-mahs
I don't want to spend more than ___ yen.	___円以下のものが，欲しいのです が。___ehn EE-kah noh moh-noh gah, hoh-SHEE noh dehs gah
Could you suggest something?	何がいいでしょうか。 NAH-nee gah ee deh-shoh kah
Could you show me your selection of bamboo baskets?	竹かごを見せてください。 tah-KEH kah-goh oh, MEE-seh-teh koo-dah-sah-ee
blown glass	口吹きガラス koo-CHEE-boo-kee gah-rah-soo
carved objects	彫刻品 $\overline{CHOH}$-koh-koo heen
ceramics	陶磁器 $\overline{TOH}$-jee-kee
chopsticks	はし $\overline{HAH}$-shee
cloisonné	七宝焼 sheep-$\overline{POH}$ yah-kee
fabric	布／生地 noo-$\overline{NOH}$/ $\overline{KEE}$-jee
fans	扇／扇子 $\overline{OH}$-gee/ sehn-soo

Japanese chests of drawers	たんす *TAHN-soo*
Japanese dolls	日本人形 *nee-HOHN neen-gyoh*
Japanese folk toys	民芸玩具 *MEEN-geh gahn-goo*
Japanese games	日本伝統のゲーム *nee-HOHN dehn-toh noh geh-moo*
Japanese swords	日本刀 *nee-HOHN toh*
kimonos	着物 *kee-MOH-noh*
kites	たこ *TAH-koh*
lacquerware	塗り物／漆器 *noo-REE moh-noh/ sheek-KEE*
lanterns	ちょうちん *CHOH-cheen*
masks	お面 *oh-MEHN*
origami paper	折り紙 *oh-REE-gah-mee*
papier–mâché	張り子細工 *hah-REE-koh zah-ee-koo*
porcelain	磁器 *JEE-kee*
sake bottles	とっくり *tohk-KOO-ree*
sake cups	盃 *sah-KAH-zoo-kee*
scrolls	掛け軸 *kah-KEH jee-koo*
tea bowls	茶道のお茶碗 *SAH-doh noh oh-CHAH-wahn*
tea cups	湯飲み茶碗 *yoo-NOH-mee jah-wahn*
tea pots	急須／土びん *KYOO-soo/ doh-BEEN*
woodblock prints	木版画 *moh-KOO hahn-gah*
Is this handmade?	それは，手製ですか。 *soh-REH wah, teh-SEH dehs KAH*
Where in Japan is it from?	どの地方の産ですか。 *DOH-noh chee-HOH noh sahn dehs KAH*

STATIONERY ITEMS

I want to buy <u>a ballpoint pen</u>.	ボールペンをください。 *<u>BOH-roo</u> pehn oh koo-dah-sah-ee*
a fountain pen	万年筆 *MAHN-nehn hee-tsoo*
a deck of cards	トランプ *toh-RAHM-poo*
some envelopes	封筒 *FOO-toh*
an eraser	消ゴム *keh-SHEE-goh-moo*
some glue	接着剤／のり *seht-CHAH-koo zah-ee／ noh-REE*
a notebook	ノート *NOH-toh*
some pencils	鉛筆 *EHN-pee-tsoo*
a pencil sharpener	鉛筆削り *EHN-pee-tsoo kch-zoo-ree*
some rubber bands	ゴムバンド *goh-MOO bahn-doh*
a ruler	定規 *JOH-gee*
some Scotch tape	セロテープ *seh-ROH teh-poo*
some string	ひも *hee-MOH*
some typing paper	タイプ用紙 *tah-EE-poo yoh-shee*
some wrapping paper	包装用紙 *HOH-soh yoh-shee*
a writing pad	筆記用紙 *heek-KEE yoh-shee*
some writing paper	便せん *BEEN-sehn*

TOBACCO

A pack of cigarettes, please.	たばこを，一箱ください。 *tah-BAH-koh oh, hee-TOH hah-koh koo-dah-sah-ee*
I'd like <u>filtered</u> cigarettes.	フィルター付きのたばこをください。 *<u>fee-ROO-tah tsoo-kee noh</u> tah-bah-koh oh koo-dah-sah-ee*

unfiltered	フィルターの付いていない *fee-ROO-tah noh tsoo-ee-teh ee-nah-ee*
menthol	はっか入りの *hahk-KAH ee-ree noh*
king size	キング・サイズの *KEEN-goo sah-ee-zoo noh*
mild	マイルドな *MAH-ee-roo-doh nah*
low tar	ニコチンが少ない *nee-KOH-cheen gah soo-koo-nah-ee*
Are these cigarettes strong/ mild?	そのたばこは，強い／軽いですか。*soh-NOH tah-bah-koh wah, tsoo-YOH-ee/ kah-ROO-ee dehs KAH*
Do you have American cigarettes?	アメリカのたばこが，ありますか。*ah-MEH-ree-kah noh tah-bah-koh gah, ah-ree-mahs KAH*
What brands?	どんな種類がありますか。*DOHN-nah shoo-roo-ee gah ah-ree-mahs KAH*

Please give me some matches too.	マッチもください。 *MAHT-chee moh koo-dah-sah-ee*
Do you sell <u>chewing tobacco</u>?	かみたばこは，売っていますか。 <u>*kah-MEE tah-bah-koh*</u> *wah, oot-TEH ee-mahs KAH*
cigarette holders	シガレット・ホールダー *shee-GAH-reht-toh hoh-roo-dah*
cigars	葉巻 *hah-MAH-kee*
flints	ライターの石 *RAH-ee-tah noh ee-shee*
lighter fluid/ gas	ライターの油／ガス *RAH-ee-tah noh ah-BOO-rah/ gah-soo*
lighters	ライター *RAH-ee-tah*
pipes	パイプ *PAH-ee-poo*
pipe tobacco	きざみたばこ *kee-ZAH-mee tah-bah-koh*
snuff	かぎたばこ *kah-GEE tah-bah-koh*

Smoking

Would you like a cigarette?	たばこは，いかがですか。 *tah-BAH-koh wah, ee-KAH-gah dehs KAH*
May I trouble you for a <u>cigarette</u>?	たばこを<u>一本</u>，お願いできますか。 *tah-BAH-koh oh <u>eep-pohn</u>, oh-neh-gah-ee deh-kee-mahs KAH*
light	たばこの火を *tah-BAH-koh noh hee oh*
No thanks, I don't smoke.	けっこうです。たばこはすいません。 *KEHK-koh dehs. tah-BAH-koh wah soo-ee-mah-sehn.*
I've given it up.	たばこは，やめました。 *tah-BAH-koh wah, yah-meh-mah-shtah*
Do you mind if I smoke?	たばこをすっても，かまいませんか。 *tah-BAH-koh oh soot-teh-moh, kah-MAH-ee-mah-sehn KAH*

I don't mind if you smoke.	どうぞ，おすいください。 *DOH-zoh, oh-soo-ee koo-dah-sah-ee*
Would you mind putting out the cigarette?	たばこを，消していただけますか。 *tah-BAH-koh oh, keh-SHEE-teh ee-tah-dah-keh-mahs KAH*

TOILETRIES

Is there a store that carries American/ European toiletries?	アメリカ／ヨーロッパの化粧品類を売っている，店がありますか。 *ah-MEH-ree-kah/ YOH-rohp-pah noh keh-SHOH-heen-roo-ee oh oot-teh-ee-roo, mee-SEH gah ah-ree-mahs KAH*
Do you have <u>after-shave lotion</u>?	アフター・シェーブローションが，ありますか。 *ahf-tah SHEH-boo roh-shohn gah, ah-ree-mahs KAH*
bobby pins	ヘアー・ピン *heh-AH peen*
body lotion	ボディー・ローション *boh-DEE roh-shohn*
brushes	ブラシ *boo-RAH-shee*
cleansing cream	クレンジング・クリーム *koo-REHN-jeen-goo koo-ree-moo*
cologne	オーデコロン *OH-deh-koh-rohn*
combs	くし *koo-shee*
cream rinse	クリーム・リンス *koo-REE-moo reen-soo*
curlers	カーラー *KAH-rah*
deodorant	デオドラント *deh-OH-doh-rahn-toh*
emery boards	爪やすり *tsoo-MEH yah-soo-ree*
eye liner	アイ・ライナー *ah-EE rah-ee-nah*
eye pencil	アイ・ペンシル *ah-EE pehn-shee-roo*
eye shadow	アイ・シャドー *ah-EE shah-doh*

eyebrow pencil	まゆずみ *mah-YOO zoo-mee*
face powder	おしろい *oh-SHEE-roh-ee*
hair color	毛染め *keh ZOH-meh*
hair spray	ヘアー・スプレー *heh-AH spoo-reh*
hand lotion	ハンド・ローション *HAHN-doh roh-shohn*
lipstick	口紅 *koo-CHEE beh-nee*
mascara	マスカラ *mah-SOO-kah-rah*
mirrors	鏡 *kah-GAH-mee*
nail brushes	爪ブラシ *tsoo-MEH boo-rah-shee*
nail clippers	爪切り *tsoo-MEH kee-ree*
nail files	爪やすり *tsoo-MEH yah-soo-ree*
nail polish	マニキュア液／エナメル *mah-NEE-kyoo-ah eh-kee/ eh-NAH-meh-roo*
nail polish remover	マニキュア落し／除光液 *mah-NEE-kyoo-ah oh-toh-shee/ joh-KOH-eh-kee*
perfume	香水 *KOH-soo-ee*
razors	かみそり *kah-MEE-soh-ree*
razor blades	かみそりの刃 *kah-MEE-soh-ree noh hah*
rouge, blusher	ほおべに *hoh-OH beh-nee*
safety pins	安全ピン *ahn-zehn peen*
(cuticle) scissors	（あま皮用の）はさみ *(ah-MAH-kah-wah yoh noh) hah-SAH-mee*
setting lotion	セット・ローション *seht-TOH roh-shohn*
shampoo	シャンプー *SHAHN-poo*
shaving lotion	シェービング・ローション *SHEH-been-goo roh-shohn*
soap	石けん *sehk-KEHN*

sponges	スポンジ *soo-POHN-gee*
sunscreen	日焼け止め *hee-YAH-keh doh-meh*
suntan lotion	サンタン・ローション *SAHN-tahn roh-shohn*
tissues	ちり紙／ティッシュー *chee-REE gah-mee／ TEES-shoo*
toothbrushes	歯ブラシ *hah-BOO-rah-shee*
toothpaste	練歯みがき *neh-REE hah-mee-gah-kee*
towels	タオル *TAH-oh-roo*
tweezers	毛抜き *keh-NOO-kee*

PERSONAL CARE AND SERVICES

If your hotel doesn't offer these services, ask the desk clerk to recommend someone nearby.

AT THE BARBER

Don't be surprised if you get a shave along with your haircut, even if you haven't requested it. In many Japanese barber shops, you get both for the price of the haircut. Although tipping for services is not common practice, it is expected at some hair salons in large tourist hotels. If so, you'll see a sign; 10% would be appropriate.

Does this hotel have a barber shop?	このホテルには，床屋があります か。 *koh-NOH hoh-teh-roo nee-wah, toh-KOH-yah gah ah-ree-mahs KAH*
Do you know where a good barber shop is?	上手な床屋がどこにあるか，知って いますか。 *JOH-zoo nah toh-koh-yah gah DOH-koh nee ah-roo kah, sheet-TEH-ee-mahs KAH*
Do I have to wait long?	だいぶ，待たなければなりません か。 *dah-ee-boo, mah-TAH-nah-keh-reh-bah nah-ree-mah-sehn KAH*
How much does a haircut cost there?	そこでの散髪は，いくらしますか。 *soh-KOH deh-noh sahn-pah-tsoo wah, EE-koo-rah shee-mahs KAH*
Whose turn is it?	誰の番ですか。 *DAH-reh noh bahn dehs KAH*
I don't have much time.	あまり，時間がありません。 *ah-mah-ree, jee-KAHN gah ah-ree-mah-sehn*
I want a haircut.	散髪してください。 *SAHN-pah-tsoo shteh koo-dah-sah-ee*

I want a shave.	ひげをそってください。 hee-GEH oh soht-teh koo-dah-sah-ee
Don't cut it too short, please.	あまり，短く刈らないでください。 ah-MAH-ree, mee-jee-kah-koo kah-RAH-nah-ee deh koo-dah-sah-ee
Just a trim, please.	形を，整えるだけでいいです。 kah-TAH-chee oh, toh-TOH-noh-eh-roo dah-keh deh ee dehs
Short in back, long in front.	前は長め，うしろは短かめにしてください。 MAH-eh wah nah-gah-meh, oo-SHEE-roh wah mee-jee-kah-meh nee shteh koo-dah-sah-ee
Leave it long.	全体，長目のままでいいです。 ZEHN-tah-ee, nah-GAH-meh noh mah-mah deh ee dehs
I want it (very) short.	（かなり）短か目にしてください。 (KAH-nah-ree) mee-JEE-kah-meh nee shee-teh koo-dah-sah-ee
You can cut a little <u>in back</u>.	うしろを，ちょっと刈ってください。 oo-SHEE-roh oh, choht-toh kaht-teh koo-dah-sah-ee
in front	前 MAH-eh
off the top	てっぺん tehp-PEHN
on the sides	両側 RYOH gah-wah
I part my hair <u>on the left</u>.	分け目は，左側です。 wah-KEH-meh wah, hee-DAH-ree gah-wah dehs
on the right	右側 mee-GEE gah-wah
in the middle	真中 MAHN-nah-kah
I comb my hair straight back.	髪は，いつもまっすぐうしろへとかしています。 kah-MEE wah, ee-tsoo moh mahs-SOO-goo oo-shee-roh eh toh-kahsh-teh ee-mahs
Cut a little bit more here.	ここを，もうちょっと刈ってください。 koh-KOH oh, moh CHOHT-toh kaht-teh koo-dah-sah-ee
That's enough.	それで，十分です。 soh-REH deh, joo-boon dehs

It's fine that way.	それで，_結構です。 *soh-REH deh, kehk-koh dehs*
I don't want tonic.	ヘアー・トニックは，つけないでください。 *heh-AH toh-neek-koo wah, tsoo-KEH-nah-ee-deh koo-dah-sah-ee*
I don't want grease.	ヘアー・オイルは，使わないでください。 *heh-AH oh-ee-roo wah, tsoo-KAH-wah-nah-ee-deh koo-dah-sah-ee*
I don't want hair spray.	ヘアー・スプレーは，使わないでください。 *heh-AH spoo-reh wah, tsoo-KAH-wah-nah-ee-deh koo-dah-sah-ee*
Use the scissors only.	はさみだけで，刈ってください。 *hah-SAH-mee dah-keh deh, kaht-teh koo-dah-sah-ee*
Please trim my <u>beard</u>.	<u>あごひげ</u>を，刈り込んでください。 *ah-GOH hee-geh oh, kah-ree-kohn-deh koo-dah-sah-ee*
mustache	口ひげ *koo-CHEE hee-geh*
sideburns	もみあげ *moh-MEE-ah-geh*
Thank you very much.	どうも，ありがとうございました。 *DOH-moh, ah-REE-gah-toh goh-zah-ee-mah-shtah*
How much do I owe you?	いかほどですか。 *ee-KAH-hoh-doh dehs KAH*

AT THE BEAUTY PARLOR

Check under "Barber Shop", page 272, for tipping hints.

Is there a beauty parlor (hairdresser) <u>near</u> the hotel?	ホテルの<u>近くに</u>，美容院があります か。 *HOH-teh-roo noh chee-KAH-koo nee, bee-YOH een gah ah-ree-mahs KAH*
in	中に *NAH-kah nee*
Do you know where a good beauty parlor (hairdresser) is?	上手な美容院がどこにあるか，御存 知ですか。 *JOH-zoo nah bee-YOH een gah, DOH-koh nee ah-roo kah goh-ZOHN-jee dehs KAH*
What are the business hours?	何時から何時まで，やっています か。 *NAHN-jee kah-rah NAHN-jee mah-deh, yaht-teh ee-mahs KAH*
Are they used to foreigners' hair?	外人の髪の毛に，慣れていますか。 *gah-EE-jeen noh kah-mee noh keh nee, NAH-reh-teh ee-mahs KAH*
Is it an expensive place?	そこは，高いですか。 *soh-koh wah, tah-KAH-ee dehs KAH*
Can you give me a <u>color rinse</u>?	<u>カラー・リンスをして</u>ください。 *kah-RAH reen-soo oh shteh koo-dah-sah-ee*
facial massage	美顔術をして *bee-GAHN joo-tsoo oh shteh*
haircut	カットをして *KAHT-toh oh shteh*
manicure	マニキュアをして *mah-NEE-kyoo-ah oh shteh*
permanent	パーマをかけて *PAH-mah oh kah-keh-teh*
shampoo	シャンプーをして *SHAHN-poo oh shteh*
shampoo and blow dry	シャンプーのあと，ブロー・ドラ イして *SHAHN-poo noh ah-toh, boo-ROH doh-rah-ee shteh*

wash and set	シャンプーとセットをして *SHAHN-poo toh SEHT-toh oh shteh*
I'd like to see a color chart.	色の表を，見せてください。 *ee-ROH noh hyoh oh, MEE-seh-teh koo-dah-sah-ee*
I want <u>auburn</u>.	<u>とび色</u>を，お願いします。 <u>*toh-BEE ee-roh*</u> *oh, oh-neh-gah-ee shee-mahs*
blond	ブロンド *boo-ROHN-doh*
brunette	ブルネット *boo-ROO-neht-toh*
a darker color	もっと濃い色 *moht-toh KOH-ee ee-roh*
a lighter color	もっと薄い色 *moht-toh oo-SOO-ee ee-roh*
the same color	同じ色 *oh-NAH-jee ee-roh*
Don't apply any hair spray.	ヘアー・スプレーは，<u>使わないで</u>ください。 *heh-AH spoo-reh wah, tsoo-KAH-wah-nah-ee deh koo-dah-sah-ee*
Not too much hair spray.	ヘアー・スプレーは，あまりかけないでください。 *heh-AH spoo-reh wah, ah-mah-ree kah-KEH-nah-ee-deh koo-dah-sah-ee*
I want <u>bangs</u>.	<u>前髪をさげて</u>ください。 <u>*mah-EH gah-mee oh SAH-geh-teh*</u> *koo-dah-sah-ee*
a bun	シニヨン・スタイルにして *shee-NEE-yohn soo-tah-ee-roo nee shteh*
it curly	巻き毛／カーリーにして *mah-KEE geh／KAH-ree nee shteh*
it wavy	ウェーブをかけて *WEH-boo oh kah-keh-teh*
Is it done?	終りましたか。 *oh-WAH-ree-mahsh-tah KAH*
Thank you very much.	どうも，ありがとうございました。 *DOH-moh, ah-REE-gah-toh goh-zah-ee-mahsh-tah*
How much do I owe you?	おいくらですか。 *oh-EE-koo-rah dehs KAH*

LAUNDRY AND DRY CLEANING

Do you have laundry service in this hotel?	このホテルには，洗濯のサービスがありますか。 *koh-NOH hoh-teh-roo nee-wah, SEHN-tah-koo noh sah-bee-soo gah ah-ree-mahs KAH*
Do you have dry cleaning service in this hotel?	このホテルには，ドライ・クリーニングのサービスがありますか。 *koh-NOH hoh-teh-roo nee-wah, doh-RAH-ee koo-ree-neen-goo noh sah-bee-soo gah ah-ree-mahs KAH*
Where is the nearest laundry?	一番近い洗濯屋は，どこですか。 *ee-CHEE-bahn chee-kah-ee sehn-tah-koo yah wah, DOH-koh dehs KAH*
laundromat	コイン・ランドリー *koh-EEN rahn-doh-ree*
dry cleaner	ドライ・クリーニング屋 *doh-RAH-ee koo-ree-neen-goo yah*
I want this dry cleaned.	これを，ドライ・クリーニングしてください。 *koh-REH oh, doh-RAH-ee koo-ree-neen-goo shteh koo-dah-sah-ee*
I want this ironed/pressed.	これに，アイロンをかけてください。 *koh-REH nee, ah-EE-rohn oh kah-keh-teh koo-dah-sah-ee*
I want this mended.	これを，繕ってください。 *koh-REH oh, tsoo-KOO-roht-teh koo-dah-sah-ee*
I want this washed.	これを，洗濯してください。 *koh-REH oh, SEHN-tah-koo shteh koo-dah-sah-ee*
When will it be ready?	いつできますか。 *EE-tsoo deh-kee-mahs KAH*
I need it for tonight.	今晩必要なんですが。 *KOHN-bahn hee-tsoo-yoh nahn dehs gah*
tomorrow	あした *ah-SHTAH*
the day after tomorrow	あさって *ah-SAHT-teh*

Could you do it as soon as possible?	出来るだけ早く、やってもらえますか。 *deh-KEE-roo dah-keh hah-yah-koo, yaht-TEH moh-rah-eh-mahs KAH*
Can you get the stain out?	このしみを、抜いてもらえますか。 *koh-NOH shee-mee oh, noo-EE-teh moh-rah-eh-mahs KAH*
Can you sew this button on?	このボタンを、つけてもらえますか。 *koh-NOH boh-tahn oh, tsoo-KEH-teh moh-rah-eh-mahs KAH*
I want my shirts <u>well</u> starched.	ワイシャツには、のりを<u>よく</u>きかせてください。 *wah-EE-shah-tsoo nee wah, noh-ree oh <u>YOH-koo</u> kee-kah-seh-teh koo-dah-sah-ee*
lightly	軽く *kah-ROO-koo*
I don't want my shirts starched.	ワイシャツに、のりはいりません。 *wah-EE-shah-tsoo nee, noh-ree wah ee-REE-mah-sehn*
I want my shirts <u>boxed</u>.	ワイシャツは、<u>箱に入れて</u>ください。 *wah-EE-shah-tsoo wah, <u>hah-KOH nee ee-reh-teh</u> koo-dah-sah-ee*
folded	たたんで *tah-TAHN-deh*
on hangers	つるして *tsoo-ROO-shteh*
What time shall I come for them?	何時に、取りにくればいいですか。 *<u>NAHN</u>-jee nee, toh-ree-nee koo-reh-bah ee dehs KAH*

SHOE REPAIRS

The heel of my high-heeled shoes <u>came off</u>.	ハイヒールのかかとが、<u>とれてしまいました</u>。 *hah-EE-hee-roo noh kah-kah-toh gah, <u>TOH-reh-teh</u> shee-mah-ee-mah-shtah*
broke	折れて *OH-reh-teh*
Can you fix it while I wait?	待っている間に、なおしてもらえますか。 *MAHT-teh ee-roo ah-ee-dah nee, nah-OH-shteh moh-rah-eh-mahs KAH*

I want these shoes repaired.	このくつを，なおしてください。 *koh-NOH koo-tsoo oh, nah-OH-shteh koo-dah-sah-ee*
I need new <u>heels</u>.	新しい<u>かかと</u>に，かえてください。 *ah-TAH-rah-shee kah-kah-toh nee, kah- EH-teh koo-dah-sah-ee*
soles	くつ底 *koo-TSOO zoh-koh*
heels and soles	かかととくつ底 *kah-KAH-toh toh koo-TSOO zoh-koh*
Would you polish them, too?	くつも，みがいておいてもらえます か。 *koo-tsoo moh, mee-GAH-ee-teh oh- ee-teh moh-rah-eh-mahs KAH*
When will they be ready?	いつできますか。 *EE-tsoo deh-kee- mahs KAH*

WATCH REPAIRS

I need a battery for this watch.	この時計用の電池が，欲しいのです が。 *koh-noh toh-<u>KEH</u> yoh noh DEHN- chee gah, hoh-shee noh dehs gah*
Can you fix this watch/clock?	この時計を，直してもらえますか。 *koh-noh toh-<u>KEH</u> oh, nah-OH-shteh moh-rah-eh-mahs KAH*
Can you look at it?	どこが悪いか，みてもらえますか。 *DOH-koh gah wah-roo-ee kah, MEE- teh moh-rah-eh-mahs KAH*
Can you clean it?	そうじしてもらえますか。 *<u>SOH</u>-jee shteh moh-rah-eh-mahs KAH*
I dropped it.	おっことしてしまいました。 *ohk- KOH-toh-shteh shee-mah-ee-mah-shtah*
It doesn't run well.	調子が，よくないんです。 *CHOH- shee gah, YOH-koo-nah-een-dehs*
It's <u>slow</u>.	<u>遅れ</u>がちです。 *oh-KOO-reh gah-chee dehs*
fast	進み *soo-SOO-mee*

It's stopped.	動きません。 *oo-GOH-kee-mah-sehn*
I need <u>a crystal</u>.	ガラスぶたを、つけてください。 <u>*gah-RAH-soo boo-tah*</u> *oh, tsoo-KEH-teh koo-dah-sah-ee*
an hour hand	時針／短針 *jee SHEEN／ TAHN sheen*
a minute hand	分針／長針 *FOON sheen／ CHOH sheen*
a screw	ねじ *NEH-jee*
a second hand	秒針 *BYOH sheen*
a spring	ぜんまい／バネ *ZEHN-mah-ee／ BAH-neh*
When will it be ready?	いつできますか。 *EE-tsoo deh-kee-mahs KAH*
May I have a receipt?	領収書を、お願いします。 *RYOH-shoo shoh oh, oh-NEH-gah-ee shee-mahs*

CAMERA REPAIRS

There's something wrong with this camera.	カメラの調子が、悪いのですが。 *KAH-meh-rah noh choh-shee gah wah-ROO-ee noh dehs gah*
Can you fix it?	直してもらえますか。 *nah-OH-shteh moh-rah-eh-mahs KAH*
There's a problem with the <u>exposure counter</u>.	フイルムの駒数計が、おかしいのですが。 <u>*foo-EE-roo-moo noh koh-MAH-soo keh*</u> *gah, oh-KAH-shee noh dehs gah*
film winder	フイルムの巻き上げ *foo-EE-roo-moo noh mah-KEE-ah-geh*
light meter	露出計 *roh-SHOO-tsoo keh*
range finder	距離計 *kyoh-REE keh*
shutter	シャッター *SHAHT-tah*

How much will it cost to fix it?	修理には，いくらかかりますか。 *SHOO-ree nee-wah, EE-koo-rah kah-kah-ree-mahs KAH*
I'd like it as soon as possible.	できるだけ早く，直してもらいたいのですが。 *deh-KEE-roo dah-keh hah-yah-koo, nah-OH-shteh moh-rah-ee-tah-ee noh dehs gah*
When will it be ready?	いつできますか。 *EE-tsoo deh-kee-mahs KAH*

HEALTH AND MEDICAL CARE

THE PHARMACY

Where is the nearest pharmacy?	一番近い薬屋は，どこにあります か。 *ee-CHEE-bahn chee-kah-ee koo-SOO-ree yah wah, DOH-koh nee ah-ree-mahs KAH*
Is there an all-night pharmacy?	終夜営業の薬屋がありますか。 *SHOO-yah eh-gyoh noh koo-SOO-ree yah gah, ah-ree-mahs KAH*
Where is the all-night pharmacy?	終夜営業の薬屋は，どこにあります か。 *SHOO-yah eh-gyoh noh koo-SOO-ree yah wah, DOH-koh nee ah-ree-mahs KAH*
What time does the pharmacy open?	その薬屋は，何時に，あきますか。 *soh-noh koo-SOO-ree yah wah, NAHN-jee nee ah-kee-mahs KAH*
close	しまります *shee-mah-ree-mahs*
Is there a pharmacy that carries American/European products?	アメリカ／ヨーロッパ製品を売って いる，薬屋がありますか。 *ah-MEH-ree-kah/ YOH-rohp-pah seh-heen oh oot-teh ee-roo koo-SOO-ree-yah gah ah-ree-mahs KAH*
I need something for a burn.	やけどの薬をください。 *yah-KEH-doh noh koo-soo-ree oh koo-dah-sah-ee*
a cold	風邪 *kah-ZEH*
constipation	便秘 *BEHN-pee*
a cough	せき *seh-KEE*
diarrhea	下痢 *geh-REE*
a fever	熱 *neh-TSOO*
hay fever	花粉症 *kah-FOON shoh*

a headache	頭痛 *zoo-TSOO*
insomnia	不眠症 *foo-MEEN shoh*
nausea	吐き気 *hah-KEE-keh*
a sunburn	日焼け *hee-YAH-keh*
a toothache	歯痛／歯いた *shee-TSOO／ hah-EE-tah*
an upset stomach	胃がおかしいとき *ee gah oh-KAH-shee toh-kee*

Is a prescription needed for the medicine?	その薬には，処方せんが必要です か。 *soh-NOH koo-soo-ree nee-wah, shoh-HOH sehn gah hee-tsoo-yoh dehs KAH*
Can you fill this pre-scription for me now?	この処方せんの薬を，今もらえます か。 *koh-noh shoh-HOH-sehn noh koo-soo-ree oh, EE-mah moh-rah-eh-mahs KAH*
It's an emergency.	急病です。 *KYOO byoh dehs*
Can I wait for it?	薬は，待っていたらもらえますか。 *koo-soo-ree wah, MAHT-teh ee-tah-rah moh-rah-eh-mahs KAH*
How long will it take?	薬をもらうのに，どの位時間がかか りますか。 *koo-SOO-ree oh moh-rah-oo noh nee, doh-NOH koo-rah-ee jee-kahn gah kah-kah-ree-mahs KAH*
When can I come for it?	いつ取りに来ましょうか。 *EE-tsoo toh-ree nee kee-mah-shoh KAH*
Do you have contact lens care products for <u>soft</u> <u>lenses</u>?	ソフト・コンタクト・レンズの，手 入れ用の品がありますか。 *soh-FOO-toh kohn-tahk-toh rehn-zoo noh, teh-EE-reh yoh noh shee-nah gah ah-ree-mahs KAH*
hard lenses	ハード・コンタクト・レンズ *hah-doh KOHN-tahk-toh rehn-zoo*
May I see what you have?	何があるか，見せてもらえますか。 *NAH-nee gah ah-roo kah, MEE-seh-teh moh-rah-eh-mahs KAH*

I need a carrying case for <u>hard lenses</u>.	ハード・コンタクト・レンズの，携帯用ケースがいります。 *hah-doh KOHN-tahk-toh rehn-zoo noh, KEH-tah-ee yoh kehs gah ee-ree-mahs*
soft lenses	ソフト・コンタクト・レンズ *soh-FOO-toh kohn-tahk-toh rehn-zoo*
I would like <u>some adhesive tape</u>.	ばんそうこうを，ください。 *BAHN-soh-koh oh, koo-dah-sah-ee*
some alcohol	アルコール *ah-ROO-koh-roo*
an antacid	胃散 *ee-SAHN*
an antiseptic	消毒薬 *SHOH-doh-koo yah-koo*
some aspirin	アスピリン *ah-SOO-pee-reen*
an aspirin-free pain-killer	アスピリンを含まない鎮痛剤 *ah-SOO-pee-reen oh foo-koo-mah-nah-ee CHEEN-tsoo zah-ee*
some bandages	包帯 *HOH-tah-ee*
some bandaids	バンド・エイド *BAHN-doh eh-ee-doh*
some corn plasters	魚の目膏薬 *oo-OH noh meh koh-yah-koo*
some cotton	脱脂綿 *dahs-SHEE mehn*
some cough drops	せきどめドロップ *seh-KEE doh-meh doh-rohp-poo*
some cough syrup	せきどめシロップ *seh-KEE doh-meh shee-rohp-poo*
some (disposable) diapers	（使いすての）おしめ *(tsoo-KAH-ee soo-teh noh) oh-shee-meh*
some ear drops	耳薬 *mee-MEE goo-soo-ree*
some eye drops	目薬 *meh GOO-soo-ree*
a first aid kit	救急箱 *KYOO-kyoo bah-koh*
some gauze	ガーゼ *GAH-zeh*
some insect repellent	防虫剤 *BOH choo zah-ee*
some iodine	ヨード・チンキ *YOH-doh cheen-kee*

a laxative	下剤／通じ薬 *geh-ZAH-ee／ TSOO-jee yah-koo*
a razor	かみそり *kah-MEE-soh-ree*
some razor blades	かみそりの刃 *kah-MEE-soh-ree noh hah*
some sanitary napkins	生理ナプキン *SEH-ree nahp-keen*
some sleeping pills	睡眠薬 *soo-EE-meen yah-koo*
some suppositories	座薬 *zah YAH-koo*
some talcum powder	シッカロール *sheek-KAH-roh-roo*
some tampons	タンポン *TAHN-pohn*
a thermometer	体温計 *tah-EE-ohn keh*
some tissues	ちり紙／ティッシュー *chee-REE gah-mee／ TEES-shoo*
some toilet paper	トイレット・ペーパー *toh-EE-reht-toh peh-pah*
a toothbrush	歯ブラシ *hah BOO-rah-shee*
some toothpaste	練歯みがき *neh-REE hah-mee-gah-kee*
some tranquillizers	トランキライザー *toh-RAHN-kee-rah-ee-zah*
some vitamins	ビタミン剤 *bee-TAH-meen zah-ee*

ACCIDENTS AND EMERGENCIES

The telephone number for an ambulance in emergencies is 119 nationwide. A call to this number will secure an ambulance in 5 or 10 minutes, but the operator speaks Japanese <u>only</u>, and gets off the line quickly. For similar service with more time to make yourself understood, some additional numbers are: Tokyo: 212-2323; Kobe: 391-6931; Kyoto: 231-3511; Osaka: 531-0601. The first four phrases listed here will work on the telephone. For more information on securing medical help, see p. 287.

Hello. It's an emergency!	もしもし。緊急事態です。 *MOH-shee moh-shee. KEEN-kyoo jee-tah-ee dehs*
I'm hurt.	私は，けがをしてしまいました。 *wah-TAHK-shee wah keh-GAH oh shee-teh shee-mah-ee-mah-shtah*
My husband's	主人が *SHOO-jeen gah*
My wife's	家内が *KAH-nah-ee gah*
My child's	子供が *koh-DOH-moh gah*
Somebody's	誰か *DAH-reh-kah*
Can you send an ambulance immediately?	大至急，救急車をよこしてください。 *dah-EE-shee-kyoo KYOO-kyoo shah oh yoh-KOH-shteh koo-dah-sah-ee*
We're located at ___.	場所は，___ です。 *bah-SHOH wah ___ dehs*
Help!	助けて *tahs-KEH-teh*
Help me, somebody!	誰か，助けてください。 *DAH-reh kah, tahs-KEH-teh koo-dah-sah-ee*
Get a <u>doctor</u>, quick!	すぐ<u>医者</u>を，呼んでください。 *soo-goo ee-SHAH oh, yohn-deh koo-dah-sah-ee*
nurse	看護婦（夫） *KAHN-goh foo*
Call an ambulance!	救急車を，呼んでください。 *KYOO-kyoo shah oh, yohn-deh koo-dah-sah-ee*
I need first aid.	応急処置が，必要です。 *OH-kyoo shoh-chee gah, hee-tsoo-yoh dehs*
I've fallen.	ころんでしまいました。 *koh-REHN-deh shee-mah-ee-mah-shtah*
I was knocked down.	突き倒されました。 *tsoo-KEE tah-oh-sah-reh-mah-shtah*
I've had a heart attack.	心臓麻痺です。 *SHEEN-zoh mah-hee dehs*
I burned myself.	やけどしました。 *yah-KEH-doh shee-mah-shtah*
I cut myself.	切り傷です。 *kee-REE kee-zoo dehs*

I'm bleeding.	出血しています。 *shook-KEH-tsoo shteh ee-mahs*
I've lost a lot of blood.	ずい分，出血しました。 *ZOO-ee-boon, shook-KEH-tsoo shee-mah-shtah*
The <u>wrist</u> is sprained.	手首を，ねんざしました。 *TEH koo-bee oh, NEHN-zah shee-mah-shtah*
ankle	足首 *ah-SHEE koo-bee*
I can't bend my <u>elbow</u>.	ひじが，曲りません。 *hee-JEE gah, mah-GAH-ree-mah-sehn*
knee	ひざ *hee-ZAH*
I can't move my <u>arm</u>.	腕が，動かせません。 *oo-DEH gah, oo-GOH-kah-seh-mah-sehn*
leg	足 *ah-SHEE*
I think the bone is <u>broken</u>.	骨が折れたようです。 *hoh-NEH gah OH-reh-tah yoh dehs*
dislocated	脱臼した *dahk-KYOO shtah*
The leg is swollen.	足が，はれています。 *ah-SHEE gah, hah-REH-teh ee-mahs*

Finding a Doctor

At a large tourist hotel, the staff can usually help you find a doctor. If you're on your own, here are a few hospitals with English-speaking doctors and staff members:

TOKYO	St. Luke's International Hospital, 541-5151
	International Catholic Hospital, 951-1111
YOKO-HAMA	Bluff Hospital, 641-6961
KYOTO	Japan Baptist Hospital, 781-5194
OSAKA	Yodogawa Christian Hospital, 322-2250

Although many Japanese physicians and dentists speak good English, you can't count on finding them everywhere; it's best to be prepared with some Japanese phrases.

Do you know a doctor who speaks English?	英語を話す医者を，知っていますか。 *EH-goh oh hah-nah-soo ee-SHAH oh, sheet-TEH ee-mahs KAH*

Do you know an American doctor?	アメリカ人の医者を，知っていますか。 *ah-MEH-ree-kah-jeen noh ee-shah oh, sheet-TEH ee-mahs KAH*
Where is the <u>office</u>?	その医者の診療所／オフィスは，どこですか。 *soh-NOH ee-shah noh <u>SHEEN-rhoh</u> joh/ <u>OH-fee-soo</u> wah, DOH-koh dehs KAH*
hospital	病院 *BYOH-een*
What are the office hours?	診療時間は，何時から何時までですか。 *SHEEN-ryoh jee-kahn wah, NAHN-jee kah-rah NAHN-jee mah-deh dehs KAH*
Can I just walk in?	予約なしに，行けますか。 *yoh-YAH-koo nah-shee nee, ee-KEH-mahs KAH*
Do I need to make an appointment?	予約の必要が，ありますか。 *yoh-YAH-koo noh hee-tsoo-yoh gah, ah-REE-mahs KAH*
What's the telephone number of the <u>office</u>?	オフィスの電話番号は，何番ですか。 *<u>OH-fee-soo</u> noh dehn-wah bahn-goh wah, NAHN-bahn dehs KAH*
hospital	病院 *BYOH-een*
I want to see <u>an internist</u>.	内科の医者に，行きたいのですが。 *<u>nah-EE-kah noh ee-shah</u> nee, ee-kee-TAH-ee noh dehs gah*
an ear, nose, and throat specialist	耳鼻咽喉科の医者 *jee-bee-EEN koh kah noh ee-shah*
a dermatologist	皮膚科の医者 *hee-FOO-kah noh ee-shah*
a gynecologist	婦人科医 *foo-JEEN-kah ee*
an obstetrician	産科医 *SAHN-kah ee*
an ophthalmologist	眼科医 *GAHN-kah ee*
an orthopedic specialist	整形外科の医者 *SEH-keh geh-kah noh ee-shah*

WITH THE DOCTOR

This section is divided into two parts: **Telling the Doctor** and **What the Doctor Says**. You use the phrases under **Telling the Doctor** and hand the book to the doctor so he or she can point to the appropriate phrases under **What the Doctor Says**.

Please point to the phrase in the book.	この本の，適当な文を指さしてください。 *koh-NOH hohn noh, teh-KEE-toh nah boon oh yoo-BEE sah-shteh koo-dah-sah-ee*

Telling the Doctor

I don't feel well.	気分が，すぐれません。 *KEE-boon gah, soo-goo-reh-mah-sehn*
I feel sick.	気分が，悪いです。 *KEE-boon gah, wah-ROO-ee dehs*
I'm dizzy.	めまいがします。 *meh-MAH-ee gah shee-mahs*
I feel weak.	体に，力が入りません。 *kah-RAH-dah nee, chee-kah-rah gah hah-ee-ree-mah-sehn*
It hurts me here.	ここが，痛みます。 *koh-KOH gah, ee-tah-mee-mahs*
My whole body hurts.	体全体が，痛みます。 *kah-RAH-dah zehn-tah-ee gah, ee-tah-mee-mahs*
I feel faint.	気が，遠くなりそうです。 *kee gah, TOH-koo nah-ree-soh dehs*
I feel nauseated.	吐き気がします。 *hah-KEE-keh gah shee-mahs*
I feel a chill.	悪寒がします。 *oh-KAHN gah shee-mahs*
I've been vomiting	吐いています。 *HAH-ee-teh ee-mahs*
I'm pregnant.	妊娠中です。 *NEEN-sheen choo dehs*
I want to sit down for a while.	ちょっと，すわりたいのですが。 *CHOHT-toh, soo-WAH-ree-tah-ee noh dehs gah*

My temperature is normal (98.6°F, 37°C).	熱は，平熱です。	*neh-TSOO wah, heh-neh-tsoo dehs*
I feel all right now.	今は，大丈夫です。	*EE-mah wah, dah-EE-joh-boo dehs*
I feel better.	今は，よくなりました。	*ee-MAH wah, YOH-koo nah-ree-mah-shtah*
I feel worse.	気分が，前より悪くなっています。	*KEE-boon gah, mah-eh yoh-ree WAH-roo-koo naht-teh ee-mahs*
My <u>ankle</u> hurts.	足首が，痛いんですが。	*ah-SHEE koo-bee gah, ee-TAH-een-dehs gah*

arm	腕	*oo-DEH*
back	背中	*seh-NAH-kah*
chest	胸	*moo-NEH*
ear	耳	*mee-MEE*
elbow	ひじ	*hee-JEE*
eye	目	*MEH*
face	顔	*kah-OH*
finger	指	*yoo-BEE*
foot	足	*ah-SHEE*
hand	手	*TEH*
head	頭	*ah-TAH-mah*
heel	かかと	*kah-KAH-toh*
joint	関節	*KAHN-seh-tsoo*
knee	ひざ	*hee-ZAH*
leg	足	*ah-SHEE*
muscle	筋肉	*KEEN-nee-koo*
neck	首	*koo-BEE*
nose	鼻	*hah-NAH*
rib	ろっ骨	*rohk-KOH-tsoo*

shoulder	肩 *KAH-tah*
skin	肌 *HAH-dah*
spine	背骨 *seh BOH-noh*
stomach	胃 *ee*
thigh	太もも *foo-TOH moh-moh*
throat	のど *NOH-doh*
thumb	親指 *oh-YAH yoo-bee*
toe	足の指 *ah-SHEE noh yoo-bee*
tongue	舌 *SHTAH*
wrist	手首 *TEH koo-bee*
I have an abcess.	腫れ物ができました。 *hah-REH moh-noh gah deh-kee-mah-shtah*
I have a bee sting.	蜂にさされました。 *hah-CHEE nee, sah-sah-reh-mah-shtah*
I have a bruise.	打撲傷です。 *dah-BOH-koo shoh dehs*
I have a burn.	やけどしました。 *yah-KEH-doh shee-mah-shtah*
I have the chills.	悪感がします。 *oh-KAHN gah shee-mahs*
I have a cold.	風邪をひきました。 *kah-ZEH oh hee-KEE-mah-shtah*
a chest cold	せきの出る風邪 *seh-KEE noh deh-roo kah-zeh*
a head cold	鼻風邪 *hah-NAH kah-zeh*
I'm constipated.	便秘しています。 *BEHN-pee shteh ee-mahs*
I have cramps.	おなかが，痛んでいます。 *oh-NAH-kah gah, ee-TAHN-deh ee-mahs*
I have a cut.	切り傷です。 *kee-REE kee-zoo dehs*
I have diarrhea.	下痢をしています。 *geh-REE oh shteh ee-mahs*
I have a fever.	熱があります。 *neh-TSOO gah ah-ree-mahs*

I have a headache.	頭痛がします。	*zoo-TSOO gah shee-mahs*
I have indigestion.	消化不良です。	*SHOH-kah foo-ryoh dehs*
I have an infection.	化膿している所があります。	*kah-NOH shteh ee-roo toh-koh-roh gah ah-ree-mahs*
I have an insect bite.	虫にさされました。	*moo-SHEE nee sah-sah-reh-mah-shtah*
I have a lump.	しこりがあります。	*shee-KOH-ree gah ah-ree-mahs*
I have a sore throat.	のどが痛いです。	*NOH-doh gah, ee-TAH-ee dehs*
I have a stomach ache.	おなかが，痛いです。	*oh-NAH-kah gah, ee-TAH-ee-dehs*
I have a swelling.	はれている所があります。	*hah-REH-teh ee-roo toh-koh-roh gah ah-ree-mahs*
I have a wound.	けがをしました。	*keh-GAH oh shee-mah-shtah*
I think I have a <u>broken bone/ fracture</u>.	骨が折れたらしいです。	<u>*hoh-NEH gah oh-reh-tah* </u>*rah-shee dehs*
dysentery	赤痢	*SEH-kee-ree*
the flu	流感	*RYOO-kahn*
a stomach ulcer	胃潰瘍	*ee-KAH-ee-yoh*
I've had this pain since <u>this morning</u>.	けさから，痛みがあります。	<u>*KEH-sah* </u>*kah-rah, ee-TAH-mee gah ah-ree-mahs*
last night	きのうの晩	*kee-NOH noh bahn*
yesterday	きのう	*kee-NOH*
the day before yesterday	おととい	*oh-TOH-toh-ee*
last week	先週	*SEHN-shoo*
I'm having chest pain.	胸に，痛みがあります。	*moo-NEH nee, ee-tah-mee gah ah ree-mahs*

I had a heart attack __ years ago.	____年前，心臓麻痺の発作がありました。 ____ nehn mah-eh, SHEEN-zoh mah-hee noh hohs-SAH gah ah-ree-mah-shtah
I'm a diabetic.	私には，糖尿病があります。 wah-TAHK-shee nee-wah, TOH-nyoh byoh gah ah-ree-mahs
I'm taking this medicine.	今，この薬を使っています。 ee-mah, koh-NOH koo-soo-ree oh tsoo-KAHT-teh ee-mahs
insulin	インシュリン EEN-shoo-reen
I'm allergic to antibiotics.	抗生物質に過敏です。 KOH-seh boos-shee-tsoo nee kah-BEEN dehs
aspirin	アスピリン ah-SOO-pee-reen
penicillin	ペニシリン peh-NEE-shee-reen
There's a history of ____ in my family.	家族には，____の歴史があります。 KAH-zoh-koo nee-wah, ____ noh reh-kee-shee gah ah-ree-mahs
There's no history of ____ in my family.	家族には，____の歴史はありません。 KAH-zoh-koo nee-wah, ____ noh reh-kee-shee wah ah-ree-mah-sehn
Do you know what's wrong with me?	どこが，悪いですか。 DOH-koh gah, wah-roo-ee dehs KAH
Do I have ____?	____でしょうか。 ____ deh-shōh kah
Is it ____?	____でしょうか。 ____ deh-shōh kah

[See page 294, under what the doctor says, for a list of medical ailments.]

Is it serious?	重いですか。 oh-MOH-ee dehs KAH
Is it contagious?	うつる恐れがありますか。 oo-TSOO-roo oh-soh-reh gah ah-ree-mahs KAH
Do I have to stay in bed?	寝ていなければ，なりませんか。 neh-TEH ee-nah-keh-reh-bah, nah-ree-mah-sehn KAH
How long do I have to stay in bed?	どの位，寝ていなければなりませんか。 doh-NOH koo-rah-ee, neh-TEH-ee-nah-keh-reh-bah nah-ree-mah-sehn KAH

Do I have to go to the hospital?	入院しなければ，なりませんか。 *NYOO-een shee-nah-keh-reh-bah, nah-ree-mah-sehn KAH*
Are you going to give me a prescription?	処方せんがいりますか。 *shoh-HOH sehn gah ee-ree-mahs KAH*
What kind of medicine is it?	どんな種類の薬ですか。 *DOHN-nah shoo-roo-ee noh koo-soo-ree dehs KAH*
Will it make me sleepy?	それを飲むと眠くなりますか。 *soh-REH oh noh-moo toh, neh-MOO-koo nah-ree-mahs KAH*
How often must I take this medicine?	この薬は，一日何回飲むのですか。 *koh-NOH koo-soo-ree wah, ee-chee nee-chee NAHN-kah-ee noh-moo noh dehs KAH*
When can I continue my trip?	いつから，旅行を続けられますか。 *EE-tsoo-kah-rah, ryoh-koh oh tsoo-ZOO-keh-rah-reh-mahs KAH*
Thank you very much.	どうもありがとうございました。 *doh-moh, ah-REE-gah-toh goh-zah-ee-mah-shtah*
Where do I pay?	どこで払えば，よろしいですか。 *DOH-koh deh hah-rah-eh-bah, yoh-ROH-shee dehs KAH*

What the Doctor Says

Where were you before you came to Japan?	日本に来る前は，どこにいましたか。 *nee-HOHN nee koo-roo mah-eh wah, DOH-koh nee ee-mah-shtah KAH*
I'm going to take your temperature.	熱を計ります。 *neh-TSOO oh hah-kah-ree-mahs*
I'm going to take your blood pressure.	血圧を計ります。 *keh-TSOO ah-tsoo oh hah-kah-ree-mahs*
Open your mouth, please.	口をあけてください。 *koo-CHEE oh ah-keh-teh koo-dah-sah-ee*
Stick out your tongue, please.	舌を出してください。 *shee-TAH oh dah-shteh koo-dah-sah-ee*
Cough, please.	せきをしてください。 *seh-KEE oh shteh koo-dah-sah-ee*

Breathe deeply, please.	深呼吸をして／深く息を吸ってください。 *SHEEN koh-kyoo oh shteh/ foo-kah-koo EE-kee oh soot-teh koo-dah-sah-ee*
Roll up your sleeve, please.	そでを，まくってください。 *soh-DEH noh, mah-KOOT-teh koo-dah-sah-ee*
Take off your clothing to the waist, please.	上半身をぬいでください。 *JOH hahn-sheen oh NOO-ee-deh koo-dah-sah-ee*
Remove your trousers/ skirt and underwear, please.	ズボン／スカートと，下着を脱いでください。 *zoo-BOHN/ soo-KAH-toh toh, shee-TAH gee oh NOO-ee-deh koo-dah-sah-ee*
Lie down, please.	横になってください。 *yoh-KOH nee naht-teh koo-dah-sah-ee*
Does it hurt when I press here?	ここを押すと，痛みますか。 *koh-KOH oh oh-soo toh, ee-TAH-mee-mahs KAH*
Stand up, please.	立ってください。 *TAHT-teh koo-dah-sah-ee*
Get dressed, please.	服を着てください。 *foo-KOO oh kee-teh koo-dah-sah-ee*
Have you ever had this before?	前，こんなになったことがありますか。 *MAH-eh, KOHN-nah nee naht-tah koh-toh gah ah-ree-mahs KAH*
Are you having short-ness of breath?	息切れがしますか。 *ee-KEE gee-reh gah shee-mahs KAH*
Do you have any numb-ness here?	ここは，感覚が鈍いですか。 *koh-KOH wah, KAHN-kah-koo gah nee-boo-ee dehs KAH*
What medicine have you been taking?	どんな薬を，使っていますか。 *DOHN-nah koo-soo-ree oh, tsoo-KAHT-teh ee-mahs KAH*
What dosage of insulin do you take?	インシュリンの使用量は，一回どの位ですか。 *EEN-soo-reen noh shoo-YOH ryoh wah, eek-kah-ee doh-NOH koo-rah-ee dehs KAH*

Is it by injection, or oral?	注射ですか，飲み薬ですか。 *CHOO-shah dehs KAH, noh-MEE goo-soo-ree dehs KAH*
What treatment have you been having?	どんな治療を，受けていますか。 *DOHN-nah chee-ryoh oh, OO-keh-teh ee-mahs KAH*
Is there a history of _____ in your family?	家族に，_____ の歴史がありますか。 *KAH-zoh-koo nee, _____ noh reh-kee-shee gah ah-ree-mahs KAH*
When is your baby due?	出産予定日は，いつですか。 *shoos-SAHN yoh-teh bee wah, EE-tsoo dehs KAH*
I want a <u>urine</u> sample.	尿の検査をします。 *NYOH noh KEHN-sah oh shee-mahs*
stool	便 *BEHN*
blood	血液 *keh-TSOO-eh-kee*
I want you to have an X ray.	レントゲンをとります。 *REHN-toh-gehn oh toh-REE-mahs*
When was your last tetanus shot?	破傷風の予防注射は，いつしましたか。 *hah-SHOH-foo noh yoh-boh choo-shah wah, EE-tsoo shee-mah-shtah KAH*
I'm going to send you to <u>a specialist</u>.	専門医のところへ，行ってもらいます。 *SEHN-mohn-ee noh toh-koh-roh eh, eet-TEH moh-rah-ee-mahs*
a dermatologist	皮膚科の医者 *hee-FOO-kah noh ee-shah*
an ear, nose, and throat specialist	耳鼻咽喉科医 *jee-bee-EEN-koh-kah ee*
a gynecologist	婦人科医 *foo-JEEN-kah ee*
an obstetrician	産科医 *SAHN-kah ee*
an ophthalmologist	眼科医 *GAHN-kah ee*
an orthopedist	整形外科医 *SEH-keh geh-kah ee*
a surgeon	外科医 *geh-KAH ee*
It's minor.	たいしたことありません。 *TAH-ee-shtah koh-toh ah-ree-mah-sehn*

It's acute. 急性の病気です。 *KYOO-seh noh byoh-kee dehs*

It's infected. 化膿しています。 *kah-NOH shteh ee-mahs*

It's broken. 折れています。 *OH-reh-teh ee-mahs*

It's sprained. ねんざしています。 *NEHN-zah shteh ee-mahs*

It's dislocated. 脱臼しています。 *dahk-KYOO shteh ee-mahs*

It's inflamed. 炎症を，起しています。 *EHN-shoh oh, oh-KOH-shteh ee-mahs*

I'll have to take stitches. ぬわなければ，なりません。 *noo-WAH-nah-keh-reh-bah, nah-ree-mah-sehn*

I'll have to lance it. 切開しなければ，なりません。 *SEHK-kah-ee shee-nah-keh-reh-bah, nah-ree-mah-sehn*

I'll have to tape it. テープで，固定しなければなりません。 *TEH-poo deh, koh-TEH shee-nah-keh-reh-bah nah-ree-mah-sehn*

You can't travel until ＿＿＿. 旅行は，＿＿＿までひかえてください。 *ryoh-KOH wah, ＿＿＿ mah-deh hee-KAH-eh-teh koo-dah-sah-ee*

I want you to go to the hospital for some tests. 検査のために，病院へ行ってください。 *KEHN-sah noh tah-meh nee, BYOH-een eh eet-teh koo-dah-sah-ee*

I want you to go to the hospital for treatment. 治療のために，病院へ行ってください。 *chee-RYOH noh tah-meh nee, BYOH-een eh eet-teh koo-dah-sah-ee*

I want you to go to the hospital for surgery. 手術のために，病院へ行ってください。 *SHOO-joo-tsoo noh tah-meh nee, BYOH-een eh eet-teh koo-dah-sah-ee*

Shall I make the arrangements for you to go to the hospital? 病院へ行く手はずを整えましょうか。 *BYOH-een eh ee-koo TEH-hah-zoo oh, toh-TOH-noh-eh-mah-shoh KAH*

You've had a mild heart attack.	軽い心臓発作です。 *kah-roo-ee SHEEN-zoh hohs-SAH dehs*
Are you allergic to ____?	____ に，アレルギー体質ですか。 *____ nee, ah-REH-roo-gee tah-ee-shee-tsoo dehs KAH*
Are you allergic to any medicines?	アレルギー反応のある薬があります か。 *ah-REH-roo-gee hahn-noh noh ah-roo koo- SOO-ree gah ah-ree-mahs KAH*
I'm giving you an injection of penicillin.	ペニシリンの注射をします。 *peh-NEE-shee-reen noh choo-shah oh shee-mahs*
I'm prescribing an antibiotic.	抗生物質を処方します。 *KOH-seh boos-shee-tsoo oh, shoh-hoh shee-mahs*
I'm giving you some medicine to take.	薬をあげます。 *koo-SOO-ree oh ah-geh-mahs*
I'm writing a prescription for you.	処方せんを，書きましょう。 *shoh-HOH sehn oh, kah-kee-mah-shoh*
We don't use ____ in Japan.	____ は，日本では使っていません。 *____ wah, nee-HOHN deh-wah tsoo-KAHT-teh ee-mah-sehn*
This is quite similar to ____.	これは，____ に非常に似ています。 *koh-REH wah, ____ nee hee-JOH nee nee-teh ee-mahs*
Take ____ teaspoons of this medicine at a time.	この薬を，一度にさじ ____ 杯飲んで ください。 *koh-NOH koo-soo-ree oh, ee-chee doh nee sah-jee ____ pah-ee/ hah-ee/ bah-ee nohn-deh koo-dah-sah-ee*
Take it every ____ hours.	____ 時間ごとに，飲んでください。 *____ jee-kahn goh-toh nee, NOHN-deh koo-dah-sah-ee*
Take ____ tablets with a glass of water.	これを ____ 錠，水で飲んでくださ い。 *koh-reh oh ____ joh, mee-zoo deh NOHN-deh koo-dah-sah-ee*
Take it ____ times a day.	一日に ____ 回，飲んでください。 *ee-CHEE nee-chee nee ____ kah-ee, NOHN-deh koo-dah-sah-ee*

Take it after meals.	食後に飲んでください。 *shoh-KOO-goh nee, NOHN-deh koo-dah-sah-ee*
Take it before meals.	食前に，飲んでください。 *shoh-KOO-zehn nee, NOHN-deh koo-dah-sah-ee*
Take it in the morning.	朝飲んでください。 *AH-sah nohn-deh koo-dah-sah-ee*
Take it at night.	夜飲んでください。 *YOH-roo nohn-deh koo-dah-sah-ee*
Use an ice pack on it.	氷のうをあててください。 *HYOH-noh oh ah-teh-teh koo-dah-sah-ee*
Use wet heat on it.	温湿布をあててください。 *OHN sheep-poo oh ah-teh-teh koo-dah-sah-ee*
I want you to come back after _____ day(s).	_____ たったら，また来てください。 *_____ TAHT-tah-rah, mah-tah kee-TEH koo-dah-sah-ee*
I think it's _____.	_____ だと思います。 *_____ dah toh oh-moh-ee-mahs*
an allergy	アレルギー *ah-REH-roo-gee*
appendicitis	盲腸炎 *MOH-choh ehn*
a bacterial infection	細菌性炎症 *sah-EE-keen seh ehn-shoh*
a bladder infection	ぼうこう炎 *BOH-koh ehn*
bronchitis	気管支炎 *kee-KAHN-shee ehn*
a common cold	普通の風邪 *foo-TSOO noh kah-zeh*
conjunctivitis	結膜炎 *keh-TSOO-mah-koo ehn*
dysentery	赤痢 *SEH-kee-ree*
gastroenteritis	胃腸炎 *ee-CHOH ehn*
the heart	心臓 *SHEEN-zoh*
hepatitis	肝炎 *KAHN ehn*
influenza	インフルエンザ／流感 *EEN-foo-roo-ehn-zah／RYOO-kahn*
a muscle spasm	筋肉のけいれん *KEEN-nee-koo noh keh-rehn*

muscular	筋肉 *KEEN-nee-koo*
pneumonia	肺炎 *hah-EE ehn*
an ulcer	潰瘍 *kah-EE-yoh*
a urinary infection	尿道炎 *NYOH-doh ehn*

AT THE DENTIST

This section is divided into two parts: **Patient** and **Dentist**. You use the phrases under **Patient**, and hand the book to the dentist so he or she can point to the appropriate phrases under **Dentist**.

| Please point to the phrase in the book. | この本の，適当な文を指さしてください。 *koh-NOH hohn noh, teh-KEE-toh nah boon oh yoo-BEE sah-shteh koo-dah-sah-ee* |

Patient

I have to go to a dentist.	歯医者に，行かなければなりません。 *HAH ee-shah nee, ee-KAH-nah-keh-reh-bah nah-ree-mah-sehn*
Can you recommend a dentist?	歯医者を，紹介してもらえますか。 *HAH ee-shah oh, shoh-kah-ee shteh moh-rah-eh-mahs KAH*
I'd like an appointment with the dentist.	歯医者の予約をしたいのですが。 *HAH ee-shah noh yoh-YAH-koo oh shee-tah-ee noh dehs gah*
I need to see the dentist immediately.	すぐ，歯医者に行かなければなりません。 *SOO-goo, hah ee-shah nee ee-KAH-nah-keh-reh-bah nah-ree-mah-sehn*
I have a really bad toothache.	歯が，ひどく痛みます。 *HAH gah, HEE-doh-koo ee-tah-mee-mahs*
I think I have a cavity.	虫歯のようですが。 *moo-SHEE bah noh yoh dehs gah*
an abscess	うんでいる *OON-deh ee-roo*

I've lost a filling.	歯のつめ物を，なくしてしまいました。 *HAH noh tsoo-meh-moh-noh oh, nah-KOO-shteh shee-mah-ee-mah-shtah*
I've broken a tooth.	歯を，折ってしまいました。 *HAH oh, OHT-teh shee-mah-ee-mah-shtah*
I can't chew.	かむことが，できません。 *KAH-moo koh-toh gah, deh-kee-mah-sehn*
My gums hurt.	歯ぐきが，痛んでいます。 *HAH goo-kee gah, ee-TAHN-deh ee-mahs*
Can you give me <u>a temporary</u> filling?	仮のつめ物を，してもらえますか。 <u>*kah-REE*</u> *noh tsoo-meh-moh-noh oh, shteh moh-rah-eh-mahs KAH*
a silver	銀の *GEEN noh*
a gold	金の *KEEN noh*
a porcelain	磁器製の *jee-KEE seh noh*
Can you fix this <u>bridge</u>?	この<u>ブリッジ</u>を，直してもらえますか。 *koh-noh boo-REEJ-jee oh, nah-OH-shteh moh-rah-eh-mahs KAH*
crown	金冠 *KEEN kahn*
denture	入れ歯 *ee-REH-bah*

Dentist

I see the problem.	どこが悪いか，わかりました。 *DOH-koh gah wah-roo-ee kah, wah-KAH-ree-mah-shtah*
I want to take an X ray.	レントゲンを，とります。 *REHN-toh-gehn oh, toh-REE-mahs*
We should do it now.	今，しなければなりません。 *EE-mah, shee-NAH-keh-reh-bah nah-ree-mah-sehn*
It can wait until you get home.	帰国するまで，大丈夫です。 *kee-KOH-koo soo-roo mah-deh, dah-EE-joh-boo dehs*

I'm going to give you a <u>temporary</u> filling.	仮のつめ物をしましょう。 *kah-REE noh tsoo-MEH-moh-noh oh shee-mah-shoh*
silver	銀の *GEEN noh*
gold	金の *KEEN noh*
porcelain	磁器製の *jee-KEE-seh noh*
Would you like some <u>novocain</u>?	<u>ノボカイン</u>をしましょうか。 *noh-BOH-kah-een oh shee-mah-shoh KAH*
gas	麻酔ガス *mah-SOO-ee gah-soo*
Does this hurt?	痛みますか。 *ee-TAH-mee-mahs KAH*
Is it tender?	敏感ですか。 *BEEN-kahn dehs KAH*
I'm giving you a prescription.	処方せんを，あげましょう。 *shoh-HOH sehn oh, ah-geh-mah-shoh*
Rinse with this ____ times daily.	一日____回，これですすいでください。 *ee-CHEE nee-chee ____ kah-ee, koh-REH deh soo-soo-ee-deh koo-dah-sah-ee*
This is <u>an antibiotic</u>.	これは，<u>抗生物質</u>です。 *koh-REH wah, KOH-seh boos-shee-tsoo dehs*
a painkiller	痛み止め *ee-TAH-mee doh-meh*
Take ____ tablets/ capsules at a time.	錠剤／カプセルを，一度に____錠飲んでください。 *JOH-zah-ee/ KAH-poo-seh-roo oh ee-chee-doh nee, ____ joh nohn-deh koo-dah-sah-ee*
Take it/ them every ____ hours.	____時間ごとに，飲んでください。 *____ jee-kahn goh-toh nee, NOHN-deh koo-dah-sah-ee*

TRADITIONAL TREATMENTS

Acupressure (Shiatsu) and Acupuncture (Hari)

Although most Westerners think of acupuncture as Chinese, it's also widely practiced in Japan. You can have acupuncture or acu-

pressure treatment at the therapist's office, or where you're staying.
Payment is usually by the hour.

Where can I get <u>acu-pressure</u>?	指圧は、どこでうけられますか。 *shee-AH-tsoo wah, DOH-koh deh oo-keh-rah-reh-mahs KAH*
acupuncture	針療治 *hah-REE ryoh-jee*
Do you know a good <u>acupressurist</u>?	上手な指圧師を、知っていますか。 *JOH-zoo nah shee-AH-tsoo shee oh, sheet-TEH ee-mahs KAH*
acupuncturist	針の療治師 *HAH-ree noh ryoh-jee shee*
Does he/ she come to my place?	私の所へ、来てくれますか。 *wah-TAHK-shee noh toh-koh-roh eh, kee-TEH koo-reh-mahs KAH*
How much is it for an hour?	一時間いくらですか。 *ee-CHEE jee-kahn EE-koo-rah dehs KAH*
Do I need to make an appointment?	予約するべきですか。 *yoh-YAH-koo soo-roo beh-kee dehs KAH*
Could you get me one?	よんでもらえますか。 *YOHN-deh moh-rah-eh-mahs KAH*

With the Acupressurist or Acupuncturist

My problem is here.	ここの具合が、よくありません。 *koh-KOH noh goo-ah-ee gah, YOH-koo ah-ree-mah-sehn*
My <u>neck</u> is (are) stiff.	首が、こっています。 <u>*koo-BEE*</u> *gah, koht-teh ee-mahs*
shoulders	肩 *KAH-tah*
back	背中 *seh-NAH-kah*
My <u>head</u> ache (s).	頭が、痛いんです。 <u>*ah-TAH-mah*</u> *gah, ee-TAH-een dehs*
arms	腕 *oo-DEH*
waist	腰 *koh-SHEE*
stomach	胃 *ee*
legs	足 *ah-SHEE*

With the Acupressurist

It's too hard. 強すぎます。 *tsoo-YOH-soo-gee-mahs*

Can you do it more gently? もうちょっと，弱くしてください。 *MOH choht-toh, YOH-wah-koo shteh koo-dah-sah-ee*

I can take it harder. もうちょっと，強くてもいいです。 *MOH choht-toh TSOO-yoh-koo-teh-moh ee dehs*

WITH THE OPTICIAN

Can you repair these glasses for me? 眼鏡を，直してもらえますか。 *MEH-gah-neh oh, nah-OH-shteh moh-rah-eh-mahs KAH*

I've broken a lens. レンズを，わってしまいました。 *REHN-zoo oh, waht-TEH shee-mah-ee-mah-shtah*

I've broken the frame. わくを，こわしてしまいました。 *wah-KOO oh, koh-WAH-shteh shee-mah-ee-mah-shtah*

Can you put in a new lens? 新しいレンズを，入れてもらえますか。 *ah-TAH-rah-shee rehn-zoo oh, ee-REH-teh moh-rah-eh-mahs KAH*

Can you get the prescription from the old lens? 古いレンズから，度をとってもらえますか。 *foo-ROO-ee rehn-zoo kah-rah, doh oh TOHT-teh moh-rah-eh-mahs KAH*

Can you tighten the screw? ねじを，しめてもらえますか。 *NEH-jee oh, SHEE-meh-teh moh-rah-eh-mahs KAH*

I need the glasses as soon as possible. 眼鏡は，できるだけ早く欲しいのですが。 *MEH-gah-neh wah, deh-KEE-roo dah-keh hah-yah-koo hoh-SHEE noh dehs gah*

I don't have any others. かわりの眼鏡は，ありません。 *kah-WAH-ree noh meh-gah-neh wah, ah-ree-mah-sehn*

I'd like a new pair of eyeglasses.	新しい眼鏡が，欲しいのですが。 *ah-TAH-rah-shee meh-gah-neh gah, hoh-SHEE noh dehs gah*
Can you give me a new prescription?	度を，計ってもらえますか。 *doh oh, hah-KAHT-teh moh-rah-eh-mahs KAH*
I'd like the lenses tinted.	レンズに，軽く色をつけてください。 *REHN-zoo nee, kah-roo-koo ee-ROH oh tsoo-KEH-teh koo-dah-sah-ee*
Do you sell <u>contact lenses</u>?	<u>コンタクトレンズ</u>は，売っていますか。 <u>*KOHN-tah-koo-toh rehn-zoo*</u> *wah, oot-TEH ee-mahs KAH*
soft contact lenses	ソフト・コンタクトレンズ *soh-foo-toh KOHN-tah-koo-toh rehn-zoo*
Do you sell sun glasses?	サングラスは，売っていますか。 *SAHN-goo-rah-soo wah, oot-TEH ee-mahs KAH*

COMMUNICATIONS

POST OFFICE

Post offices are identified by this symbol. 〒 It looks like a capital T with a bar above it. Mailboxes on the street have this sign, too; the mailboxes are red. Post offices are open from 9 A.M. to 5 P.M. weekdays, and 9 A.M. to noon Saturdays. You can buy stamps at shops and kiosks that display the red symbol.

I want to mail a letter.	手紙を出したいのですが。 *teh-GAH-mee oh dahsh-TAH-ee noh dehs gah*
Where is a <u>mailbox</u>?	<u>ポスト</u>は，どこにありますか。 *POH-soo-toh wah, DOH-koh nee ah-ree-mahs KAH*
post office	郵便局 *YOO-been kyoh-koo*
Which window sells stamps?	切手の窓口は，どこですか。 *keet-TEH noh mah-doh goo-chee wah, DOH-koh dehs KAH*
What's the postage for <u>a letter</u> to the United States?	アメリカへの<u>手紙</u>は，いくらです か。 *ah-MEH-ree-kah eh noh teh-GAH-mee wah, EE-koo-rah dehs KAH*
an airmail letter	航空便 *KOH-koo been*
a registered letter	書留 *kah-KEE-toh-meh*
a special delivery letter	速達 *soh-KOO-tah-tsoo*
a postcard	葉書 *hah-GAH-kee*
I'd like <u>5 aerograms</u>.	<u>航空書簡／エアログラムを５枚</u>くだ さい。 *KOH-koo shoh-kahn/ eh-AH-roh-goo-rah-moo oh goh mah-ee koo-dah-sah-ee*
6 airmail stamps for Europe	ヨーロッパへの，エアメール用の 切手を６枚 *YOH-rohp-pah eh noh, eh-AH-meh-roo yoh noh keet-teh oh roh-KOO-mah-ee*

7 postcard stamps for South America	南米への，葉書用の切手を 7 枚 *NAHN-beh eh noh, hah-GAH-kee yoh noh keet-teh oh nah-NAH mah-ee*
I want pretty stamps.	きれいな切手をください。 *KEE-reh-nah keet-teh oh koo-dah-sah-ee*
I'd like to send this parcel.	この小包を，送りたいのですが。 *koh-noh koh-ZOO-tsoo-mee oh, oh-KOO-ree-tah-ee noh dehs gah*
Is there a big difference in <u>price</u> between airmail and sea mail?	航空便と船便では，値段にかなりの差がありますか。 *KOH-koo been toh foo-NAH been deh-wah, neh-DAHN nee KAH-nah-ree no sah gah ah-ree-mahs KAH*
arrival time	かかる日数 *kah-KAH-roo nees-SOO*
How much will it be by <u>air</u>?	航空便だと，いくらかかりますか。 *KOH-koo been dah toh, EE-koo-rah kah-kah-ree-mahs KAH*
sea	船便 *foo-NAH been*
Do I need to fill out a customs declaration form?	税関の申告書に，記入しなければなりませんか。 *ZEH-kahn noh sheen-koo-koo shoh nee, kee-NYOO shee-nah-keh-reh-bah nah-REE-mah-sehn KAH*

TELEGRAPH

Where can I send a telegram/ cable?	電報は，どこでうてますか。 *DEHN-poh wah, DOH-koh deh oo-teh-mahs KAH*
Where's the telegraph office?	電報取扱局は，どこにありますか。 *DEHN-poh toh-ree-ah-tsoo-KAH-ee kyoh-koo wah, DOH-koh nee ah-ree-mahs KAH*
How early is it open?	何時から，やっていますか。 *NAHN-jee kah-rah, yaht-teh ee-mahs KAH*
late	まで *mah-deh*

I'd like to send a telegram/ cable to ___.	___ へ、電報をうちたいのですが。 ___ *eh, DEHN-poh oh oo-CHEE-tah-ee noh dehs gah*
I'd like to send an urgent telegram/ cable to ___.	___ へ、至急電報をうちたいのですが。 ___ *eh, shee-KYOO dehn-poh oh oo-CHEE-tah-ee noh dehs gah*
How much is it per word?	一語いくらですか。 *ee-CHEE-goh EE-koo-rah dehs KAH*
I want to send it collect.	料金先方払いで、送りたいのですが。 *ryoh-keen SEHN-poh bah-rah-ee deh, oh-KOO-ree-tah-ee noh dehs gah*
When will it arrive?	いつ着きますか。 *EE-tsoo tsoo-kee-mahs KAH*

TELEPHONE

Telephone service in Japan is very good. It costs 10 yen to speak for 3 minutes for a local call on a public telephone. You lift the receiver, wait for a dial tone, and deposit your coins. If you are going to speak more than 3 minutes, insert the coins at the beginning; otherwise you risk being cut off abruptly. If you've used up your time and have not inserted an extra coin, you'll hear a warning tone, and unless you put more money in immediately, the line will be cut. If you deposit more money than you need at the beginning, your unused coins will be returned at the end.

Phones for public use come in four colors: they differ according to where they're located and how many coins they hold:

RED   outside shops, they take 10-yen coins only, up to **6** coins at a time.

PINK   inside shops such as bars, coffee shops, and restaurants, they operate like the red ones.

BLUE   in telephone booths in public places, the wall-mounted type takes up to **10** 10-yen coins at once, the desk-top type takes **6**.

YELLOW   take both 10-yen (up to **10** at a time) and 100-yen (up to **9** at a time) coins, making these phones the best choice for long-distance calls.

Visitors to Japan will find Japan Travel-Phone helpful. If you're having difficulty communicating, or if you want more detailed information for sightseeing or travel plans, use Travel-Phone — you'll find an English-speaking travel expert on the line to help solve your problems!

JAPAN TRAVEL-PHONE

Use private phones, or BLUE or YELLOW public phones. In the Tokyo or Kyoto area, the charge is the regular 10 yen per 3 minutes. The phone numbers are:

Tokyo Area 502-1461 (Tokyo Tourist Information Center)

Kyoto Area 371-5649 (Kyoto Tourist Information Center)

Elsewhere in Japan Insert a 10-yen coin, dial 106, and tell the operator (in English): "Collect call, TIC." Your money will be returned after the call.

Where is a <u>public telephone</u>?	公衆電話は，どこにありますか。 *KOH-shoo dehn-wah wah, DOH-koh nee ah-ree-mahs KAH*
telephone booth	電話ボックス *DEHN-wah bohk-koo-soo*
Is there an English telephone directory?	英語の電話帳が，ありますか。*EH-goh noh dehn-wah choh gah, ah-ree-mahs KAH*
I'd like to make a phone call. Could you give me some change?	電話をかけるのに，こまかくしてもらえますか。*DEHN-wah oh kah-keh-roo noh-nee, koh-MAH-kah-koo shee-TEH moh-rah-eh-mahs KAH*
May I use your phone?	電話をはいしゃくできますか。*DEHN-wah oh hah-ee-shah-koo deh-kee-mahs KAH*
I want to make a <u>local call</u>.	市内電話を，かけたいのですが。*shee-NAH-ee dehn-wah oh, kah-KEH-tah-ee noh dehs gah*
long distance call	長距離電話 *CHOH-kyoh-ree dehn-wah*
person to person call	パーソナル・コール *PAH-soh-nah-roo koh-roo*
collect call	料金先方払いの電話 *RYOH-keen sehn-poh bah-rah-ee noh dehn-wah*

Please tell me how to call this number.	この番号のかけ方を，教えてください。 *koh-NOH bahn-goh noh kah-KEH-kah-tah oh, oh-SHEE-eh-teh koo-dah-sah-ee*
Can I dial direct?	ダイヤル直通ですか。 *dah-ee-yah-roo choh-KOO-tsoo dehs KAH*
Do I need an operator's assistance?	交換手を，呼ぶ必要がありますか。 *KOH-kahn shoo oh, yoh-BOO hee-tsoo-yoh gah ah-ree-mahs KAH*
Is there an operator who speaks English?	英語を話す交換手が，いますか。 *EH-goh oh hah-nah-soo KOH-kahn shoo gah, ee-mahs KAH*
What's the number for the operator?	交換手の番号は，何番ですか。 *KOH-kahn shoo noh bahn-goh wah, NAHN-bahn dehs KAH*

With the Telephone Operator

I want Tokyo 111-2222	東京111の2222を，お願いします。 *TOH-kyoh ee-CHEE ee-chee ee-chee noh NEE nee nee nee oh, oh-NEH-gah-ee shee-mahs*
I want this to be a <u>person to person call</u>.	これは，パーソナル・コールでお願いします。 *koh-REH wah, PAH-soh-nah-roo koh-roo deh oh-neh-gah-ee shee-mahs*
collect call	料金先方払い *RYOH-keen sehn-poh bah-rah-ee*
The name of the person I want to talk to is ____ ____.	先方の名前は，(姓，名) です。 *SEHN-poh noh nah-mah-eh wah, (last name, first name) dehs*
Would you tell me the cost when I'm finished?	終ったら，いくらだったか教えてもらえますか。 *oh-WAHT-tah-rah, EE-koo-rah daht-tah kah oh-SHEE-eh-teh moh-rah eh-mahs KAH*

With the Other Party

Hello!	もしもし *MOH-shee moh-shee*
Is this Mr./ Mrs./ Miss/ Ms. ____'s residence?	(姓) さんの，お宅ですか。 (last name) *sahn noh oh-TAH-koo dehs KAH*
May I speak to ____? (Mr.)	(姓) さんを，お願いします。 (last name) *sahn oh, oh-neh-gah-ee shee-mahs*
(Mrs.)	(姓) さんの奥さん (last name) *sahn noh OHK-sahn*
(son or daughter)	(名) さん (first name) *sahn*
Is this (company name)?	(会社の名前) ですか。 ____ *dehs KAH*
I want extension ____.	内線の ____ 番を，お願いします。 *nah-EE-sehn noh* ____ *bahn oh, oh-neh-gah-ee shee-mahs*
Is Mr./ Mrs./ Miss/ Ms. ____ in?	(姓) さんは，いらっしゃいますか。 (last name) *sahn wah, ee-RAHS-shah-ee-mahs KAH*
Hello! Is this ____?	もしもし，____ さんですか。 *MOH-shee moh-shee.* ____ *sahn dehs KAH*
____ speaking.	私は，(名前) ですが。 *wah-TAHK-shee wah,* (name) *dehs gah*

If the Person Isn't There

When will he/ she be back?	いつ，おもどりになりますか。 *EE-tsoo, oh-MOH-doh-ree nee nah-ree-mahs KAH*
Will you tell him/ her that ____ called?	____ が電話したと，お伝えいただけますか。 ____ *gah DEHN-wah shtah toh, oh-TSOO-tah-eh ee-tah-dah-keh-mahs KAH*
Would you tell him/ her to call me?	私に電話するように，伝えていただけますか。 *wah-TAHK-shee nee dehn-wah soo-roo yoh nee, tsoo-TAH-eh-teh ee-tah-dah-keh-mahs KAH*

My phone number is ____.	私の電話番号は，____番です。 *wah-TAHK-shee noh dehn-wah bahn-goh wah, ____ dehs*
My extension is ____.	内線は，____番です。 *nah-EE-sehn wah, ____ bahn dehs*
Please tell him/ her to leave a message if I'm not here.	もし私が出なかったら，伝言を残すようにお伝えください。 *MOH-shee wah-tahk-shee gah DEH-nah-kaht-tah-rah, DEHN-gohn oh noh-koh-soo yoh nee oh-TSOO-tah-eh koo-dah-sah-ee*
I'll call him/ her again.	また電話します。 *mah-TAH dehn-wah shee-mahs*
Thank you very much. Goodbye.	どうも，ありがとうございました。では，ごめんください。 *DOH-moh, ah-REE-gah-toh goh-zah-ee-mah-shtah. DEH-wah, goh-MEHN koo-dah-sah-ee.*

DRIVING A CAR

Foreigners driving in Japan must contend with certain realities: The steering wheel is on the right side of the car, and you drive on the left side of the road; most expressway signs are in Japanese; non-express roads may be narrow and usually have no sidewalks. Speedometers are only in kilometers, streets are crowded with pedestrians, bicycles, vendors, and cars, and penalties for accidents are high. In short, for the visitor to Japan, driving is not recommended. Do you still want to? If so, you'll need an International Driving Permit. You'll also need to be familiar with Japanese road signs and traffic signs, some of which are shown at the end of this section. Many are International Traffic Signs, which are clear and easy to read. The Japan Automobile Federation in Tokyo has a useful booklet called "Rules of the Road," which you might want to read if you're planning on driving. One final note: There are road checkpoints for drivers under the influence of alcohol, and penalties can be severe.

RENTING A CAR

Where can I rent a car?	どこで，車が借りられますか。 *DOH-koh deh, koo-ROO-mah gah kah-REE-rah-reh mahs KAH*
I'd like to rent a car.	車を借りたいのですが。 *koo-ROO-mah oh, kah-REE-tah-ee noh dehs gah*
Do you have a <u>small car</u>?	小さい車が，ありますか。 <u>*CHEE-sah-ee koo-ROO-mah gah, ah-ree-mahs KAH*</u>
mid-size car	中型車 *CHOO-gah-tah-shah*
large car	大型車 *OH-gah-tah-shah*
sports car	スポーツ・カー *soo-POH-tsoo kah*
May I see your list of rates?	料金表を，見せてもらえますか。 *RYOH-keen hyoh oh, MEE-seh-teh moh-rah-eh-mahs KAH*

I prefer a car with automatic transmission.	自動変速の車が，欲しいのですが。 *jee-DOH hehn-soh-koo noh koo-roo-mah gah, hoh-SHEE noh dehs gah*
Do you have a car that's cheap and easy to handle?	安くて，運転しやすい車がありますか。 *yah-SOO-koo-teh, OON-tehn shee-YAH-soo-ee koo-roo-mah gah ah-ree-mahs KAH*
I'd like it for <u>a day</u>.	それを<u>一日</u>借りたいのですが。 *soh-reh oh, <u>ee-CHEE-nee-chee</u> kah-REE-tah-ee noh dehs gah*
a week	一週間 *eesh-SHOO-kahn*
What's the rate for <u>a day</u>?	<u>一日</u>の料金は，いくらですか。 *ee-CHEE-nee-chee noh RYOH-keen wah, EE-koo-rah dehs KAH*
a week	一週間 *eesh-SHOO-kahn*
Does the rate include <u>mileage</u>?	それには，<u>キロ数</u>も入っていますか。 *soh-REH nee-wah, kee-ROH-soo moh HAH-eet-teh ee-mahs KAH*
gas	ガソリン代 *gah-SOH-reen dah-ee*
insurance	保険 *hoh-KEHN*
How much is the insurance?	保検は，いくらですか。 *hoh-KEHN wah, EE-koo-rah dehs KAH*
Do I have to leave a deposit?	保証金が，必要ですか。 *hoh-SHOH keen gah, hee-TSOO-yoh dehs KAH*
What's the deposit?	保証金は，いくらですか。 *hoh-SHOH-keen wah, EE-koo-rah dehs KAH*
Do you take credit cards?	クレジット・カードで，払えますか。 *koo-REH-jeet-toh KAH-doh deh, hah-RAH-eh-mahs KAH*
Can you deliver it to <u>my hotel</u>?	車を，<u>私のホテル</u>までとどけてもらえますか。 *koo-ROO-mah oh, <u>wah-TAHK-shee noh HOH-teh-roo</u> mah-deh, toh-DOH-keh-teh moh-rah-eh-mahs KAH*
this address	この住所 *koh-NOH joo-shoh*

Here's my International Driving Permit.	これが, 私の国際免許書です。 *koh-REH gah, wah-TAHK-shee noh kohk-sah-ee MEHN-kyoh-shoh dehs*
Please give me some emergency telephone numbers.	緊急の場合によべる電話番号を, 教えてください。 *KEEN-kyoo noh bah-ah-ee nee yoh-beh-roo DEHN-wah bahn-goh oh, oh-SHEE-eh-teh koo-dah-sah-ee*

INFORMATION AND DIRECTIONS

Excuse me, but ____	ちょっとすみませんが, ____ *CHOHT-toh soo-mee-mah-sehn gah,*
How do I get to ____?	____へは, どういけばいいですか。 *____ eh wah, DOH ee-keh-bah ee dehs KAH*
I think we're lost.	道に, 迷ってしまったようです。 *mee-CHEE nee, mah-YOHT-teh shee-maht-tah yoh dehs*
Which is the road to ____?	____へ行く道は, どれですか。 *____ eh ee-KOO mee-chee wah, DOH-reh dehs KAH*
Is this the road to ____?	____へ行くには, この道ですか。 *____ eh ee-KOO nee-wah, koh-NOH mee-chee dehs KAH*
What's the name of this town?	この町の名前は, 何ですか。 *koh-NOH mah-chee noh nah-MAH-eh wah, NAHN dehs KAH*
Is the next town far?	次の町は, 遠いですか。 *tsoo-GEE noh mah-chee wah, TOH-ee dehs KAH*
gas station	ガソリン・スタンド *gah-SOH-reen soo-tahn-doh*
How far away is ____? (distance)	____へは, どの位距離があります か。 *____ eh wah, doh-NOH koo-rah-ee kyoh-ree gah ah-ree-mahs KAH*

How far away is ____? (time)	____まで，どの位時間がかかりますか。 ____ *mah-deh, doh-NOH koo-rah-ee jee-KAHN gah kah-kah-ree-mahs KAH*
Do you have a road map?	道路地図がありますか。 *DOH-roh chee-zoo gah, ah-REE-mahs KAH*
Could you show me where ____ is on the map?	____がどこか，地図で教えてください。 ____*gah DOH-koh kah, CHEE-zoo deh oh-SHEE-eh-teh koo-dah-sah-ee*
Could you show me where I am on the map?	私がどこにいるのか，地図で教えてください。 *wah-TAHK-shee gah DOH-koh nee ee-roo kah, CHEE-zoo deh oh-SHEE-eh-teh koo-dah-sah-ee*
Is this the fastest way?	これが，一番速い行き方ですか。 *koh-REH gah, ee-CHEE bahn hah-yah-ee ee-KEE-kah-tah dehs KAH*
Do I go straight?	まっすぐ行くのですか。 *mahs-SOO-goo ee-koo noh dehs KAH*
Do I turn to the right?	右に曲がるのですか。 *mee-GEE nee mah-GAH-roo noh dehs KAH*
left	左 *hee-DAH-ree*
Where is the entrance to the highway?	高速道路への入口は，どこですか。 *KOH-soh-koo doh-roh eh noh ee-REE-goo-chee wah, DOH-koh dehs KAH*
tourist information center	旅行案内所 *ryoh-KOH ahn-nah-ee joh*
gas station	ガソリン・スタンド *gah-SOH-reen soo-tahn-doh*

THE SERVICE STATION

Is there a gas station nearby?	近くに，ガソリン・スタンドがありますか。 *chee-KAH-koo nee, gah-SOH-reen soo-tahn-doh gah ah-ree-mahs KAH*

LIQUID MEASURES (APPROXIMATE)		
LITERS	U.S.GALLONS	IMPERIAL GALLONS
30	8	6
40	10	8
50	13	11
60	15	13
70	18	15
80	21	17

I need some gas.	ガソリンをください。 *gah-SOH-reen oh koo-DAH-sah-ee*
How much is a liter of <u>regular</u>?	レギュラーは，１リットルいくらですか。 *REH-gyoo-rah wah, ee-CHEE reet-toh-roo EE-koo-rah dehs KAH*
super	スーパー／ハイオク *SOO-pah/ hah-EE-oh-koo*
unleaded	無鉛ガソリン *moo-EHN gah-soh-reen*
diesel	ディーゼル *DEE-zeh-roo*
Give me 10 liters of regular please.	レギュラーを，十リットルください。 *REH-gyoo-rah oh, JOO reet-toh-roo koo-dah-sah-ee*
20	二十 *nee-JOO*
30	三十 *SAHN-joo*
Give me 3000 yen worth of super, please.	スーパーを，三千円分ください。 *SOO-pah oh, SAHN-zehn ehn boon koo-dah-sah-ee*
4000	四千 *YOHN-sehn*
5000	五千 *goh-SEHN*
Fill it up, please.	満タンにしてください。 *MAHN-tahn nee shteh koo-DAH-sah-ee*
Please check the <u>battery</u>.	バッテリーを，調べてください。 *baht-TEH-ree oh, shee-RAH-beh-teh koo-dah-sae-ee*

brake fluid	ブレーキ・オイル *boo-REH-kee oh-ee-roo*
clutch fluid	クラッチ・オイル *koo-RAHT-chee oh-ee-roo*
oil	エンジン・オイル *EHN-jeen oh-ee-roo*
spark plugs	スパーク・プラグ *soo-PAH-koo poo-rah-goo*
tires	タイヤ *tah-EE-yah*
tire pressure	タイヤの空気圧 *tah-EE-yah no KOO-kee ah-tsoo*
water	ラジエーターの水 *rah-JEE-eh-tah noh mee-zoo*
Add 1 liter of oil, please.	エンジン・オイルを一リットルたしてください。 *EHN-jeen oh-ee-roo oh, ee-CHEE reet-toh-roo tah-SHEE-teh koo-dah sah-ee*
2 liters	ニリットル *nee REET-toh-roo*
3 liters	三リットル *SAHN reet-toh-roo*

TIRE PRESSURES			
LBS. PER SQ.IN.	KG.PER CM.	LBS. PER SQ. IN.	KG.PER CM.
17	1.2	30	2.1
18	1.3	31	2.2
20	1.4	33	2.3
21	1.5	34	2.4
23	1.6	36	2.5
24	1.7	37	2.6
26	1.8	38	2.7
27	1.9	40	2.8
28	2.0		

Put distilled water in the battery, please.	バッテリーに，蒸留水を入れてください。 *baht-TEH-ree nee, JOH-ryoo-soo-ee oh ee-reh-teh koo-dah-sah-ee*
Put water in the radiator, please.	ラジエーターに，水を入れてください。 *rah-JEE-eh-tah nee, mee-ZOO oh ee-reh-teh koo-dah-sah-ee*
Charge the battery, please	バッテリーを，充電してください。 *baht-TEH-ree oh, JOO-dehn shteh koo-dah-sah¡-ee*
Can you fix a flat tire?	パンクを，修理してもらえますか。 *PAHN-koo oh, SHOO-ree shteh moh-rah-eh mahs KAH*
Change this tire, please.	このタイヤを，かえてください。 *koh-NOH tah-ee-yah oh, kah-EH-teh koo-dah-sah-ee*
Tighten the fan belt, please.	ファン・ベルトを，しめてください。 *FAHN beh-roo-toh oh, SHEE-meh-teh koo-dah-sah-ee*
Would you clean the windshield?	フロント・グラスをふいてもらえますか。 *foo-ROHN-toh goo-rahs oh foo-EE-teh moh-rah-eh-mahs KAH*
Do you have a road map of this area?	この地域の，道路地図がありますか。 *koh-NOH chee- ee-kee noh, DOH-roh chee-zoo gah ah-ree-mahs KAH*
Where are the rest rooms?	トイレは，どこですか。 *TOH-ee-reh wah, DOH-koh dehs KAH*

DISTANCE MEASURES (APPROXIMATE)	
KILOMETERS	MILES
1	.75
5	3
10	6
20	12
50	31
100	62

PARKING

Parking can be a problem in the cities. There's little street parking available in Tokyo, and not much in other cities either. All-night street parking is not allowed. In fact, Japanese must prove they have an off-street parking space when they obtain an automobile license. A parking garage or parking lot may be your best bet. Some hotels offer parking facilities for their guests.

Excuse me, but ____.	ちょっとすみませんが、 _____ *CHOHT-toh soo-mee-mah-sehn gah,*
Can I park here?	ここに駐車できますか。 *koh-KOH nee, CHOO-shah deh-kee-mahs KAH*
Is it illegal to park here?	ここは、駐車禁止ですか。 *koh-KOH wah, CHOO-shah keen-shee dehs KAH*
Is there any street parking nearby?	近くに、路上駐車できる場所があります か。 *chee-KAH-koo nee, roh-JOH choo-shah deh-kee-roo bah-SHOH gah ah-ree-mahs KAH*
Is there a parking garage nearby?	近くに、駐車場がありますか。 *chee-KAH-koo nee, CHOO-shah joh gah ah-ree-mahs KAH*
When does the parking garage <u>open</u>?	駐車場は、何時に開きますか。 *CHOO-shah-joh wah, NAHN-jee nee ah-kee-mahs KAH*
close	閉まります *shee-mah-ree-mahs*
What's the parking fee?	駐車料は、いくらですか。 *CHOO-shah ryoh wah, EE-koo-rah dehs KAH*
I'd like to park <u>for one hour</u>.	一時間駐車したいのですが。 *ee-CHEE jee-kahn choo-shah shee-TAH-ee noh dehs gah*
for two hours	二時間 *nee-JEE-kahn*
till noon	昼まで *hee-ROO mah-deh*
till 5 o'clock	五時まで *GOH-jee mah-deh*

overnight	一晩 *hee-TOH bahn*
for a day	一日 *ee-CHEE nee-chee*
for two days	二日 *foo-TSOO-kah*
Do I leave the key in the car?	鍵は、車にのこしますか。 *kah-GEE wah, koo-roo-mah nee noh-KOH-shee-mahs KAH*

ACCIDENTS AND REPAIRS

Could you help me?	助けてもらえますか。 *tahs-KEH-teh moh-rah-eh-mahs KAH*
I have a flat tire.	パンクです。 *PAHN-koo dehs*
Could you help me change the tire?	タイヤをかえるのを、手伝ってもらえますか。 *tah-EE-yah oh kah-eh-roo noh oh, teh-TSOO-daht-teh moh-rah-eh-mahs KAH*
I've run out of gas.	ガス欠です。 *gah-SOO keh-tsoo dehs*
Could you give me some gas?	ガソリンを少し、わけてもらえますか。 *gah-SOH-reen oh SKOH-shee, WAH-keh-teh moh-rah-eh-mahs KAH*
The car is overheated.	オーバー・ヒートです。 *OH-bah HEE-toh dehs*
Can I get some water?	水をすこし、もらえますか。 *mee-ZOO oh SKOH-shee, moh-rah-eh mahs KAH*
The car is stuck in the <u>mud</u>.	車がぬかるみにはまって、でられません。 *koo-ROO-mah gah noo-KAH-roo-mee nee hah-maht-teh, deh-RAH-reh-mah-sehn*
ditch	みぞ *mee-ZOH*
Could you give me a <u>hand</u>?	手助けしてもらえますか。 *teh-DAH-soo-keh shee-teh moh-rah-ee-mahs KAH*
push it	押して *oh-SHEE-teh*
pull it	引っぱって *heep-PAHT-teh*

The battery is dead.	バッテリーが，あがってしまいました。 *baht-TEH-ree gah, ah-GAHT-teh shee-mah-ee-mahsh-tah*
Do you have a jumper cable?	ジャンパーを，お持ちですか。 *JAHN-pah oh, oh-MOH-chee dehs KAH*
The radiator is leaking.	ラジエーターが，もっています。 *rah-JEE-eh-tah gah, MOHT-teh ee-mahs*
The keys are locked inside the car.	鍵を車の中に残したまま，ドアをロックしてしまいました。 *kah-GEE oh koo-ROO-mah noh nah-kah nee noh-KOHSH-tah mah-mah, DOH-ah oh ROHK-koo shteh shee-mah-ee-mahsh-tah*
I don't have any tools.	修理道具は，持っていません。 *SHOO-ree doh-goo wah, MOHT-teh ee-mah-sehn*
Could you lend me a <u>flashlight</u>?	懐中電燈を，かしてもらえますか。 *kah-EE-choo dehn-toh oh, kah-SHEE-teh moh-rah-eh-mahs KAH*
hammer	ハンマー *HAHN-mah*
jack	ジャッキ *JAHK-kee*
monkey wrench	モンキー・レンチ *MOHN-kee rehn-chee*
pliers	ペンチ *PEHN-chee*
screwdriver	ドライバー *doh-RAH-ee-bah*
My car has broken down.	車が，故障してしまいました。 *koo-ROO-mah gah, koh-shoh shteh shee-mah-ee-mahsh-tah*
The engine won't start.	エンジンが，かかりません。 *EHN-jeen gah, kah-KAH-ree-mah-sehn*
The car doesn't go.	車が，動きません。 *koo-ROO-mah gah, oo-GOH-kee-mah-sehn*
I need <u>an auto mechanic</u>.	車の整備士が必要です。 *koo-ROO-mah noh SEH-bee-shee gah, hee-tsoo-yoh dehs*

a tow truck	レッカー車 *rehk-KAH shah*
Is there a repair shop/ garage near here?	この近くに，修理工場があります か。*koh-noh chee-KAH-koo nee, SHOO ree koh-joh gah ah-ree-mahs KAH*
Do you know the phone number of a nearby garage?	近くの修理工場の電話番号を御存知 ですか。*chee-KAH-koo noh SHOO-ree koh-joh noh, DEHN-wah bahn-goh oh goh-ZOHN-jee dehs KAH*
Could you send a <u>mechanic</u>?	<u>修理できる人</u>を，よこしてもらえま すか。*SHOO-ree deh-kee-roo hee-toh oh, yoh-KOHSH-teh moh-rah-eh-mahs KAH*
tow truck	レッカー車 *rehk-KAH shah*

At the Garage

There's something wrong with my car.	どこか，車の調子がよくないのです が。*DOH-koh kah, koo-ROO-mah noh choh-shee gah YOH-koo-nah-ee noh dehs gah*
I don't know what's wrong with the car.	どこが悪いのか，わかりません。 *DOH-koh gah wah-roo-ee noh kah, wah-KAH-ree-mah-sehn*
I think there's something wrong with the <u>battery</u>.	<u>バッテリー</u>が，よくないみたいで す。*baht-TEH-ree gah, YOH-koo-nah-ee mee-tah-ee dehs*
brakes	ブレーキ *boo-REH-kee*
clutch	クラッチ *koo-RAHT-chee*
electrical system	電気装置 *DEHN-kee soh-chee*
engine	エンジン *EHN-jeen*
fan belt	ファン・ベルト *FAHN-beh-roo-toh*
fuel pump	ガソリン・ポンプ *gah-SOH-reen pohn-poo*
gears	ギヤ *GEE-yah*
ignition	点火装置 *TEIIN-kah soh-chee*

starter	スターター soo-*TAH*-*tah*
steering wheel	ハンドル *HAHN-doh-roo*
suspension	サスペンション sah-*SOO-pehn-shohn*
transmission	トランスミッション toh-*RAHN-soo-mees-shohn*
water pump	ウォーター・ポンプ *WOH-tah pohn-poo*
Can you take a look at the <u>carburetor</u>?	キャブレターを，チェックしてもらえますか。 *kyah-BOO-reh-tah oh, CHEHK-koo shteh moh-rah-eh-mahs KAH*
distributor	ディストリビューター *dee-SOO-toh-ree-byoo-tah*
gear box	ギヤ・ボックス *gee-YAH bohk-koos*
ignition coil	イグニッション・コイル *ee-GOO-nees-shohn koh-ee roo*
thermostat	サーモスタット *SAH-moh-soo-tuht-toh*
What's the problem?	どこが，よくないですか。 *DOH-koh gah, YOH-koo-nah-ee dehs KAH*
Is it fixable?	直りますか。 *nah-OH-ree-mahs KAH*
Do you have the necessary parts?	必要な部品が，ありますか。 *hee-TSOO-yoh nah boo-HEEN gah, ah-ree-mahs KAH*
Is it possible to get it fixed <u>now</u>?	<u>今</u>直してもらえるでしょうか。 *EE-mah nah-OH-shteh moh-RAH-eh-roo deh-shoh kah*
today	今日中に *KYOH joo nee*
How long will it take?	修理には，どの位時間がかかりますか。 *SHOO-ree nee-wah, doh-NOH koo-rah-ee jee-kahn gah kah-KAH-ree-mahs KAH*
Can you repair it temporarily?	仮の修理をしてもらえますか。 *kah-REE noh shoo-ree oh, SHTEH moh-rah-eh-mahs KAH*

Can you give me an estimate for the repair?	修理の見積りを，教えてください。 *SHOO-ree noh mee-TSOO-moh-ree oh,* *oh-SHEE-eh-teh koo-dah-sah-ee*
Is everything okay now?	直りましたか。 *nah-OH-ree-mah-* *shtah KAH*
May I have an itemized bill and a receipt?	明細書と領収書を，お願いします。 *MEH-sah-ee shoh toh RYOH-shoo shoh* *oh, oh-NEH-gah-ee shee-mahs*
Thank you very much for your help.	おかげで，本当に助かりました。 *oh-* *KAH-geh deh, HOHN-toh nee tahs-* *KAH-ree-mah-shtah*

ROAD SIGNS IN JAPANESE

Most road signs will be of the visual kind. But you may see some with just Japanese writing. This list may help you recognize them and understand what they mean.

入口	entrance
出口	exit
次の出口	next exit
料金所	toll gate
国道	national highway
県道	state (prefectural) highway
非常電話	emergency telephone
通行止め	road closed
車両通行止め	no vehicles
車両進入禁止	no entry
転回禁止	no U turn
行き止まり	dead end
駐車禁止	no parking
駐停車禁止	no stopping

徐行	slow down
止まれ	stop
一方通行	one way
追越し禁止	no passing
路肩弱し	soft shoulder
道路工事中	road under construction
まわり道（回り道）	detour
歩行者専用道路	road strictly for pedestrians

Guide Signs

 Emergency Telephone

 Parking

 National Highway

 Prefectural Highway

 Entrance to Expressway

Service Area

  Toll Gate

  Next Exit

 Exit

 Detour

Caution Signs

  Caution

  Slippery

Regulation Signs

Road Closed

No Vehicles

No Entry

No Entry for Vehicles

No Entry for Vehicles or Motorcycles

No Right Turn

No U Turn

No Passing

No Parking, No Standing

No Parking

No Parking Over 60 Minutes

Maximum Speed

Minimum Speed

Cars Only

Bicycles Only

Pedestrians and Bicycles Only

Pedestrians Only

  One Way

 This Lane for Motorcycles and Lightweight Cars

 Stop

 Slow Down

 Sound Horn

 End of Speed Limit Restriction

Indication Signs

Parking Permitted

Standing Permitted

Two Way Traffic Dividing Line

Traffic Island

Auxiliary Signs

日曜・祝日を除く

8－20

Except Sundays and Holidays

追越し禁止

No Passing

路肩弱し

Soft Shoulder

注　意

Caution

End of Restriction

Indication Board

Left Turn Permitted

GENERAL INFORMATION

TELLING TIME

A.M.	午前	*GOH-zehn*
P.M.	午後	*GOH-goh*
noon	正午	*SHŌH-goh*
midnight	真夜中／午前零時	*mah-YOH-nah-kah／ GOH-zehn reh jee*
o'clock	時	*jee*

First, a list of hours, then a list of minutes, then we'll put them together!

Hours

1 o'clock	一時	*ee-CHEE jee*
2 o'clock	二時	*NEE jee*
3 o'clock	三時	*SAHN jee*
4 o'clock	四時	*YOH jee*
5 o'clock	五時	*GOH jee*
6 o'clock	六時	*roh-KOO jee*
7 o'clock	七時	*shee-CHEE jee*
8 o'clock	八時	*hah-CHEE jee*
9 o'clock	九時	*KOO jee*
10 o'clock	十時	*JŌŌ jee*
11 o'clock	十一時	*JŌŌ ee-chee jee*
12 o'clock	十二時	*JŌŌ nee jee*

Minutes

1 minute	一分	*EEP-poon*
2 minutes	二分	*NEE foon*
3 minutes	三分	*SAHN poon*
4 minutes	四分	*YOHN poon*
5 minutes	五分	*GOH foon*
6 minutes	六分	*ROHP-poon*
7 minutes	七分	*nah-NAH foon*
8 minutes	八分	*HAHP-poon*
9 minutes	九分	*KYOO foon*
10 minutes	十分	*JOOP-poon*
11 minutes	十一分	*joo EEP-poon*
12 minutes	十二分	*joo NEE foon*
13 minutes	十三分	*joo SAHN poon*
14 minutes	十四分	*joo YOHN poon*
15 minutes	十五分	*joo GOH foon*
16 minutes	十六分	*joo ROHP-poon*
17 minutes	十七分	*joo nah-NAH foon*
18 minutes	十八分	*joo HAHP-poon*
19 minutes	十九分	*joo KYOO foon*
20 minutes	二十分	*nee JOOP-poon*
21 minutes	二十一分	*NEE joo eep-poon*
22 minutes	二十二分	*NEE joo nee foon*
23 minutes	二十三分	*NEE joo sahn poon*
24 minutes	二十四分	*NEE joo yohn poon*
25 minutes	二十五分	*NEE joo goh foon*
26 minutes	二十六分	*NEE joo rohp-poon*
27 minutes	二十七分	*NEE joo nah-nah foon*
28 minutes	二十八分	*NEE joo hahp-poon*

29 minutes	二十九分	*NEE jōo kyōo foon*
30 minutes	三十分	*SAHN joop-poon*
31 minutes	三十一分	*SAHN jōo eep-poon*
32 minutes	三十二分	*SAHN jōo nee foon*
33 minutes	三十三分	*SAHN jōo sahn poon*
34 minutes	三十四分	*SAHN jōo yohn poon*
35 minutes	三十五分	*SAHN jōo goh foon*
36 minutes	三十六分	*SAHN jōo rohp-poon*
37 minutes	三十七分	*SAHN jōo nah-nah foon*
38 minutes	三十八分	*SAHN jōo hahp-poon*
39 minutes	三十九分	*SAHN jōo kyōo foon*
40 minutes	四十分	*YOHN joop-poon*
41 minutes	四十一分	*YOHN jōo eep-poon*
42 minutes	四十二分	*YOHN jōo nee foon*
43 minutes	四十三分	*YOHN jōo sahn poon*
44 minutes	四十四分	*YOHN jōo yohn poon*
45 minutes	四十五分	*YOHN jōo goh foon*
46 minutes	四十六分	*YOHN jōo rohp-poon*
47 minutes	四十七分	*YOHN jōo nah-nah foon*
48 minutes	四十八分	*YOHN jōo hahp-poon*
49 minutes	四十九分	*YOHN jōo kyōo foon*
50 minutes	五十分	*goh JOOP-poon*
51 minutes	五十一分	*goh jōo EEP-poon*
52 minutes	五十二分	*goh jōo NEE foon*
53 minutes	五十三分	*goh jōo SAHN poon*
54 minutes	五十四分	*goh jōo YOHN poon*
55 minutes	五十五分	*goh jōo GOH foon*
56 minutes	五十六分	*goh jōo ROHP-poon*

57 minutes	五十七分	*goh jōo nah-NAH foon*
58 minutes	五十八分	*goh jōo HAHP-poon*
59 minutes	五十九分	*goh jōo KYŌO foon*

a quarter after <u>ten</u>

JŌO jee jōo GOH foon

or *JŌO jee jōo goh FOON soo-gee*

[*Note*: using "soo-gee," which means "past" or "after," is optional.]

a quarter to <u>ten</u>

JŌO jee jōo goh FOON mah-eh

[*Note*: start using "mah-eh," which means "to" or "before," at 15 minutes before the hour.]

half past <u>ten</u>

JŌO jee hahn

[*Note*: "hahn" means "half."]

What time is it?	何時ですか。 *NAHN-jee dehs KAH*	
It's <u>5:00</u> o'clock.	<u>五時</u>です。 *GOH jee dehs*	
5:05	五時五分 *GOH jee GOH foon*	
5:10	五時十分 *GOH jee JOOP-poon*	
5:15	五時十五分 *GOH jee jōo GOH foon*	
5:20	五時二十分 *GOH jee nee JOOP-poon*	
5:25	五時二十五分 *GOH jee NEE jōo goh foon*	
5:30	五時半 *goh JEE hahn*	
5:35	五時三十五分 *GOH jee SAHN jōo goh foon*	
5:40	五時四十分 *GOH jee YOHN joop-poon*	

5:45/ a quarter to six	五時四十五分／六時十五分前	*GOH jee YOHN joo goh foon / roh-KOO jee joo goh FOON mah-eh*
5:50 (ten to six)	六時十分前	*roh-KOO jee joop-POON mah-eh*
5:55 (five to six)	六時五分前	*roh-KOO jee goh FOON mah-eh*

For time schedules, as in railway and airline timetables, numbers 1 to 59 are used for minutes, <u>not</u> "a quarter to," or "ten to" the hour.

My train leaves at 1:48 P.M.	私の汽車は，午後一時四十八分に出ます。	*wah-TAHK-shee noh kee-shah wah, GOH-goh ee-CHEE jee YOHN joo HAHP-poon nee deh-mahs*
My plane arrives at 10:53 A.M.	私の飛行機は，午前十時五十三分に着きます。	*wah-TAHK-shee noh hee-koh-kee wah, GOH-zehn JOO jee goh joo SAHN poon nee tskee-mahs*

Note that transportation timetables are based on the 24–hour clock. Airline and train schedules are expressed in terms of a point within a 24–hour sequence.

DAYS OF THE WEEK

Sunday	日曜日	*nee-CHEE-yoh bee*
Monday	月曜日	*geh-TSOO-yoh bee*
Tuesday	火曜日	*kah-YOH bee*
Wednesday	水曜日	*soo-EE-yoh bee*
Thursday	木曜日	*moh-KOO-yoh bee*
Friday	金曜日	*KEEN-yoh bee*
Saturday	土曜日	*doh-YOH bee*

MONTHS OF THE YEAR

January	一月	*ee-CHEE gah-tsoo*
February	二月	*nee GAH-tsoo*
March	三月	*SAHN gah-tsoo*
April	四月	*shee GAH-tsoo*
May	五月	*GOH gah-tsoo*
June	六月	*roh-KOO gah-tsoo*
July	七月	*shee-CHEE gah-tsoo*
August	八月	*hah-CHEE gah-tsoo*
September	九月	*KOO gah-tsoo*
October	十月	*JOO gah-tsoo*
November	十一月	*JOO ee-chee gah-tsoo*
December	十二月	*JOO nee gah-tsoo*

THE FOUR SEASONS

spring	春	*HAH-roo*
summer	夏	*nah-TSOO*
fall	秋	*AH-kee*
winter	冬	*foo-YOO*

TIME PHRASES

today	今日	*KYOH*
yesterday	きのう	*kee-NOH*
the day before yesterday	おととい	*oh-TOH-toh-ee*

tomorrow	あした *ah-SHTAH*
the day after tomorrow	あさって *ah-SAHT-teh*
this week	今週 *KOHN shoo*
last week	先週 *SEHN shoo*
next week	来週 *rah-EE shoo*
for one week	一週間 *ees-SHOO kahn*
for two weeks	二週間 *nee SHOO kahn*
in one week	一週間で *ees-SHOO kahn deh*
in two weeks	二週間で *nee SHOO kahn deh*
for two days	二日間 *foo-TSOO-kah kahn*
in one day	一日で *ee-CHEE nee-chee deh*
in two days	二日で *foo-TSOO-kah deh*
three days ago	三日前 *meek-KAH mah-eh*
four months ago	四カ月前 *YOHN kah geh-tsoo mah-eh*
five years ago	五年前 *goh NEHN mah-eh*
this year	今年 *koh-TOH-shee*
last year	去年 *KYOH-nehn*
next year	来年 *rah-EE-nehn*
this morning	けさ *KEH-sah*
this afternoon	今日の午後 *KYOH noh GOH-goh*
tonight	今晩 *KOHN-bahn*
tomorrow night	あしたの晩 *ah-SHTAH noh bahn*
for six years	六年間 *roh-KOO nehn kahn*
for seven months	七カ月間 *nah-NAH kah geh-tsoo kahn*
in the morning	午前中 *goh-ZEHN choo*
in the afternoon	午後 *GOH-goh*
in the early evening	夕方 *YOO-gah-tah*
in the evening	夜 *YOH-roo*
in summer	夏に *nah-TSOO nee*
in winter	冬に *foo-YOO nee*

by Tuesday	火曜日までに	*kah-YOH bee mah-deh nee*
by June	六月までに	*roh-KOO gah-tsoo mah-deh nee*
by morning	朝までに	*AH-sah mah-deh nee*
What's today's date?	今日は，何日ですか。	*KYOH wah, NAHN-nee-chee dehs KAH*
It's ____.	今日は，____ です。	*KYOH wah, ____ dehs*
What day is today?	今日は，何曜日ですか。	*KYOH wah, nah-NEE yoh-bee dehs KAH*
It's ____.	今日は，____ です。	*KYOH wah, ____ dehs*

DAYS OF THE MONTH

1st	一日	*tsoo-EE-tah-chee*
2nd	二日	*foo-TSOO-kah*
3rd	三日	*meek-KAH*
4th	四日	*yohk-KAH*
5th	五日	*ee-TSOO-kah*
6th	六日	*moo-EE-kah*
7th	七日	*nah-NOH-kah*
8th	八日	*YOH-kah*
9th	九日	*koh-KOH-noh-kah*
10th	十日	*TOH-kah*
11th	十一日	*JOO ee-chee nee-chee*
12th	十二日	*JOO nee nee-chee*
13th	十三日	*JOO sahn nee-chee*
14th	十四日	*JOO yohk-kah*
15th	十五日	*JOO goh nee-chee*

16th	十六日 *JOO roh-koo nee-chee*
17th	十七日 *JOO shee-chee nee-chee*
18th	十八日 *JOO hah-chee nee-chee*
19th	十九日 *JOO koo nee-chee*
20th	二十日 *hah-TSOO-kah*
21st	二十一日 *NEE-joo ee-chee nee-chee*
22nd	二十二日 *NEE joo nee nee-chee*
23rd	二十三日 *NEE joo sahn nee-chee*
24th	二十四日 *NEE joo yohk-kah*
25th	二十五日 *NEE joo goh nee-chee*
26th	二十六日 *NEE joo roh-koo nee-chee*
27th	二十七日 *NEE joo shee-chee nee-chee*
28th	二十八日 *NEE joo hah-chee nee-chee*
29th	二十九日 *NEE joo koo nee-chee*
30th	三十日 *SAHN joo nee-chee*
31st	三十一日 *SAHN joo ee-chee nee-chee*

COUNTING YEARS

one year	一年	*ee-CHEE nehn*
two years	二年	*NEE nehn*
three years	三年	*SAHN nehn*
four years	四年	*yoh NEHN*
five years	五年	*goh NEHN*
six years	六年	*roh-KOO nehn*
seven years	七年	*nah-NAH nehn*
eight years	八年	*hah-CHEE nehn*
nine years	九年	*koo NEHN*
ten years	十年	*JOO nehn*

COUNTING DAYS

one day	一日	*ee-CHEE nee-chee*
two days	二日	*foo-TSOO-kah*
three days	三日	*meek-KAH*
four days	四日	*yohk-KAH*
five days	五日	*ee-TSOO-kah*
six days	六日	*moo-EE-kah*
seven days	七日	*nah-NOH-kah*
eight days	八日	*YOH-kah*
nine days	九日	*koh-KOH-noh-kah*
ten days	十日	*TOH-kah*
eleven days	十一日	*JOO ee-chee nee-chee*
twelve days	十二日	*JOO nee nee-chee*

COUNTING WEEKS

one week	一週間	*ees-SHOO kahn*
two weeks	二週間	*nee SHOO kahn*
three weeks	三週間	*SAHN shoo kahn*
four weeks	四週間	*YOHN shoo kahn*
five weeks	五週間	*goh SHOO kahn*
six weeks	六週間	*roh-KOO shoo kahn*
seven weeks	七週間	*nah-NAH shoo kahn*
eight weeks	八週間	*hahs-SHOO-kahn*
nine weeks	九週間	*KYOO shoo kahn*
ten weeks	十週間	*joos-SHOO kahn*

COUNTING DIFFERENT KINDS OF THINGS

	1 (one)	2 (two)	3 (three)	4 (four)	5 (five)
people	*hee-TOH-ree* 一人	*foo-TAH-ree* 二人	*SAHN neen* 三人	*yoh NEEN* 四人	*goh NEEN* 五人
long, skinny objects (pencils, sticks, bottles, and so forth)	*EEP-pohn* 一本	*NEE-hohn* 二本	*SAHN bohn* 三本	*YOHN hohn* 四本	*goh HOHN* 五本
thin, flat objects (paper, bills, cloth, dishes, tickets, and so forth)	*ee-CHEE mah-ee* 一枚	*NEE mah-ee* 二枚	*SAHN mah-ee* 三枚	*YOHN mah-ee* 四枚	*goh MAH-ee* 五枚
bound objects (books, magazines, notebooks, and so forth)	*ees-SAH-tsoo* 一冊	*NEE sah-tsoo* 二冊	*SAHN sah-tsoo* 三冊	*YOHN sah-tsoo* 四冊	*GOH sah-tsoo* 五冊
liquid or dry measures (glasses or cups of water, coffee, tea, sugar, and so forth)	*EEP-pah-ee* 一杯	*NEE hah-ee* 二杯	*SAHN bah-ee* 三杯	*YOHN hah-ee* 四杯	*goh HAH-ee* 五杯
vehicles, machines	*ee-CHEE dah-ee* 一台	*NEE dah-ee* 二台	*SAHN dah-ee* 三台	*YOHN dah-ee* 四台	*goh DAH-ee* 五台
things to wear (jackets, sweaters, shirts, coats, and so forth)	*eet-CHAH-koo* 一着	*NEE chah-koo* 二着	*SAHN chah-koo* 三着	*YOHN chah-koo* 四着	*GOH chah-koo* 五着

pairs of things to wear on feet or legs (socks, shoes, slippers, and so forth)

ees-SOH-koo 一足	NEE soh-koo 二足	SAHN zoh-koo 三足	YOHN soh-koo 四足	GOH soh-koo 五足

sets of dishes, pairs of people, and so forth

hee-TOH koo-mee 一組	foo-TAH koo-mee 二組	MEE koo-mee 三組	YOH koo-mee 四組	ee-TSOO koo-mee 五組

boxes, cases, and so forth

hee-TOH hah-koh 一箱	foo-TAH hah-koh 二箱	MEE hah-koh 三箱	YOH hah-koh 四箱	ee-TSOO hah-koh 五箱

floors of buildings

eek-KAH-ee 一階	nee KAH-ee 二階	SAHN gah-ee 三階	yohn kah-ee 四階	goh KAH-ee 五階

houses, buildings

EEK-kehn 一軒	NEE kehn 二軒	SAHN gehn 三軒	YOHN kehn 四軒	GOH-kehn 五軒

animals, insects, fish

eep-PEE-kee 一匹	NEE hee-kee 二匹	SAHN bee-kee 三匹	YOHN hee-kee 四匹	GOH hee-kee 五匹

large animals (horses, cows, elephants, and so forth)

EET-toh 一頭	NEE toh 二頭	SAHN toh 三頭	YOHN toh 四頭	GOH toh 五頭

birds

| ee-CHEE wah 一羽 | NEE wah 二羽 | SAHN bah 三羽 | YOHN wah 四羽 | GOH wah 五羽 |

bunches (grapes, bananas, and so forth)

| hee-TOH foo-sah 一房 | foo-TAH foo-sah 二房 | MEE foo-sah 三房 | YOH foo-sah 四房 | ee-TSOO foo-sah 五房 |

copies (newspapers, documents, books, and so forth)

| ee-CHEE boo 一部 | NEE boo 二部 | SAHN boo 三部 | YOH boo 四部 | GOH boo 五部 |

portions, servings

| ee-CHEE neen mah-eh 一人前 | nee NEEN mah-eh 二人前 | SAHN neen mah-eh 三人前 | yoh NEEN mah-eh 四人前 | goh-NEEN mah-eh 五人前 |

slices

| hee-TOH kee-reh 一切れ | foo-TAH kee-reh 二切れ | MEE kee-reh 三切れ | YOH kee-reh 四切れ | ee-TSOO kee-reh 五切れ |

small objects not in the categories listed above

| EEK-koh / hee-TOH-tsoo 一個／一つ | NEE koh / foo-TAH-tsoo 二個／二つ | SAHN koh / meet-TSOO 三個／三つ | YOHN koh / yoht-TSOO 四個／四つ | GOH koh / ee-TSOO-tsoo 五個／五つ |

NATIONAL HOLIDAYS

January 1
   New Years Day | 元旦 | *GAHN-tahn*

January 15
   Adulthood Day | 成人の日 | *SEH-jeen noh hee*

February 11
   National Founda-
   tion Day | 建国記念日 | *KEHN-koh-koo kee-
   nehn-bee*

March 20 or 21
   Vernal Equinox
   Day | 春分の日 | *SHOON-boon noh
   hee*

April 29
   Emperor's
   Birthday | 天皇誕生日 | *TEHN-noh tahn-joh-
   bee*

May 3
   Constitution Day | 憲法記念日 | *KEHN-poh kee-
   NEHN-bee*

May 5
   Children's Day | 子供の日 | *koh-DOH-moh noh
   hee*

September 15
   Respect for the
   Aged Day | 敬老の日 | *KEH-roh noh hee*

September 23 or 24
   Autumnal Equinox
   Day | 秋分の日 | *SHOO-boon noh hee*

October 10
   Health-Sports
   Day | 体育の日 | *TAH-ee-ee-koo noh
   hee*

November 3
   Culture Day | 文化の日 | *BOON-kah noh hee*

November 23

Labor Thanksgiv-   勤労感謝の日   *KEEN-roh kahn-*
ing Day   *shah noh hee*

COUNTRIES

Argentina	アルゼンチン	*ah-ROO-zehn-cheen*
Australia	オーストラリア	*OH-soo-toh-rah-ree-ah*
Austria	オーストリア	*OH-soo-toh-ree-ah*
Belgium	ベルギー	*beh-ROO-gee*
Bolivia	ボリビア	*boh-REE-bee-ah*
Brazil	ブラジル	*boo-RAH-jee-roo*
Burma	ビルマ	*BEE-roo-mah*
Canada	カナダ	*KAH-nah-dah*
Chile	チリ	*CHEE-ree*
China	中国	*CHOO-goh-koo*
Colombia	コロンビア	*koh-ROHN-bee-ah*
Czechoslovakia	チェコスロバキア	*CHEH-koh-soo-ROH-bah-kee-ah*
Denmark	デンマーク	*DEHN-mah-koo*
Ecuador	エクアドル	*eh-KOO-ah-doh-roo*
Egypt	エジプト	*eh-JEE-poo-toh*
England	イギリス	*ee-GEE-ree-soo*
Finland	フィンランド	*FEEN-rahn-doh*
France	フランス	*foo-RAHN-soo*
Greece	ギリシャ	*GEE-ree-shah*
Holland	オランダ	*oh-RAHN-dah*
India	インド	*EEN-doh*
Indonesia	インドネシア	*EEN-doh-neh-shee-ah*
Iran	イラン	*EE-rahn*

Ireland	アイルランド	*ah-EE-roo-rahn-doh*
Israel	イスラエル	*ee-SOO-rah-eh-roo*
Italy	イタリア	*ee-TAH-ree-ah*
Jordan	ヨルダン	*YOH-roo-dahn*
Korea	韓国	*KAHN-koh-koo*
Kuwait	クウェート	*koo-WEH-toh*
Lebanon	レバノン	*REH-bah-nohn*
Malaysia	マレーシア	*mah-REH-shee-ah*
Mexico	メキシコ	*meh-KEE-shee-koh*
New Zealand	ニュージーランド	*nyoo-jee-rahn-doh*
Norway	ノルウェー	*NOH-roo-weh*
Pakistan	パキスタン	*pah-KEE-soo-tahn*
Peru	ペルー	*PEH-roo*
Philippines	フィリッピン	*fee-REEP-peen*
Poland	ポーランド	*POH-rahn-doh*
Portugal	ポルトガル	*poh-ROO-toh-gah-roo*
Saudi Arabia	サウジアラビア	*sah-OO-jee ah-rah-bee-ah*
Singapore	シンガポール	*SHEEN-gah-poh-roo*
South Africa	南アフリカ	*mee-NAH-mee ah-foo-ree-kah*
Soviet Union	ソ連	*SOH-rehn*
Spain	スペイン	*soo-PEH-een*
Sweden	スウェーデン	*soo-WEH-dehn*
Switzerland	スイス	*SOO-ee-soo*
Thailand	タイ国	*TAH-ee-koh-koo*
Turkey	トルコ	*TOH-roo-koh*
United States	アメリカ	*ah-MEH-ree-kah*
Uruguay	ウルグアイ	*oo-ROO-goo-ah-ee*
Venezuela	ベネズエラ	*beh-NEH-zoo-eh-rah*

| West Germany | 西ドイツ | *nee-SHEE doh-ee-tsoo* |
| Yugoslavia | ユーゴスラビア | *YOO-goh-soo-rah-bee-ah* |

NATIONALITIES

To express nationality, add **jeen** to the Japanese expressions for the countries listed above. For example, to say "American," look up the country **United States**, which is **ah-MEH-ree-kah**, and add **jeen**. Thus **American** is **ah-MEH-ree-kah jeen**. *Jeen* literally means "person."

| person | 人 | *jeen* |

Exceptions: For Russian and German, use these expressions:

| Russian | ロシア人 | *roh-SHEE-ah jeen* |
| German (both East and West) | ドイツ人 | *doh-EE-tsoo jeen* |

COUNTING TIMES

once	一度	*ee-CHEE doh*
twice	二度	*nee DOH*
three times	三度	*sahn DOH*
four times	四度	*YOHN doh*
five times	五度	*GOH-doh*
the first time	初めて	*hah-JEE-meh-teh*
the second time	二度目	*nee-DOH meh*
the third time	三度目	*SAHN-doh meh*
the fourth time	四度目	*YOHN-doh meh*
the fifth time	五度目	*goh-DOH meh*

SIGNS

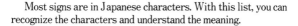

Most signs are in Japanese characters. With this list, you can recognize the characters and understand the meaning.

入口	Entrance
出口	Exit
東口	East exit
西口	West exit
南口	South exit
北口	North exit
便所	Lavatory
お手洗	Lavatory
男	Men
女	Women
大人	Adult
小人	Child
危険	Danger
立入禁止	Keep Out
消火器	Fire Extinguisher
火気厳禁	No Matches
有料	Fee Required
無料	Free Admission
本日休業	Closed Today
準備中	Temporarily Closed
禁煙	No Smoking
土足禁止	No Shoes (no street shoes allowed on the floor)
コインロッカー	Pay Locker
指定席	Reserved Seat
自由席	Nonreserved Seat

満席	Full
駐車場	Parking Place
病院	Hospital
空き	Vacant
使用中	Occupied
ベルを押してください	Please Ring
引く	Pull
押す	Push
注意	Caution
非常口	Emergency Exit
触れるな	Don't Touch
案内所	Information
猛犬に注意	Beware of Dog
会計	Cashier
貸し出し／貸します	For Rent, For Hire
ノックせずにお入りください	Enter Without Knocking
入場禁止	No Entry
入場お断わり	No Admittance
私有地	Private Property
警告	Warning
止まれ	Stop
売り切れ	Sold Out
魚釣禁止	No Fishing
水泳禁止	No Swimming

METRIC CONVERSIONS

If you're not used to the metric system, you'll need the tables and conversion charts for your visit to Japan.

Some Convenient Rough Equivalents

These are rough approximations, but they'll help you to "think metric" when you don't have your pocket calculator handy.

3 kilometers	=	2 miles
30 grams	=	1 ounce
100 grams	=	3.5 ounces
1 kilogram	=	2 pounds
1 liter	=	1 quart
1 hectare	=	1 acre

CENTIMETERS/INCHES

It is usually unnecessary to make exact conversions from your customary inches to the metric system, but to give you an approximate idea of how they compare, we give you the following guide.

To convert **centimeters** into inches, multiply by .39.

To convert inches into **centimeters,** multiply by 2.54.

Centimeters

Inches

METERS/FEET

1 meter	=	39.37 inches	1 foot	=	0.3 meters
	=	3.28 feet	1 yard	=	0.9 meters
	=	1.09 yards			

How tall are you in meters? See for yourself.

FEET/INCHES	METERS/CENTI-METERS
5	1.52
5 1	1.545
5 2	1.57
5 3	1.595
5 4	1.62
5 5	1.645
5 6	1.68
5 7	1.705
5 8	1.73
5 9	1.755
5 10	1.78
5 11	1.805
6	1.83
6 1	1.855

LIQUID MEASUREMENTS

1 liter =1.06 quarts
4 liters =1.06 gallons

For quick approximate conversion, multiply the number of gallons by 4 to get liters. Divide the number of liters by 4 to get gallons.

WHEN YOU WEIGH YOURSELF

1 kilogram   2.2 pounds
1 pound   0.45 kilogram

KILOGRAMS	POUNDS
40	88
45	99
50	110
55	121
60	132
65	143
70	154
75	165
80	176
85	187
90	198
95	209
100	220

QUICK GRAMMAR GUIDE

Japanese is a complex language, and a detailed grammatical presentation is far beyond the scope of this book. However, this list of some major characteristics of the language may give you an idea of how Japanese works and can help you use the phrases with confidence. Note that in this Grammar Guide the romaji spellings are used for the Japanese, in addition to, or instead of, the pronunciation.

WORD ORDER

The word order of a Japanese sentence is subject-object-verb. The verb always comes at the end. Subordinate clauses must come before the main clause. For example, the sentence *I'm studying Japanese* becomes *Japanese-am-studying. I won't go if it rains* becomes: *It-rains-if I-won't-go.* Notice how the subordinate clause, *if it rains,* changes position so that the main clause can be at the end of the sentence.

ARTICLES

There are no articles in Japanese. That is, there is nothing that corresponds to the English words *a, an,* or *the.*

NOUNS

Japanese nouns do *not* have plural forms. 本 hon *(hohn)* means *a book, the book, books* or *the books*.

PARTICLES

Japanese contains many particles, short words which are often called postpositions because they come after other words. These particles help to identify the relationship of the word they follow to other important parts of the sentence. The most commonly used particles are the following:

ROMAJI/ PRONUNCIATION

wa/ ga	*wah/gah*	Subject markers (More accurately, they occur with words that translate the English subject)
o	*oh*	Direct object marker
ka	*kah*	Question marker
no	*noh*	Possessive marker
ni	*nee*	Translates English *to* (or *at* when it indicates where something is located)
e	*eh*	Translates English *to*
de	*deh*	Translates English *at* when it indicates where an action takes place

Note that many other English prepositions are translated by Japanese noun phrases. An example of such a Japanese noun phrase is:

sūpa no mae ni   (*SOO-pah noh MAH-eh nee*)

This means "(located) in front of the supermarket." The word *MAH-eh* (front) is a noun.

PRONOUNS

The subject and object pronouns are usually omitted if the meaning is clear without them. They can be included when necessary. For example:

| I'm an American. | *Amerikajin desu.* | *ah-MEH-ree-kah jeen* |
| | American am | *dehs.* |

ADJECTIVES

In English, adjectives (such as *big, small, attractive*) are related to nouns. In Japanese, however, many are really a type of verb. That is, the endings change according to tense and the like. On the other hand, some Japanese adjectives are part of the noun system. These are invariable in form and are usually followed by the word *na,* as in kirei na hito (*KEE-reh nah hee-toh*), which means "a pretty person" (the adjective is kirei , "pretty").

VERBS

There are two tenses in Japanese: non-past and past. We can think of the non-past as including the present and future tense meanings:

I study at the library.

<u>Toshokan</u> <u>de</u> <u>benkyō shimasu</u>.
 library at study

I'm studying at the library.

<u>Toshokan</u> <u>de</u> <u>benkyō shite imasu</u>.
 library at studying am

I'll study at the library soon.

<u>Sugu</u> <u>toshokan</u> <u>de</u> <u>benkyō shimasu</u>.
 soon library at study will

The past tense looks like this:

I studied at the library.

<u>Toshokan</u> <u>de</u> <u>benkyō shimashita</u>.
 library at studied

Negatives of non-past verbs are made by changing -masu to -masen:

I understand.　　　　　　Wakarimasu.
I don't understand.　　　　Wakarimasen.

In the case of the past, -mashita becomes -masen deshita:

I understood.　　　　　　Wakarimashita.
I didn't understand.　　　　Wakarimasen deshita

LEVELS OF LANGUAGE

The Japanese language reflects the importance of interpersonal relationships in Japanese society. Other languages, of course, have ways of expressing varying degrees of formality in a relationship or a situation. But Japanese has many more ways than most. To fulfill the linguistic requirments of dealing with respect, courtesy, and relative social status in Japanese takes a knowledge of the culture and the language that ordinarily results from considerable time and study.

Many of the social and other distinctions are conveyed in the verbs. There are entire sets of endings for different levels of language. This book uses a level of politeness that will be appropriate for your trip. We may characterize it as "polite" (formal), as opposed to "plain" (informal).

	polite	plain
I understand	wakarimasu	wakaru
I'm eating	tabete imasu	tabete iru

You should be aware that there is much more to this dimension of the Japanese language, and that while you will be correct in using the verb forms presented in this book, you will hear a great many others.

MALE AND FEMALE LANGUAGE

Another aspect of the interpersonal distinctions in Japanese is the difference between male and female language. Japanese men and women are bound by certain rules of language usage, and some of these carry over to foreigners as well. The only difference that we treat here is the use of the polite or honorific particle before certain words. We indicate this for you in the pronunciation by an *oh* in parenthesis.

Japanese rice wine   *(oh) sah-KEH*

This means that a woman should pronounce the *oh*. For a man, it's optional.

NUMBERS

A word about numbers may be helpful here. Japanese uses classifiers for counting different categories of things. For speakers of English or other European languages, this can be confusing at first. It means that when you've learned to count from 1 to 10 or to 100 or 1,000, you can't necessarily use those numbers for counting books or days or people. For example, some cardinal numbers:

one	ichi	*ee-chee*
two	ni	*nee*
three	san	*sahn*

But:

| one *book* | hon o issatsu | *HOHN oh ees-SAH-tsoo* |
| one *dog* | inu o ippiki | *ee-NOO oh eep-PEE-kee* |

Not an ichi in sight! So, before you count anything, check for the classifier, or counter, you need. You'll find many listed throughout the book, under the appropriate headings. Others appear on page 332, General Information section.

WRITING SYSTEM

You probably won't be reading or writing Japanese on your trip, but you will see those fascinating characters everywhere, and you might want to know something about them. You might even get to recognize a few!

Traditionally, Japanese is written vertically, from top to bottom and from right to left. But it is also written horizontally and from left to right as in English. There are three kinds of characters used in the writing:

kanji	*KAHN-jee*
hiragana	*hee-RAH-gah-nah*
katakana	*kah-TAH-kah-nah*

All three are used together in Japanese words and sentences.

Kanji

Although Japanese and Chinese are completely separate languages, Japanese adopted written symbols and much vocabulary from Chinese, beginning in the fourth or fifth century. In Japan these symbols or Chinese characters are called kanji. They represent both meaning and sound, and it is often the case that one kanji has more than one reading (or pronunciation) and meaning. Japanese people learn about 2,000 kanji by the end of high school. Those are the basic characters used in newspapers, magazines, and school textbooks. Most Japanese know several thousand additional kanji as well.

Kanji can be very simple, with one or two strokes, or quite complicated, with many strokes needed to make one character. Some kanji look like pictures, or line drawings, of the words they represent:

mountain	yama	*yah-MAH*	山
river	kawa	*kah-WAH*	川

Put these two together, and you have the Japanese family name Yamakawa.

Hiragana and Katakana

Hiragana and katakana are used to represent the sounds of syllables. Each is a kind of alphabet of 46 characters or sounds. Hiragana is used for native Japanese words, and katakana for words of foreign origin.

Welcome to Japan, Mr. Smith.	スミス	さん，	日本	へようこそ。
	kata-kana	hira-gana	kanji	hiragana

HIRAGANA

	a	i	u	e	o	
	a あ *ah*	i い *ee*	u う *oo*	e え *eh*	o お *oh*	
k	ka か *kah*	ki き *kee*	ku く *koo*	ke け *keh*	ko こ *koh*	
s	sa さ *sah*	shi し *shee*	su す *soo*	se せ *seh*	so そ *soh*	
t	ta た *tah*	chi ち *chee*	tsu つ *tsoo*	te て *teh*	to と *toh*	
n	na な *nah*	ni に *nee*	nu ぬ *noo*	ne ね *neh*	no の *noh*	ん n
h	ha は *hah*	hi ひ *hee*	fu ふ *hoo*	he へ *heh*	ho ほ *hoh*	
m	ma ま *mah*	mi み *mee*	mu む *moo*	me め *meh*	mo も *moh*	
y	ya や *yah*		yu ゆ *yoo*		yo よ *yoh*	
r	ra ら *rah*	ri り *ree*	ru る *roo*	re れ *reh*	ro ろ *roh*	
w	wa わ *wah*				o を *oh*	

KATAKANA

	a	i	u	e	o	
	a ア *ah*	i イ *ee*	u ウ *oo*	e エ *eh*	o オ *oh*	
k	ka カ *kah*	ki キ *kee*	ku ク *koo*	ke ケ *keh*	ko コ *koh*	
s	sa サ *sah*	shi シ *shee*	su ス *soo*	se セ *seh*	so ソ *soh*	
t	ta タ *tah*	chi チ *chee*	tsu ツ *tsoo*	te テ *teh*	to ト *toh*	
n	na ナ *nah*	ni ニ *nee*	nu ヌ *noo*	ne ネ *neh*	no ノ *noh*	ン n
h	ha ハ *hah*	hi ヒ *hee*	fu フ *hoo*	he ヘ *heh*	ho ホ *hoh*	
m	ma マ *mah*	mi ミ *mee*	mu ム *moo*	me メ *meh*	mo モ *moh*	
y	ya ヤ *yah*		yu ユ *yoo*		yo ヨ *yoh*	
r	ra ラ *rah*	ri リ *ree*	ru ル *roo*	re レ *reh*	ro ロ *roh*	
w	wa ワ *wah*				o ヲ *oh*	

ENGLISH-JAPANESE DICTIONARY

A

abalone *AH-wah-bee* あわび

accident *JEE-koh* 事故

acupressure *shee-AH-tsoo* 指圧

acupressurist *shee-AH-tsoo shee* 指圧師

acupuncture *hah-REE ryoh-jee* 針療治

acupuncturist *HAH-ree noh ryoh-jee shee* 針の療治師

ad *KOH-koh-koo* 広告

adapter plug *POO-rah-goo noh ah-DAH-poo-tah* プラグのアダプター

address *JOO-shoh* 住所

adhesive tape *BAHN-soh-koh* ばんそうこう

admission fee *NYOO-joh ryoh* 入場料

aerogram *KOH-koo shoh kahn* 航空書簡

Africa *ah-FOO-ree-kah* アフリカ

after _____ *noh AH-toh deh* _____ の あとで

afternoon *GOH-goh* 午後

again *MOH ee-chee-doh* もう一度

age limit *NEHN-reh seh-gehn* 年齢制限

air conditioner *REH-boh* 冷房

airplane *hee-KOH-kee* 飛行機

airport *KOH-koh* 空港

aisle *TSOO-roh* 通路

alcohol *ah-ROO-koh-roo* アルコール

ale *EH-roo* エール

allergy *ah-REH-roo-gee* アレルギー

almonds *AH-mohn-doh* アーモンド

alone *hee-TOH-ree* ひとり

also *moh/ mah-TAH* も／また

to alter (clothing) *nah-OH-soo* 直す

altogether *ZEHN-boo* 全部

always *EE-tsoo moh* いつも

ambulance *KYOO-kyoo shah* 救急車

America *ah-MEH-ree-kah* アメリカ

American (adj.) *ah-MEH-ree-kah noh* アメリカの

American *ah -MEH-ree-kah-jeen* アメリカ人

American music *ah-MEH-ree-kah noh ohn-gah-koo* アメリカの音楽

American products *ah-MEH-ree-kah seh-heen* アメリカ製品

and (between nouns) *toh* と

and (between sentences) *sohsh-TEH* そして

ankle *ah-SHEE koo-bee* 足首

another *hoh-kah-noh* 外の

antacid *ee-SAHN* 胃散

antibiotics *KOH-seh boos-shee-tsoo* 抗生物質

antiques *koht-TOH heen* こっとう品

antiseptic *SHOH-doh-koo yah-koo* 消毒薬

aperitif *ah-PEH-ree-chee-foo* アペリチフ

appendicitis *MOH-choh ehn* 盲腸炎

appetizers *ZEHN-sah-ee/ tsoo-MAH-mee* 前菜／つまみ

apple *REEN-goh* りんご

appointment *yoh-YAH-koo* 予約

April *shee-GAH-tsoo* 四月

aquamarine *ah-koo-ah mah-reen* アクアマリン

aquarium *soo-EE-zoh-koo kahn* 水族館

Arabic (lang.) *ah-RAH-bee-ah goh* アラビア語

architect *KEHN-chee-koo kah* 建築家

architecture *KEHN-chee-koo* 建築

area *chee-ee-kee* 地域

arm *oo-DEH* 腕

around (approximate time) *GOH-roh* 〜頃

arrival *TOH-chah-koo* 到着

arrival time *TOH-chah-koo noh jee-kahn* 到着の時間

to arrive *tsoo-koo* 着く

art *BEE-joo-tsoo* 美術

art gallery *gah-ROH* 画廊

artist *GEH-joo-tsoo kah* 芸術家

to go ashore *JOH-ree-koo soo-roo* 上陸する

ashtray *hah-EE-zah-rah* 灰皿

aspirin *ah-SOO-pee-reen* アスピリン

aspirin-free painkiller *ah-SOO-pee-reen oh foo-koo-mah-nah-ee CHEEN-tsoo zah-ee* アスピリンを含まない鎮痛剤

assorted food *moh-REE-ah-wah-seh* 盛り合せ

at ____ deh ____で

atmosphere *foon-ee-kee* 雰囲気

attache case *ah-TAHSH-sheh kehs* アタッシェ・ケース

attractions *mee-MOH-noh* みもの

main attractions *OH-moh nah mee-MOH-noh* 主なみもの

auburn *toh-BEE ee-roh* とび色

August *hah-CHEE-gah-tsoo* 八月

aunt (someone else's) *oh-BAH-sahn* おばさん

aunt (your own) *oh-BAH* 叔母

Australia *OH-soo-toh-rah-ree-ah* オーストラリア

author *CHOH-shah* 著者

auto mechanic *koo-ROO-mah noh SEH-bee-shee* 車の整備士

auto repair shop *SHOO-ree koh-joh* 修理工場

automatic transmission *jee-DOH hehn-soh-koo* 自動変速

autumn leaves *KOH-yoh* 紅葉

awful-tasting *mah-ZOO-ee* まずい

B

baby *ah-KAHM-boh* 赤ん坊

baby sitter *koh-MOH-ree* 子守り

back (location) *oo-SHEE-roh* うしろ

back (body) *seh-NAH-kah* 背中

bacon *BEH-kohn* ベーコン

bad *wah-ROO-ee* 悪い

badminton *bah-DOH-meen-tohn* バドミントン

baggage *NEE-moh-tsoo* 荷物

baked *BAH-pee deh yah-ee-tah* 天火で焼いた

bakery *PAHN yah* パン屋

balcony (theater) *nee-KAH-ee noh seh-kee* 二階の席

ballet *BAH-reh* バレー

　　classical ballet *koh-TEHN bah-reh* 古典バレー

　　modern ballet *moh-DAHN bah-reh* モダン・バレー

　　ballet theater *bah-REH geh-kee joh* バレー劇場

ballpoint pen *BOH-roo pehn* ボールペン

bamboo *tah-KEH* 竹

bamboo basket *tah-KEH noh kah-goh* 竹のかご

bamboo craft shop *tah-KEH zah-ee-koo noh mee-seh* 竹細工の店

banana *BAH-nah-nah* バナナ

band *gah-koo dahn* 楽団

bandages *HOH-tah-ee* 包帯

bandaids *BAHN-doh eh-ee-doh* バンドエイド

bangs *mah-EH gah-mee* 前髪

bank *GEEN-koh* 銀行

bar *BAH* バー

barbershop *toh-KOH-yah* 床屋

barn *NAH-yah* 納屋

baseball *yah-KYOO* 野球

  ball game *shee-AH-ee* 試合

  professional baseball *poo-ROH yah-kyoo* プロ野球

  ballpark *yah-KYOO joh* 野球場

basket *kah-goh* かご

basketball *bah-SOO-keht-toh boh-roo* バスケット・ボール

bath *yoh-KOOSHTS/ (oh)-FOO-roh* 浴室／（お）風呂

bathing suit *mee-ZOO-gee* 水着

bathtub *(oh)-FOO-roh/ yoh-KOO-soh* （お）風呂／浴そう

bathroom *oh-TEH-ah-rah-ee/ TOH-ee-reh/ oh-BEHN-joh* お手洗／トイレ／お便所

batter-fried food *TEHM-poo-rah* 天ぷら

battery *DEHN-chee* 電池

battery (car) *baht-TEH-ree* バッテリー

bay *wahn* 湾

beach *kah-ee-gahn* 海岸

  beach umbrella *BEE-chee PAH-rah-soh-roo* ビーチ・パラソル

bean curd *TOH-foo* 豆腐

beard *ah-GOH hee-geh* あごひげ

beautiful, pretty *KEE-reh* きれい

beauty parlor *bec-YOH-een* 美容院

bed *BEHD-doh* ベッド

beef *gyoo-nee-koo/ bee-foo* 牛肉／ビーフ

  roast beef *ROH-soo-toh bee-foo* ロースト・ビーフ

beef cooked in broth *shah-BOO shah-boo* しゃぶしゃぶ

beef cooked in seasoned sauce *SKEE-yah-kee* すき焼き

beer *BEE-roo* ビール

before ___ *noh MAH-eh nee* ___ の前に

bellhop *boh-ee* ボーイ

belt *beh-ROO-toh* ベルト

better *MOHT-toh ee* もっといい

bicycle, bike *jee-TEHN-shah* 自転車

bicycling *SAH-ee-koo-reen-goo* サイクリング

bicycling course *sah-EE-koo-reen-goo koh-soo* サイクリング・コース

big *OH-kee* 大きい

bills (currency) *oh-SAH-tsoo* お札

bird *toh-REE* 鳥

birthdate *SEH-nehn gahp-pee* 生年月日

biscuits *bee-SOO-keht-toh* ビスケット

black *koo-ROH-ee* 黒い

black and white *shee-ROH-koo-roh* 白黒

blanket *MOH-foo* 毛布

blender *MEE-kee-sah* ミキサー

blond *boo-ROHN-doh* ブロンド

blood *chee* 血

blood pressure *keh-TSOO ah-tsoo* 血圧

blouse *boo-RAH-oo-soo* ブラウス

blow dry *boo-ROH doh-rah-ee* ブロー・ドライ

blown glass *koo-CHEE-boo-kee gah-rah-soo* 口吹きガラス

blue *ah-OH-ee* 青い

boat *BOH-toh* ボート

bobby pins *heh-$\overline{AH}$ peen* ヘ
アー・ピン

body *kah-RAH-dah* 体

body lotion *boh-$\overline{DEE}$ roh-shohn*
ボディー・ローション

boiled *YOO-deh-tah/ nee-TAH* ゆ
でた／煮た

bone *hoh-NEH* 骨

book *HOHN* 本

bookstore *HOHN yah* 本屋

boots *$\overline{BOO}$-tsoo* ブーツ

bottle *been* びん

　　large bottle *$\overline{OH}$-been* 大びん

　　medium-size bottle
　　CHOO-been 中びん

　　small bottle *koh-BEEN* 小び
　　ん

bourbon *$\overline{BAH}$-bohn* バーボン

bow *oh-JEE-gee* おじぎ

to bow *oh-JEE-gee soo-roo* おじぎ
する

bowl *$\overline{boh}$-roo* ボール

boxed *hah-KOH nee ee-reh-teh* 箱
に入れて

box office *keep-poo OO-ree-bah* 切
符売り場

bra, brassiere *boo-RAH-jah* ブラ
ジャー

bracelet *boo-REH-soo-reht-toh* ブ
レスレット

brakes *boo-$\overline{REH}$-kee* ブレーキ

brake fluid *boo-$\overline{REH}$-kee oh-ee-roo*
ブレーキ・オイル

Brazil *boo-RAH-jee-roo* ブラジル

Brazilian *boo-RAH-jee-roo noh* ブ
ラジルの

bread *PAHN* パン

　　French bread *foo-RAHN-soo pahn*
　　フランス・パン

to break down *koh-shoh soo-roo*
故障する

breakfast *CHOH-shoh-koo/ ah-
SAH goh-hahn* 朝食／朝ご飯

bridge *hah-SHEE* 橋

bright *hah-DEH-yah-kah nah* はで
やかな

British *ee-GEE-ree-soo noh* イギ
リスの

Britisher *ee-GEE-ree-soo-jeen* イ
ギリス人

Broadway hits *boo-$\overline{ROH}$-doh-$\overline{weh}$
noh heet-toh* ブロード・ウェー
のヒット

broccoli *boo-ROHK-koh-ree* ブ
ロッコリ

broiled *jee-KEE-bee deh yah-ee-tah*
直火で焼いた

broken *oh-reh-tah* 折れた

broken, out of order (mechanical)
koh-WAH-reh-teh こわれて

brooch *boo-$\overline{ROH}$-chee* ブローチ

brown *chah-EE-roh-ee* 茶色い

bruise *dah-BUH-koo shoh* 打撲傷

brunette *boo-ROO-neht-toh* ブル
ネット

brushes *boo-RAH-shee* ブラシ

Buddhist temples *oh-TEH-rah* お
寺

buffet car *byoof-FEH shah*
ビュッフェ車

building *bee-roo* ビル

(to be) built *kehn-$\overline{zoh}$ sah-reh-roo*
建造される

burn *yah-KEH-doh* やけど

bus *BAH-soo* バス

　　hotel bus *HOH-teh-roo noh
　　bah-soo* ホテルのバス

　　limousine bus *ree-MOO-jeen
　　bah-soo* リムジン・バス

　　shuttle bus *shah-TOH-roo bah-
　　soo* シャトル・バス

bus stop *BAH-soo noh noh-REE-
bah* バスの乗り場

business *shee-goh-toh/ BEE-jee-
nehs* 仕事／ビジネス

business district *bee-JEE-neh-soo
gah-ee* ビジネス街

business trip *shee-GOH-toh noh
ryoh-$\overline{koh}$* 仕事の旅行

but _KEH-reh-doh-moh/ DEH-moh_ けれども／でも

butcher _nee-KOO yah_ 肉屋

butter _BAH-tah_ バター

button _boh-TAHN_ ボタン

to buy _kah-oo_ 買う

by (means of) ____ _deh_ ____で

by the aisle _TSOO-roh gah-wah_ 通路側

by the hour _jee-KAHN deh_ 時間で

by the way _toh-KOH-roh deh_ ところで

by the window _mah-DOH gee-wah_ 窓ぎわ

C

cabaret _KYAH-bah-reh_ キャバレー

cabbage _KYAH-beh-tsoo_ キャベツ

cable car _KEH-boo-roo kah_ ケーブル・カー

caddy _KYAH-dee_ キャディー

cake _KEH-kee_ ケーキ

  cheesecake _CHEE-zoo keh-kee_ チーズ・ケーキ

  chocolate cake _choh-KOH-reh-toh keh-kee_ チョコレート・ケーキ

calendar _kah-REHN-dah_ カレンダー

to call (telephone) _DEHN-wah soo-roo_ 電話する

camera _KAH-meh-rah_ カメラ

camera shop _kah-MEH-rah yah_ カメラ屋

camping _KYAHN-poo_ キャンプ

camping site _KYAHN-poo joh_ キャンプ場

can _kahn_ かん

Canada _KAH-nah-dah_ カナダ

Canadian _kah-NAH-dah-jeen_ カナダ人

candy _KYAHN-dee_ キャンディー

candy store _oh-KAH-shee yah_ お菓子屋

capital _SHOO-toh_ 首都

car _koo-ROO-mah_ 車

  large car _OH-gah-tah shah_ 大型車

  medium-sized car _CHOO-gah-tah shah_ 中型車

  small car _koh-GAH-tah shah_ 小型車

  sports car _soo-POH-tsoo kah_ スポーツ・カー

car rental agency _REHN-tah-kah noh OH-fees_ レンタカーのオフィス

carburetor _kyah-BOO-reh-tah_ キャブレター

card (business, personal) _MEH-shee_ 名刺

cardigan _KAH-dee-gahn_ カーディガン

cards (playing) _toh-RAHM-poo_ トランプ

carp _koh-ee_ 鯉

carrots _NEEN-jeen_ 人参

carry-on _KEE-nah-ee moh-CHEE-koh-mee heen_ 機内持ち込み品

cartridges _KAH-toh-reej-jee_ カートリッジ

  8-track _eh-EE-toh kah-toh-reej-jee teh-poo_ エイトカートリッジ・テープ

carved objects _CHOH-koh-koo heen_ 彫刻品

cassette _kah-SEHT-toh_ カセット

cassette recorder _kah-SEHT-toh reh-koh-dah_ カセット・レコーダー

castle _oh-SHEE-roh_ お城

____ **castle** ____ _joh_ ____城

catalog _kah-TAH-roh-goo_ カタログ

cavity _moo-SHEE bah_ 虫歯

celery _SEH-roh-ree_ セロリ

center *CHOO-oh* 中央

ceramics *TOH-jee-kee* 陶磁器

ceramics store *seh-TOH-moh-noh yah* 瀬戸物屋

cereal *SHEE-ree-ah-roo* シリアル

chain *chehn/ koo-SAH-ree* チェーン／鎖

chamber music *shee-TSOO-nah-ee gah-koo* 室内楽

change (money) *oh-TSOO-ree* おつり

to change *kah-EH-roo* 変える／代える／替える／換える

to change (transportation) *noh-REE-kah-eh-roo* 乗り換える

channel (TV) *CHAHN-neh-roo* チャンネル

chauffeur *OON-tehn-shoo* 運転手

cheap *yah-SOO-ee* 安い

check, bill *KAHN-joh/ CHEHK-koo/ kah-EE-keh* 勘定／チェック／会計

check (personal) *koh-JEEN yoh koh-GEET-teh* 個人用小切手

checks (pattern) *CHEHK-koo/ ee-CHEE-mah-tsoo moh-yoh* チェック／市松模様

to check (baggage) *ah-ZOO-keh-roo* あずける

to check (examine) *shee-RAH-beh-roo* 調べる

to check in *chehk-KOO een soo-roo* チェック・インする

cheek *HOH-hoh* ほほ

cheese *CHEE-zoo* チーズ

cherries *sah-KOO-rahn-boh/ CHEH-ree* さくらんぼ／チェリー

cherry blossoms *sah-KOO-rah* 桜

chest *moo-NEH* 胸

chestnuts *koo-REE* くり

chicken *nee-WAH-toh-ree* にわとり

chicken skewered and grilled *yah-KEE-toh-ree* 焼き鳥

chicken soup *chee-KEEN soo-poo* チキン・スープ

child (someone else's) *oh-KOH-sahn* お子さん

child (your own) *koh-doh-moh* 子供

chill *oh-KAHN* 悪寒

china *seh-TOH-moh-noh* 瀬戸物

China *CHOO-goh-koo* 中国

Chinese *CHOO-goh-koo noh* 中国の

Chinese (lang.) *CHOO-goh-koo goh* 中国語

Chinese tile game *mah-jahn* マージャン

mahjong parlor *JAHN soh* ジャン荘

mahjong set *mah-jahn noh SEHT-toh* マージャンのセット

chocolate *choh-KOH-reh-toh* チョコレート

hot chocolate *KOH-koh-ah* ココア

chopsticks *HAH-shee* はし

chopstick rest *hah-SHEE oh-kee* はし置き

church *kyoh-kah-ee* 教会

cigarettes *tah-BAH-koh* たばこ／タバコ

filtered cigarettes *fee-ROO-tah tsoo-kee noh tah-bah-koh* フィルター付きのたばこ

cigarette lighter *RAH-ee-tah* ライター

a pack of cigarettes *tah-BAH-koh oh hee-TOH hah-koh* たばこを一箱

cigars *hah-MAH-kee* 葉巻き

citizen *shee-meen* 市民

city *shee/ toh-shee* 市／都市

big city *toh-KAH-ee* 都会

clams *hah-MAH-goo-ree* はまぐり

classical music *koo-RAH-sheek-koo myoo-jeek-koo* クラシック・ミュージック

clean *KEE-reh nah* きれいな

to clean (tidy)
kah-TAH-zoo-keh-roo 片付ける

cleansing cream
koo-REHN-jeen-goo koo-ree-moo
クレンジング・クリーム

clear sky *HAH-reh* 晴れ

clerk *tehn-een* 店員

climate *kee-KOH* 気候

to climb *noh-BOH-roo* 登る

clock *toh-KEH* 時計

　　alarm clock
　　meh-ZAH-mah-shee doh-keh 目覚
　　し時計

　　travel alarm clock *ryoh-KOH
　　yoh noh meh-ZAH-mah-shee doh-
　　keh* 旅行用の目覚し時計

cloisonné *sheep-POH yah-kee* 七
宝焼

to close (v.i.) *shee-mah-roo* 閉まる

to close (v.t.) *shee-meh-roo* 閉める

clothes *foo-koo-soh* 服装

clothing store *YOH-foo-koo yah*
洋服屋

　　children's clothing
　　koh-DOH-moh foo-koo 子供服

　　children's clothing store
　　*koh-DOH-moh foo-koo noh mee-
　　seh* 子供服の店

　　men's clothing store
　　SHEEN-shee foo-koo noh mee-seh
　　紳士服の店

　　women's clothing store
　　foo-JEEN foo-koo noh mee-seh 婦
　　人服の店

cloudy *koo-MOH-ree* 曇り

club soda *TAHN-sahn/ koo-RAH-
boo soh-dah* 炭酸／クラブ・
ソーダ

clutch *koo-RAHT-chee* クラッチ

clutch fluid *koo-RAHT-chee oh-ee-
roo* クラッチ・オイル

coast *kah-cc gahn* 海岸

cocktails *KAH-koo-teh-roo* カクテ
ル

cocktail lounge *kah-KOO-teh-roo
rah-oon-jee* カクテル・ラウンジ

cocoa *KOH-koh-ah* ココア

coffee *KOH-hee* コーヒー

　　iced coffee *ah-EE-soo koh-hee*
　　アイス・コーヒー

　　instant coffee *EEN-stahn-toh
　　koh-hee* インスタント・コー
　　ヒー

coffee shop *KOH-hee shohp-poo*
コーヒー・ショップ

　　Japanese coffee shop
　　kees-SAH-tehn 喫茶店

coins *KOH-kah* 硬貨

cold (weather, climate)
sah,MOO-ee 寒い

cold (food, drink) *tsoo-MEH-tah-ee*
冷たい

cold (head, chest) *kah-ZEH* 風邪

colleague *DOH-ryoh* 同僚

cologne *OH-deh-koh-rohn* オーデ
コロン

color *ee-roh* 色

color chart *ee-ROH noh hyoh* 色
の表

color rinse *kah-RAH reen-soo* カ
ラー・リンス

comb *koo-shee* くし

to come *koo-roo* 来る

comedy *KEE-geh-kee* 喜劇

company *kah-EE-shah* 会社

company executive *kah-EE-shah
noh JOO-yah-koo* 会社の重役

company president *kah-EE-shah
noh shah-CHOH* 会社の社長

concert *kohn-SAH-toh* コンサー
ト

concert hall *kohn-SAH-toh hoh-
roo* コンサート・ホール

concerto *KYOH-soh kyoh-koo* 協奏
曲

confectionary *oh-KAH-shee yah*
お菓子屋

constipation *BEHN-pee* 便秘

consulate *RYOH-jee kahn* 領事館

contact lenses *KOHN-tahk-toh rehn-zoo* コンタクト・レンズ

soft lenses *soh-FOO-toh kohn-tahk-toh rehn-zoo* ソフト・コンタクトレンズ

convenient *BEHN-ree nah* 便利な

to cook *RYOH-ree-soo-roo* 料理する

cookies *KOOK-kee* クッキー

cooking facilities *RYOH-ree noh seh-tsoo-bee* 料理の設備

cooking utensils *soo-EE-jee yoh-goo* 炊事用具

cool *soo-ZOO-shee* 涼しい

coral *SAHN-goh* さんご

corn *KOHN/ toh-moh-roh-koh-shee* コーン／とうもろこし

corner *KAH-doh* 角

corn flakes *KOHN foo-REH-koo* コーン・フレーク

corn plasters *oo-OH noh meh koh-yah-koo* 魚の目膏薬

correct *tah-DAH-shee* 正しい

cosmetics shop *keh-SHOH-heen tehn* 化粧品店

cottage *koh-YAH* 小屋

cotton *dahs-SHEE mehn* 脱脂綿

cotton (fabric) *moh-MEHN* 木綿

cough *seh-KEE* せき

cough drops *seh-KEE doh-meh doh-rohp-poo* せきどめドロップ

cough syrup *seh-KEE doh-meh SHEE-rohp-poo* せきどめシロップ

counter *kah-OON-tah* カウンター

country (nation) *koo-NEE* 国

countryside *chee-HOH/ ee-NAH-kah* 地方／田舎

cover charge *kah-BAH chah-jee* カバー・チャージ

cozy *ee-GOH-koh-chee noh ee* 居心地のいい

crab *kah-NEE* かに

crackers *koo-RAHK-kah* クラッカー

rice crackers *(oh)-SEHN-beh* おせんべ

crafts *KOH-geh* 工芸

craftsman *KOH-geh kah* 工芸家

cramp *hee-KEE-tsoo-ree* ひきつり

cramps (stomach) *foo-KOO tsoo* 腹痛

cream *MEE-roo-koo* ミルク

cream rinse *koo-REE-moo reen-soo* クリーム・リンス

credit card *koo-REH-jeet-toh KAH-doh* クレジット・カード

crib *beh-bee BEHD-doh* ベビー・ベッド

croissant *koo-ROH-wahs-sahn* クロワッサン

to cross *wah-TAH-roo* 渡る

crowded *KOHN-deh* 混んで

cruise *KOH-kah-ee* 航海

cruise ship *YOO-rahn-sehn* 遊覧船

crystal (watch) *gah-RAH-soo boo-tah* ガラスぶた

cucumber *KYOO-ree* きゅうり

cufflinks *kah-FOO-soo boh-tahn* カフス・ボタン

curfew *MOHN-gehn* 門限

curlers *KAH-rah* カーラー

curly *mah-KEE geh/ KAH-ree* 巻き毛／カーリー

currency *tsoo-kah* 通貨

foreign currency *GAH-ee-kah* 外貨

custard *kahs-TAH-doh* カスタード

customs *ZEH-kahn* 税関

customs inspection *ZEH-kahn KEHN-sah* 税関検査

customs declaration form *ZEH-kahn noh sheen-koh-koo shoh* 税関の申告書

to cut *kee-roo* 切る

D

daily *MAH-ee-nee-chee noh* 毎日の

dancing *oh-DOHT-teh* おどって

Danish pastry *DĒH-neesh-shoo peh-stoh-ree/ kah-SHEE pahn* デーニッシュ・ペーストリー／菓子パン

dark *koo-RAH-ee* 暗い

date *hee-ZOO-keh* 日付

daughter (someone else's) *oh-JŌH-sahn* おじょうさん

daughter (your own) *moo-SOO-meh* 娘

day *hee* 日

  a day *ee-CHEE nee-chee* 一日

  day after tomorrow *ah-SAHT-teh* あさって

  a few days *SŌŌ jee-tsoo* 数日

  a half day *HAHN nee-chee* 半日

  two days *foo-TSOO-kah* 二日

  by the day *ee-CHEE nee-chee goh-toh* 一日ごと

  per day *ee-chee nee-chee* 一日

decaffeinated coffee *kah-FEH-een noo-kee noh KŌH-hee* カフェイン抜きのコーヒー

December *JŌŌ-nee-gah-tsoo* 十二月

delicious *oh-EE-shee* おいしい

demonstration *jee-TSOO-ehn* 実演

dentist *HAH-ee-shah* 歯医者

denture *ee-REH-bah* 入れ歯

deodorant *deh-OH-doh-rahn-toh* デオドラント

to depart (transportation) *deh-roo* 出る

department store *deh-PAH-toh* デパート

departure *shoop-PAH-tsoo* 出発

departure gate *shoop-PAH-tsoo goo-chee* 出発口

departure time *shoop-PAH-tsoo noh jee-kahn* 出発の時間

deposit *hoh-SHŌH-keen* 保証金

dessert *deh-ZĀH-toh* デザート

detective stories *TAHN-teh shoh-seh-tsoo* 探偵小説

detour *mah-WAH-ree mee-chee* 回り道

to develop (film) *gehn-zoh soo-roo* 現像する

diamond *dah-EE-yah* ダイヤ

diapers (disposable) *(tsoo-KAH-ee soo-teh noh) oh-shee-meh* （使いすての）おしめ

diarrhea *geh-REE* 下痢

dictionary *jee-shoh* 辞書

  English-Japanese dictionary *eh-wah jee-tehn* 英和辞典

  pocket dictionary *poh-KEHT-toh bahn oh jee-shoh* ポケット版の辞書

diesel (gas) *DĒE-zeh-roo* ディーゼル

diet *DAH-ee-eht-toh* ダイエット

diet soda *DAH-ee-eht-toh noh noh-MEE-moh-noh* ダイエットの飲み物

difference *chee-gah-ee* 違い

different *chee-GAH-oo* 違う

difficult *moo-ZOO-kah-shee* 難しい

dining car *shoh-KOO-doh shah* 食堂車

dining room *shoh-KOO-dōh* 食堂

dinner *BAHN-goh-hahn/ YOO-shoh-koo* 晩ご飯／夕食

direct dial *dah-ee-yah-roo choh-KOO-tsoo* ダイヤル直通

  directional signal *HŌH-koh shee-jee kee* 方向指示器

director (sports, film) *kahn toh-koo* 監督

director (theater, TV) *EHN-shoo-tsoo kah* 演出家

dirty *kee-TAH-nah-ee* きたない

disco _DEES-koh_ ディスコ

discount _wah-REE-bee-kee_ 割引き

dislocated _dahk-KYOO shtah_ 脱臼した

ditch _mee-ZOH_ みぞ

doctor _ee-SHAH_ 医者

documents _SHOH-roo-ee_ 書類

dollar _DOH-roo_ ドル

door _toh/ doh-ah_ 戸／ドア

doughnuts _DOH-naht-tsoo_ ドーナッツ

down ___ _noh SHTAH nee_ ___ の下に

downtown area _HAHN-kah gah-ee_ 繁華街

dress _DOH-reh-soo_ ドレス

dressing room _shee-CHAH-koo shee-tsoo_ 試着室

drinking water _noh-MEE mee-zoo_ 飲み水

drinks _noh-MEE-moh-noh_ 飲み物

drinks (alcoholic) _oh-SAH-keh_ お酒

to drink _NOH-moo_ 飲む

dry _KAHN-soh shteh ee-roo_ 乾燥している

dry cleaner _koo-REE-neen-goo yah_ クリーニング屋

dry cleaning service _doh-RAH-ee koo-ree-neen-goo noh sah-bee-soo_ ドライ・クリーニングのサービス

dubbed (film) _foo-KEE-kah-eh-rah-reh-teh_ 吹き替えられて

duck _ah-HEE-roo_ あひる

during ___ _noh ah-EE-dah nee_ ___ の間に

Dutch _oh-RAHN-dah-jeen_ オランダ人

E

ear _mee-MEE_ 耳

ear drops _mee-MEE goo-soo-ree_ 耳薬

early _hah-YAH-ee_ 早い

earrings _ee-YAH-reen-goo_ イヤリング

　　earrings for pierced ears _PEE-ah-soo noh ee-yah-reen-goo_ ピアスのイヤリング

earthquake _jee-SHEEN_ 地震

east _hee-GAH-shee_ 東

easy _yah-sah-shee_ やさしい

to eat _tah-BEH-roo_ 食べる

eclair _eh-KOO-reh-ah_ エクレア

egg _tah-MAH-goh_ たまご

eggplant _NAH-soo_ なす

elbow _hee-JEE_ ひじ

elder brother (someone else's) _oh-NEE-sahn_ お兄さん

elder brother (your own) _AH-nee_ 兄

elder sister (someone else's) _oh-NEH-sahn_ お姉さん

elder sister (your own) _ah-NEH_ 姉

electrical appliance _DEHN-kee seh-heen_ 電気製品

electrical appliance store _DEHN-kee kee-goo tehn_ 電気器具店

electrical transformer _HEHN-ah-tsoo-kee_ 変圧器

electricity _DEHN-kee_ 電気

electric razor _DEHN-kee kah-mee-soh-ree_ 電気カミソリ

elevator _eh-REH-beh-tah_ エレベーター

embassy _tah-EE-shee kahn_ 大使館

emerald _eh-MEH-rah-roo-doh_ エメラルド

emergency _KEEN-kyoo_ 緊急

emery boards *tsoo-MEH yah-soo-ree* 爪やすり

emperor *TEHN-noh* 天皇

engine *EHN-jeen* エンジン

engineer *EHN-jee-nee-ah* エンジニア

England *ee-GEE-ree-soo* イギリス

English (lang.) *EH-goh* 英語

English-speaking *EH-goh oh hah-nah-seh-roo* 英語を話せる

to enjoy *tah-NOH-shee-moo* 楽しむ

enlargement *hee-KEE-noh-bah-shee* 引き伸し

entertainment *moh-YOH-shee moh-noh* 催し物

entrance *ee-REE-goo-chee* 入口

envelope *FOO-toh* 封筒

eraser *keh-SHEE-goh-moo* 消しゴム

error *mah-CHEE-gah-ee* 間違い

estimate *mee-TSOO-moh-ree* 見積り

European products *YOH-rohp-pah seh-heen* ヨーロッパ製品

evening *YOO-gah-tah* 夕方

evening gown *ee-BOO-neen-goo doh-reh-soo* イブニング・ドレス

to exchange *KOH-kahn soo-roo* 交換する

exchange rate *KOH-kahn ree-tsoo* 交換率

Excuse me. *goh-MEHN-nah-sah-ee/ shee-TSOO-reh shee-mahs* ごめんなさい／失礼します

to exhibit *TEHN-jee soo-roo* 展示する

exit *DEH-goo-chee* 出口

expensive *tah-KAH-ee* 高い

to explain *seh-TSOO-meh soo-roo* 説明する

eye *MEH* 目

eyebrow pencil *mah-YOO zoo-mee* まゆずみ

eyeglasses *MEH-gah-neh* 眼鏡

frames *wah-KOO* わく

lenses *REHN-zoo* レンズ

eye liner *ah-EE rah-ee-nah* アイ・ライナー

eye pencil *ah-EE pehn-shee-roo* アイ・ペンシル

eye shadow *ah-EE shah-doh* アイ・シャドー

F

fabric *noo-NOH/ kee-jee* 布／生地

face *kah-OH* 顔

face powder *oh-SHEE-roh-ee* おしろい

facial massage *bee-GAHN joo-tsoo* 美顔術

fall *AH-kee* 秋

family *kah-zoh-koo* 家族

famous *yoo-meh* 有名

fan *OH-gee* 扇

fan belt *FAHN beh-roo-toh* ファン・ベルト

fancy *shah-REH-tah* しゃれた

far *TOH-ee* 遠い

fare *ryoh-keen* 料金

farm *hah-TAH-keh* 畑

fast, quick *hah-YAH-ee* 速い

father (someone else's) *oh-TOH-sahn* お父さん

father (your own) *chee-CHEE* 父

February *nee-GAH-tsoo* 二月

female, woman *OHN-nah noh hee-toh* 女の人

ferry *REHN-rahk-sehn* 連絡船

festival *oh-MAH-tsoo-ree* お祭り

fever *neh-TSOO* 熱

few, a little *SKOH-shee* 少し

fields *NOH-hah-rah* 野原

filet *hee-REII nee-koo* ひれ肉

filet mignon *hee-REH MEE-nee-ohn* ヒレミニオン

to fill (gas tank) *MAHN tahn nee soo-roo* 満タンにする

filling (tooth)
HAH noh tsoo-meh-moh-noh 歯のつめもの

temporary filling
kah-REE noh tsoo-meh-moh-noh 仮のつめもの

film *foo-EE-roo-moo* フィルム

filter (camera) *fee-roo-tah* フィルター

fine *GEHN-kee* 元気

Fine, thank you. *HAH-ee, oh-KAH-geh-sah-mah deh* はい，おかげさまで

finger *yoo-BEE* 指

to finish (v.i.) *oh-wah-roo* 終わる

It's over./ I'm finished.
oh-WAH-ree-mah-shtah 終わりました。

first aid kit *KYOO-kyoo bah-koh* 救急箱

first class *ee-CHEE ryoo noh* 一流の

first class (train) *GREEN-shah* グリーン車

first run film *FOO-kee-ree noh eh-gah* 封切りの映画

first time *hah-JEE-meh-teh* 初めて

fish *sah-KAH-nah* さかな

raw fish *sah-SHEE-mee* 刺身

raw fish and vinegared rice
SOO-shee すし

fishing *sah-KAH-nah tsoo-ree* さかなつり

fishing boat *tsoo-REE boo-neh* 釣船

fishing equipment *tsoo-REE doh-goo* 釣道具

fishing spot *tsoo-ree bah* 釣場

fish market *sah-KAH-nah yah* さかな屋

to fit *ah-oo* 合う

to fix *nah-OH-soo* 直す

fixable *nah-OH-seh-roo* 直せる

flash bulbs *foo-RAHS-shoo bah-roo-boo* フラッシュ・バルブ

flashlight *kah-EE-choo dehn-toh* 懐中電燈

flat tire *PAHN-koo* パンク

flight number *been-meh* 便名

connecting flight *noh-REE-tsoo gee been* 乗りつぎ便

direct flight *chohk-KOH-been* 直行便

nonstop flight
nohn-STOHP-poo ノン・ストップ

floor show *foo-ROH-ah shoh* フロア・ショー

florist *hah-NAH yah* 花屋

flounder *hee-RAH-meh* 平目

flower *hah-NAH* 花

flower arrangement *KAH-doh/ee-KEH-bah-nah/ oh-HAH-nah* 華道／活け花／お花

headmaster *ee-EH-moh-toh* 家元

flu *RYOO-kahn* 流感

flying time *hee-KOH jee-kahn* 飛行時間

folded *tah-TAHN-deh* たたんで

folk art *MEEN-geh* 民芸

folk song *FOH-koo sohn-goo* フォーク・ソング

folkware shop *MEEN-geh yah* 民芸屋

food *tah-beh-moh-noh* 食べ物

Japanese food *nee-HOHN shoh-koo-heen* 日本食品

Western food *SEH-yoh shoh-koo-heen* 西洋食品

foot (body) *ah-SHEE* 足

football *foot-TOH boh-roo* フットボール

for example *tah-TOH-eh-bah* 例えば

forbidden *keen-shee* 禁止

forehead *hee-TAH-ee* ひたい

foreign *gah-EE-koh-koo noh* 外国の

foreigner *gah-EE-koh-koo-jeen* 外国人

forest *moh-REE* 森

fork *FOH-koo* フォーク

formal clothing *SEH-soh* 正装

forward *MAH-eh noh* 前の

fortress *JOH-sah-ee* 城塞

fountain pen *MANN-nehn hee-tsoo* 万年筆

four seasons *SHEE-kee* 四季

fractured *hoh-NEH gah oh-reh-tah* 骨が折れた

fragile (goods) *koh-WAH-reh-moh-noh* こわれもの

franc *FOO-rahn* フラン

free (unoccupied) *ah-ee-teh* 空いて

free time *jee-YOO jee-kahn* 自由時間

French *foo-RAHN-soo noh* フランスの

French (lang.) *foo-RAHN-soo goh* フランス語

frequency (radio station) *SHOO-hah soo* 周波数

fresh *SHEEN-sehn nah* 新鮮な

Friday *KEEN-yoh-bee* 金曜日

fried (*ah-BOO-rah deh*) *ah-geh-tah* (油で) あげた

friend *YOO-jeen/ toh-MOH-dah-chee* 友人／友達

from ____ *kah-rah* ____から

front *MAH-eh* 前

fruit *koo-DAH-moh-noh* 果物

fruit compote *foo-ROOTS kahp-poo* フルーツ・カップ

fuel pump *gah-SOH-reen pohn-poo* ガソリン・ポンプ

full (I'm full) *oh-NAH-kah gah, eep-PAH-ee dehs* おなかが、いっぱいです。

furniture *KAH-goo* 家具

G

garden *nee-WAH/ TEH-ehn* 庭／庭園

garlic *GAH-reek-koo/ NEEN-nee-koo* ガーリック／にんにく

gas *GAH-soo* ガス

gasoline *gah-SOH-reen* ガソリン

  unleaded *moo-EHN gah-soh-reen* 無鉛ガソリン

  regular *REH-gyoo-rah* レギュラー

  super *SOO-pah/ hah-EE-oh-koo* スーパー／ハイオク

gas station *gah-SOH-reen soo-tahn-doh* ガソリン・スタンド

to gather (v.i.) *ah-tsoo-mah-roo* 集まる

gauze *GAH-zeh* ガーゼ

gears *GEE-yah* ギヤ

German *DOH-ee-tsoo noh* ドイツの

German (lang.) *doh-EE-tsoo goh* ドイツ語

Germany *DOH-ee-tsoo* ドイツ

to get off *oh-ree-roo* 降りる

to get on *noh-roo* 乗る

gift *oh-MEE-yah-geh* おみやげ

  return gift *oh-KAH-eh-shee* おかえし

gift shop *bah-EE-tehn* 売店

gin *JEEN* ジン

ginger *SHOH-gah* しょうが

glass *GOO-rah-soo* グラス

glass (drinking) *kohp-POO* コップ

gloves *teh-BOO-koo-roh* 手袋

glue *seht-CHAH-koo zah-ee/ noh-REE* 接着剤／のり

to go *ee-koo* 行く

  Let's go. *ee-KEE-mah-shoh* 行きましょう。

  Shall we go? *ee-KEE-mah-shoh KAH* 行きましょうか。

gold *KEEN* 金

   solid gold *JOON keen* 純金

gold plated *KEEN mehk-kee* 金メッキ

golf *GOH-roo-foo* ゴルフ

golf ball *goh-ROO-foo boh-roo* ゴルフ・ボール

golf clubs *goh-ROO-foo koo-rah-boo* ゴルフ・クラブ

golf course *goh-ROO-foo koh-soo* ゴルフ・コース

to play golf *GOH-roo-foo oh soo-roo* ゴルフをする

good, fine *EE* いい

good afternoon *KOHN-nee-chee-wah* こんにちは

goodbye *sah-YOH-nah-rah* さようなら

good evening *KOHN-bahn-wah* こんばんは

good morning *oh-HAH-yoh goh-zah-ee-mahs* おはようございます

good night *oh-YAH-soo-mee nah-sah-ee* おやすみなさい

good quality *JOH-toh / JOH-shee-tsoo* 上等／上質

grammar *boon-poh* 文法

grammar book *boon-poh noh hohn* 文法の本

grandfather (someone else's) *oh-JEE-sahn* おじいさん

grandfather (your own) *SOH-foo* 祖父

grandmother (someone else's) *oh-BAH-sahn* おばあさん

grandmother (your own) *SOH-boh* 祖母

grapefruit *goo-REH-poo foo-ROO-tsoo* グレープ・フルーツ

grapes *boo-DOH* ぶどう

gray *goo-REH noh* グレーの

Greek *GEE-ree-shah noh* ギリシャの

green *goo-REEN noh* グリーンの

grocery store *shoh-KOO-ryoh-heen tehn* 食料品店

grilled *yah-KEE-ah-mee deh yah-ee-tah* 焼網で焼いた

ground beef *GYOO noh hee-KEE nee-koo* 牛のひき肉

guidebook *gah-EE-doh book-koo* ガイド・ブック

gym *JEE-moo* ジム

H

hair *kah-mee noh keh* 髪の毛

hair color *keh ZOH-meh* 毛染め

haircut *SAHN-pah-tsoo* 散髪

hairdresser *bee-YOH een* 美容院

hair dryer *heh-AH doh-rah-ee-yah* ヘアー・ドライヤー

hair spray *heh-AH spoo-reh* ヘアー・スプレー

ham *HAH-moo* ハム

hamburger *HAHN-bah-gah* ハンバーガー

hamburger steak *HAHN-bah-goo soo-TEH-kee* ハンバーグ・ステーキ

hammer *HAHN-mah* ハンマー

hand *TEH* 手

handmade *teh-ZOO-koo-ree noh / teh SEH noh* 手作りの／手製の

handicrafts *shoo-KOH-geh heen* 手工芸品

handicrafts shop *KOH-geh noh mee-seh* 工芸の店

harbor, port *mee-NAH-toh* 港

hardware store *dah-EE-koo doh-goo-yah* 大工道具屋

hat *BOH-shee* 帽子

Hawaiian *HAH-wah-ee noh* ハワイの

hay fever *kah-FOON shoh* 花粉症

he *KAH-reh gah* 彼が

head *ah-TAH-mah* 頭

headache zoo-TSOO 頭痛

headlight hehd-DOH rah-ee-toh ヘッド・ライト

health club heh-ROOS koo-rah-boo ヘルス・クラブ

heater DAHN-boh 暖房

heart SHEEN-zoh 心臓

heart attack SHEEN-zoh mah-hee 心臓麻痺

heavy oh-MOH-ee 重い

heel kah-kah-toh かかと

height tah-KAH-sah 高さ

hello (telephone/ getting someone's attention) MOH-shee-moh-shee もしもし

helmet heh-ROO-meht-toh ヘルメット

to help tahs-KEH-roo 助ける

Help! tahs-KEH-teh 助けて

here koh-KOH ここ

high tah-KAH-ee 高い

highway KOH-soh-koo doh-roh 高速道路

hiking HAH-ee-keen-goo ハイキング

hiking trail hah-EE-keen-goo koh-soo ハイキング・コース

hill oh-KAH 丘

historical drama jee-DAH-ee moh-noh 時代物

historical sites KYOO-seh-kee 旧跡

history reh-KEE-shee 歴史

history books reh-KEE-shee noh hohn 歴史の本

hire (taxis, limousines) HAH-ee-yah ハイヤー

horn KEH-teh-kee 警笛

horseradish (Japanese) WAH-sah-bee わさび

hospital BYOH een 病院

hostess HOH-soo-tehs ホステス

hot ah-TSOO-ee 暑い

hot (peppery food) kah-RAH-ee からい

hot dog hoht-TOH dohg-goo ホットドッグ

hot springs OHN-sehn 温泉

hotel HOH-teh-roo ホテル

business hotel bee-JEE-nehs HOH-teh-roo ビジネス・ホテル

hotel reservation center HOH-teh-roo noh yoh-YAH-koo kah-OON-tah ホテルの予約カウンター

hour jee-KAHN 時間

by the hour jee-KAHN deh 時間で

per hour ee-CHEE jee-kahn 一時間

house ee-EH/ oo-chee 家／うち

housewares kah-TEH yoh heen 家庭用品

housewife SHOO-foo 主婦

hovercraft HOH-bah koo-rahf-toh ホーバー・クラフト

how DOH-yaht-teh どうやって

How are you? oh-GEHN-kee dehs KAH お気気ですか

How do you do? hah-JEE-meh-mahsh-teh, DOH-zoh yoh-ROH-shee-koo はじめまして，どうぞよろしく。

How do you do? (reply) hah-JEE-meh-mahsh-teh, koh-CHEE-rah koh-soh yoh-ROH-shee-koo はじめまして，こちらこそよろしく。

How long? doh-NOH koo-rah-ee どの位

How much? doh-NOH koo-rah-ee どの位

How much money? EE-koo-rah いくら

humid, damp shee-MEHT-teh ee-roo 湿っている

hungry *oh-NAH-kah gah, soo-EE-teh ee-mahs* おなかが，すいています。

husband (someone else's) *goh-SHOO-jeen* 御主人

husband (your own) *SHOO-jeen* 主人

hydrofoil *soo-EE-choo yohk-sehn* 水中翼船

I

I *wah-TAHK-shee gah* 私が

ice *KOH ree* 氷

ice cream *ah-EES-koo-ree-moo* アイスクリーム

ice pack *HYOH-noh* 氷のう

ice water *uh-EE-soo woh-tah* アイス・ウォーター

ignition *TEHN-kah soh-chee* 点火装置

imported *gah-EE-koh-koo noh* 外国の

I'm sorry *goh-MEHN-nah-sah-ee/ soo-MEE-mah-sehn* ごめんなさい／すみません

in ___ *nee* ___に

in advance *mah-eh-MOHT-teh* 前もって

incense *(oh)-SEHN-koh* （お）線香

Indian *EEN-doh noh* インドの

indigestion *SHOH-kah foo-ryoh* 消化不良

Indonesian *EEN-doh-neh-shee-ah noh* インドネシアの

industrialist *jee-TSOO-gyoh-kah* 実業家

inexpensive *tah-KAH-koo-nah-ee* 高くない

infection *kah-NOH* 化膿

information center *AHN-nah-ee joh* 案内所

injection *choo-shah* 注射

injury *keh-GAH* けが

insect bite *moo-SHEE sah-sah-reh* 虫さされ

insect repellent *BOH choo zah-ee* 防虫剤

inside ___ *noh NAH-kah nee* ___の中に

insomnia *foo-MEEN shoh* 不眠症

insulin *EEN-shoo-reen* インシュリン

insurance *hoh-KEHN* 保険

intelligent *ree-KOH nah* 利口な

interesting, fun *oh-MOH-shee-roh-ee* おもしろい

intermission *toh-CHOO noh KYOO-keh* 途中の休憩

interpreter *TSOO-yah-koo* 通訳

intersection *KOH-sah-tehn* 交差点

to introduce (oneself) *jee-KOH-shoh-kah-ee soo-roo* 自己紹介する

to invite *oh-MAH-neh-kee soo-roo* お招きする

iodine *YOH-doh cheen-kee* ヨードチンキ

iron *ah-EE-rohn* アイロン

Is that so? *SOH-dehs kah* そうですか

island *shee-MAH* 島

Italian *ee-TAH-ree-ah noh* イタリアの

Italian (lang.) *ee-TAH-ree-ah goh* イタリア語

Italy *ee-TAH-ree-ah* イタリア

It doesn't matter. *kah-MAH-ee-mah-sehn* かまいません。

itemized bill *MEH-sah-ee shoh* 明細書

itinerary *ryoh-KOH keh-kah-koo* 旅行計画

It's all right. *dah-ee-JOH-boo dehs* 大丈夫です。

ivory *ZOH-geh* 象牙

J

jack *JAHK-kee* ジャッキ

jacket *jah-KEHT-toh* ジャケット

jade *hee-SOO-ee* ひすい

jam *JAH-moo* ジャム

January *ee-CHEE-gah-tsoo* 一月

Japan *neep-POHN/ nee-HOHN* 日本

Japanese (lang.) *nee-HOHN goh* 日本語

Japanese board game *goh* 碁
　go board and stones
　goh-BAHN toh goh-EE-shee 碁盤と碁石

Japanese board game *shoh-gee* 将棋
　shogi board and pieces
　SHOH-gee bahn toh koh-mah 将棋盤と駒

Japanese chest of drawers *TAHN-soo* たんす

Japanese classical drama *kah-BOO kee* 歌舞伎
　Kabuki runway *hah-NAH mee-chee* 花道

Japanese classics *nee-HOHN noh koh-tehn* 日本の古典

Japanese dolls *nee-HOHN neen gyoh* 日本人形

Japanese doll shop *nee-HOHN neen-gyoh yah* 日本人形屋

Japanese folk toys *MEEN-geh gahn-goo* 民芸玩具

Japanese games *nee-HOHN dehn-toh noh geh-moo* 日本伝統のゲーム

Japanese gardens *nee-HOHN teh-ehn* 日本庭園

Japanese grammar book *nee-HOHN-goh noh boon-poh noh hohn* 日本語の文法の本

Japanese guest house *MEEN-shoo-koo* 民宿

Japanese martial arts *BOO-joo-tsoo* 武術
　judo *JOO-doh* 柔道
　karate *kah-RAH-teh* 空手
　kendo *KEHN-doh* 剣道
　black belt *koo-ROH oh-bee* 黒おび
　____ practice ____ *noh keh-koh* ____のけい古

Japanese masked dance-drama *NOH* 能
　Noh masks *NOH mehn* 能面

Japanese puppet theater *BOON-rah-koo* 文楽
　puppets *NEEN-gyoh* 人形

Japanese inn *ryoh-KAHN* 旅館

Japanese painting *nee-HOHN gah* 日本画

Japanese pinball *pah-CHEEN-koh* パチンコ
　pachinko balls *pah-CHEEN-koh dah-mah* パチンコ玉
　pachinko parlor *pah-CHEEN-koh yah* パチンコ屋
　prize *keh-heen* 景品

Japanese-style *wah SHEE-kee noh* 和式の

Japanese swords *nee-HOHN toh* 日本刀

Japanese sword shop *kah-TAH-nah yah* 刀屋

Japanese wrestling *soo-MOH* 相撲
　sumo judge *gyoh-jee* 行司
　sumo match *toh-REE-koo-mee* 取組み
　sumo ring *doh-hyoh* 土俵
　sumo tournament *bah-shoh* 場所
　sumo wrestlers *ree-KEE-shee* 力士

jazz *JYAH-zoo* ジャズ

jeans *boo-ROO jeen/ jeen-zoo* ブルー・ジーン／ジーンズ

jewelry *HOH-seh-kee* 宝石

jewelry store *HOH-seh-kee tehn* 宝石店

jogging *joh-GEEN-goo* ジョギング

jogging path *joh-GEEN-goo koh-soo* ジョギング・コース

joint (body) *KAHN-seh-tsoo* 関節

juice *JOO-soo* ジュース

  apple juice *REEN-goh JOO-soo* りんごジュース

  grapefruit juice *GREH-poo-foo-ROO-tsoo JOO-soo* グレープ・フルーツ・ジュース

  orange juice *oh-REHN-jee JOO-soo* オレンジ・ジュース

  pineapple juice *pah-EE-nahp-poo-roo JOO-soo* パイナップル・ジュース

  tomato juice *toh-MAH-toh JOO-soo* トマト・ジュース

July *shee-CHEE-gah-tsoo* 七月

June *roh-KOO-gah-tsoo* 六月

K

karat

  14 karat *joo-yohn keen* 14金

  18 karat *joo-hahk keen* 18金

  22 karat *NEE-joo-nee keen* 22金

  24 karat *NEE-joo-yohn keen* 24金

ketchup *keh-CHAHP-poo* ケチャップ

key *kah-GEE* 鍵

kilogram *kee-roh* キロ

  half kilogram *goh-HYAH-koo GOO-rah-moo* 五百グラム

kimono *kee-MOH-noh* 着物

kimono store *goh-FOO-koo yah* 呉服屋

kind (adj.) *SHEEN-seh-tsoo nah* 親切な

kite *TAH-koh* たこ

knee *hee-ZAH* ひざ

knife *NAH-ee-foo* ナイフ

Korea *KAHN-koh-koo* 韓国

Korean *KAHN-koh-koo noh* 韓国の

L

lacquer bowls *oo-ROO-shee noo-ree noh oo-tsoo-wah* うるし塗りのうつわ

lacquer trays *oo-ROO-shee noo-ree noh oh-BOHN* うるし塗りのお盆

lacquerware *noo-REE-moh-noh/ sheek-KEE* 塗り物／漆器

ladies' room *joh-SHEE yoh noh TOH-ee-reh* 女子用のトイレ

lake *mee-ZOO-oo-mee* 湖

lamb *koh-HEE-tsoo-jee* 子羊

lamb chop *rah-MOO chohp-poo* ラム・チョップ

lamp *RAHN-poo* ランプ

landscape *keh-shee-kee* 景色

lanterns *CHOH-cheen* ちょうちん

large (big) *OH-kee* 大きい

large (size) *DAH-ee* 大

late *oh-SOH-ee* おそい

later *AH-toh deh* あとで

laundromat *koh-EEN rahn-doh-ree* コイン・ランドリー

laundry (clothes) *SEHN-tah-koo moh-noh* 洗濯物

laundry (shop) *SEHN-tah-koo yah* 洗濯屋

laundry service *SEHN-tah-koo noh sah-bee-soo* 洗濯のサービス

lawyer *BEHN-goh-shee* 弁護士

laxative *geh-ZAH-ee/ TSOO-jee yah-koo* 下剤／通じ薬

to leak *moh-reh-roo* もれる

leather *kah-WAH* 皮

left *hee-DAH-ree* 左

leg *ah-SHEE* 足

lemon *REH-mohn* レモン

lemonade *reh-MOH-neh-doh* レモ ネード

lens *rehn-zoo* レンズ

lesson *rehs-soon* レッスン

Let's ___ *SAH* さあ

letter *teh-GAH-mee* 手紙

lettuce *REH-tah-soo* レタス

library *toh-SHOH-kahn* 図書館

lifeguard *mee-HAH-ree* 見張り

light (shade, color) *ah-KAH-roo-ee* 明るい

light (weight) *kah-ROO-ee* 軽い

light bulb *DEHN-kyoo* 電球

lighter fluid/ gas *RAH-ee-tah noh ah-BOO-rah/ gah-soo* ライターの 油/ガス

limit *SEH-gehn* 制限

line (train) *sehn* 線

linen *ah-SAH/ REEN-neh-roo* 麻 /リンネル

lip *koo-CHEE-bee-roo* 口びる

liquor store *sah-KAH yah* 酒屋

lira *REE-rah* リラ

list *hyoh* 表

liter *reet-toh-roo* リットル

a little, few *SKOH-shee* 少し

to live (reside) *soo-moo* 住む

liver *KAHN-zoh/ REH-bah* 肝臓/ レバー

lobby *roh-bee* ロビー

lobster *ee-SEH eh-bee/ ROH-boo-stah* 伊勢えび/ロブスター

to lock *ROHK-koo soo-roo* ロック する

lodging *shoo-KOO-hah-koo* 宿泊

long *nah-GAH-ee* 長い

long distance call *CHOH-kyoh-ree DEHN-wah* 長距離電話

to look around *MEE-teh mah-wah-roo* 見て回る

loose (clothes) *yoo-ROO-ee* ゆるい

to lose *nah-koo-soo* なくす

lost *nah-KOO-shee-tah* なくした

to be lost *mee-CHEE nee mah-yoh-oo* 道に迷う

lost and found *ee-SHEE-tsoo boo-tsoo gah-kah-ree* 遺失物係り

a lot, many *tahk-SAHN* たくさん

low *hee-KOO-ee* 低い

luggage *ryoh-KOH kah-bahn* 旅行 かばん

luggage rack *NEE-moh-tsoo noh oh-KEE dah-ee* 荷物の置き台

lunch (box lunch) *(oh)-BEHN-toh* （お）弁当

M

magazine *zahs-shee* 雑誌

magnificent *reep-PAH* 立派

maid *MEH-doh* メード

mail *yoo-been/ teh-gah-mee* 郵便/ 手紙

  airmail *KOH-koo been* 航空便

  mail box *YOO-been pohs-toh* 郵便ポスト

  registered mail *kah-KEE-toh-meh* 書留

  special delivery *soh-KOO-tah-tsoo* 速達

to mail a letter *teh-GAH-mee oh dah-soo* 手紙を出す

to make *tskoo-roo* 作る

male *oh-TOH-koh (noh hee-toh)* 男 （の人）

man *oh-TOH-koh (noh hee-toh)* 男 （の人）

manager *mah-NEH-jah* マネー ジャー

mandarin orange *MEE-kahn* み かん

mango *MAHN-goh* マンゴー

manicure *mah-NEE-kyoo-ah* マニキュア

many, a lot *tahk-SAHN* たくさん

map *CHEE-zoo* 地図

March *SAHN-gah-tsoo* 三月

margarine *MAH-gah-reen* マーガリン

mark *MAH-roo-koo* マルク

market *EE-chee-bah* 市場

married *kehk-KOHN shteh* 結婚して

masks *oh-MEHN* お面

masseur, masseuse *AHN-mah sahn* あんまさん

matches *MAHT-chee* マッチ

matinee *MAH-chee-neh* マチネー

maybe *TAH-boon* 多分

mayonnaise *mah-YOH-neh-zoo* マヨネーズ

meal *shoh-KOO-jee* 食事

  light meal *kah-ROO-ee shoh-koo-jee* 軽い食事

meal service *shoh-KOO-jee noh SAH-bee-soo* 食事のサービス

measurements *sah-ee-zoo* サイズ

meatballs *MEE-toh BOH-roo/ nee-KOO dahn-goh* ミートボール／肉だんご

medicine *koo-soo-ree* 薬

medium (meat) *MEE-dee-ah-moo* ミディアム

medium (size) *CHOO* 中

to meet *oh-AH-ee soo-roo* お会いする

melon *MEH-rohn* メロン

to mend *tsoo-KOO-roh-oo* 繕う

men's clothing *SHEEN-shee foo-koo* 紳士服

men's room *DAHN-shee yoh noh TOH-ee-reh* 男子用のトイレ

menu *MEH-nyoo* メニュー

message *mehs-SEH-jee* メッセージ

metal *KEEN-zoh-koo* 金属

meter (taxi) *MEH-tah* メーター

Mexican *meh-KEE-shee-koh noh* メキシコの

Mexico *meh-KEE-shee-koh* メキシコ

mezzanine *CHOO-nee-kah-ee* 中二階

micro cassette recorder *mah-EE-koo-roh kah-seht-toh reh-koh-dah* マイクロ・カセット・レコーダー

mileage *kee-ROH-soo* キロ数

military (personnel) *GOON-jeen* 軍人

milk *MEE-roo-koo / GYOO-nyoo* ミルク／牛乳

  hot milk *ah-TAH-tah-kah-ee GYOO-nyoo* あたたかい牛乳

milkshake *mee-ROO-koo SEH-kee* ミルクセーキ

I don't mind. *EE-dehs-yoh / kah-MAH-ee-mah-sehn* いいですよ／かまいません

minicalculator *poh-KEHT-toh gah-tah keh-sahn kee / poh-KEHT-toh dehn-tah-koo* ポケット型計算器／ポケット電卓

miniature TV *CHOO koh-gah-tah teh-reh-bee* 超小型テレビ

minimum charge *sah-EE-teh ryoh-keen* 最低料金

minister *boh-KOO-shee* 牧師

mirror *kah-GAH-mee* 鏡

modern *moh-DAHN nah* モダンな

modern dance *moh-DAHN dahns* モダン・ダンス

modern Japanese novels *KEEN-dah-ee nee-HOHN shoh-seh-tsoo* 近代日本小説

modern music *moh-DAHN myoo-jeek-koo* モダン・ミュージック

Monday *geh-TSOO-yoh-bee* 月曜日

money *oh-KAH-neh* お金

money exchange *RYOH-gah-eh-joh* 両替所

monkey wrench *MOHN-kee rehn-chee* モンキー・レンチ

monorail *moh-NOH-reh-roo* モノレール

month *tskee* 月

morning *ah-sah* 朝

this morning *KEH-sah* けさ

mosque *KAH-ee-kyoh noh jee-een* 回教の寺院

mother (someone else's) *oh-KAH-sahn* お母さん

mother (your own) *HAH-hah* 母

mountain *yah-MAH* 山

mountain range *SAHN-myah-koo* 山脈

mousse *MOO-soo* ムース

movie, film *EH-gah* 映画

movie theater *EH-gah kahn* 映画館

Mr./ Mrs./ Miss /Ms. ____ *sahn* ____さん

MSG (monosodium glutamate) *kah-GAH-koo CHOH-mee-ryoh* 化学調味料

mud *noo-KAH-roo-mee* ぬかるみ

muscle *KEEN-nee-koo* 筋肉

museum *hah-KOO-boo-tsoo kahn* 博物館

mushrooms *mahs-SHOO-roo-moo/ SHAHN-pee-nee-ohn* マッシュルーム／シャンピニオン

shiitake mushrooms *SHEE-tah-keh* しいたけ

music *OHN-gah-koo* 音楽

musical *MYOO-jee-kah-roo* ミュージカル

mustache *koo-CHEE hee-geh* 口ひげ

mustard *mah-SOO-tah-doh/ kah-RAH-shee* マスタード／からし

my *wah-TAHK-shee noh* 私の

myself *jee-BOON deh* 自分で

mystery *MEE-soo-teh-ree* ミステリー

N

nail file *tsoo-MEH yah-soo-ree* 爪やすり

nail polish *mah-NEE-kyoo-ah eh-kee/ eh-NAH-meh-roo* マニキュア液／エナメル

nail polish remover *mah-NEE-kyoo-ah oh-toh-shee/ joh-KOH-eh-kee* マニキュア落し／除光液

name *nah-MAH-eh* 名前

napkin *NAH-poo-keen* ナプキン

narrow *seh-MAH-ee* せまい

nationality *koh-KOO-seh-kee* 国籍

national park *koh-KOO-ree-tsoo KOH-ehn* 国立公園

nausea *hah-KEE-keh* 吐き気

near *chee-KAH-ee* 近い

nearby ____ *noh chee-KAH-koo nee* ____の近くに

necessary *hee-TSOO-yoh nah* 必要な

neck *koo-BEE* 首

necklace *NEHK-koo-reh-soo* ネックレス

nectarine *neh-KOO-tah-reen* ネクタリン

to need *ee-roo/ hee-TSOO-yoh dah* いる／必要だ

needles (record player) *reh-KOH-doh bah-ree* レコード針

new *ah-TAH-rah-shee* 新しい

New Zealand *nyoo-jee-rahn-doh* ニュージーランド

news magazines *NYOO-soo kahn-keh noh zahs-SHEE* ニュース関係の雑誌

newspaper *sheen-boon* 新聞

newsstand *SHEEN-boon OO-ree-bah* 新聞売り場

next *tsoo-GEE* 次

night *YOH-roo* 夜

nightclub *nah-EE-toh koo-rah-boo* ナイト・クラブ

no *ee-EH* いいえ

No, it isn't. *ee-EH, chee-GAH-ee-mahs* いいえ、違います。

noisy *yah-KAH-mah-shee* やかましい

noodles (Japanese) *oo-dohn/ soh-bah/ rah-mehn* うどん／そば／ラーメン

noodle soup *noo-doh-roo SOO-poo* ヌードル・スープ

noon *hee-ROO* 昼

north *kee-TAH* 北

nose *hah-NAH* 鼻

no smoking section *KEEN-ehn seh-kee* 禁煙席

No thank you. *ee-EH, KEHK-koh dehs* いいえ、けっこうです。

notebook *NOH-toh* ノート

notions *koh-MAH-moh-noh* 小間物

novel *shoh-seh-tsoo* 小説

November *JOO-ee-chee-gah-tsoo* 十一月

now *EE-mah* 今

number *BAHN-goh/ kah-zoo* 番号／数

nurse *KAHN-goh-foo* 看護婦

nuts *KEE-noh-mee* 木の実

nylon *NAH-ee-rohn* ナイロン

O

oatmeal *OH-toh MEE-roo* オートミール

occupation *shoh-koo-gyoh* 職業

ocean *OO-mee* 海

October *JOO-gah-tsoo* 十月

of course *moh-CHEE-rohn* もちろん

office *OH-fee-soo* オフィス

office worker (male) *sah-RAH-ree mahn* サラリーマン

office worker (female) *oh-eh-roo* オーエル

oil (car) *EHN-jeen oh-ee-roo* エンジン・オイル

oil (food) *ah-BOO-rah* 油

olive oil *oh-REE-boo yoo* オリーブ油

old (people) *tohsh-TOHT-tah* 年とった

old (things) *foo-ROO-ee* 古い

How old are you? *oh-EE-koo-tsoo dehs KAH* おいくつですか。

I'm ____ years old. *____ sah-ee dehs ____歳です。

old town *KYOO shee-gah-ee* 旧市街

omelet *oh-MOO-reh-tsoo* オムレツ

on *____ noh oo-EH nee* ____の上に

on board (ship) *FOO-neh nee* 船に

on foot *ah-ROO-ee-teh* 歩いて

on one's own *jee-BOON deh* 自分で

on time *jee-KAHN doh-ree nee* 時間通りに

one way *kah-TAH-mee-chee* 片道

one-way ticket *kah-TAH-mee-chee keep-poo* 片道切符

onion *tah-MAH-neh-gee* 玉ねぎ

onion soup *oh-NEE-ohn soo-poo* オニオンスープ

onyx *shee-MAH meh-noh* しまめのう

to open (v.i.) *ah-koo* 開く

to open (v.t.) *ah-keh-roo* 開ける

opera *OH-peh-rah* オペラ

opera house *oh-PEH-rah geh-kee joh* オペラ劇場

optician *meh-GAH-neh yah* 眼鏡屋

or *soh-REH-toh-moh/ mah-TAH-wah/ ah-ROO-ee-wah* それとも／または／あるいは

orange *oh-REHN-jee* オレンジ

orchestra *kahn-gehn-gah-koo dahn/ OH-kehs-toh-rah* 管弦楽団／オーケストラ

orchestra (theater) *BOO-tah-ee nee chee-KAH-ee seh-kee* 舞台に近い席

order *CHOO-mohn* 注文

to order *CHOO-mohn soo-roo* 注文する

origami paper *oh-REE-gah-mee* 折り紙

original *MOH-toh noh mah-mah* 元のまま

other *hoh-kah noh* 外の

out of order *koh-WAH-reh-teh* こわれて

outside _____ *noh SOH-toh nee* ___の外に

outside line (phone) *SHEE-nah-ee* 市内

It's over./ I'm finished. *oh-WAH-ree-mah-shtah* 終わりました。

overcoat *OH-bah* オーバー

overheated *OH-bah HEE-toh* オーバー・ヒート

overnight *hee-TOH bahn* 一晩

oysters *KAH-kee* かき

P

package *NEE-moh-tsoo* 荷物

pain *ee-TAH-mee/ koo-tsoo* 痛み／苦痛

to paint (art) *kah-koo* 描く

painter *gah-KAH* 画家

palace *KYOO-dehn* 宮殿

pancakes *hoht-TOH keh-kee* ホット・ケーキ

panda *PAHN-dah* パンダ

pants *soo-RAHK-ksoo* スラックス

pantyhose *pahn-tee STOHK-keen-goo* パンティー・ストッキング

paper shop *kah-MEE yah/ wah-SHEE yah* 紙屋／和紙屋

papier mâché *hah-REE-koh zah-ee-koo* 張り子細工

parcel *koh-ZOO-tsoo-mee* 小包

Pardon me, but _____ *soo-MEE-mah-sehn gah* _____ すみませんが

parfait *pah-FEH* パフェー

park *KOH-ehn* 公園

to park *choo-shah soo-roo* 駐車する

parking fee *CHOO-shah ryoh* 駐車料

parking garage *CHOO-shah joh* 駐車場

street parking *roh-JOH choo-shah* 路上駐車

passenger *JOH-kyah-koo* 乗客

passport *pah-SOO-poh-toh* パスポート

pastry *PEH-soo-toh-ree* ペーストリー

pastry shop *oh-KAH-shee yah* お菓子屋

paté *PAH-teh* パテ

path *mee-chee* 道

peach *moh-MOH* 桃

peanuts *PEE-naht-tsoo* ピーナッツ

pear *YOH nah-shee* 洋なし

Japanese pear *nah-SHEE* なし

pearls *SHEEN-joo/ PAH-roo* 真珠／パール

cultured pearls *YOH-shoh-koo sheen-joo* 養殖真珠

pencil *EHN-pee-tsoo* 鉛筆

pencil sharpener *EHN-pee-tsoo keh-zoo-ree* 鉛筆削り

pendant *PEHN-dahn-toh* ペンダント

pepper *koh-SHOH* こしょう

green pepper *PEE-mahn* ピーマン

performance *JOH-ehn* 上演

performer *shoo-TSOO-ehn shah* 出演者

perfume *KOH-soo-ee* 香水

permanent wave *PAH-mah* パーマ

per person *hee-TOH-ree (ah-tah-ree)* 一人 (当り)

persimmon *kah-KEE* 柿

person *hee-toh* 人

personal AM-FM stereo cassette player *mee-nee EH-eh-moo eh-FOO-eh-moo STEH-reh-oh kah-seht-toh poo-reh-yah* ミニ・エーエム・エフエムステレオ・カセット・プレーヤー

personal stereo cassette recorder/ player *mee-nee STEH-reh-oh kah-seht-toh reh-KOH-dah/ poo-REH-yah* ミニ・ステレオカセット・レコーダー／プレーヤー

peso *PEH-soh* ペソ

pharmacy *yahk-KYOH-koo/ koo-SOO-ree yah* 薬局／薬屋

  all-night pharmacy *SHOO-yah eh-gyoh noh yahk-KYOH-koo* 終夜営業の薬局

Philippines *fee-REEP-peen* フィリッピン

photograph, picture *shah-SHEEN* 写真

photography shop *kah-MEH-rah yah* カメラ屋

pickles (Japanese) *(oh)-TSKEH-moh-noh* （お）つけ物

picture postcards *eh-HAH-gah-kee* 絵葉書

pie *PAH-ee* パイ

  apple pie *ahp-POO-roo PAH-ee* アップル・パイ

  lemon meringue pie *reh-MOHN meh-REHN-geh* レモン・メレンゲ

pier *foo-TOH* 埠頭

pillow *MAH-koo-rah* 枕

pin (jewelry) *kah-ZAH-ree peen* 飾りピン

pineapple *pah-EE-nahp-poo-roo* パイナップル

ping pong *PEEN-pohn* ピンポン

pink *PEEN-koo noh* ピンクの

pipe *PAH-ee-poo* パイプ

pipe tobacco *kee-ZAH-mee tah-bah-koh* きざみタバコ

plaid *KOH-shee jee-mah* 格子じま

plants *koo-SAH* 草

plastic *poo-RAH-soo-cheek-koo/ bee-NEE-roo* プラスチック／ビニール

plate *oh-SAH-rah* お皿

platinum *poo-RAH-chee-nah* プラチナ

play (theater) *EHN-geh-kee* 演劇

playground *ah-SOH-bee bah* 遊び場

pleasant *tah-NOH-shee* 楽しい

please ___ *oh koo-dah-sah-ee/ ___ oh oh-NEH-gah-ee shee-mahs* ___をください／___をお願いします

please (come in/ sit down/ begin/ have some/ go first/ etc.) *DOH-zoh* どうぞ

Pleased to meet you. *hah-JEE-meh-teh oh-MEH-nee kah-kah-ree-mahs* 初めて、おめにかかります。

pliers *PEHN-chee* ペンチ

plum *POO-rah-moo/ soo-MOH-moh* プラム／すもも

points of interest *MEH-shoh* 名所

police *KEH-sah-tsoo* 警察

police officer *KEH-kahn* 警官

to polish *mee-GAH-koo* みがく

politician *SEH-jee kah* 政治家

polyester *poh-REE-eh-steh-roo* ポリエステル

pond *ee-KEH* 池

popcorn *pohp-POO kōhn* ポップ コーン

popular *neen-kee gah ah-roo* 人気 がある

popular songs *poh-PYOO-rah sohn-goo* ポピュラー・ソング

porcelain *JEE-kee* 磁器

pork *boo-TAH nee-koo* 豚肉

pork chop *PŌH CHOHP-poo* ポーク・チョップ

portable component stereo system *keh-tah-ee KOHM-poh steh-reh-oh soh-chee* 携帯コンボ ステレオ装置

portable radio *PŌH-tah-boo-roo rah-jee-oh* ポータブル・ラジオ

porter *PŌH-tah* ポーター

poter (train station) *ah-KAH-boh* 赤帽

Portuguese *poh-ROO-toh-gah-roo noh* ボルトガルの

postcard *hah-GAH-kee* 葉書

post office *YŌO-been kyoh-koo* 郵 便局

potato *PŌH-teh-toh/ jah-GAH-ee-moh* ポテト／じゃがいも

  baked potato *BĒH-koo-doh POH-teh-toh* ベークド・ポテト

  French fries *foo-REHN-chee FOO-rah-ee* フレンチ・フライ

  mashed potatoes *mahsh-SHOO poh-teh-toh* マッ シュ・ポテト

  sweet potato *soo-EE-toh POH-teh-toh/ sah-TSOO-mah ee-moh* スイート・ポテト／さつまいも

  potato chips *poh-TEH-toh cheep-poo* ポテトチップ

pottery *TŌH-kee* 陶器

pottery shop *seh-TOH-moh-noh yah/ TŌH-kee noh mee-seh* 瀬戸 物屋／陶器の店

pounds (currency) *POHN-doh* ポ ンド

to pray *oh-EE-noh-ree soo-roo* お 祈りする

prefectural capital *KEHN-choh shoh-ZAH-ee-chee* 県庁所在地

prefecture *kehn* 県

to prefer *koh-noh-moo* 好む

pregnant *NEEN-sheen choo* 妊娠 中

prescription *shoh-HŌH sehn* 処方 せん

pretty, beautiful *KEE-reh nah* きれいな

price *neh-DAHN* 値段

priest *SHEEN-poo* 神父

print (pattern) *poo-REEN-toh* プ リント

print (photo) *yah-KEE-tsoo-keh* 焼 付け

problem *mohn-dah-ee* 問題

professor *KYŌH-joo* 教授

program *bahn-goo-mee* 番組

prosciutto *nah-MAH hah-moo* 生 ハム

public transportation *KŌH-kyoh koh-tsoo kee-kahn* 公共交通機関

pudding *POO-reen* プリン

  chocolate pudding *choh-KOH-rēh-toh POO-reen* チョコレート・プリン

purple *moo-RAH-sah-kee ee-roh noh* 紫色の

purpose *moh-KOO-teh-kee* 目的

purse *HAHN-doh bahg-goo* ハンド バック

Q

question *shee-TSOO-mohn* 質問

quick, fast *hah-YAH-ee* 速い

quiet *SHEE-zoo-kah* 静か

R

rabbi *RAH-bee* ラビ

racket *rah-KEHT-toh* ラケット

radiator *rah-JEE-eh-tah* ラジエーター

radio *RAH-jee-oh* ラジオ

radio station *rah-JEE-oh kyoh-koo* ラジオ局

radish *RAH-deesh-shoo/ hah-TSOO-kah DAH-ee-kohn* ラディッシュ／二十日大根

rain *AH-meh* 雨

raincoat *reh-EEN koh-toh* レイン・コート

rainy season *tsoo-YOO* 梅雨

raisins *hoh-SHEE boo-doh* 干しぶどう

rare (meat) *REH-ah* レア

rate *RYOH-keen* 料金

raw *NAH-mah* なま

razor *kah-MEE-soh-ree* かみそり

razor blades *kah-MEE-soh-ree noh hah* かみそりの刃

to read *yoh-moo* 読む

Really? *SOH-dehs-KAH / hohn-TOH* そうですか／本当

to the rear *oo-SHEE-roh noh* うしろの

receipt *RYOH-shoo-shoh* 領収書

to recommend *soo-EE-sehn soo-roo / soo-SOO-meh-roo* 推薦する／勧める

to reconfirm *sah-EE-kah-koo-neen soo-roo* 再確認する

record *reh-KOH-doh* レコード

record album *reh-KOH-doh AH-roo-bah-moo* レコード・アルバム

record player *reh-KOH-doh poo-reh-yah* レコード・プレイヤー

record store *reh-KOH-doh yah* レコード屋

red *ah-KAH-ee* 赤い

refund *hehn-keen* 返金

regular *foo-TSOO* 普通

religious *SHOO-kyoh noh* 宗教の

religious service *REH-hah-ee* 礼拝

to rent *kah-REE-roo* 借りる

repair *SHOO-ree* 修理

repair tools *SHOO-ree doh-goo* 修理道具

to repair *SHOO-ree soo-roo* 修理する

repeat it *MOH ee-chee-doh* もう一度

reputation *hyoh-bahn* 評判

reservation *yoh-YAH-koo* 予約

reserved seats (train) *zah-SEH-kee shee-teh* 座席指定

   unreserved seats (train) *jee-YOO seh-kee* 自由席

restrooms *TOH-ee-reh* トイレ

restaurant *REH-soo-toh-rahn* レストラン

rib *rohk-KOH-tsoo* ろっ骨

rice (Japanese)

   cooked *GOH-hahn* ご飯

   uncooked *koh-MEH* 米

rice (Western) *RAH-ee-soo* ライス

rice paddy *soo-EE-dehn* 水田

right (correct) *tah-DAH-shee* 正しい

right (direction) *mee-GEE* 右

ring (jewelry) *yoo-BEE-wah* 指輪

river *kah-WAH* 川

road *mee-chee* 道

road map *DOH-roh chee-zoo* 道路地図

roasted *ah-BOO-ree yah-kee nee shtah/ ROH-stoh nee shtah* あぶり焼きにした／ローストにした

robe *keh-SHOH-gee* 化粧着

rock'n'roll *rohk-KOON roh-roo* ロックンロール

rolls (bread) *ROH-roo pahn* ロール・パン

romance (movie) *REHN-ah-ee moh-noh* 恋愛物

room *heh-YAH* 部屋

Japanese room (restaurant) *oh-ZAH-shkee* お座敷

private room (restaurant) *koh-SHEE-tsoo* 個室

room service *ROO-moo SAH-bee-soo* ルーム・サービス

rouge *hoh-OO-beh-nee* ほお紅

round *mah-ROO-ee* 丸い

round trip *oh-foo-koo* 往復

round trip ticket *OH-foo-koo kehn* 往復券

rubber bands *goh-MOO bahn-doh* ゴム・バンド

ruby *ROO-bee* ルビー

ruler *JOH-gee* 定規

Rumanian *ROO-mah-nee-ah noh* ルーマニアの

rush hour *rahsh-SHOO ah-wah* ラッシュ・アワー

Russian *ROH-see-ah noh* ロシアの

Russian (lang.) *roh-SHEE-ah goh* ロシア語

S

safe (adj.) *AHN-zehn nah* 安全な

safe (valuables) *KEEN-koh* 金庫

safety pins *AHN-zehn peen* 安全ピン

sailboat *YOHT-toh* ヨット

sake bottle *tohk-KOO-ree* とっくり

sake cup *sah-KAH zoo-kee* 盃

salad *SAH-rah-dah* サラダ

Caesar salad *SHEE-zah SAH-rah-dah* シーザー・サラダ

salami *sah-RAH-mee soh-seh-jee* サラミ・ソーセージ

sale *SEH-roo/ toh-KOO-bah-ee* セール／特売

salmon *SAH-keh* さけ

salt *shee-OH* 塩

same *oh-NAH-jee* 同じ

sandals *SAHN-dah-roo* サンダル

sandwich *sahn-doh-EET-chee* サンドイッチ

sanitary napkins *SEH-ree nahp-keen* 生理ナプキン

sapphire *sah-FAH-ee-ah* サファイア

sardines *SAH-deen/ ee-WAH-shee* サーディン／いわし

Saturday *doh-YOH-bee* 土曜日

saucer *oo-KEH-zah-rah* 受け皿

sauna *SAH-oo-nah* サウナ

sausage *soh-SEH-jee* ソーセージ

sauteed *soh-TEH nee shtah* ソテーにした

scallops *kah-EE-bah-shee-rah* 貝柱

Scandinavian *soo-KAHN-jee-nah-bee-uh-noh* スカンジナビアの

scarf *SKAH-foo* スカーフ

schedule *SKEH-joo-roo* スケジュール

school *gahk-KOH* 学校

science fiction *sah-EE-ehn-soo fee-koo-shohn* サイエンス・フィクション

scissors *hah-SAH-mee* はさみ

cuticle sissors *ah-MAH-kah-wah yoh noh hah-SAH-mee* あま皮用のはさみ

scotch (whisky) *SKOHT-chee* スコッチ

Scotch tape *seh-ROH teh-poo* セロテープ

screwdriver *doh-RAH-ee-bah* ドライバー

scroll *kah-KEH jee-koo* 掛け軸

sculptor *CHOH-koh-koo kah* 彫刻家

sculpture *CHOH-koh-koo* 彫刻

sea *oo-mee* 海

sea mail *foo-NAH been* 船便

seashore *kah-ee-gahn* 海岸

seasickness *foo-NAH-yoh-ee* 船酔い

season *KEE-seh-tsoo* 季節

seat *SEH-kee* 席

seaweed *noh-REE* のり

secretary *HEE-shoh* 秘書

to see *MEE-roo* 見る

Oh, I see *ah, SOH* ああ, そう

to sell *oo-roo* 売る

to send *oh-koo-roo* 送る

senior citizens *toh-SHEE yoh-ree* 年寄り

September *KOO-gah-tsoo* 九月

service charge *SAH-bee-soo ryoh* サービス料

setting lotion *seht-TOH roh-shohn* セットローション

to sew *noo-oo* ぬう

shampoo *SHAHN-poo* シャンプー

sharks *sah-MEH* さめ

shave *hee-GEH soh-ree* ひげそり

shaving lotion *SHEH-been-goo roh-shohn* シェービング・ローション

aftershave lotion *ahf-tah SHEH-boo roh-shohn* アフターシェーブ・ローション

shave and shampoo *hee-GEH soh-ree toh sehn-pah-tsoo* ひげそりと洗髪

she *KAH-noh-joh gah* 彼女が

sherbet *SHAH-beht-toh* シャーベット

lemon sherbet *reh-mohn SHAH-beht-toh* レモンシャーベット

Shinto ceremony *SHEEN-toh noh gee-shee-kee* 神道の儀式

ship *FOO-neh* 船

shirt *wah-ee-shah-tsoo* ワイシャツ

shoes *koo-TSOO* くつ

to take off one's shoes *koo-TSOO oh noo-goo* くつをぬぐ

shoe repair shop *koo-TSOO noh shoo-ree yah* くつの修理屋

shoe store *koo-TSOO yah* くつ屋

shoelaces *koo-TSOO hee-moh* くつひも

shopping *shohp-PEEN-goo/ kah-EE-moh-noh* ショッピング／買い物

shopping arcade *shohp-PEEN-goo ah-keh-doh* ショッピング・アーケード

shopping area *shohp-PEEN-goo gah-ee* ショッピング街

short *mee-JEE-kah-ee* 短い

shortcut *chee-KAH mee-chee* 近道

short story books *TAHN-pehn shoh-seh-tsoo* 短編小説

shorts (briefs) *boo-REE-foo* ブリーフ

shoulder *KAH-tah* 肩

show (stage, floor) *SHOH* ショー

Broadway show *boo-ROH-doh-weh kah-rah noh shoh* ブロード・ウェーからのショー

first show *sah-EE-shoh noh-shoh* 最初のショー

last show *SAH-ee-goh noh shoh* 最後のショー

to show *mee-seh-roo* 見せる

shower *SHAH-wah* シャワー

shrimp *eh-BEE* えび

shrine *jeen-jah* 神社

sick *BYOH-kee* 病気

sightseeing bus *KAHN-koh bahs* 観光バス

sightseeing tour *KAHN-koh ryoh-koh* 観光旅行

signature *shoh-MEH* 署名

silk *KEE-noo/ SHEE-roo-koo* 絹／
シルク

silver *GEEN* 銀

singer *KAH-shoo* 歌手

singing *oo-TAHT-teh* 歌って

single (marital status) *doh-KOO-sheen* 独身

sink *SEHN-mehn-dah-ee* 洗面台

size *SAH-ee-zoo* サイズ

skiing *SKEE* スキー

skis *SKEE* スキー

ski lift *REE-foo-toh* リフト

ski poles *soo-TOHK-koo* ストック

ski resort *skee jōh* スキー場

ski shoes *SKEE goo-tsoo* スキー
ぐつ

skim milk *soo-KEE-moo MEE-roo-koo* スキム・ミルク

skin *hah-dah* 肌

skin diving equipment *soo-KEEN dah-ee-been-goo yōh goo* スキン・ダイビング用具

skirt *SKAH-toh* スカート

to sleep *neh-roo* 寝る

sleeping car *SHEEN-dah-ee shah* 寝台車

sleeping pills *soo-EE-meen yah-koo* 睡眠薬

sleepy *neh-MOO-ee* ねむい

sleeves *soh-deh* そで

long sleeves *nah-GAH soh-deh* 長そで

short sleeves *HAHN soh-deh* 半そで

slides *soo-RAH-ee-doh* スライド

slip *SREEP-poo* スリップ

slippers *SREEP-pah* スリッパ

slow *oh-SOH-ee* おそい

small *CHEE-sah-ee* 小さい

small (size) *SHŌH* 小

to smile *wah-RAII-oo* 笑う

to smoke *tah-BAH-koh oh soo-oo* たばこを吸う

snack *soo-NAHK-koo* スナック

snack bar *soo-NAHK-koo bāh* スナック・バー

sneakers *OON-dōh goo-tsoo/ soo-NEE-kah* 運動ぐつ／スニーカー

snow *yoo-KEE* 雪

soap *sehk-KEHN* 石けん

soccer *SAHK-kāh* サッカー

soccer match *SAHK-kāh noh shee-ah-ee* サッカーの試合

soccer stadium *SAHK-kāh noh kyōh-gee jōh* サッカーの競技場

socks *koo-TSOO-shtah/ SOHK-koo-soo* くつ下／ソックス

sole *koo-TSOO zoh-koh* くつ底

solid color *MOO-jee* 無地

some *SKOH-shee* 少し

somebody, someone *DAH-reh-kah* 誰か

son (someone else's) *moo-SOO-koh sahn* 息子さん

son (your own) *moo-SOO-koh* 息子

soon *MŌH soo-goo dehs* もうすぐ
です

soup *soo-poo* スープ

bean paste soup *mee-SOH shee-roo* みそしる

clear soup *soo-EE-moh-noh* 吸い物

south *mee-NAH-mee* 南

souvenir *oh-MEE-yah-geh* おみやげ

souvenir shop *oh-MEE-yah-geh yah* おみやげ屋

soy sauce *SHŌH-yoo* しょう油

spaghetti *soo-PAH-geht-tee* スパゲッティー

Spain *soo-PEH-een* スペイン

Spanish *soo-PEH-een noh* スペインの

Spanish (lang.) *SPEH-een goh* スペイン語

spark plugs　*soo-PAH-koo poo-rah-goo* スパーク・プラブ

special　*toh-KOO-beh-tsoo noh* 特別の

to spend (money)　*tskah-oo* 使う

spinach　*HOH-rehn-soh* ほうれん草

spine　*seh BOH-neh* 背骨

sponge　*soo-POHN-jee* スポンジ

sporting goods store　*OON-doh-goo tehn* 運動具店

to sprain　*NEHN-zah soo-roo* ねんざする

spring　*HAH-roo* 春

square　*shee-KAH-koo-ee* 四角い

squid　*ee-KAH* いか

stainless steel　*STEHN-rehs* ステンレス

stamps　*keet-TEH* 切手

to stand　*tah-tsoo* 立つ

starched (laundry)　*noh-REE oh kee-KAH-seh-teh* のりをきかせて

to start (v.i.)　*hah-jee-mah-roo* 始まる

station (train)　*eh-kee* 駅

stationery shop　*BOON-boh-goo tehn* 文房具店

to stay　*toh-MAH-roo* 泊まる

steak　*STEH-kee* ステーキ

steering wheel　*HAHN-doh-roo* ハンドル

stock exchange　*SHOH-kehn toh-ree-hee-kee joh* 証券取引所

stockings　*STOHK-keen-goo* ストッキング

stolen　*noo-SOO-mah-reh-teh* 盗まれて

stomach　*ee* 胃

　　upset stomach　*ee NOH choh-shee gah yoh-koo-nah-ee* 胃の調子がよくない

stone (jewelry)　*hoh-seh-kee* 宝石

to stop　*yah-meh-roo* やめる

to stop (transportation)　*toh-mah-roo* 止まる

store　*oh-MEE-seh* お店

story (movie, play)　*soo-jee* 筋

straight (direction)　*mahs-SOO-goo* まっすぐ

strawberries　*ee-CHEE-goh* いちご

stream　*oh-GAH-wah* 小川

street　*TOH-ree* 通り

string　*hee-MOH* ひも

string beans　*sah-YAH ehn-doh* さやえんどう

stripes　*shee-MAH moh-yoh* しま模様

strong　*tsoo-YOH-ee* 強い

student　*gahk-SEH* 学生

stupid　*BAH-kah nah* ばかな

style　*STAH-ee-roo* スタイル

subtitles (film)　*jee-MAH-koo* 字幕

subway　*chee-KAH-teh-tsoo* 地下鉄

sudden illness　*KYOO byoh* 急病

sugar　*sah-TOH* 砂糖

sugar substitute　*dah-EE-eht-toh kahn-mee-ryoh* ダイエット甘味料

suit　*SOO-tsoo* スーツ

summer　*nah-TSOO* 夏

sunburn　*hee-YAH-keh* 日焼け

sundae　*SAHN-deh* サンデー

Sunday　*nee-CHEE-yoh-bee* 日曜日

sunglasses　*SAHN goo-rah-soo* サングラス

sunscreen　*hee-YAH-keh doh-meh* 日焼け止め

suntan lotion　*SAHN-tahn roh-shohn* サンタン・ローション

supermarket　*SOO-pah* スーパー

suppositories　*zah YAH-koo* 座薬

sweater　*SEH-tah* セーター

sweet　*ah-MAH-ee* 甘い

to swim *oh-YOH-goo* 泳ぐ
swimming pool *poo-roo* プール
Swiss *SOO-ee-soo noh* スイスの
swollen *hah-REH-teh* はれた
swordfish *mah-KAH-jee-kee* まかじき
symphony *SHEEN-foh-nee* シンフォニー
synagogue *yoo-DAH-yah kyoh noh jee-een* ユダヤ教の寺院
syrup *SHEE-rohp-poo* シロップ

T

Tabasco *tah-BAHS-koh* タバスコ
table *TEH-boo-roo* テーブル
tablespoon *OH-sah-jee* 大さじ
tailor *shee-TAH-teh yah* 仕立て屋
to take a picture *shah-SHEEN oh toh-roo* 写真をとる
talcum powder *sheek-KAH-roh-roo* シッカロール
tampons *TAHN-pohn* タンポン
tangerine *MEE-kahn* みかん
tapes (recording) *roh-KOO-ohn teh-poo* 録音テープ
tape recorder *TEH-poo reh-koh-dah* テープ・レコーダー
tax *ZEH-keen* 税金
taxi *TAHK-shee* タクシー
taxi stand *tahk-SHEE noh-ree-bah* タクシー乗り場
tea *KOH-chah* 紅茶
   iced tea *ah-EES tee* アイスティー
   Japanese tea *oh-CHAH* お茶
   Japanese green tea *ryoh-koo-chah* 緑茶
   Japanese roasted tea *HOH-jee-chah* ほうじ茶
tea ceremony *SAH-doh* 茶道
   etiquette of the preparation of tea *tah-TEH mah-eh* 点前

tea bowl *SAH-doh noh oh-CHAH-wahn/ chah-WAHN* 茶道のお茶碗/茶碗
teacup *yoo-NOH-mee jah-wahn/ chah-WAHN* 湯飲み茶碗/茶碗
teacher *KYOH-shee/ SEHN-seh* 教師/先生
team *chee-moo* チーム
teapot *KYOO-soo/ doh-BEEN* 急須/土びん
teaspoon *koh-SAH-jee* 小さじ
tee shirt *TEE shah-tsoo* ティーシャツ
telegram, cable *dehn-poh* 電報
telephone *dehn-wah* 電話
telephone booth *DEHN-wah bohk-koo-soo* 電話ボックス
   public telephone *KOH-shoo dehn-wah* 公衆電話
telephone call *dehn-wah* 電話
   collect call *RYOH-keen sehn-poh bah-rah-ee noh dehn-wah* 料金先払いの電話
   local call *shee-NAH-ee dehn-wah* 市内電話
   long distance call *CHOH-kyoh-ree dehn-wah* 長距離電話
   person to person call *PAH-soh-nah-roo koh-roo* パーソナル・コール
   English telephone directory *EH-goh noh dehn-wah choh* 英語の電話帳
telephone number *DEHN-wah bahn-goh* 電話番号
   extension number *nah-EE-sehn* 内線
telephone operator *KOH-kahn-shoo* 交換手
television, TV *TEH-reh-bee* テレビ
television set *TEH-reh-bee* テレビ
to tell *oh-SHEE-eh-roo* 教える
temperature, fever *neh-TSOO* 熱

temple *oh-TEH-rah* お寺

tennis *TEH-nees* テニス

tennis ball *teh-NEES boh-roo* テニス・ボール

tennis court *teh-NEES koh-toh* テニス・コート

to play tennis *TEH-nees oh soo-roo* テニスをする

tent *TEHN-toh* テント

terrace *TEH-rah-soo* テラス

Thai (adj.) *TAH-ee koh-koo noh* タイ国の

Thai *tah-EE-koh-koo jeen* タイ国人

thank you *DOH-moh ah-REE-gah-toh* どうもありがとう

that/ that over there (adj.) *soh-NOH/ ah-NOH* その／あの

that/ that over there (n.) *soh-REH/ ah-REH* それ／あれ

thatch roof *wah-RAH-boo-kee yah-neh* わらぶき屋根

theater *geh-KEE joh* 劇場

theft *toh-nahn* 盗難

theme *TEH-mah* テーマ

there/ over there *soh-KOH / ah-SOH-koh* そこ／あそこ

thermometer *tah-EE-ohn keh* 体温計

themostat (car) *SAH-moh-soo-taht-toh* サーモスタット

they *KAH-reh-rah gah* 彼らが

thick *ah-TSOO-ee* 厚い

thigh *foo-TOH moh-moh* 太もも

thin *oo-SOO-ee* 薄い

to think *oh-moh-oo* 思う

I don't think so. *SOH oh-MOH-ee-mah-sehn* そう思いません。

I think so. *SOH-dah toh oh-moh-ee-mahs* そうだと思います。

thirsty *NOH-doh gah, kah-WAH-ee-teh ee-mahs* のどが、かわいています。

this (adj.) *koh-NOH* この

this (n.) *koh-REH* これ

thriller, horror movie *SOO-ree-rah* スリラー

throat *NOH-doh* のど

thumb *oh-YAH yoo-bee* 親指

Thursday *moh-KOO-yoh-bee* 木曜日

ticket *kehn/ keep-POO* 券／切符

ticket (air) *KOH-koo kehn* 航空券

ticket machine (train) *keep-POO noh HAHN-bah-ee-kee* 切符の販売機

ticket window/ counter *keep-POO OO-ree-bah* 切符売り場

tie *NEHK-tah-ee* ネクタイ

tight (clothing) *kee-TSOO-ee* きつい

to tighten *shee-MEH-roo* 締める

time *jee-KAHN* 時間

What time is it? *ee-mah NAHN-jee dehs KAH* いま何時ですか。

timetable *jee-KOHK hyoh* 時刻表

tire *tah-EE-yah* タイヤ

tire pressure *tah-EE-yah noh KOO-kee ah-tsoo* タイヤの空気圧

spare tire *soo-PEH-yah tah-ee-yah* スペヤ・タイヤ

tired *tsoo-KAH-reh-teh ee-mahs* つかれています

tissues *chee-REE gah-mee/ TEES-shoo* ちり紙／ティッシュー

title *dah-ee meh* 題名

to ___ *eh / nee ___* へ／に

toast (bread) *TOH-soo-toh* トースト

toast (drinks) *kahn-pah-ee* 乾杯

toaster *TOH-stah* トースター

tobacco shop *tah-BAH-koh yah* たばこ屋

today *KYOH* 今日

for today *KYOH* noh 今日の

toe *ah-SHEE* noh yoo-bee 足の指

together *ees-shoh* nee 一緒に

toilet *TOH-ee-reh* トイレ

toilet paper toh-EE-reht-toh *PEH-pah* トイレット・ペーパー

toiletries shop keh-*SHOH* heen tehn 化粧品店

tomato *TOH-mah-toh* トマト

tomorrow ahsh-*TAH*/ ah-*SOO* あした／あす

tomorrow night ah-*SHTAH* noh bahn あしたの晩

tongue *SHTAH* 舌

tonight *KOHN-bahn* 今晩

tonsils *HEHN-toh* sehn 扁桃腺

toothache shee-*TSOO*/ hah-EE-tah 歯痛／歯いた

toothbrush hah-*BOO-rah-shee* 歯ブラシ

toothpaste neh-*REE-hah-mee-gah-kee* 練歯みがき

toothpicks *YOH-jee* ようじ

topaz *TOII-pah-zoo* トパーズ

tour tsoo-*ah* ツアー

group tour goo-*ROO-poo* tsoo-*ah* グループ・ツアー

tour guide *KAHN-koh* gah-ee doh 観光ガイド

guided tour *AHN-nah-ee* tsoo-kee noh kehn-boo-tsoo 案内付きの見物

tourist *KAHN-koh* kyah-koo 観光客

tourist information center ryoh-*KOH* ahn-nah-ee joh 旅行案内所

towels *TAH-oh-roo* タオル

town mah-*CHEE* 町

tow truck rehk-*KAH* shah レッカー車

toy store oh-*MOH-chah* yah おもちゃ屋

traditional *DEHN-toh* teh-kee nah 伝統的な

train kee-shah/ rehs-shah 汽車／列車

commuter train *DEHN-shah* 電車

express train kah-*EE-soh-koo* 快速

limited express tohk-*KYOO* 特急

local train foo-*TSOO* 普通

ordinary express *KYOO-koh* 急行

super express *SHEEN-kahn-sehn* 新幹線

platform hoh-moo ホーム

track sehn 線

tragedy *HEE-geh-kee* 悲劇

tranquilizers toh-*RAHN-kee-rah-ee-zah* トランキライザー

to translate *HOHN-yah-koo* soo-roo 翻訳する

translation *HOHN-yah-koo* 翻訳

transportation koh-tsoo kee-kahn 交通機関

travel agency ryoh-*KOH* dah-ee-ree tehn 旅行代理店

travelers check toh-*RAH-beh-rah* *CHEHK-koo* トラベラー・チェック

tree *KEE* 木

trip ryoh-*KOH*/ tah-bee 旅行／旅

trout mah-*SOO* ます

to try on shee-*CHAH-koo* soo-roo 試着する

Tuesday kah-*YOH-bee* 火曜日

tuna mah-*GOO-roh* まぐろ

to turn mah-*GAH-roo* 曲がる

turquoise toh-*ROO-koh* ee-shee トルコ石

tweezers keh-*NOO-kee* 毛抜き

type, kind shoo-roo-ee 種類

typewriter *tah-EE-poo rah-ee-tah* タイプライター

typing paper *tah-EE-poo yoh-shee* タイプ用紙

typhoon *tah-EE-foo* 台風

typical *dah-EE-hyoh-teh-kee nah* 代表的な

U

ugly *mee-NEE-koo-ee* みにくい

uncle (someone else's) *oh-JEE-sahn* おじさん

uncle (your own) *oh-JEE* 叔父

undershirt *AHN-dah shah-tsoo/ hah-DAH gee* アンダーシャツ／肌着

to understand *wah-KAH-roo* わかる

    I understand
    wah-KAH-ree-mahs わかります

underwear *SHTAH-gee* 下着

United States *ah-MEH-ree-kah* アメリカ

university *dah-EE-gah-koo* 大学

up _____ *noh oo-EH nee* _____ の上に

urgent *shee-KYOO* 至急

to use *tsoo-kah-oo* 使う

V

vacation *bah-KEH-shohn* バケーション

valley *tah-NEE* 谷

veal *koh-OO-shee* 子牛

vegetables *yah-sah-ee* 野菜

venetian blind *boo-RAH-een-doh* ブラインド

video equipment shop *bee-DEH-oh soh-chee noh mee-seh* ビデオ装置の店

Vietnamese *beh-TOH-nah-moo noh* ベトナムの

view *nah-GAH-meh* ながめ

village *moo-RAH* 村

vinegar *SOO* 酢

vinyl *bee-NEE-roo* ビニール

vitamins *bee-tah-meen zah-ee* ビタミン剤

vodka *WOHK-kah* ウォッカ

volcano *KAH-zahn* 火山

voltage *DEHN-ah-tsoo* 電圧

W

to wait *MAH-tsoo* 待つ

waiting room *mah-CHEE-ah-ee shee-tsoo* 待合室

to walk *ah-roo-koo* 歩く

wallet *sah-EE-foo* さいふ

walnuts *koo-ROO-mee* くるみ

to want *hoh-SHEE* 欲しい

    I don't want it.
    ee-REE-mah-sehn/ KEHK-koh dehs いりません／けっこうです

warm *ah-TAH-tah-kah-ee* あたたかい

warmup suit *toh-REH-neen-goo weh-ah* トレーニング・ウェア

to wash *ah-rah-oo* 洗う

wash and set *SHAHN-poo toh seht-toh* シャンプーとセット

watch and clock store *toh-KEH yah* 時計屋

watch repair shop *toh-KEH noh shoo-ree yah* 時計の修理屋

water *mee-zoo* 水

    water (car) *rah-JEE-eh-tah noh mee-zoo* ラジエーターの水

    hot water *oh-YOO* お湯

    mineral water *mee-NEH-rah-roo WOH-tah* ミネラル・ウォーター

    running water *soo-EE-doh* 水道

waterfall *tah-KEE* 滝

water fountain *mee-ZOO noh-mee bah* 水飲み場

watermelon *soo-EE-kah* 西瓜

water skis *soo-EE-joh skee* 水上スキー

waves (hair) *WEH-boo* ウェーブ

waves (water) *nah-mee* 波

we *wah-TAHK-shee-tah-chee gah* 私たちが

weak *yoh-WAH-ee* 弱い

to wear *kee-ROO* 着る

weather *TEHN-kee* 天気

weather forecast *TEHN-kee yoh-hoh* 天気予報

Wednesday *soo-EE-yoh-bee* 水曜日

week *shoo* 週

weekend *SHOO-mah-tsoo* 週末

this week *KOHN-shoo* 今週

to welcome *KAHN-geh soo-roo* 歓迎する

well done (meat) *YOH-koo yah-KEH-tah* よく焼けた

west *nee-SHEE* 西

western (film) *SEH-boo geh-kee* 西部劇

Western-style *YOH shee-kee noh* 洋式

what *NAH-nee* 何

what time *NAHN-jee* 何時

when *EE-tsoo* いつ

where *DOH-koh* どこ

which *DOH-reh / DOH-chee-rah* どれ／どちら

whiskey *oo-EE-skee* ウイスキー

white *shee-ROH-ee* 白い

who *DAH-reh / DOH-nah-tah* 誰／どなた

why *NAH-zeh / DOH-shteh* なぜ／どうして

wide *hee-ROH-ee* 広い

wife (someone else's) *OH-koo-sahn* 奥さん

wife (your own) *KAH-nah-ee* 家内

wind *kah-ZEH* 風

window *MAH-doh* 窓

to window shop *WEEN-doh shohp-peen-goo oh soo-roo* ウインドー・ショッピングをする

windshield *foo-ROHN-toh gah-rahs* フロント・ガラス

windshield wiper *WAH-ee-pah* ワイパー

wine *WAH-een* ワイン

red wine *rehd-DOH WAH-een* レッド・ワイン

white wine *hoh-WAH-ee-toh WAH-een* ホワイト・ワイン

Japanese rice wine *sah-KEH / oh-SAH-keh* 酒／お酒

winter *foo-YOO* 冬

to wipe *foo-koo* ふく

with pleasure *yoh-ROH-kohn-deh* 喜んで

woman, female *OHN-nah / joh-seh* 女／女性

women's clothing *foo-JEEN foo-koo* 婦人服

wonderful *soo-BAH-rah-shee* 素晴しい

wood *KEE* 木

wooden *moh-KOO-seh noh* 木製の

woodblock prints *moh-KOO hahn-gah* 木版画

woodblock print shop *HAHN-gah yah* 版画屋

wool *OO-roo* ウール

wrapping paper *HOH-soh yoh-shee* 包装用紙

wrist *TEH koo-bee* 手首

wrist TV *oo-DEH doh-keh shkee teh-reh-bee* 腕時計式テレビ

wristwatch *oo-DEH doh-keh* 腕時計

digital watch *DEH-jee-tah-roo noh toh-kee* デジタルの時計

quartz watch *koo-OH-tsoo noh toh-keh* クォーツの時計

to write *kah-koo* 書く

writer *sahk-KAH* 作家

writing pad *heek-KEE yoh-shee* 筆記用紙

writing paper *BEEN-sehn* 便せん

wrong *mah-CHEE-gaht-tah/wah-ROO-ee* 間違った／悪い

XYZ

X-ray *REHN-toh-gehn* レントゲン

yellow *KEE-roh-ee* 黄色い

yen *EHN* 円

yes *HAH-ee/EH* はい／ええ

Yes, it is. *HAH-ee, SOH dehs* はい、そうです。

you (sing.) *ah-NAH-tah gah* あなたが

you (pl.) *ah-NAH-tah tah-chee gah* あなたたちが

You're welcome. *ee-EH, doh-ee-TAH-shee mahsh-teh* いいえ、どういたしまして。

young *wah-KAH-ee* 若い

young people *wah-KAH-ee hee-toh* 若い人

younger brother (someone else's) *oh-TOH-toh-sahn* 弟さん

younger brother (your own) *oh-TOH-toh* 弟

younger sister (someone else's) *ee-MOH-toh sahn* 妹さん

younger sister (your own) *ee-MOH-toh* 妹

your *ah-NAH-tah noh* あなたの

zipper *CHAHK-koo* チャック

zoo *DOH-boo-tsoo ehn* 動物園

zucchini *zook-KEE-nee* ズッキーニ

JAPANESE-ENGLISH DICTIONARY

A

ah-BOO-rah oil (food) 油

ah-BOO-rah deh ah-geh-tah fried 油であげた

ah-BOO-ree yah-kee nee shtah/ ROH-stoh nee shtah roasted あぶり焼きにした/ローストにした

ah-EE pehn-shee-roo eye pencil アイ・ペンシル

ah-EE rah-ee-nah eye liner アイ・ライナー

ah-EE-rohn iron アイロン

ah-EE-soo tee iced tea アイス・ティー

ah-EE shah-doh eye shadow アイ・シャドー

ah-EES-koo-ree-moo ice cream アイスクリーム

ah-EE-soo koh-hee iced coffee アイス・コーヒー

ah-EE-soo woh-tah ice water アイス・ウォーター

ah-ee-teh free (unoccupied) あいて

ah-FOO-ree-kah Africa アフリカ

ahf-tah SHEH-boo roh-shohn aftershave lotion アフター・シェーブ・ローション

ah-GOH hee-geh beard あごひげ

ah-HEE-roo duck あひる

ah-KAH-boh porter (train station) 赤帽

ah-KAH-ee red 赤い

ah-KAHM-boh baby 赤ん坊

ah-KAH-roo-ee light (shade, color) 明るい

AH-kee fall, autumn 秋

ah-keh-roo to open (v.t.) 開ける

ah-koo to open (v.i.) 開く

ah-koo-ah-mah-reen aquamarine アクアマリン

ah-MAH-ee sweet 甘い

ah-MAH-kah-wah yoh noh hah-SAH-mee cuticle scissors あま皮用のはさみ

AH-meh rain 雨

AH-MEH-ree-kah United States アメリカ

AH-MEH-ree-kah-jeen American アメリカ人

ah-MEH-ree-kah noh American (adj.) アメリカの

ah-MEH-ree-kah noh ohn-gah-koo American music アメリカの音楽

ah-MEH-ree-kah seh-heen American products アメリカ製品

AH-mohn-doh almonds アーモンド

ah-NAH-tah gah you (sing.) あなたが

ah-NAH-tah noh your あなたの

ah-NAH-tah-tah-chee you (pl.) あなたたち

AHN-dah shah-tsoo/ hah-DAH gee undershirt アンダーシャツ/肌着

AH-nee elder brother (your own) 兄

ah-NEH elder sister (your own) 姉

AHN-mah sahn masseur, masseuse あんまさん

AHN-nah-ee joh information center 案内所

AHN-nah-ee tsoo-kee noh kehn-boo-tsoo guided tour 案内付きの見物

AHN-zehn nah safe (adj.) 安全な

AHN-zehn peen safety pins 安全ピン

ah-OH-ee blue 青い

ah-oo to fit 合う

ah-PEH-ree-chee-foo apertif アペリチフ

ahp-POO-roo PAH-ee apple pie アップル・パイ

ah-RAH-bee-ah goh Arabic (lang.) アラビア語

ah-rah-oo to wash 洗う

ah-REH-roo-gee allergy アレルギー

ah-ROO-ee-teh on foot 歩いて

ah-ROO-ee-koh-roo alcohol アルコール

ah-roo-koo to walk 歩く

ah-sah morning 朝

ah-SAH/REEN-neh-roo linen 麻／リンネル

ah-SHEE foot, leg 足

ah-SHEE koo-bee ankle 足首

ah-SHEE noh yoo-bee toe 足の指

ah-SHTAH/ah-SOO tomorrow あした／あす

ah-SHTAH noh bahn tomorrow night あしたの晩

ah, SOH oh, I see ああ，そう

ah-SOH-bee-bah playground 遊び場

ah-SOO-pee-reen aspirin アスピリン

ah-SOO-pee-reen oh foo-koo-mah-nee CHEEN-tsoo zah-ee aspirin-free painkiller アスピリンを含まない鎮痛剤

ah-SAHT-teh day after tomorrow あさって

ah-TAH-mah head 頭

ah-TAH-rah-shee new 新しい

ah-TAHSH-sheh kehs attaché case アタッシェ・ケース

ah-TAH-tah-kah-ee warm あたたかい

ah-TAH-tah-kah-ee GYOO-nyoo hot milk あたたかい牛乳

AH-toh deh later あとで

ah-TSOO-ee hot 暑い

ah-TSOO-ee thick 厚い

ah-tsoo-mah-roo to gather (v.i.) 集まる

AH-wah-bee abalone あわび

ah-ZOO-keh-roo to check (baggage) あずける

B

BAH bar バー

BAH-bohn bourbon バーボン

bah-DOH-meen-tohn badminton バドミントン

bah-EE-tehn gift shop 売店

BAH-kah nah stupid ばかな

bah-KEH-shohn vacation バケーション

BAH-nah-nah banana バナナ

BAHN-doh eh-ee-doh band aids バンド・エイド

BAHN-goh/kah-zoo number 番号／数

BAHN-goh-hahn/YOO-shoh-koo dinner 晩ご飯／夕食

bahn-goo-mee   program 番組

BAHN-soh-koh   adhesive tape ば
んそうこう

BAH-reh   ballet バレー

bah-REH geh-kee joh   ballet
theater バレー劇場

bah-shoh   place 場所

bah-shoh   tournament (sumo) 場所

BAH-soo   bus バス

bah-SOO-keht-toh boh-roo
basketball バスケット・ボール

BAH-soo noh noh-REE-bah   bus
stop バスの乗り場

BAH-tah   butter バター

baht-TEH-ree   battery バッテ
リー

BEE-chee PAH-rah-soh-roo
beach umbrella ビーチ・パラソ
ル

bee-DEH-oh soh-chee noh mee-seh   video equipment shop ビ
デオ装置の店

bee-GAHN joo-tsoo   facial
massage 美顔術

bee-JEE-nehs HOH-teh-roo
business hotel ビジネス・ホテ
ル

bee-JEE-neh-soo gah-ee
business district ビジネス街

BEE-joo-tsoo   art 美術

been   bottle びん

bee-NEE-roo   vinyl ビニール

been-meh   flight number 便名

BEEN-sehn   writing paper 便せ
ん

bee-roo   building ビル

BEE-roo   beer ビール

bee-SOO-keht-toh   biscuits ビス
ケット

bee-tah-meen zah-ee   vitamins ビ
タミン剤

bee-YOH een   hairdresser, beauty
parlor 美容院

beh-bee BEHD-doh   crib ベ
ビー・ベッド

BEHD-doh   bed ベッド

BEH-kohn   bacon ベーコン

BEH-koo-doh POH-teh-toh
baked potato ベークド・ポテト

BEHN-goh-shee   lawyer 弁護士

BEHN-pee   constipation 便秘

BEHN-ree nah   convenient 便利
な

beh-ROO-toh   belt ベルト

beh-TOH-nah-moo noh
Vietnamese ベトナムの

BOH-choo zah-ee   insect
repellant 防虫剤

boh-DEE roh-shohn   body lotion
ボディー・ローション

boh-ee   bellhop ボーイ

boh-KOO-shee   minister 牧師

boh-roo   bowl ボール

BOH-roo pehn   ballpoint pen
ボールペン

BOH-shee   hat 帽子

boh-TAHN   button ボタン

BOH-toh   boat ボート

boo-DOH   grapes ぶどう

BOO-joo-tsoo   Japanese martial
arts 武術

BOON-boh-goo tehn   stationery
shop 文房具店

boon-poh   grammar 文法

boon-poh noh hohn   grammar
book 文法の本

BOON-rah-koo   Japanese puppet
theater 文楽

boo-RAH-een-doh   venetian blind
ブラインド

boo-RAH-jah   bra, brassiere ブラ
ジャー

boo-RAH-jee-roo Brazil ブラジル

boo-RAH-jee-roo noh Brazilian ブラジルの

boo-RAH-oo-soo blouse ブラウス

boo-RAH-shee brushes ブラシ

boo-REE-foo shorts (briefs) ブリーフ

boo-REH-kee brakes ブレーキ

boo-REH-kee oh-ee-roo brake fluid ブレーキ・オイル

boo-REH-soo-reht-toh bracelet ブレスレット

boo-ROH-chee brooch ブローチ

boo-ROH doh-rah-ee blow dry ブロー・ドライ

boo-ROH-doh-weh kah-rah noh shoh Broadway show ブロード・ウェーからのショー

boo-ROH-doh-weh noh heet-toh Broadway hits ブロード・ウェーのヒット

boo-ROHK-koh-ree broccoli ブロッコリ

boo-ROHN-doh blond ブロンド

boo-ROO jeen/jeen-zoo jeans ブルージーン／ジーンズ

boo-ROO-neht-toh brunette ブルネット

BOO-tah-ee nee chee-KAH-ee seh-kee orchestra (theater) 舞台に近い席

boo-TAH nee-koo pork 豚肉

BOO-tsoo boots ブーツ

BYOH-een hospital 病院

BYOH-kee sick 病気

byoof-FEH shah buffet car ビュッフェ車

C

chah-EE-roh-ee brown 茶色い

CHAHK-koo zipper チャック

CHAHN-neh-roo channel (TV) チャンネル

chee blood 血

chee-CHEE father (your own) 父

chee-ee-kee area 地域

chee-gah-ee difference 違い

chee-GAH-oo different 違う

chee-HOH/ ee-NAH-kah countryside 地方／田舎

chee-KAH-ee near 近い

chee-KAH mee-chee short cut 近道

chee-KAH-teh-tsoo subway 地下鉄

chee-KEEN soo-poo chicken soup チキン・スープ

chee-moo team チーム

chee-REE gah-mee/ TEES-shoo tissues ちり紙／ティッシュー

CHEE-sah-ee small 小さい

CHEE-zoo map 地図

CHEE-zoo cheese チーズ

CHEE-zoo keh-kee cheesecake チーズ・ケーキ

CHEHK-koo/ ee-CHEE-mah-tsoo moh-yoh checks (pattern) チェック／市松模様

chehk-KOO een soo-roo to check in チェック・インする

chehn/ koo-SAH-ree chain チェーン／鎖

CHOH-cheen lanterns ちょうちん

chohk-KOH-been direct flight 直行便

CHOH koh-gah-tah teh-reh-bee miniature TV 超小型テレビ

CHOH-koh-koo sculpture 彫刻

CHOH-koh-koo kah sculptor 彫刻家

CHOH-koh-koo heen carved objects 彫刻品

choh-KOH-reh-toh chocolate チョコレート

choh-KOH-reh-toh keh-kee chocolate cake チョコレート・ケーキ

choh-KOH-reh-toh POO-reen chocolate pudding チョコレート・プリン

CHOH-kyoh-ree DEHN-wah long-distance call 長距離電話

CHOH-shah author 著者

CHOH-shoh-koo/ ah-SAH goh-hahn breakfast 朝食／朝ご飯

CHOO medium size 中

CHOO-been medium-size bottle 中びん

CHOO-gah-tah shah medium-sized car 中型車

CHOO-goh-koo China 中国

CHOO-goh-koo goh Chinese (lang.) 中国語

CHOO-goh-koo noh Chinese 中国の

CHOO-mohn order 注文

CHOO-mohn soo-roo to order 注文する

CHOO-nee-kah-ee mezzanine 中二階

CHOO-oh center 中央

choo-shah injection 注射

CHOO-shoh joh parking garage 駐車場

CHOO-shah ryoh parking fee 駐車料

choo-shah soo-roo to park 駐車する

D

dah-BOH-koo shoh bruise 打撲傷

DAH-ee large (size) 大

DAH-ee-eht-toh diet ダイエット

dah-EE-eht-toh kahn-mee-ryoh sugar substitute ダイエット甘味料

DAH-ee-eht-toh noh noh-MEE-moh-noh diet soda ダイエットの飲み物

dah-EE-gah-koo university 大学

dah-EE-hyoh teh-kee nah typical 代表的な

dah-ee-JOH-boo dehs It's all right だいじょうぶです

dah-EE-koo doh-goo yah hardware store 大工道具屋

dah-ee meh title 題名

dah-EE-yah diamond ダイヤ

dah-ee-yah-roo choh-KOO-tsoo direct dial ダイヤル直通

dahk-KYOO shtah dislocated 脱臼した

DAHN-boh heater 暖房

DAHN-shee yoh noh TOH-ee-reh men's room 男子用のトイレ

DAH-reh/ DOH-nah-tah who 誰／どなた

DAH-reh-kah somebody, someone 誰か

dahs-SHEE mehn cotton 脱脂綿

DEES-koh disco ディスコ

DEE-zeh-roo diesel (gas) ディーゼル

____ *deh* at; by (means of) 〜で

DEH-goo-chee exit 出口

DEH-jee-tah-roo noh toh-keh digital watch デジタルの時計

DEHN-ah-tsoo voltage 電圧

DEHN-chee battery 電池

DEH-neesh-shoo peh-stoh-ree/ kah-SHEE pahn Danish pastry デーニッシュ・ペーストリー／菓子パン

DEHN-kee electricity 電気

DEHN-kee kah-mee-soh-ree electric razor 電気カミソリ

DEHN-kee kee-goo tehn
electrical appliance store 電気
器具店

DEHN-kee seh-heen electrical
appliance 電気製品

DEHN-kyoo light bulb 電球

dehn-poh telegram, cable 電報

DEHN-shah commuter train 電
車

DEHN-toh teh-kee nah traditional 伝統的な

dehn-wah telephone, telephone
call 電話

DEHN-wah bahn-goh telephone
number 電話番号

DEHN-wah bohk-koo-soo
telephone booth 電話ボックス

DEHN-wah soo-roo to call
(telephone) 電話する

deh-OH-doh-rahn-toh deodorant
デオドラント

deh-PAH-toh department store
デパート

deh-roo depart (v.) (transportation) 出る

deh ZAH-toh dessert デザート

DOH-boo-tsoo ehn zoo 動物園

DOH-ee-tsoo Germany ドイツ

doh-EE-tsoo goh German (lang.)
ドイツ語

DOH-ee-tsoo noh German ドイツ
の

doh-hyoh sumo ring 土俵

DOH-koh where どこ

doh-KOO-sheen single (marital
status) 独身

DOH-moh ah-REE-gah-toh
thank you どうもありがとう

DOH-nah-tsoo doughnuts ドー
ナッツ

doh-NOH koo-rah-ee how long,
how much どの位

doh-RAH-ee-bah screwdriver ド
ライバー

***doh-RAH-ee koo-ree-neen-goo
noh sah-bee-soo*** dry cleaning
service ドライ・クリーニング
のサービス

DOH-reh/ DOH-chee-rah which
どれ／どちら

DOH-reh-soo dress ドレス

DOH-roh chee-zoo road map 道
路地図

DOH-roo dollar (s) ドル

DOH-ryoh colleague 同僚

DOH-yaht-teh how どうやって

doh-YOH-bee Saturday 土曜日

DOH-zoh please (come in/ sit
down/ begin/ have some/ go
first/ etc.) どうぞ

E

EE good, fine いい

ee stomach 胃

ee-BOO-neen-goo DOH-reh-soo
evening gown イブニング・ドレ
ス

EE-chee-bah market 市場

ee-CHEE-gah-tsoo January 一月

ee-CHEE-goh strawberries いち
ご

ee-CHEE jee-kahn per hour 一
時間

ee-CHEE nee-chee a day; per
day 一日

ee-CHEE nee-chee goh-toh by
the day 一日ごと

ee-CHEE ryoo noh first class 一
流の

***EE-dehs-yoh/ kah-MAH-ee-mah-
sehn*** I don't mind いいですよ
／かまいません

ee-EH no いいえ

ee-EH/ oo-chee house 家／うち

ee-EH, chee-GAH-ee-mahs No, it isn't いいえ、違います

ee-EH, doh-ee-TAH-shee-mahsh-teh You're welcome いいえ、どういたしまして

ee-EH, KEHK-koh dehs No, thank you いいえ、けっこうです

ee-EH-moh-toh headmaster (flower arrangement) 家元

ee-GEE-ree-soo England イギリス

ee-GEE-ree-soo-jeen Britisher イギリス人

ee-GEE-ree-soo noh British イギリスの

ee-GOH-koh-chee noh ee cozy 居心地のいい

ee-KAH squid いか

ee-KEE-mah-shoh Let's go 行きましょう

ee-KEE-mah-shoh KAH Shall we go? 行きましょうか

ee-KEH pond 池

ee-koo to go 行く

EE-koo-rah how much (money) いくら

EE-mah now 今

ee-mah NAHN-jee dehs KAH What time is it? いま何時ですか

ee-MOH-toh younger sister (your own) 妹

ee-MOH-toh sahn younger sister (someone else's) 妹さん

EEN-doh-neh-shee-ah noh Indonesian インドネシアの

EEN-doh noh Indian インドの

ee NOH choh-shee gah yoh-koo-mah-ee upset stomach 胃の調子がよくない

EEN-shoo-reen insulin インシュリン

EEN-stahn-toh koh-hee instant coffee インスタント・コーヒー

ee-REE-goo-chee entrance 入口

___ gah ee-REE-mahs/ gah hee-TSOO-yoh dehs I need ___ ～がいります／～が必要です

ee-REE-mah-sehn/ KEHK-koh dehs I don't want it いりません／けっこうです

ee-REH-bah denture 入れ歯

ee-roh color 色

ee-ROH noh hyoh color chart 色の表

ee-SAHN antacid 胃散

ee-SEH eh-bee/ ROH-boo-stah lobster 伊勢えび／ロブスター

ee-SHAH doctor 医者

ee-SHEE-tsoo boo-tsoo gah-kah-ree lost and found 遺失物係り

ees-shoh nee together 一緒に

ee-TAH-mee/ koo-tsoo pain 痛み／苦痛

ee-TAH-ree-ah Italy イタリア

ee-TAH-ree-ah goh Italian (lang.) イタリア語

ee-TAH-ree-ah noh Italian イタリアの

EE-tsoo when いつ

EE-tsoo moh always いつも

ee-YAH-reen-goo earrings イヤリング

___ eh/ nee to ___へ／___に

eh-BEE shrimp えび

eh-EE-toh kah-too-reej-jee teh-poo 8-track cartridges エイト・カートリッジ・テープ

EH-gah movie, film 映画

EH-gah kahn movie theater 映画館

EH-goh English (lang.) 英語

EH-goh noh dehn-wah choh English telephone directory 英語の電話帳

EH-goh oh hah-nah-seh-roo English-speaking 英語を話せる

eh-HAH-gah-kee picture postcards 絵葉書

eh-kee station (train) 駅

eh-KOO-reh-ah eclair エクレア

eh-MEH-rah-roo-doh emerald エメラルド

EHN yen 円

EHN-geh-kee play (theater) 演劇

EHN-jeen engine エンジン

EHN-jee-nee-ah engineer エンジニア

EHN-jeen oh-ee-roo oil (car) エンジン・オイル

EHN-pee-tsoo pencil 鉛筆

EHN-pee-tsoo keh-zoo-ree pencil sharpener 鉛筆削り

EHN-shoo-tsoo kah director (theater, TV) 演出家

eh-REH-beh-tah elevator エレベーター

EH-roo ale エール

EH-wah jee-tehn English-Japanese dictionary 英和辞典

F

FAHN beh-roo-toh fan belt ファン・ベルト

fee-REEP-peen Philippines フィリッピン

fee-roo-tah filter (camera) フィルター

fee-ROO-tah tsoo-kee noh tah-bah-koh filtered cigarettes フィルター付きのたばこ

FOH-koo fork フォーク

FOH-koo sohn-goo folk songs フォーク・ソング

foo-EE-roo-moo film フィルム

foo-JEEN foo-koo women's clothing 婦人服

foo-JEEN foo-koo noh mee-seh women's clothing store 婦人服の店

foo-KEE-kah-eh-rah reh-teh dubbed (film) 吹き替えられて

FOO kee-ree noh eh-gah first-run film 封切りの映画

foo-koo to wipe ふく

foo-koo-soh clothes 服装

foo-KOO tsoo cramps (stomach) 腹痛

foo-MEEN shoh insomnia 不眠症

foo-NAH been sea mail 船便

foo-NAH-yoh-ee seasickness 船酔い

foon-ee-kee atmosphere 雰囲気

FOO-neh ship 船

FOO-neh nee on board (ship) 船に

FOO-rahn franc フラン

foo-RAHN-soo goh French (lang.) フランス語

foo-RAHN-soo noh French フランスの

foo-RAHN-soo pahn French bread フランス・パン

foo-RAHS-shoo bah-roo-boo flash bulbs フラッシュ・バルブ

foo-REHN-chee FOO-rah-ee French fries フレンチ・フライ

(oh)-FOO-roh/ yoh-KOO-soh bathtub （お)風呂/浴そう

foo-ROH-ah shoh floor show フロア・ショー

foo-ROHN-toh gah-rahs windshield フロント・ガラス

foo-ROO-ee old (things) 古い

foo-ROOTS kahp-poo fruit compote フルーツ・カップ

foo-TOH pier 埠頭

FOO-toh envelopes 封筒

foot-TOH boh-roo football フットボール

foo-TOH moh-moh thigh 太もも

foo-TSOO regular, ordinary 普通

foo-TSOO-kah two days 二日

foo-YOO winter 冬

G

gah-EE-doh book-koo guide book ガイド・ブック

GAH-ee-kah foreign currency 外貨

gah-EE-koh-koo jeen foreigner 外国人

gah-EE-koh-koo noh foreign, imported 外国の

gah-KAH painter 画家

gahk-KOH school 学校

gah-koo-dahn band 楽団

gahk-SEH student 学生

gah-RAH-soo boo-tah crystal (watch) ガラスぶた

GAH-reek-koo/ NEEN-nee-koo garlic ガーリック／にんにく

gah-ROH art gallery 画廊

gah-SOH-reen gasoline ガソリン

gah-SOH-reen pohn-poo fuel pump ガソリン・ポンプ

gah-SOH-reen soo-tahn-doh gas station ガソリン・スタンド

GAH-soo gas ガス

GAH-zeh gauze ガーゼ

GEEN silver 銀

GEEN-koh bank 銀行

GEE-ree-shah noh Greek ギリシャの

GEE-yah gears ギヤ

GEH-joo-tsoo kah artist 芸術家

geh-KEE joh theater 劇場

GEHN-kee fine 元気

gehn-zoh soo-roo to develop (film) 現像する

geh-REE diarrhea 下痢

geh-TSOO-yoh-bee Monday 月曜日

geh-ZAH-ee/ TSOO-jee yah-koo laxative 下剤／通じ薬

goh Japanese board game 碁

goh-BAHN toh goh EE-shee go board and stones 碁盤と碁石

goh-FOO-koo yah kimono store 呉服屋

GOH-gah-tsoo May 五月

GOH-goh afternoon 午後

GOH-hahn Japanese rice, cooked ご飯

goh-HYAH-koo GOO-rah-moo half kilogram 五百グラム

goh-MEHN-nah-sah-ee/ soo-MEE-mah-sehn I'm sorry ごめんなさい／すみません

goh-MEHN-nah-sah-ee/ shee-TSOO-reh shee-mahs Excuse me ごめんなさい／失礼します

goh-MOO bahn-doh rubber bands ゴム・バンド

GOH-roh around (approximate time) ～頃

GOH-roo-foo golf ゴルフ

goh-ROO-foo boh-roo golf ball ゴルフ・ボール

goh-ROO-foo koh-soo golf course ゴルフ・コース

goh-ROO-foo koo-rah-boo golf clubs ゴルフ・クラブ

GOH-roo-foo oh soo-roo to play golf ゴルフをする

goh-SHOO-jeen husband (someone else's) 御主人

GOON-jeen military (personnel) 軍人

GOO-rah-soo glass グラス

goo-REEN noh green グリーンの

goo-REH noh gray グレーの

goo-REH-poo foo-ROO-tsoo grapefruit グレープ・フルーツ

goo-ROO-poo tsoo-ah group tour グループ・ツアー

GREEN-shah first class (train...green car) グリーン車

GREH-poo-foo-ROO-tsoo JOO-soo grapefruit juice グレープ・フルーツ・ジュース

gyoh-jee sumo judge 行司

gyoo-nee-koo/ bee-foo beef 牛肉／ビーフ

GYOO noh hee-KEE nee-koo ground beef 牛のひき肉

H

hah-BOO-rah-shee toothbrush 歯ブラシ

hah-CHEE-gah-tsoo August 八月

hah-dah skin 肌

hah-DEH-yah-kah-nah bright はでやかな

HAH-ee/ EH yes はい／ええ

HAH-ee-keen-goo hiking ハイキング

hah-EE-keen-goo koh-soo hiking trail ハイキング・コース

HAH-ee, oh-KAH-geh-sah-mah deh Fine, thank you. はい、おかげさまで

HAH-ee-shah dentist 歯医者

HAH-ee, SOH dehs Yes, it is. はい、そうです

HAH-ee-yah hire (limousines, taxis) ハイヤー

hah-EE-zah-rah ashtray 灰皿

hah-GAH-kee postcard 葉書

HAH-hah mother (your own) 母

hah-jee-mah-roo to start (v.i.) 始まる

hah-JEE-meh-mahsh-teh DOH-zoh yoh-ROH-shee-koo How do you do? はじめまして、どうぞよろしく

hah-JEE-meh-mahsh-teh koh-CHEE-rah koh-soh yoh-ROH-shee-koo How do you do? (reply) はじめまして、こちらこそよろしく

hah-JEE-meh-teh first time 初めて

hah-JEE-meh-teh oh-MEH-nee kah-kah-ree-mahs Pleased to meet you. 初めて、おめにかかります

hah-KEE-keh nausea 吐き気

hah-KOH nee ee-reh-teh boxed 箱に入れて

hah-KOO-boo-tsoo kahn museum 博物館

hah-MAH-goo-ree clams はまぐり

hah-MAH-kee cigars 葉巻き

HAH-rʂoo ham ハム

hah-NAH nose 鼻

hah-NAH flower 花

hah-NAH mee-chee Kabuki runway 花道

hah-NAH yah florist 花屋

HAHN-b̄ah-ḡah hamburger ハンバーガー

HAHN-bah-goo soo-TĒH-kee hamburger steak ハンバーグ・ステーキ

HAHN-doh bahg-goo handbag ハンド・バッグ

HAHN-doh-roo steering wheel ハンドル

HAHN-gah yah woodblock print shop 版画屋

HAHN-kah-gah-ee downtown area 繁華街

HAHN-m̄ah hammer ハンマー

HAHN nee-chee a half day 半日

HAH noh tsoo-meh-moh-noh filling (tooth) 歯のつめもの

HAHN soh-deh short sleeves 半そで

hah-REE-koh zah-ee-koo papier mâché 張り子細工

HAH-ree noh ryōh-jee shee acupuncturist 針の療治師

hah-REE ryōh-jee acupuncture 針療治

HAH-reh clear sky 晴れ

hah-REH-teh swollen はれて

HAH-roo spring 春

hah-SAH-mee scissors はさみ

hah-SHEE bridge 橋

HAH-shee chopsticks はし

hah-SHEE oh-kee chopstick rest はし置き

hah-TAH-keh farm 畑

HAH-wah-ee noh Hawaiian ハワイの

hah-YAH-ee early 早い

hah-YAH-ee fast, quick 速い

hee day 日

hee-DAH-ree left 左

hee-GAH-shee east 東

HEE-geh-kee tragedy 悲劇

hee-GEH soh-ree shave ひげそり

hee-GEH soh-ree toh sehn-pah-tsoo shave and shampoo ひげそりと洗髪

hee-JEE elbow ひじ

hee-KEE-noh-bah-shee enlargement 引き伸し

hee-KEE-tsoo-ree cramp ひきつり

heek-KEE yōh-shee writing pad 筆記用紙

hee-KŌH jee-kahn flying time 飛行時間

hee-KŌH-kee airplane 飛行機

hee-KOO-ee low 低い

hee-MOH string ひも

hee-RAH-meh flounder 平目

hee-REH MEE-nee-ohn filet mignon ヒレミニオン

hee-REH nee-koo filet ひれ肉

hee-ROH-ee wide 広い

hee-ROO noon 昼

HEE-shoh secretary 秘書

hee-SOO-ee jade ひすい

hee-TAH-ee forehead ひたい

hee-toh person 人

hee-TOH bahn overnight 一晩

hee-TOH-ree alone ひとり

hee-TOH-ree (ah-tah-ree) per person 一人（当り）

hee-TSOO-yōh nah necessary 必要な

hee-YAH-keh sunburn 日焼け

hee-YAH-keh doh-meh sunscreen 日焼け止め

hee-ZAH knee ひざ

hee-ZOO-keh date 日付

heh-ĀH doh-rah-ee-yāh hair dryer ヘアー・ドライヤー

heh-AH peen bobby pins ヘアー・ピン

heh-AH spoo-reh hair spray ヘアー・スプレー

hehd-DOH rah-ee-toh headlight ヘッド・ライト

HEHN-ah-tsoo-kee electrical transformer 変圧器

hehn-keen refund 返金

HEHN-toh sehn tonsils 扁桃腺

heh-ROO-meht-toh helmet ヘルメット

heh-ROOS koo-rah-boo health club ヘルス・クラブ

heh-YAH room 部屋

HOH-bah koo-rahf-toh hovercraft ホーバー・クラフト

HOH-hoh cheek ほほ

HOH-jee-chah Japanese roasted tea ほうじ茶

hoh-kah noh another, other 外の

hoh-KEHN insurance 保険

HOH-koh shee-jee kee directional signal 方向指示器

hoh-moo platform ホーム

HOHN book 本

hoh-NEH bone 骨

hoh-NEH gah oh-reh-tah fractured 骨が折れた

hohn-TOH Really? 本当

HOHN yah bookstore 本屋

HOHN-yah-koo translation 翻訳

HOHN-yah-koo soo-roo to translate 翻訳する

HOH-rehn-soh spinach ほうれん草

hoh-seh-kee stone (jewelry) 宝石

HOH-seh-kee tehn jewelry store 宝石店

hoh-SHEE to want 欲しい

hoh-SHEE boo-doh raisins 干しぶどう

hoh-SHOH-keen deposit 保証金

HOH-soh yoh-shee wrapping paper 包装用紙

HOH-soo-tehs hostess ホステス

HOH-tah-ee bandages 包帯

HOH-teh-roo hotel ホテル

HOH-teh-roo noh bah-soo hotel bus ホテルのバス

HOH-teh-roo noh yoh-YAH-koo kah-OON-tah hotel reservation counter ホテルの予約カウンター

hoht-TOH dohg-goo hot dog ホットドッグ

hoht-TOH keh-kee pancakes ホット・ケーキ

hoh-WAH-ee-toh WAH-een white wine ホワイト・ワイン

hyoh list 表

hyoh-bahn reputation 評判

HYOH-noh ice pack 氷のう

J

jah-KEHT-toh jacket ジャケット

JAHK-kee jack ジャッキ

JAH-moo jam ジャム

JAHN soh mahjong parlor ジャン荘

jee-BOON deh on one's own 自分で

jee-DAH-ee moh-noh historical drama 時代物

jee-DOH hehn-soh-koo automatic transmission 自動変速

jee-KAHN time, hour 時間

jee-KAHN deh by the hour 時間で

jee-KAHN dōh-ree nee on time 時間通りに

JEE-kee porcelain 磁器

jee-KEE-bee deh yah-ee-tah broiled 直火で焼いた

JEE-koh accident 事故

jee-KOHK hyōh timetable 時刻表

jee-KOH-shoh-kah-ee soo-roo to introduce (oneself) 自己紹介する

jee-MAH-koo subtitles (film) 字幕

JEE-moo gym ジム

JEEN gin ジン

jeen-jah shrine 神社

jee-SHEEN earthquake 地震

jee-shoh dictionary 辞書

jee-TEHN-shah bicycle, bike 自転車

jee-TSOO-ehn demonstration 実演

jee-TSOO-gyōh-kah industrialist 実業家

jee-YŌŌ jee-kahn free time 自由時間

jee-YŌŌ seh-kee unreserved seats (train) 自由席

___ *jōh* ___ castle ～城

JŌH-ehn performance 上演

JŌH-gee ruler 定規

joh-GEEN-goo jogging ジョギング

joh-GEEN-goo KŌH-soo jogging path ジョギング・コース

joh-KŌH-eh-kee nail polish remover 除光液

JŌH-kyah-koo passenger 乗客

JŌH-ree-koo soo-roo to go ashore 上陸する

JŌH-sah-ee fortress 城塞

joh-SHEE-yoh noh TOH-ee-reh ladies' room 女子用のトイレ

JŌH-toh/ JŌH-shee-tsoo good quality 上等／上質

JŌO-doh judo 柔道

JŌO-ee-chee-gah-tsoo November 十一月

JŌO-gah-tsoo October 十月

joo-hahk-keen 18 karat 18金

JOON keen solid gold 純金

JŌO-nee-gah-tsoo December 十二月

JŌO-shoh address 住所

JŌO-soo juice ジュース

joo-yohn-keen 14 karat 14金

JYAH-zoo jazz ジャズ

K

kah-BĀH chah-jee cover charge カバー・チャージ

kah-BOO-kee Japanese classical drama 歌舞伎

KĀH-dee-gahn cardigan カーディガン

kah-doh corner 角

KAH-doh/ ee-KEH-bah-nah/ oh-HAH-nah flower arrangement 華道／活け花／お花

kah-EE bah-shee-rah scallops 貝柱

kah-EE-choo dehn-toh flashlight 懐中電燈

kah-ee-gahn coast, beach, seashore 海岸

KAH-ee-kyōh noh jee-een mosque 回教の寺院

kah-EE-moh-noh shopping 買い物

kah-EE-shah company (business) 会社

kah-EE-shah noh JOO-yah-koo company executive 会社の重役

kah-EE-shah noh shah-CHOH company president 会社の社長

kah-EE-soh-koo express train 快速

kah-EH-roo to change 変える／代える／替える／換える

kah-FEH-een noo-kee noh KOH-hee decaffeinated coffee カフェイン抜きのコーヒー

kah-FOON shoh hay fever 花粉症

kah-FOO-soo boh-tahn cufflinks カフス・ボタン

kah-GAH-koo CHOH-mee-ryoh MSG (monosodium glutamate) 化学調味料

kah-GAH-mee mirror 鏡

kah-GEE key 鍵

kah-goh basket かご

KAH-goo furniture 家具

KAH-kah-toh heel かかと

KAH-kee oysters かき

kah-KEE persimmon 柿

kah-KEE-toh-meh registered mail 書留

kah-KEH jee-koo scroll 掛け軸

kah-koo to paint (art) 描く

kah-koo to write 書く

KAH-koo-teh-roo cocktails カクテル

kah-KOO-teh-roo rah-oon-jee cocktail lounge カクテル・ラウンジ

kah-MAH-ee-mah-sehn It doesn't matter かまいません

kah-mee noh keh hair 髪の毛

kah-MEE-soh-ree razor かみそり

kah-MEE-soh-ree noh hah razor blades かみそりの刃

kah-MEE yah/ wah-SHEE yah paper shop 紙屋／和紙屋

KAH-meh-rah camera カメラ

kah-MEH-rah yah camera shop, photography shop カメラ屋

kahn can かん

KAH-nah-dah Canada カナダ

KAH-nah-dah-jeen Canadian カナダ人

KAH-nah-ee wife (your own) 家内

kah-NEE crab かに

kahn-gehn-gah-koo-dahn orchestra 管弦楽団

KAHN-geh soo-roo to welcome 歓迎する

KAHN-goh-foo nurse 看護婦

KAHN-joh/ CHEHK-koo/ kah-EE-keh check, bill 勘定／チェック／会計

KAHN-koh ahn-nah-ee-joh tourist information center 観光案内所

KAHN-koh bahs sightseeing bus 観光バス

KAHN-koh gah-ee-doh tour guide 観光ガイド

KAHN-koh-koo Korea 韓国

KAHN-koh-koo noh Korean 韓国の

KAHN-koh kyah-koo tourist 観光客

KAHN-koh ryoh-koh sightseeing tour 観光旅行

kah-NOH infection 化膿

KAH-noh-joh gah she 彼女が

kahn-pah-ee toast (drinks) 乾杯

KAHN-seh-tsoo joint (body) 関節

KAHN-soh shteh ee-roo dry 乾燥している

kahn-toh-koo director (sports/ film) 監督

KAHN-zoh/ REH-bah liver 肝臓 /レバー

kah-OH face 顔

kah-oo to buy 買う

kah-OON-tah counter カウン ター

____ *kah-rah* from ____から

KAH-rah curlers カーラー

kah-RAH-dah body 体

kah-RAH-ee hot (peppery food) からい

kah-RAH reen-soo color rinse カラー・リンス

kah-RAH-teh karate (martial art) 空手

kah-REE-noh tsoo-meh-moh-noh temporary filling 仮のつめもの

kah-REE-roo to rent 借りる

KAH-reh gah he 彼が

kah-REHN-dah calendar カレン ダー

KAH-reh-rah gah they 彼らが

kah-ROO-ee light (weight) 軽い

kah-ROO-ee shoh-koo-jee light meal 軽い食事

kah-SEHT-toh cassettes カセッ ト

kah SEHT-toh reh-koh-dah cassette recorder カセット・レ コーダー

keh-SHOH-heen tehn toiletries shop 化粧品店

KAH-shoo singer 歌手

kahs-TAH-doh custard カスター ド

KAH-tah shoulder (body) 肩

kah-TAH-mee-chee one way 片 道

kah-TAH-mee-chee keep-poo one-way ticket 片道切符

kah-TAH-nah yah Japanese sword shop 刀屋

kah-TAH-roh-goo catalog カタロ グ

kah-TAH-zoo-keh-roo to clean (tidy) 片付ける

kah-TEH yoh-heen housewares 家庭用品

KAH-toh-reej-jee cartridges カ ートリッジ

kah-WAH leather 皮

kah-WAH river 川

kah-YOH-bee Tuesday 火曜日

KAH-zahn volcano 火山

kah-ZAH-ree peen pin (jewelry) 飾りピン

kah-ZEH cold (head, chest) 風邪

kah-ZEH wind 風

kah-zoh-koo family 家族

KEE tree, wood 木

KEE-geh-kee comedy 喜劇

kee-jee fabric 生地

kee-KOH climate 気候

kee-MOH-noh kimono 着物

KEEN gold 金

KEE-nah-ee moh-CHEE-koh-mee heen carry-on 機内持込品

KEEN-dah-ee nee-HOHN shoh-seh-tsoo modern Japanese novels 近代日本小説

KEEN-ehn seh-kee no-smoking section 禁煙席

KEEN-koh safe 金庫

KEEN-kyoo emergency 緊急

KEEN mehk-kee gold plated 金 メッキ

KEEN-nee-koo muscle 筋肉

KEE-noh-mee nuts 木の実

KEE-noo/ SHEE-roo-koo silk 絹 /シルク

keen-shee forbidden 禁止

KEEN-yoh-bee Friday 金曜日

KEEN-zoh-koo metal 金属

keep-POO noh HAHN-bah-ee-kee ticket machine (trains) 切符の販売機

keep-poo OO-ree-bah box office, ticket window/ counter 切符売り場

KEE-reh nah pretty, beautiful きれいな

KEE-reh nah clean きれいな

kee-roh kilogram キロ

KEE-roh-ee yellow 黄色い

kee-ROH-soo mileage キロ数

KEE-roo to cut 切る

kee-ROO to wear 着る

KEE-seh-tsoo season 季節

kee-shah/ rehs-shah train 汽車／列車

kees-SAH-tehn Japanese coffee shop 喫茶店

kee-TAH north 北

kee-TAH-nah-ee dirty きたない

kee-TSOO-ee tight (clothing) きつい

keet-TEH stamps 切手

kee-ZAH-mee tah-bah-koh pipe tobacco きざみたばこ

KEH-boo-roo kah cable car ケーブル・カー

keh-CHAHP-poo ketchup ケチャップ

keh-GAH injury けが

keh-heen prize 景品

KEH-kahn police officer 警官

KEH-kee cake ケーキ

kehk-KOHN shteh married 結婚して

kehn prefecture 県

kehn/ keep-POO ticket 券／切符

KEHN-chee-koo architecture 建築

KEHN-chee-koo kah architect 建築家

KEHN-choh shoh-ZAH-ee-chee prefectural capital 県庁所在地

KEHN-doh kendo (martial art) 剣道

keh-NOO-kee tweezers 毛抜き

kehn-zoh sah-reh-roo to be built 建造される

KEH-reh-doh-moh/ DEH-moh but けれども／でも

KEH-sah this morning けさ

KEH-sah-tsoo police 警察

keh-SHEE-goh-moo eraser 消ゴム

keh-shee-kee landscape 景色

keh-SHOH-gee robe 化粧着

keh-SHOH-heen tehn cosmetics shop 化粧品店

keh-tah-ee KOHM-poh steh-reh-oh soh-chee portable component stereo system 携帯コンポステレオ装置

KEH-teh-kee horn 警笛

keh-TSOO ah-tsoo blood pressure 血圧

keh ZOH-meh hair color 毛染め

koh-BEEN small bottle 小びん

KOH-chah tea 紅茶

koh-doh-moh child (your own) 子供

koh-DOH-moh foo-koo children's clothing 子供服

koh-DOH-moh foo-koo noh mee-seh children's clothing store 子供服の店

koh-ee carp 鯉

koh-EEN rahn-doh-ree laundromat コイン・ランドリー

KOH-ehn park 公園

koh-GAH-tah shah small car 小
型車

KOH-geh crafts 工芸

KOH-geh kah craftsman 工芸家

KOH-geh noh mee-seh
handicrafts shop 工芸の店

KOH-hee coffee コーヒー

KOH-hee shohp-poo coffee shop
コーヒー・ショップ

KOH-HEE-tsoo-jee lamb 子羊

koh-JEEN yoh koh-GEET-teh
personal check 個人用小切手

KOH-kah coins 硬貨

KOH-kah-ee cruise 航海

KOH-kahn ree-tsoo exchange
rate 交換率

KOH-kahn-shoo telephone
operator 交換手

KOH-kahn soo-roo to exchange
交替する

koh-KOH here ここ

KOH-koh-ah cocoa, hot chocolate
ココア

KOH-koh-koo ad 広告

KOH-koo been airmail 航空便

KOH-koo kehn ticket (air) 航空
券

koh-KOO-ree-tsoo KOH-ehn
national park 国立公園

KOH-koo-seh-kee nationality 国
籍

KOH-koo shoh-kahn aerogram
航空書簡

KOH-kyoh koh-tsoo kee-kahn
public transportation 公共交通
機関

koh-MAH-moh-noh notions 小間
物

koh-MEH Japanese rice,
uncooked 米

koh-MOH-ree baby sitter 子守り

KOHN/ TOH-moh-roh-koh-shee
corn コーン／とうもろこし

KOHN-bahn tonight 今晩

KOHN-bahn-wah Good evening
こんばんは

KOHN-deh crowded 混んで

KOHN foo-REH-koo corn flakes
コーン・フレーク

KOHN-nee-chee-wah Good
afternoon こんにちは

koh-NOH this (adj.) この

koh-noh-moo to prefer 好む

kohn-SAH-toh concert コンサー
ト

kohn-SAH-toh hoh-roo concert
hall コンサート・ホール

KOHN-shoo this week 今週

KOHN-tahk-toh rehn-zoo
contact lenses コンタクト・レ
ンズ

koh-OO-shee veal 子牛

kohp-POO glass (drinking) コッ
プ

KOH-ree ice 氷

koh-REH this (noun) これ

koh-SAH-jee teaspoon 小さじ

KOH-sah-tehn intersection 交差
点

KOH-seh boos-shee-tsoo antibiotics 抗生物質

KOH-shee jee-mah plaid 格子じ
ま

koh-SHEE-tsoo private room
(restaurant) 個室

koh-SHOH pepper こしょう

koh-shoh soo-roo to break down
故障する

KOH-shoo dehn-wah public
telephone 公衆電話

KŌH-soh-koo dŌh-roh highway 高速道路

KŌH-soo-ee perfume 香水

koh-TEHN bah-reh classical ballet 古典バレー

koh-tsoo kee-kahn transportation 交通機関

koht-TŌH heen antiques こっとう品

koht-TŌH yah antique shop こっとう屋

koh-WAH-reh-moh-noh fragile (goods) こわれ物

koh-WAH-reh-teh broken, out of order (mechanical) こわれて

koh-YAH cottage 小屋

KŌH-yoh autumn leaves 紅葉

koh-zoo-tsoo-mee parcel 小包

koo-BEE neck 首

koo-CHEE-bee-roo lip 唇

koo-CHEE beh-nee lipstick 口紅

koo-CHEE-boo-kee GAH-rah-soo blown glass 口吹きガラス

koo-CHEE hee-geh mustache 口ひげ

koo-DAH-moh-noh fruit 果物

KOO-gah-tsoo September 九月

KOOK-kee cookies クッキー

KŌO-koh airport 空港

koo-MOH-ree cloudy 曇り

koo-NEE country 国

koo-ŌH-tsoo noh toh-keh quartz watch クオーツの時計

koo-RAH-boo soh-dah club soda クラブ・ソーダ

koo-RAH-ee dark 暗い

koo-RAHK-kah crackers クラッカー

koo-RAH-sheek-koo myoo-jeek-koo classical music クラシック・ミュージック

koo-RAHT-chee clutch クラッチ

koo-RAHT-chee oh-ee-roo clutch fluid クラッチ・オイル

koo-REE chestnuts くり

koo-REE-moo reen-soo cream rince クリーム・リンス

koo-REE-neen-goo yah dry cleaner クリーニング屋

koo-REH-jeet-toh KAH-doh credit card クレジット・カード

koo-REHN-jeen-goo koo-ree-moo cleansing cream クレンジング・クリーム

koo-ROH-ee black 黒い

koo-ROH oh-bee black belt 黒おび

koo-ROH-wahs-sahn croissant クロワッサン

koo-roo come (v.) 来る

koo-ROO-mah car 車

koo-ROO-mah noh SEH-bee-shee auto mechanic 車の整備士

koo-ROO-mee walnuts くるみ

koo-SAH plants 草

koo-shee comb くし

koo-soo-ree medicine 薬

koo-TSOO shoes くつ

koo-TSOO hee-moh shoelaces くつひも

koo-TSOO noh shoo-ree yah shoe repair shop くつの修理屋

koo-TSOO oh noo-goo to take off one's shoes くつをぬぐ

koo-TSOO-shtah/SOHK-koo-soo socks くつ下／ソックス

koo-TSOO yah shoe store くつ屋

koo-TSOO zoh-koh sole くつ底

KYAH-bah-reh cabaret キャバレー

KYAH-beh-tsoo cabbage キャベツ

kyah-BOO-reh-tah carburetor キャブレター

KYAH-dee caddy キャディー

KYAHN-dee candy キャンディー

KYAHN-poo camping キャンプ

KYAHN-poo joh camping site キャンプ場

KYOH today 今日

KYOH-joo professor 教授

kyoh-kah-ee church 教会

KYOH noh for today 今日の

KYOH-shee teacher 教師

KYOH-soh kyoh-koo concerto 協奏曲

KYOO byoh sudden illness 急病

KYOO-dehn palace 宮殿

KYOO-koh ordinary express train 急行

KYOO-kyoo bah-koh first aid kit 救急箱

KYOO-kyoo shah ambulance 救急車

KYOO-ree cucumber きゅうり

KYOO-seh-kee historical sites 旧跡

KYOO-shee-gah-ee old town 旧市街

KYOO-soo/ doh-BEEN teapot 急須／土びん

M

mah-CHEE town 町

mah-CHEE-ah-ee shee-tsoo waiting room 待合室

mah-CHEE-gah-ee error 間違い

mah-CHEE-gaht-tah/ wah-ROO-ee wrong 間違った／悪い

MAH-chee-neh matinee マチネー

MAH-doh window 窓

mah-DOH gee-wah by the window 窓ぎわ

mah-EE-koo-roh kah-seht-toh-reh-koh-dah microcassette recorder マイクロ・カセット・レコーダー

MAH-ee-nee-chee noh daily 毎日の

MAH-eh front 前

mah-EH gah-mee bangs 前髪

mah-eh-MOHT-teh in advance 前もって

MAH-eh noh forward 前の

MAH-gah-reen margarine マーガリン

mah-GAH-roo to turn 曲がる

mah-GOO-roh tuna まぐろ

mah-jahn mahjong; Chinese tile game マージャン

mah-jahn noh SEHT-toh mahjong set マージャンのセット

mah-KAH-jee-kee swordfish まかじき

mah-KEE geh/ KAH-ree curly 巻き毛／カーリー

MAH-koo-rah pillow 枕

mah-NEE-kyoo-ah manicure マニキュア

mah-NEE-kyoo-ah eh-kee/ eh-NAH-meh-roo nail polish マニキュア液／エナメル

mah-NEE-kyoo-ah oh-toh-shee nail polish remover マニキュア落し

mah-NEH-jah manager マネージャー

MAHN-goh mango マンゴー

MAHN-nehn hee-tsoo fountain pen 万年筆

MAHN-tahn nee soo-roo to fill (gas tank) 満タンにする

mah-ROO-ee round 丸い

MAH-roo-koo mark マルク

mahsh-SHOO poh-teh-toh mashed potatoes マッシュ・ポテト

mah-SOO trout ます

mah-SOO-tah-doh/ kah-RAH-shee mustard マスタード／からし

mahs-SHOO-roo-moo/ SHAHN-pee-nee-ohn mushrooms マッシュルーム／シャンビニオン

mahs-SOO-goo straight (direction) まっすぐ

MAHT-chee matches マッチ

MAH-tsoo to wait 待つ

mah-WAH-ree mee-chee detour 回り道

mah-YOH-neh-zoo mayonnaise マヨネーズ

mah-YOO zoo-mee eyebrow pencil まゆずみ

mah-ZOO-ee awful-tasting まずい

mee-chee road, path 道

mee-CHEE nee mah-yoh-oo to be lost 道に迷う

MEE-dee-ah-moo medium (meat) ミディアム

mee-GAH-koo to polish みがく

mee-GEE right (direction) 右

mee-HAH-ree lifeguard 見張り

mee-JEE-kah-ee short 短い

MEE-kahn mandarin orange, tangerine みかん

MEE-kee-sah blender ミキサー

mee-MEE ear 耳

mee-MEE goo-soo-ree ear drops 耳薬

mee-MOH-noh attractions みもの

mee-NAH-mee south 南

mee-NAH-toh harbor, port 港

mee-nee EH-eh-moo eh-FOO-eh-moo STEH-reh-oh kah-seht-toh poo-reh-yah personal AM-FM stereo cassette player ミニ・エーエム・エフエム・ステレオ・カセット・プレーヤー

mee-NEE-koo-ee ugly みにくい

mee-nee STEH-reh-oh kah-seht-toh reh-KOH-dah/ poo-REH-yah personal stereo cassette recorder/ player ミニ・ステレオ・カセット・レコーダー／プレーヤー

mee-NEH-rah-roo WOH-tah mineral water ミネラル・ウォーター

MEEN-geh folk art 民芸

MEEN-geh gahn-goo Japanese folk toys 民芸玩具

MEEN-geh yah folkware shop 民芸屋

MEEN-shoo-koo Japanese guest house 民宿

MEE-roo to see 見る

MEE-roo-koo/ GYOO-nyoo milk, cream ミルク／牛乳

mee-ROO-koo SEH-kee milkshake ミルクセーキ

mee-seh-roo to show 見せる

mee-SOH shee-roo bean paste soup みそしる

MEE-soo-teh-ree mystery ミステリー

MEE-teh mah-wah-roo to look around 見て回る

MEE-toh BOH-roo/ nee-KOO dahn-goh meatballs ミートボール／肉だんご

mee-TSOO-moh-ree estimate 見積り

mee-ZOH ditch みぞ

mee-zoo water 水

mee-ZOO-gee bathing suit 水着

mee-ZOO noh-mee-bah water fountain 水飲み場

mee-ZOO-oo-mee lake 湖

MEH eye 目

MEH-doh maid メイド

MEH-gah-neh eyeglasses 眼鏡

meh-GAH-neh yah optician 眼鏡屋

meh-KEE-shee-koh Mexico メキシコ

meh-KEE-shee-koh noh Mexican メキシコの

MEH-nyoo menu メニュー

MEH-rohn melon メロン

MEH-sah-ee shoh itemized bill 明細書

mehs-SEH-jee message メッセージ

MEH-shee card (business, personal) 名刺

MEH-shoh points of interest 名所

MEH-tah meter (taxi) メーター

meh-ZAH-mah-shee doh-keh alarm clock 目覚し時計

moh/ mah-TAH also も／また

moh-CHEE-rohn of course もちろん

MOH-choh ehn appendicitis 盲腸炎

moh-DAHN bah-reh modern ballet モダン・バレー

moh-DAHN dahns modern dance モダン・ダンス

moh-DAHN myoo-jeek-koo modern music モダン・ミュージック

moh-DAHN nah modern モダンな

MOH ee-chee-doh again, repeat it もう一度

MOH-foo blanket 毛布

moh-KOO hahn-gah woodblock prints 木版画

moh-KOO-seh noh wooden 木製の

moh-KOO-teh-kee purpose 目的

moh-KOO-yoh-bee Thursday 木曜日

moh-MEHN cotton (fabric) 木綿

moh-MOH peach 桃

mohn-dah-ee problem 問題

MOHN-gehn curfew 門限

MOHN-kee rehn-chee monkey wrench モンキー・レンチ

moh-NOH-reh-roo monorail モノレール

moh-REE forest 森

moh-REE-ah-wah-seh assorted food 盛り合せ

moh-reh-roo to leak もれる

MOH-shee-moh-shee hello (telephone/ getting someone's attention) もしもし

MOH soo-goo dehs soon もうすぐです

MOH-toh noh mah-mah original 元のまま

MOHT-toh ee better もっといい

moh-YOH-shee moh-noh entertainment 催し物

moo-EHN gah-soh-reen unleaded (gas) 無鉛ガソリン

MOO-jee solid color 無地

moo-NEH chest 胸

moo-RAH village 村

moo-RAH-sah-kee ee-roh noh purple 紫色の

moo-SHEE bah cavity 虫歯

moo-SHEE sah-sah-reh insect bite 虫ささされ

MŌŌ-soo mousse ムース

moo-SOO-koh son (your own) 息子

moo-SOO-koh sahn son (someone else's) 息子さん

moo-SOO-meh daughter (your own) 娘

moo-ZOO-kah-shee difficult 難しい

MYŌŌ-jee-kah-roo musical ミュージカル

N

NAH-ee-foo knife ナイフ

NAH-ee-rohn nylon ナイロン

nah-EE-sehn extension number 内線

nah-EE-toh koo-rah-boo nightclub ナイト・クラブ

nah-GAH-ee long 長い

nah-GAH-meh view ながめ

nah-GAH soh-deh long sleeves 長そで

nah-KOO-shee-tah lost なくした

nah-koo-soo to lose なくす

NAH-mah raw なま

nah-MAH-eh name 名前

nah-MAH hah-moo prosciutto 生ハム

nah-mee waves (water) 波

NAH-nee what 何

NAHN-jee what time 何時

nah-OH-seh-roo fixable 直せる

nah-OH-soo to fix, to alter 直す

NAH-poo-keen napkin ナプキン

NAH-SHEE pear (Japanese) なし

NAH-soo eggplant なす

nah-TSOO summer 夏

NAH-yah barn 納屋

NAH-zeh/ DŌŌ-shteh why なぜ／どうして

____ nee in ___に

nee-CHEE-yoh-bee Sunday 日曜日

nee-GAH-tsoo February 二月

nee-HOHN dehn-toh noh geh-moo Japanese games 日本伝統のゲーム

nee-HOHN gah Japanese painting 日本画

nee-HOHN goh Japanese (lang.) 日本語

nee-HOHN goh noh boon-poh noh hohn Japanese grammar book 日本語の文法の本

nee-HOHN neen-gyoh Japanese dolls 日本人形

nee-HOHN neen-gyoh yah Japanese doll shop 日本人形屋

nee-HOHN noh koh-tehn Japanese classics 日本の古典

nee-HOHN shoh-koo-heen Japanese food 日本食品

nee-HOHN teh-ehn Japanese gardens 日本庭園

nee-HOHN toh Japanese swords 日本刀

NEE-joo-nee-keen 22 karat 22金

NEE-joo-yohn-keen 24 karat 24金

nee-KAH-ee noh seh-kee balcony (theater) 二階の席

nee-KOO yah butcher 肉屋

NEE-moh-tsoo baggage, luggage, package 荷物

NEE-moh-tsoo noh oh-KEE-dah-ee luggage rack 荷物の置き台

NEEN-gyoh puppets, dolls 人形

NEEN-jeen carrots 人参

neen-kee gah ah-roo popular 人気がある

NEEN-sheen choo pregnant 妊娠中

neep-POHN/ nee-HOHN Japan 日本

nee-SHEE west 西

nee-TAH boiled 煮た

nee-WAH/ TEH-ehn garden 庭／庭園

nee-WAH-toh-ree chicken にわとり

neh-DAHN price 値段

NEHK-koo-reh-soo necklace ネックレス

neh-KOO-tah-reen nectarine ネクタリン

NEHK-tah-ee necktie ネクタイ

neh-MOO-ee sleepy ねむい

NEHN-reh seh-gehn age limit 年齢制限

NEHN-zah soo-roo to sprain ねんざする

neh-REE-hah-mee-gah-kee toothpaste 練歯みがき

neh-roo to sleep 寝る

neh-TSOO temperature, fever 熱

NOH Japanese masked dance-drama 能

____ *noh ah-EE-dah nee* during ____の間に

____ *noh AH-toh deh* after ____のあとで

noh-BOH-roo to climb 登る

____ *noh chee-KAH-koo nee* nearby ____の近くに

NOH-doh throat のど

NOH-doh gah, kah-WAH-ee-teh ee-mahs thirsty のどが、かわいています

NOH-hah-rah fields 野原

____ *noh keh-koh* judo/ karate/ kendo practice ____のけい古

____ *noh MAH-eh nee* before ____の前に

noh-MEE mee-zoo drinking water 飲み水

noh-MEE-moh-noh drinks 飲み物

NOH mehn Noh masks 能面

NOH-moo to drink 飲む

____ *noh NAH-kah nee* inside ____の中に

nohn-STOHP-poo nonstop flight ノン・ストップ

____ *noh oo-EH nee* on, up, above ____の上に

noh-REE seaweed のり

noh-REE-kah-eh-roo to change (transportation) 乗り換える

noh-REE oh kee-KAH-seh-teh starched (laundry) のりをきかせて

noh-REE-tsoo-gee been connecting flight 乗りつぎ便

noh-roo to get on (transportation) 乗る

____ *noh SHTAH nee* down ____の下に

____ *noh SOH-toh nee* outside ____の外に

NOH-toh notebook ノート

noo-doh-roo SOO-poo noodle soup ヌードル・スープ

noo-KAH-roo-mee　mud　ぬかるみ

noo-NOH　fabric　布

noo-oo　to sew　ぬう

noo-REE-moh-noh　lacquerware　塗り物

noo-SOO-mah-reh-teh　stolen　盗まれて

nyoo-jee-rahn-doh　New Zealand　ニュージーランド

NYOO-joh ryoh　admission fee　入場料

NYOO-soo kahn-keh noh zahs-SHEE　news magazines　ニュース関係の雑誌

O

oh-AH-ee soo-roo　to meet　お会いする

oh-BAH　aunt (your own)　叔母

OH-bah　overcoat　オーバー

OH-bah HEE-toh　overheated　オーバー・ヒート

oh-BAH-sahn　aunt (someone else's)　おばさん

oh-BAH-sahn　grandmother (someone else's)　おばあさん

OH-been　large bottle　大びん

(oh-)BEHN-toh　box lunch　（お）弁当

oh-CHAH　Japanese tea　お茶

OH-deh-koh-rohn　cologne　オーデコロン

oh-DOHT-teh　dancing　おどって

oh-EE-koo-tsoo dehs KAH　How old are you?　おいくつですか

oh-EE-noh-ree soo-roo　to pray　お祈りする

oh-EE-shee　delicious　おいしい

oh-eh-roo　office worker (female)　オーエル

OH-fee-soo　office　オフィス

OH-foo-koo　round trip　往復

OH-foo-koo kehn　round-trip ticket　往復券

OH-gah-tah shah　large car　大型車

oh-GAH-wah　stream　小川

OH-gee　fan　扇

oh-GEHN-kee dehs KAH　How are you?　お元気ですか

oh-HAH-yoh goh-zah-ee-mahs　Good morning　おはようございます

oh-JEE　uncle (your own)　叔父

oh-JEE-gee　bow　おじぎ

oh-JEE-gee soo-roo　to bow　おじぎする

oh-JEE-sahn　uncle (someone else's)　叔父さん

oh-JEE-sahn　grandfather (someone else's)　おじいさん

oh-JOH-sahn　daughter (someone else's)　おじょうさん

oh-KAH　hill　丘

oh-KAH-eh-shee　return gift　おかえし

oh-KAHN　chill　悪寒

oh-KAH-neh　money　お金

oh-KAH-sahn　mother (someone else's)　お母さん

oh-KAH-shee yah　candy store, confectionary, pastry shop　お菓子屋

OH-kee　big (large)　大きい

OH-keh-soo-toh-rah　orchestra　オーケストラ

oh-KOH-sahn　child (someone else's)　お子さん

____ *oh koo-dah-sah-ee*/ ____ *oh oh-NEH-gah-ee shee-mahs* please ____をください／____をお願いします

oh-koo-roo to send 送る

OH-koo-sahn wife (someone else's) 奥さん

oh-MAH-neh-kee soo-roo to invite お招きする

oh-MAH-tsoo-ree festival お祭り

oh-MEE-seh store お店

oh-MEE-yah-geh gift, souvenir おみやげ

oh-MEE-yah-geh yah souvenir shop おみやげ屋

oh-MEHN masks お面

oh-MOH-chah yah toy store おもちゃ屋

oh-MOH-ee heavy 重い

OH-moh nah mee-MOH-noh main attractions 主なみもの

oh-moh-oo to think 思う

oh-MOH-shee-roh-ee interesting/ fun おもしろい

oh-MOO-reh-tsoo omelet オムレツ

oh-NAH-jee same 同じ

oh-NAH-kah gah eep-PAH-ee dehs full (I'm full) おなかが、いっぱいです

oh-NAH-kah gah soo-EE-teh ee-mahs hungry (I'm hungry) おなかが、すいています

oh-NEE-ohn soo-poo onion soup オニオンスープ

oh-NEE-sahn elder brother (someone else's) お兄さん

oh-NEH-sahn elder sister (some-one else's) お姉さん

OHN-gah-koo music 音楽

OHN-nah/ *joh-seh* woman, female 女／女性

OHN-sehn hot springs 温泉

OH-peh-rah opera オペラ

oh-PEH-rah geh-kee joh opera house オペラ劇場

oh-RAHN-dah-jeen Dutch (person) オランダ人

oh-REE-boo yoo olive oil オリーブ油

oh-REE-gah-mee origami paper 折り紙

oh-ree-roo to get off 降りる

oh-REHN-jee orange オレンジ

oh-REHN-jee JOO-soo orange juice オレンジジュース

oh-reh-tah broken 折れた

OH-sah-jee tablespoon 大さじ

oh-SAH-keh drinks (alcoholic) お酒

oh-SAH-rah plate お皿

oh-SAH-tsoo bills (currency) お札

(oh)-SEHN-koh incense （お）線香

oh-SHEE-eh-roo to tell, teach 教える

oh-SHEE-roh castle お城

oh-SHEE-roh-ee face powder おしろい

oh-SOH-ee late, slow おそい

OH-soo-toh-rah-ree-ah Australia オーストラリア

oh-TEH-ah-rah-ee/ *TOH-ee-reh*/ *oh-BEHN-joh* bathroom お手洗／トイレ／お便所

oh-TEH-rah Buddhist temple お寺

oh-TOH-koh (noh hee-toh) man, male 男(の人)

OH-toh MEE-roo oatmeal オートミール

oh-TOH-sahn　father (someone else's)　お父さん

oh-TOH-toh　younger brother (your own)　弟

oh-TOH-toh sahn　younger brother (someone else's)　弟さん

oh-TSOO-ree　change (n.) (money)　おつり

oh-WAH-ree-mah-shtah　It's over. / I'm finished.　終わりました

oh-wah-roo　to finish, end (v.i.)　終わる

oh-YAH-soo-mee nah-sah-ee　Good night　おやすみなさい

oh-YAH yoo-bee　thumb　親指

oh-YOH-goo　to swim　泳ぐ

oh-YOO　hot water　お湯

oh-ZAH-shkee　Japanese room (restaurant)　お座敷

oo-DEH　arm　腕

oo-deh doh-keh　wristwatch　腕時計

oo-DEH doh-keh shkee teh-reh-bee　wrist TV　腕時計式テレビ

oo-DEH-wah　bracelet　腕輪

oo-dohn/ soh-bah/ rah-mehn　noodles (Japanese)　うどん/そば/ラーメン

oo-EE-skee　whiskey　ウイスキー

oo-KEH-zah-rah　saucer　受け皿

oo-mee　sea, ocean　海

OON-doh-goo tehn　sporting goods store　運動具店

OON-doh goo-tsoo/ soo-NEE-kah　sneakers　運動ぐつ/スニーカー

OON-tehn-shoo　chauffeur, driver　運転手

oo-OH noh meh koh-yah-koo　corn plasters　魚の目膏薬

oo-roo　to sell　売る

OO-roo　wool　ウール

oo-ROO-shee noo-ree noh oh-bohn　lacquer trays　うるし塗りのお盆

oo-ROO-shee noo-ree noh oo-tsoo-wah　lacquer bowls　うるし塗りのうつわ

oo-SHEE-roh　back (location)　うしろ

oo-SHEE-roh noh　to the rear　うしろの

oo-SOO-ee　thin　薄い

oo-TAHT-teh　singing　歌って

P

pah-CHEEN-koh　Japanese pinball　パチンコ

pah-CHEEN-koh dah-mah　pachinko balls　パチンコ玉

pah-CHEEN-koh yah　pachinko parlor　パチンコ屋

PAH-ee　pie　パイ

pah-EE-nahp-poo-roo　pineapple　パイナップル

pah-EE-nahp-poo-roo JOO-soo　pineapple juice　パイナップル・ジュース

PAH-ee-poo　pipe　パイプ

pah-FEH　parfait　パフェー

PAH-mah　permanent　パーマ

PAHN-dah　panda　パンダ

PAHN　bread　パン

PAHN-koo　flat tire　パンク

pahn-tee STOHK-keen-goo　pantyhose　パンティー・ストッキング

PAHN yah bakery パン屋

PAH-soh-nah-roo koh-roo
person to person call パーソナ
ル・コール

pah-SOO-poh-toh passport パス
ポート

PAH-teh paté パテ

PEE-ah-soo noh ee-yah-reen-goo
earrings for pierced ears ピア
スのイヤリング

PEE-mahn green pepper ピーマ
ン

PEE-naht-tsoo peanuts ピーナッ
ツ

PEEN-koo noh pink ピンクの

PEEN-pohn ping pong ピンポン

PEHN-chee pliers ペンチ

PEHN-dahn-toh pendant ペンダ
ント

PEH-soh peso ペソ

PEH-soo-toh-reē pastry ペース
トリー

poh-KEHT-toh bahn noh jee-shoh
pocket dictionary ポケット版の
辞書

*poh-KEHT-toh gah-tah keh-sahn
kee/ poh-KEHT-toh dehn-tah-
koo* minicalculator ポケット
型計算器／ポケット電卓

POH-koo CHOHP-poo pork chop
ポーク・チョップ

POHN-doh pounds (currency) ポ
ンド

pohp-POO koñn popcorn ポップ
コーン

poh-PYOO-rah sohn-goo popular
songs ポピュラー・ソング

poh-REE-eh-steh-roo polyester
ポリエステル

poh-ROO-toh-gah-roo noh
Portuguese ポルトガルの

POH-tah porter ポーター

POH-tah-boo-roo rah-jee-oh
portable radio ポータブル・ラ
ジオ

POH-teh-toh/ jah-GAH-ee-moh
potato ポテト／じゃがいも

poh-TEH-toh cheep-poo potato
chips ポテトチップ

poo-RAH-chee-nah platinum プ
ラチナ

*POO-rah-goo noh ah-DAH-poo-
tah* adapter plug プラグのア
ダプター

POO-rah-moo/ soo-MOH-moh
plum プラム／すもも

*poo-RAH-soo-cheek-koo/ bee-
NEE-roo* plastic プラスチッ
ク／ビニール

POO-reen pudding プリン

poo-REEN-toh print (pattern) プ
リント

poo-ROH yah-kyoo professional
baseball プロ野球

POO-roo swimming pool プール

R

RAH-bee rabbi ラビ

*RAH-deesh-shoo/ hah-TSOO-kah
DAH-ee-kohn* radish ラディ
シュ／二十日大根

RAH-ee-soo rice (Western) ライ
ス

RAH-ee-taħ cigarette lighter ラ
イター

*RAH-ee-taħ noh ah-BOO-rah/
gah-soo* lighter fluid/gas ラ
イターの油／ガス

rah-JEE-eh-teh radiator ラジエーター

rah-JEE-eh-tah noh mee-zoo water (car) ラジエーターの水

RAH-jee-oh radio ラジオ

rah-JEE-oh kyoo-koo radio station ラジオ局

rah-KEHT-toh racket ラケット

rah-MOO chohp-poo lamb chop ラム・チョップ

RAHN-poo lamp ランプ

rahsh-SHOO ah-wah rush hour ラッシュ・アワー

REE-foo-toh ski lift リフト

ree-KEE-shee sumo wrestlers 力士

ree-KOH nah intelligent 利口な

ree-MOO-jeen bah-soo limousine bus リムジン・バス

REEN-goh apple りんご

REEN-goh JOO-soo apple juice りんごジュース

reep-PAH magnificent 立派

REE-rah lira リラ

reet-toh-roo liter リットル

REH-ah rare (meat) レア

REH-boh air conditioner 冷房

rehd-DOH WAH-een red wine レッド・ワイン

reh-EEN koh-toh raincoat レイン・コート

REH-gyoo-rah regular (gas) レギュラー

REH-hah-ee religious service 礼拝

reh-KEE-shee history 歴史

reh-KEE-shee noh hohn history books 歴史の本

rehk-KAH shah tow truck レッカー車

reh-KOH-doh record レコード

reh-KOH-doh AH-roo-bah-moo record album レコード・アルバム

reh-KOH-doh bah-ree needles (record player) レコード針

reh-KOH-doh poo-reh-yah record player レコード・プレーヤー

reh-KOH-doh yah record store レコード屋

REH-mohn lemon レモン

reh-MOH-neh-doh lemonade レモネード

reh-MOHN meh-REHN-geh lemon meringue pie レモン・メレンゲ

reh-mohn SHAH-beht-toh lemon sherbet レモン・シャーベット

REHN-ah-ee moh-noh romance 恋愛物

REHN-rahk-sehn ferry 連絡船

REHN-tah-kah noh OH-fees car rental agency レンタ・カーのオフィス

REHN-toh-gehn X-ray レントゲン

rehn-zoo lens レンズ

rehs-soon lesson レッスン

REH-soo-toh-rahn restaurant レストラン

REH-tah-soo lettuce レタス

roh-bee lobby ロビー

roh-JOH choo-shah street parking 路上駐車

rohk-KOH-tsoo rib ろっ骨

rohk-KOON roh-roo rock'n'roll ロックンロール

ROHK-koo soo-roo to lock ロックする

roh-KOO-gah-tsoo June 六月

roh-KOO-ohn teh-poo tapes (recording) 録音テープ

ROH-roo pahn rolls (bread) ロール・パン

ROH-shee-ah noh Russian ロシアの

roh-SHEE-ah goh Russian (lang.) ロシア語

ROH-soo-toh bee-foo roast beef ロースト・ビーフ

ROO-bee ruby ルビー

ROO-mah-nee-ah noh Rumanian ルーマニアの

ROO-moo SAH-bee-soo room service ルーム・サービス

RYOH-gah-eh-joh money exchange 両替所

RYOH-jee kahn consulate 領事館

ryoh-KAHN Japanese inn 旅館

RYOH-keen rate, fare 料金

RYOH-keen sehn-poh bah-rah-ee noh dehn-wah collect call 料金先方払いの電話

ryoh-KOH/ tah-bee trip 旅行／旅

ryoh-KOH ahn-nah-ee joh tourist information center 旅行案内所

ryoh-KOH dah-ee-ree tehn travel agency 旅行代理店

ryoh-KOH kah-bahn luggage 旅行かばん

ryoh-KOH keh-kah-koo itinerary 旅行計画

ryoh-KOH yoh noh meh-ZAH-mah-shee doh-keh travel alarm clock 旅行用の目覚し時計

ryoh-KOO-cha Japanese tea, green 緑茶

RYOH-ree noh seh-tsoo-bee cooking facilities 料理の設備

RYOH-ree soo-roo to cook 料理する

RYOH-shoo-shoh receipt 領収書

RYOO-kahn flu 流感

S

SAH Let's さあ

SAH-bee-soo ryoh service charge サービス料

SAH-deen/ ee-WAH-shee sardines サーディン／いわし

SAH-doh tea ceremony 茶道

SAH-doh noh oh-CHAH-wahn/ chah-WAHN tea bowl (tea ceremony) 茶道のお茶碗／茶碗

____ sah-ee dehs I'm ____ years old ____才です

sah-EE-ehn-soo fee-koo-shohn science fiction サイエンス・フィクション

sah-EE-foo wallet さいふ

SAH-ee-goh noh shoh last show 最後のショー

sah-EE-kah-koo-neen soo-roo to reconfirm 再確認する

SAH-ee-koo-reen-goo bicycling サイクリング

sah-EE-koo-reen-goo koh-soo bicycling course サイクリング・コース

sah-EE-shoh noh shoh first show 最初のショー

sah-EE-teh ryoh-keen　minimum charge　最低料金

SAH-ee-zoo　size, measurements　サイズ

sah-FAH-ee-ah　sapphire　サファイア

sah-KAH-nah　fish　さかな

sah-KAH-nah tsoo-ree　fishing　さかなつり

sah-KAH-nah yah　fish market　さかな屋

sah-KAH yah　liquor store　酒屋

sah-KAH-zoo-kee　sake cup　盃

SAH-keh　salmon　さけ

sah-KEH/ oh-SAH-keh　Japanese rice wine　酒／お酒

sahk-KAH　writer　作家

SAHK-kah　soccer　サッカー

SAHK-kah noh kyoh-gee joh　soccer stadium　サッカーの競技場

SAHK-kah noh shee-ah-ee　soccer match　サッカーの試合

sah-KOO-rah　cherry blossoms　桜

sah-KOO-rahn-boh/ CHEH-ree　cherries　さくらんぼ／チェリー

sah-MEH　sharks　さめ

SAH-moh-soo-taht-toh　thermostat (car)　サーモスタット

sah-MOO-ee　cold (temperature, climate)　寒い

___ *sahn*　Mr. /Mrs. /Miss/Ms. ___さん

SAHN-dah-roo　sandals　サンダル

SAHN-deh　sundae　サンデー

sahn-doh-EET-chee　sandwich　サンドイッチ

SAHN-gah-tsoo　March　三月

SAHN-goh　coral　さんご

SAHN goo-rah-soo　sunglasses　サングラス

SAHN-myah-koo　mountain range　山脈

SAHN-pah-tsoo　haircut　散髪

SAHN tahn roh-shohn　suntan lotion　サンタン・ローション

SAH-oo-nah　sauna　サウナ

sah-rah-dah　salad　サラダ

sah-RAH-mee soh-seh-jee　salami　サラミ・ソーセージ

sah-RAH-ree mahn　office worker (male)　サラリーマン

sah-SHEE-mee　raw fish　刺身

sah-TOH　sugar　砂糖

sah-YAH chn-doh　string beans　さやえんどう

sah-YOH-nah-rah　Goodbye　さようなら

shee-CHAH-koo soo-roo　to try on　試着する

seh-BOH-neh　spine　背骨

SEH-boo geh-kee　western (film)　西部劇

SEH-gehn　limit　制限

SEH-jee kah　politician　政治家

SEH-kee　seat　席

seh-KEE　cough　せき

seh-KEE doh-meh doh-rohp-poo　cough drops　せきどめドロップ

seh-KEE doh-meh SHEE-rohp-poo　cough syrup　せきどめシロップ

sehk-KEHN　soap　石けん

seh-MAH-ee　narrow　せまい

(oh)-SEHM-beh　rice crackers　(お)せんべい

sehn　track, line (train)　線

seh-NAH-kah　back (body)　背中

SEH-nehn gahp-pee　birthdate　生年月日

SEHN-mehn-dah-ee　sink　洗面台

SEHN-seh　teacher　先生

SEHN-tah-koo moh-noh laundry (clothes) 洗濯物

SEHN-tah-koo noh sah-bee-soo laundry service 洗濯のサービス

SEHN-tah-koo yah laundry (shop) 洗濯屋

SEH-ree nahp-keen sanitary napkins 生理ナプキン

SEH-roh-ree celery セロリ

seh-ROH teh-poo Scotch tape セロテープ

SEH-roo/ toh-KOO-bah-ee sale セール／特売

SEH-soh formal clothing 正装

SEH-tah sweater セーター

seht-CHAH-koo zah-ee/ noh-REE glue 接着剤／のり

seh-TOH-moh-noh china 瀬戸物

seh-TOH-moh-noh yah/ TOH-kee noh mee-seh pottery, ceramics shop 瀬戸物屋／陶器の店

seht-TOH roh-shohn setting lotion セット・ローション

seh-TSOO-meh soo-roo to explain 説明する

SEH-yoh shoh-koo-heen Western food 西洋食品

SHAH-beht-toh sherbet シャーベット

shah-BOO-shah-boo beef cooked in broth しゃぶしゃぶ

SHAHN-poo shampoo シャンプー

SHAHN-poo toh seht-toh wash and set シャンプーとセット

shah-REH-tah fancy しゃれた

shah-SHEEN photograph picture 写真

shah-SHEEN oh toh-roo to take a picture 写真をとる

shah-SHEEN yah photographer 写真屋

shah-TOH-roo bah-soo shuttle bus シャトル・バス

SHAH-wah shower シャワー

shee/ toh-shee city 市／都市

shee-AH-ee ball game 試合

shee-AH-tsoo acupressure 指圧

shee-AH-tsoo shee acupressurist 指圧師

shee-CHAH-koo shee-tsoo dressing room 試着室

shee-CHEE-gah-tsoo July 七月

shee-GAH-tsoo April 四月

shee-goh-toh/ BEE-jee-nehs business 仕事／ビジネス

shee-GOH-toh noh ryoh-koh business trip 仕事の旅行

shee-KAH-koo-ee square 四角い

SHEE-kee four seasons 四季

sheek-KAH-roh-roo talcum powder シッカロール

sheek-KEE lacquerware 漆器

shee-KYOO urgent 至急

shee-MAH island 島

shee-mah-roo to close (v.i.) 閉まる

shee-MAH meh-noh onyx しまめのう

shee-MAH moh-yoh stripes しま模様

shee-meen citizen 市民

shee-MEH-roo to tighten 締める

shee-MEHT-teh ee-roo humid, damp 湿っている

SHEE-nah-ee outside line (telephone) 市内

shee-NAH-ee dehn-wah local call 市内電話

sheen-boon newspaper 新聞

SHEEN-boon OO-ree-bah newsstand 新聞売り場

SHEEN-dah-ee shah sleeping car 寝台車

SHEEN-foh-nee symphony シンフォニー

SHEEN-joo/ PAH-roo pearls 真珠／パール

SHEEN-kahn-sehn super express train 新幹線

SHEEN-poo priest 神父

SHEEN-sehn nah fresh 新鮮な

SHEEN-seh-tsoo nah kind (adj.) 親切な

SHEEN-shee foo-koo men's clothing 紳士服

sheen-toh noh gee-shee-kee Shinto ceremony 神道の儀式

SHEEN-zoh heart 心臓

SHEEN-zoh mah-hee heart attack 心臓麻痺

shee-OH salt 塩

sheep-POH yah-kee cloisonné 七宝焼

shee-RAH-beh-roo to check (examine) 調べる

SHEE-ree-ah-roo cereal シリアル

shee-ROH-ee white 白い

shee-ROH-koo-roh black and white 白黒

SHEE-rohp-poo syrup シロップ

SHEE-tah-keh shiitake mushroom しいたけ

shee-TAH-teh yah tailor 仕立て屋

shee-TSOO/ hah-EE-tah toothache 歯痛／歯いた

shee-TSOO-mohn question 質問

shee-TSOO-nah-ee gah-koo chamber music 室内楽

SHEE-zah SAH-rah-dah Caesar salad シーザー・サラダ

SHEE-zoo-kah quiet 静か

SHEH-been-goo roh-shohn shaving lotion シェービング・ローション

SHOH small (size) 小

SHOH show (stage or floor) ショー

SHOH-doh-koo yah-koo antiseptic 消毒薬

SHOH-gah ginger しょうが

shoh-gee Japanese board game 将棋

SHOH-gee-bahn toh koh-mah shogi board and pieces 将棋盤と駒

shoh-HOH sehn prescription 処方せん

SHOH-kah foo-ryoh indigestion 消化不良

SHOH-kehn toh-ree-hee-kee joh stock exchange 証券取引所

shoh-KOO-doh dining room 食堂

shoh-KOO-doh shah dining car 食堂車

shoh-koo-gyoh occupation 職業

shoh-KOO-jee meal 食事

shoh-KOO-jee noh SAH-bee-soo meal service 食事のサービス

shoh-KOO-ryoh heen tehn grocery store 食料品店

shoh-MEH signature 署名

shohp-PEEN-goo shopping ショッピング

shohp-PEEN-goo ah-keh-doh shopping arcade ショッピング・アーケード

shohp-PEEN-goo gah-ee shopping area ショッピング街

SHOH-roo-ee documents 書類

shoh-seh-tsoo novel 小説

SHOH-yoo soy sauce しょう油

shoo week 週

SHOO-foo housewife 主婦

SHOO-hah soo frequency (radio station) 周波数

SHOO-jeen husband (your own) 主人

shoo-KOH-geh heen handicrafts 手工芸品

shoo-KOO-hah-koo lodging 宿泊

SHOO-kyoh noh religious 宗教 の

SHOO-mah-tsoo weekend 週末

shoop-PAH-tsoo departure 出発

shoop-PAH-tsoo goo-chee departure gate 出発口

shoop-PAH-tsoo noh jee-kahn departure time 出発の時間

SHOO-ree repair 修理

SHOO-ree doh-goo repair tools 修理道具

SHOO-ree koh-joh auto repair shop 修理工場

SHOO-ree soo-roo to repair 修理 する

shoo-roo-ee type, kind 種類

SHOO-toh capital 首都

shoo-TSOO-ehn shah performers 出演者

SHOO-yah eh-gyoh noh yahk-KYOH-koo all-night pharmacy 終夜営業の薬局

SHTAH tongue 舌

SHTAH-gee underwear 下着

SKAH-foo scarf スカーフ

SKAH-toh skirt スカート

SKEE skiing, skis スキー

SKEE goo-tsoo ski shoes スキー ぐつ

skee joh ski resort スキー場

SKEE-yah-kee beef cooked in seasoned sauce すき焼き

SKEH-joo-roo schedule スケ ジュール

SKOH-shee few, a little, some 少 し

SKOHT-chee scotch (whiskey) ス コッチ

SOH-boh grandmother (your own) 祖母

SOH-dah toh oh-moh-ee-mahs I think so. そうだと思います

soh-deh sleeves そで

SOH dehs KAH Is that so? Really? そうですか

SOH-foo grandfather (your own) 祖父

soh-FOO-toh kohn-tahk-toh rehn-zoo soft contact lenses ソフ ト・コンタクト・レンズ

soh-KOH/ ah-SOH-koh there/ over there そこ／あそこ

soh-KOO-tah-tsoo special delivery 速達

soh-NOH/ ah-NOH that/ that over there (adj.) その／あの

SOH oh-MOH-ee-mah-sehn I don't think so. そう思いません

soh-REH/ ah-REH that/ that over there (noun) それ／あれ

soh-REH-toh-moh/ mah-TAH-wah/ ah-ROO-ee-wah or それ とも／または／あるいは

soh-SEH-jee sausage ソーセージ

sohsh-TEH and (between sentences) そして

soh-TEH nee shtah sauteed ソ テーにした

SOO vinegar 酢

soo-BAH-rah-shee wonderful 素 晴しい

soo-EE-choo yohk-sehn hydrofoil 水中翼船

soo-EE-dehn rice paddy 水田

soo-EE-doh running water 水道

so-EE-jee yoh-goo cooking utensils 炊事用具

soo-EE-joh skee water skis 水上スキー

soo-EE-kah watermelon 西瓜

soo-EE-meen yah-koo sleeping pills 睡眠薬

soo-EE-moh-noh clear soup 吸い物

soo-EE-sehn soo-roo/ soo-SOO-meh-roo to recommed 推薦する／勧める

SOO-ee-soo noh Swiss スイスの

soo-EE-toh POH-teh-toh/ sah-TSOO-mah ee-moh sweet potato スイート・ポテト／さつまいも

soo-EE-yoh-bee Wednesday 水曜日

soo-EE-zoh-koo kahn aquarium 水族館

soo-jee story 筋

SOO jee-tsoo a few days 数日

soo-KAHN-jee-nah-bee-ah noh Scandinavian スカンジナビアの

soo-KEE-moo MEE-roo-koo skim milk スキム・ミルク

soo-KEEN dah-ee-been-goo yoh-goo skin diving equipment スキン・ダイビング用具

soo-MEE-mah-sehn gah Pardon me, but すみませんが

soo-MOH Japanese wrestling 相撲

soo-moo to live (reside) 住む

soo-NAH-hah-mah sandy beach 砂浜

soo-NAHK-koo snack スナック

soo-NAHK-koo bah snack bar スナック・バー

SOO-pah/ hah-EE -oh-koo super (gas) スーパー／ハイオク

SOO-pah supermarket スーパー

soo-PAH-geht-tee spaghetti スパゲッティー

soo-PAH-koo poo-rah-goo spark plugs スパーク・プラグ

soo-PEH-een Spain スペイン

soo-PEH-een noh Spanish スペインの

soo-PEH-yah tah-ee-ah spare tire スペヤ・タイヤ

soo-POHN-jee sponge スポンジ

soo-POH-tsoo kah sports car スポーツ・カー

soo-poo soup スープ

soo-RAH-ee-doh slides スライド

soo-RAHK-ksoo pants スラックス

soo-REE-peen-goo bahg-goo sleeping bag (camping) スリーピング・バッグ

SOO-ree-rah thriller/ horror movie スリラー

SOO-shee raw fish and vinegared rice すし

soo-TOHK-koo ski poles ストック

SOO-tsoo suit スーツ

soo-ZOO-shee cool 涼しい

SPEH-een goh Spanish (lang.) スペイン語

SREEP-pah slippers スリッパ

SREEP-poo slip スリップ

STAH-ee-roo style スタイル

STEH-kee steak ステーキ

STEHN-rehs stainless steel ステンレス

STOHK-keen-goo stockings ストッキング

T

tah-BAH-koh   cigarettes たばこ／タバコ

tah-BAH-koh oh hee-TOH hah-koh   a pack of cigarettes たばこを一箱

tah-BAH-koh oh soo-oo   to smoke たばこを喫う

tah-BAH-koh yah   tabacco shop たばこ屋

tah-BAHS-koh   tabasco タバスコ

tah-beh-moh-noh   food 食べ物

tah-BEH-roo   to eat 食べる

TAH-boon   maybe 多分

tah-DAH-shee   correct, right 正しい

tah-EE-foo   typhoon 台風

tah-EE-koh-koo jeen   Thai タイ国人

TAH-ee-koh-koo noh   Thai (adj.) タイ国の

tah-EE ohn keh   thermometer 体温計

tah-EE-poo rah-ee-tah   typewriter タイプ・ライター

tah-EE-poo yoh-shee   typing paper タイプ用紙

tah-EE-shee kahn   embassy 大使館

tah-EE-yah   tire タイヤ

tah-EE-yah noh KOO-kee ah-tsoo   tire pressure タイヤの空気圧

tah-KAH-ee   expensive; high, tall 高い

tah-KAH-koo-nah-ee   inexpensive 高くない

tah-KAH-sah   height 高さ

tah-KEE   waterfall 滝

tah-KEH   bamboo 竹

tah-KEH noh kah-goh   bamboo baskets 竹のかご

tah-KEH zah-ee-koo noh mee-seh   bamboo craft shop 竹細工の店

TAH-koh   kite たこ

tahk-SAHN   a lot, many, much たくさん

TAHK-shee   taxi タクシー

tahk-SHEE noh-ree-bah   taxi stand タクシー乗場

tah-MAH-goh   egg 卵

tah-MAH neh-gee   onion 玉ねぎ

tah-NEE   valley 谷

tah-NOH-shee   pleasant 楽しい

tah-NOH-shee-moo   to enjoy 楽しむ

TAHN-pehn shoh-seh-tsoo   short story books 短編小説

TAHN-pohn   tampons タンポン

TAHN-sahn   club soda 炭酸

TAHN-soo   Japanese chest of drawers たんす

TAHN-teh shoh-seh-tsoo   detective stories 探偵小説

TAH-oh-roo   towels タオル

tahs-KEH-roo   to help 助ける

tahs-KEH-teh   Help! 助けて

tah-TAHN-deh   folded たたんで

tah-TEH mah-eh   etiquette of the preparation of tea 点前

tah-TOH-eh-bah   for example 例えば

tah-tsoo   to stand 立つ

TEE shah-tsoo   tee shirt ティーシャツ

TEH   hand 手

teh-BOO-koo-roh   gloves 手袋

TEH-boo-roo   table テーブル

teh-GAH-mee   letter 手紙

teh-GAH-mee oh dah-soo   to mail a letter 手紙を出す

TEH koo-bee wrist 手首

TĒH-mah theme テーマ

TEHM-poo-rah batter-fried food 天ぷら

tehn-een clerk 店員

TEH-nees tennis テニス

teh-NEES boh-roo tennis ball テニス・ボール

teh-NEES koh-too tennis court テニス・コート

TEH-nees oh soo-roo to play tennis テニスをする

TEHN-jee soo-roo to exhibit 展示する

TEHN-kah soh-chee ignition 点火装置

TEHN-kee weather 天気

TEHN-kee yoh-hoh weather forecast 天気予報

TEHN-noh emperor 天皇

TEHN-pee deh yah-ee-tah baked 天火で焼いた

TEHN-toh tent テント

TĒH-poo reh-koh-dah tape recorder テープ・レコーダー

TEH-rah-soo terrace テラス

TEH-reh-bee television, TV, television set テレビ

teh-ZOO-koo-ree noh/ teh-SĒH noh handmade 手作りの／手製の

toh and (between nouns) と

toh/ doh-ah door 戸／ドア

toh-BEE ee-roh auburn とび色

TŌH-chah-koo arrival 到着

TŌH-chah-koo noh jee-kahn arrival time 到着の時間

toh-CHOO noh KYOO-keh intermission 途中の休憩

TŌH-ee far 遠い

TOH-ee-reh toilet, rest room トイレ

toh-EE-reht-toh PĒH-pah toilet paper トイレット・ペーパー

TŌH-foo bean curd 豆腐

TŌH-jee-kee ceramics 陶磁器

toh-KAH-ee big city 都会

TŌH-kee pottery 陶器

toh-KĒH clock 時計

toh-KĒH noh shoo-ree yah watch repair shop 時計の修理屋

toh-KĒH yah watch and clock store 時計屋

tohk-KOO-ree sake bottle とっくり

tohk-KYOO limited express train 特急

toh-KOH-roh deh by the way ところで

toh-KOH-yah barber shop 床屋

toh-KOO-beh-tsoo noh special 特別の

toh-MAH-roo to stay 泊まる

toh-mah-roo to stop (transportation) 止まる

TOH-mah-toh tomato トマト

toh-MAH-toh JOO-soo tomato juice トマトジュース

toh-nahn theft 盗難

TOH-pah-zoo topaz トパーズ

toh-RAHN-poo cards (playing) トランプ

toh-RAH-beh-rah CHEHK-koo travelers check トラベラー・チェック

toh-RAHN-kee-rah-ee-zah tranquilizers トランキライザー

toh-REE bird 鳥

TŌH-ree street 通り

toh-REE-koo-mee sumo match 取り組み

toh-REH-neen-goo weh-ah warmup suit トレーニング・ウェア

toh-ROO-koh ee-shee turquoise トルコ石

toh-SHEE yoh-ree senior citizens 年寄り

toh-SHOH kahn library 図書館

TOH-stah toaster トースター

tohsh-TOHT-tah old (people) 年とった

TOH-soo-toh toast (bread) トースト

tskah-oo to spend (money), to use 使う

tskee month 月

(oh)-TSKEH-moh-noh pickles (Japanese) （お）つけ物

tskoo-roo to make 作る

tsoo-ah tour ツアー

tsoo-GEE next 次

tsoo-kah currency 通貨

(tsoo-KAH-ee soo-teh noh) oh-shee-meh diapers (disposable) （使いすての）おしめ

tsoo-KAH-reh-teh ee-mahs tired つかれています

tsoo-koo to arrive 着く

tsoo-KOO-roh-oo to mend 繕う

tsoo-MEH yah-soo-ree nail file, emery board 爪やすり

tsoo-ree bah fishing spot 釣場

tsoo-REE boo-neh fishing boat 釣船

tsoo-REE doh-goo fishing equipment 釣道具

TSOO-roh aisle 通路

TSOO-roh gah-wah by the aisle 通路がわ

TSOO-yah-koo interpreter 通訳

tsoo-YOH-ee strong 強い

tsoo-YOO rainy season 梅雨

W

WAH-een wine ワイン

WAH-ee-pah windshield wiper ワイパー

wah-EE-shah-tsoo shirt ワイシャツ

wah-KAH-ee young 若い

wah-KAH-ee hee-toh young people 若い人

wah-KAH-ree-mahs I understand わかります

wah-KAH-roo to understand わかる

wah-KOO eyeglass frames わく

wahn bay 湾

wah-RAH-boo-kee yah-neh thatch roof わらぶき屋根

wah-RAH-oo to smile 笑う

wah-REE-bee-kee discount 割引き

wah-ROO-ee bad 悪い

WAH-sah-bee horseradish (Japanese) わさび

wah SHEE-kee noh Japanese-style 和式の

wah-TAHK-shee gah I 私が

wah-TAHK-shee noh my 私の

wah-TAHK-shee-tah-chee gah we 私たちが

wah-TAH-roo to cross 渡る

WEH-boo waves (hair) ウェーブ

WOHK-kah vodka ウォッカ

WEEN-doh shohp-peen-goo oh soo-roo to window shop ウィンドー・ショッピングをする

Y

yah-KAH-mah-shee noisy やかましい

yah-KEE-ah-mee deh yah-ee-tah grilled 焼網で焼いた

yah-KEE-toh-ree chicken skewered and grilled 焼き鳥

yah-KEE-tsoo-keh print (photo) 焼付け

yah-KEH-doh burn やけど

yahk-KYOH-koo/ koo-SOO-ree yah pharmacy 薬局／薬屋

yah-KYOO baseball 野球

yah-KYOO joh baseball park 野球場

yah-MAH mountain 山

yah-meh-roo to stop やめる

yah-sah-ee vegetables 野菜

yah-sah-shee easy やさしい

yah-SOO-ee cheap 安い

YOH-doh cheen-kee iodine ヨード・チンキ

YOH-foo-koo yah clothing store 洋服屋

YOH-jee toothpicks ようじ

yoh-KOOSHTS/ (oh)-FOO-roh bath 浴室／(お)風呂

YOH-koo yah-KEH-tah well-done (meat) よく焼けた

yoh-moo to read 読む

YOH nah-shee pear 洋なし

yoh-ROH-kohn-deh with pleasure 喜んで

YOH-rohp-pah seh-heen European products ヨーロッパ製品

YOH-roo night 夜

YOH shee-kee noh Western-style 洋式の

YOH-shoh-koo sheen-joo cultured pearls 養殖真珠

YOHT-toh sailboat ヨット

yoh-WAH-ee weak 弱い

yoh-YAH-koo appointment, reservation 予約

yoo-BEE finger 指

yoo-been/ teh-gah-mee mail 郵便／手紙

YOO-been kyoh-koo post office 郵便局

YOO-been pohs-toh mail box 郵便ポスト

yoo-BEE-wah ring (jewelry) 指輪

yoo-DAH-yah kyoh noh jee-een synagogue ユダヤ教の寺院

YOO-deh-tah boiled ゆでた

YOO-gah-tah evening 夕方

YOO-jeen/ toh-MOH-dah-chee friend 友人／友達

yoo-KEE snow 雪

yoo-meh famous 有名

yoo-NOH-mee jah-wahn/ chah-WAHN tea cup 湯飲み茶碗／茶碗

YOO-rahn-sehn cruise ship 遊覧船

yoo-ROO-ee loose (clothes) ゆるい

Z

zah-SEH-kee shee-teh reserved seats (train) 座席指定

zahs-shee magazine 雑誌

zah YAH-koo suppositories 座薬

ZEH-kahn/ ZEH-kahn KEHN-sah customs/ customs inspection 税関／税関検査

zeh-kahn noh sheen-koh-koo shoh customs declaration form 税関の申告書

ZEH-keen tax 税金

ZEHN-boo altogether 全部

ZEHN-sah-ee/ tsoo-MAH-mee appetizers 前菜／つまみ

ZOH-geh ivory 象牙

zook-KEE-nee zucchini ズッキーニ

zoo-TSOO headache 頭痛

KYOTO AND ENVIRONS

– – – SHINKANSEN RR
——— NATIONAL RAILWAYS
++++++ OTHER RAILWAYS
– – – SUBWAY

(162)

Kinkakuji Temple

NISHIJIN

Ryoanji Temple

Kitano Temmangu Shrine

Takaoguchi

Ryoanjimichi

Hakubeicho

Narutaki

Tenryuji Temple

Saga

Tokiwa

Hanazono

MARUTAMACHI

Arashiyama

Katabirana-tsuji

Uzumasa

Koryuji Temple

NISHIOJI

Nijo

Arashiyama

ARASHIYAMA

SHIJO ST.

Saiin

Katsura R.

GOJO ST.

Saihoji Temple

SHICHIJO ST.

Tambaguchi

Imperial Villa

Nishioji

Toji Te

Katsura

N